Teaching World Epics

Teaching
World Epics

Edited by
Jo Ann Cavallo

Modern Language Association of America
New York   2023

© 2023 by The Modern Language Association of America
85 Broad Street, New York, New York 10004
www.mla.org

All rights reserved. MLA and the MODERN LANGUAGE ASSOCIATION
are trademarks owned by the Modern Language Association of America. To
request permission to reprint material from MLA book publications, please
inquire at permissions@mla.org.

To order MLA publications, visit www.mla.org/books. For wholesale and
international orders, see www.mla.org/bookstore-orders.

The MLA office is located on the island known as Mannahatta (Manhattan) in
Lenapehoking, the homeland of the Lenape people. The MLA pays respect to
the original stewards of this land and to the diverse and vibrant Native communities that continue to thrive in New York City.

Options for Teaching 62
ISSN 1079-2562

Library of Congress Cataloging-in-Publication Data

Names: Cavallo, Jo Ann, editor.
Title: Teaching world epics / edited by Jo Ann Cavallo.
Description: New York : Modern Language Association of America, 2023. |
   Series: Options for teaching, 1079-2562 ; 62 | Includes bibliographical
   references.
Identifiers: LCCN 2023002384 (print) | LCCN 2023002385 (ebook) |
   ISBN 9781603296175 (hardcover) | ISBN 9781603296182 (paperback) |
   ISBN 9781603296199 (EPUB)
Subjects: LCSH: Epic literature—Study and teaching (Higher) | Epic
   literature—Study and teaching (Secondary) | Epic literature—History
   and criticism.
Classification: LCC PN56.E65 T43 2023 (print) | LCC PN56.E65 (ebook) |
   DDC 809.1/32071—dc23/eng/20230411
LC record available at https://lccn.loc.gov/2023002384
LC ebook record available at https://lccn.loc.gov/2023002385

Contents

Acknowledgments	ix
Introduction Jo Ann Cavallo	1

Part I: Epics from the Ancient World

Morality and Human Nature in the *Mahabharata* Arshia Sattar	19
The Multivocal *Ramayana* Tradition of India Paula Richman	28
Understanding the World of Greek and Near Eastern Epics through Homer's *Iliad* Carolina López-Ruiz	41
Ambiguity in Virgil's *Aeneid* Christine G. Perkell	54
Bad Boys to the Rescue in Statius's *Thebaid* Charles S. Ross	64

Part II: Epics from the Tenth to the Fifteenth Century

Ideologies of Intercultural Encounter in Three Epics of Medieval France Victoria Turner	77
The Calculated Heroism of the *Poema de mio Cid* Katherine Oswald	90
The *Nibelungenlied*: Otherworld, Court, and Doom in the Classroom Stefan Seeber	100
The Middle High German *Kudrun*: A Female Protagonist's Action to End Male Violence Albrecht Classen	111

vi   Contents

Epic Tales, Ethics Codes, and Evidence of Legitimacy: The
  Intriguing Case of *The Book of Dede Korkut*   121
  Emrah Pelvanoğlu

A Buddhist Perspective on War, Exile, and Women in
  The Tale of the Heike   133
  David T. Bialock, Elizabeth Oyler, and Roberta Strippoli

Three Kingdoms: Division, Unification, and National Identity
  from the Han Dynasty to Today   147
  Moss Roberts

Part III: Literary Epics of the Sixteenth and
            Seventeenth Centuries

Epic Poems and Emotions: Anger in Ariosto's *Orlando Furioso*
  and Bigolina's *Urania*   159
  Luisanna Sardu

Teaching Spenser's *Faerie Queene* through Allegory and
  Digital Rhetoric   169
  Jason Lotz

New World Epics: Camões's *Os Lusíadas*, Ercilla's *La
  Araucana*, and Villagrá's *Historia de la Nueva México*   180
  Joseph M. Ortiz

"Thou Hast Seen One World Begin and End":
  Worldmaking with *Paradise Lost*   191
  Angelica A. Duran

Part IV: Oral-Derived Epics in the Sixteenth through
             Nineteenth Centuries

Stretching the Boundaries of Epic: *Popol Wuj*, Maya
  Literature, and Coloniality   205
  Nathan C. Henne

Finland's *Kalevala*: Folk Songs, Romantic Nationalism,
  and an Enduring National Epic   219
  Thomas A. DuBois

The Many Lessons of the Central Asian Epic *Manas*   229
  Roberta Micallef

Contents   vii

The Armenian National Folk Epic *David of Sassoun*   238
Barlow Der Mugrdechian

Part V: The Enduring Oral Tradition

To Drink from the Source: Teaching the *Mwindo* Epic   249
Frederick Turner

The Epic of *Sun-Jata* in the Light of Abrahamic and
Mande Traditions   258
John William Johnson

Orality and History in *The Epic of Askia Mohammed*   270
Thomas A. Hale

The Legend of Ponnivala Nadu: A South Indian Oral Folk Epic   281
Brenda E. F. Beck

Part VI: World Epics in Various Contexts

Epic Engagement: Giving Ancient Stories New Life in the
Secondary School Classroom   295
Zachary Hamby

Epic Youth Narratives in an Active Learning World
Literature Course   305
Ana Grinberg

Middle Eastern Epics across the Millennia: *The Epic of
Gilgamesh, Sirat Bani Hilal*, and the *Shahnameh*   314
Dwight F. Reynolds

World Epics in Comparison: The *Odyssey, Kebra Nagast*,
and the *Shahnameh*   325
Atefeh Akbari

Part VII: Resources

Resources   339
Jo Ann Cavallo

Notes on Contributors   353

Acknowledgments

Editing a volume is a collaborative undertaking by nature. I am grateful first of all to the thirty contributors for generously sharing their pedagogical insights and expertise and for their goodwill throughout the process. In addition, the reviewers provided detailed feedback on both the prospectus and the completed manuscript, the acquisitions editor James Hatch offered expert guidance at every step, and many of the contributors also offered suggestions for my introduction and for the resources section.

I owe a special debt of gratitude to the late William Theodore de Bary, my sinologist colleague at Columbia University, for having encouraged the teaching of literature from a polycentric perspective in his Faculty Workshops for a Multi-cultural Sequence in the Core Curriculum (at the Heyman Center for the Humanities, 2002–09). Following these workshops, I had the privilege of coteaching with de Bary for several years the global core seminar Nobility and Civility: East and West, which included Mesopotamian, Indian, Iranian, Japanese, and African epics along with more familiar (to me) European texts. This experience sparked my desire to explore approaches to teaching epics from around the world.

I am likewise grateful to Meredith Levin, the Western European humanities librarian at Columbia University, for helping me seek resources on teaching world epics when I first planned to design such a course as well as for confirming the paucity of available materials. Thus arose the idea for this volume.

Finally, I would like to thank M. Aurora Rodriguez Collado, a learning designer at Columbia's Center for Teaching and Learning, for her creative designing and technical support as I developed the *World Epics* website (edblogs.columbia.edu/worldepics).

Jo Ann Cavallo

Introduction

Cultures from across the globe have cherished stories relating memorable deeds by heroic characters whose actions have significant consequences for themselves and their larger communities. Such accounts often originate in oral traditions and may have been set down in writing at some point in time, whether in ancient India, as was the case with the *Mahabharata* and the *Ramayana* (*The Journey of Rama*), or in nineteenth-century Finland and Armenia, as was the case with the *Kalevala* and *David of Sassoun*, respectively. Some of these narratives have remained in circulation through oral transmission right up to the present day, and written versions have become available only thanks to transcriptions of oral retellings, as has been the case for the African epics of *Sun-Jata*, *Mwindo*, and *Askia Mohammed* and for the South Indian *Legend of Ponnivala Nadu*. Authors from various cultures have also composed original epic narratives rather than adaptations or retellings of traditional stories, and these works have occasionally become acknowledged masterpieces in a literary canon even if they are not part of popular tradition, as is the case with Virgil's *Aeneid* and Edmund Spenser's *Faerie Queene*.

While recourse to the generic label *epic* makes a volume like this possible, the term is used here as a signpost to signal core characteristics rather

1

2 Introduction

than as a sort of border control determining what works should be placed within or outside the genre's frontiers. Indeed, as far as generic conventions go, the epic is an especially unruly genre because its boundaries are so porous: narratives with features commonly regarded as epic often overlap with other categories, such as sacred history, chronicle, saga, legend, romance, myth, folklore, and the novel. Moreover, while many languages, including English, employ a term derived from the ancient Greek *epos* (word, song, or speech), use of the word *epic* and its linguistic variants is far from universal. Accordingly, this volume includes works that share some epic features but that are referred to by terms with distinct etymological origins in their respective cultures, such as *sira* in Arabic (e.g., *Sirat Bani Hilal* [*Epic of the Bani Hilal*]), *deeda* in the Songhay tradition of West Africa (e.g., *The Epic of Askia Mohammed*), *dastan* in Central Asia (e.g., *The Book of Dede Korkut*), *monogatari* in Japanese (e.g., *The Tale of the Heike*), and *yanyi* in Chinese (e.g., *Three Kingdoms*).

Like any literary category, epic has been subject to different formulations. The entry for the term in *A Glossary of Literary Terms* states that "in its strict sense, the term *epic* or *heroic poem* is applied to a work that meets at least the following criteria: it is a long verse narrative on a serious subject, told in a formal and elevated style, and centered on a heroic or quasi-divine figure on whose actions depends the fate of a tribe, a nation, or (in the instance of John Milton's *Paradise Lost*) the human race" ("Epic" 109). Beyond the entry's overreliance on Milton—already anticipated in the above passage, which singles out *Paradise Lost*—and the editors' general restriction of examples to the European canon, there is also the issue of eliding "epic" and "heroic poem" since there is in fact no consensus that an epic must be a "long verse" narrative. As the folklorist Richard M. Dorson states, "[T]here is no good reason to exclude the prose of heroic saga from our conception of the folk epic, if we identify epic as a stirring traditional narrative of perilous adventure, daring, and manhood honoring the heroes of a people" (4).[1] Frederick Turner, who includes many works of prose in his proposed list of epics from Africa, Asia, Europe, and the Americas (18–20), remarks that "the prose epic often resorts to a heightened and poetic kind of language, or to actual passages of poetry" (329). Restriction of the epic genre to poetic works, moreover, may lead to the exclusion of entire cultures. "It has sometimes been remarked," Turner goes on to say, "that China has no epic poem; but *The Journey to the West* and *Three Kingdoms* are plainly epic . . ." (331). Regarding oral epics, Richard P. Martin reminds us that "even to divide verbal art into 'poetry' and 'prose' might turn out to be misleading, from the standpoint of non-western traditions" (9).[2] Nor is sheer length a reliable criterion, as Albert Lord and others have pointed out.[3] We are undoubtedly (and perhaps inevitably) influenced even in our implicit delineation of the genre by those epics we happen to know best. Instructors may encourage students to reflect on their own working definitions of the genre when examining the configuration of particular epics.

Critical Approaches

While there is no consensus on the precise criteria that define epic, much critical work has been done since 1960, when Albert Lord's *Singer of Tales* was first published following Lord's extensive work with Milman Parry on the techniques of oral-formulaic composition and reproduction by South Slavic bards. Further intense scholarly activity has brought about the questioning of a strict dividing line between oral and written literature as well as a greater understanding and appreciation of oral literature (see Finnegan, among others). The increased interest in orality has led not only to newly available transcripts and translations, and thus greater awareness in the anglophone academy of epic narratives from around the world, but also to an ever-expanding field of oral studies within which the study of epics has a prominent place.[4] And while some scholars continue to maintain a distinction between folk epics and literary epics (Dorson), or, as C. S. Lewis put it, primary and secondary epics, others eschew a strict dichotomy between oral and written—and, more generally, between folk or popular and elite or learned—manifestations of epic stories (Turner; Beissinger et al.).

While the ethnographic attention to orality has extended the study of epic across time, space, and social hierarchies, a parallel development in the field of literary criticism has also helped to expand the epic canon. Until recent decades, classical Greco-Roman and later European epics were often treated as representative of the epic genre *tout court* in a trajectory that went from Homer to Milton (or to later English poets). In this Eurocentric perspective, Homer's works were considered the point of departure and even epitome of the epic genre. *The Epic of Gilgamesh*, which predated the Homeric epics by several centuries but was rediscovered and translated into English only in the nineteenth century, was sometimes added to the mix but not in a way that disrupted the Homeric epics' supremacy or the European contours of the epic canon. Hamid Dabashi voices his criticism

4   Introduction

of this mindset in his volume on Abolqasem Ferdowsi's *Shahnameh* (*Book of Kings*): "Given the normative hegemony of scholarship on 'Western epics,' what they [scholars of Western epics] think and write ipso facto denaturalizes other 'non-Western epics,' turns them into oddities, exceptions, abnormalities" (19). What Dabashi then proposes regarding the *Shahnameh* is applicable to the study of epic more broadly: "The task is not simply to push the Persian epic on a larger reading public as a piece of antiquarian ('Oriental') curiosity. The far more pressing and important (and pleasant and joyous I might add) task is to see what particular way this epic is pertinent, relevant, integral to the world in which we now live, and to the social and psychological issues that preoccupy it" (22).

Thankfully, as canonical classics from around the world have been increasingly translated into English and critical studies in English have become available, students in anglophone countries and classrooms have gained access to a wealth of epic narrative traditions. The resulting new awareness of world epics combines with the decentralizing of Western European cultures in academia to liberate the study of epic from its previous restrictive connection to the elite works of the Greco-Roman West. This liberation not only provides a greater opportunity for students' intellectual and cultural enrichment beyond the Western canon but also better prepares students to be citizens of the world. As Thomas A. Hale has argued with regard to African epics, "[I]f our students are to understand that African literature is more than a postcolonial phenomenon—post-Western colonial to be more precise—then we need to give some depth to reading lists by including works that refer back to the precolonial era in both form and content" (188–89).

This wider perspective recognizing epics as a global phenomenon rather than a genealogy to be traced from ancient Greece to early modern Christian Europe has been accompanied by a reconceptualization of the Homeric epics themselves in their own historical context. Rather than treat the *Iliad* in isolation as the point of departure for an ensuing tradition, we can now study it in relation to a prior cultural network stretching into the Mesopotamian past. While this shift was no doubt made possible by the rediscovery and translation of *The Epic of Gilgamesh*, the earliest known epic, some elements of which find an echo in Homer, it was recently given a new impetus and focus. Carolina López-Ruiz's *When the Gods Were Born* and Mary R. Bachvarova's *From Hittite to Homer* meticulously demonstrate the extent to which ancient Greek culture was influenced by Near Eastern traditions. López-Ruiz's anthology *Gods, Heroes, and Monsters*, moreover, has made it possible to bring this literary and historical contextualization directly into the undergraduate classroom with excerpts that situate Greek and Roman epics and mythology within a wider Mediterranean cultural heritage.

The shift in scholarly focus from exclusively written works to oral works, from a European perspective to a polycentric one, and from ancient Greece to the broader Mediterranean basin has opened up exciting new directions in the study of epic in all its myriad manifestations. As students read comparatively, moreover, they will discover that each epic text is unique and ultimately not reducible to the expectations with which they may approach the genre. Although the stories often present models of behavior to follow and to avoid, one group is not necessarily depicted as less virtuous than another. While sometimes the fiercest opponents are demonized, it may also happen that the religious or ethnic other offers instruction and even transforms a hero's worldview. Epics may instrumentalize or ignore women and others not part of an elite military class (whether of Kshatriyas, knights, or samurai). Nonetheless, in such stories we also encounter female warriors who defeat their male counterparts or bond with them across not only gender differences but also differences in religious creed and territorial affiliation. The victorious group is not always the one controlling the narrative, nor do all epic authors glorify war in their works even though conflict is an integral part of the genre. Indeed, while some epic storylines have provided a means to develop or support prevailing social, political, and cultural ideas within distinct political entities, others have resisted or undermined the status quo and have thus offered alternative ways of thinking about human relations. Students may therefore be prompted to uncover an epic's underlying ideologies—and they may end up examining their own perspectives on the world in the process.

Contours of the Volume

As David Damrosch remarks in his introduction to *Teaching World Literature*, "World literature surveys can never hope to cover the world," as "it's impossible to give equal time to every language, country, or century" (9). Nor can a collection of essays on world epics presume to be comprehensive. In *Teaching World Epics*, thirty scholars share their insights and pedagogical strategies for teaching epic narratives from Asia, Europe, Africa, and the Americas, from antiquity right up to the modern period. The volume privileges epics that have reliable English translations available for classroom

6   Introduction

use and that are not already well covered in the Modern Language Association's Approaches to Teaching World Literature series.[5]

While contributors share their own particular methodological approaches for their respective epics, they also take into account that the volume is intended for teaching in a comparative context in English-language classrooms. Thus, they focus on the principal issues raised by the epic or epics that they teach in relation to particular sociopolitical and cultural contexts as well as on themes that are especially relevant in our contemporary world and that are apt to resonate with students. They likewise present actionable materials, such as selections of episodes that can be read in the span of one or two weeks, the best available paperback or online editions in English, recommended critical reading, and resources available online (such as artwork and videos of performances).

The twenty-four essays in the first five parts of the volume, which focus on teaching individual epics—or, in a few cases, a small number of closely related epics—are grouped according to time period.[6] This chronological sequencing can lead to the emergence of patterns and rich juxtapositions between epics that were produced during the same time period even if they did not influence each other. The epics in part 3, for example, covering the sixteenth and seventeenth centuries, allow for a comparison of canonical literary works composed as original creations by single authors. The epic works examined in part 4 highlight instead narratives that had been circulating orally for centuries but that were freshly refashioned in writing and preserved by individuals who perceived them as essential to their community's cultural or national identity or even survival.

Chronological order by the date (or estimated period) of composition of the earliest extant version, however, tells only a small part of the history of those epics that had a long tradition of oral transmission before they were written down or whose earliest written versions have not survived. While this approach leads to some approximation in the ordering of the essays that discuss oral-derived epics in parts 1 and 2, it can seem downright arbitrary for the epics covered in parts 4 and 5 that were composed, synthesized, or transcribed from the sixteenth to the twentieth century but whose stories extend back several or an untold number of centuries. These latter two groupings may nonetheless invite internal comparisons. The essays in part 4 underscore the importance of the circumstances surrounding the emergence of particular versions of written texts as well as the meaning that they held for their respective source communities. Part 5, dedicated to living oral epics from Africa and South India, not only attends to the collaborative process of transcription by storytellers, scribes, and ethnographers but also points to societal parallels across political borders. As Minna Skafte Jensen notes with regard to the continued practice of oral transmission in particular areas of the globe, "Epic traditions in the modern world typically exist in communities peripheral to the centers of wealth and power" (47).

The essays in part 6 juxtapose three or more epic narratives that can be taught in survey courses. Zachary Hamby relays his original, multipronged approach to bringing canonical epics to life for high school students. Ana Grinberg describes the process of introducing various youth epic narratives to her students. Dwight Reynolds concentrates on three Middle Eastern epics across the millennia, from the ancient Mesopotamian *Epic of Gilgamesh*, to the early-eleventh-century Persian *Shahnameh*, to the orally transmitted *Sirat Bani Hilal*, which is still popular today in Egypt. Atefeh Akbari's concluding comparative essay on a Greek epic (the *Odyssey*), an Ethiopian epic (*Kebra Nagast* [*The Glory of Kings*]), and a Persian epic (*Shahnameh*) raises questions and issues that are applicable not only to the epic genre but to world literature and world literature courses more generally.

A final, seventh part directs readers to further resources, primarily critical studies but also reference works, publishing venues, and websites.

Themes and Topics

The epic genre spans millennia and is at the core of cultures from around the world, all with their own multifaceted social, religious, political, and literary histories. At the same time, however, epic narratives contain many parallel features that invite comparative analysis. Although the volume follows a roughly chronological order, instructors may want to mix and match, creating their own juxtapositions to put different epics into dialogue with one another and to bring certain features and issues into relief through unexpected correspondences or contrasts. To facilitate that approach, below I point to some topics and themes running through various contributions to this volume.

The fact that the epic genre is largely dominated by male authors and characters already prompts students to consider questions related to gender. Akbari and Brenda Beck focus in their contributions on gender, including gender dynamics and politics; Paula Richman looks at female perspectives; Grinberg, Jason Lotz, Reynolds, and Roberta Strippoli all

8   Introduction

consider the representation of women, including female warriors and rulers; and, most poignantly, Albrecht Classen and Stefan Seeber both examine episodes of violence against women. In addition, the volume includes coverage of a work written by a woman, Giulia Bigolina's *Urania*, as well as of two anonymous epics featuring female characters that may have also been composed at least in part by women, the German *Kudrun* and the Japanese *Tale of the Heike*. With respect to these last two epics, the contributions of Classen and Strippoli focus, respectively, on the agency of strong-willed women to effect change in their societies and in their own lives.

The epic is also a genre that invites an interrogation of the uses and abuses of power, and many of the contributors focus on political structures and ideologies. Moss Roberts, for example, investigates how political power is acquired, exercised, and lost in the fourteenth-century Chinese work *Three Kingdoms*. Joseph M. Ortiz addresses issues surrounding colonialism, Orientalism, and race in three early modern imperial epics. Frederick Turner suggestively considers the real-life implications of the bloodless shift from authoritarian rule to the beginnings of limited government depicted in the *Mwindo* epic of central Africa. Other contributors focus on the requirements for a good ruler, the interplay of national interests and ideological perspectives, and forms of nation building. Sometimes epic narratives ambiguously navigate between opposing political outlooks and values rather than openly espousing a single ideology: in this regard, Christine G. Perkell treats Virgil's *Aeneid* as both a celebration of empire and a warning about the moral hazards inherent in victory and power. The political may be deeply entwined with the familial, especially when the power elite is dynastic. Accordingly, Classen, John Johnson, Arshia Sattar, and Seeber devote attention in their essays to power relations at the level of family conflict, and Reynolds and Frederick Turner both focus on struggles between father and son.

Given today's globalized but also hostilely divided world, instructors might ask students what the epic genre can tell us about war and peace through the ages. World epics offer a full range of perspectives on violence, from the celebration of heroic valor in the service of protecting one's homeland, discussed in the essay by Barlow Der Mugrdechian, to an outright denunciation of military conflict as pointless violence, discussed in the essay by Charles Ross. Using the contributions by David Bialock, Elizabeth Oyler, Roberta Strippoli, and Classen, students can explore how competing values—such as those linked to romantic love, friendship, family, forgiveness, and spiritual transcendence—may subvert the warrior ethic to various degrees and thus provide an antidote to the inhumanity of war and violence.

Geography is another common topic of interest among contributors. Beck explicitly focuses on geographic concepts; Grinberg on the use of an interactive online map; Victoria Turner on material and geographic exoticism; Katherine Oswald and Oyler, separately, on exile as a frame for shifting political geographies; and Ortiz on historically contested spaces. The epic genre also provides students with a way to discuss the depiction of (and encounters with) the other across religious, ethnic, racial, political, and social divides—including the dehumanization of the enemy within an empire, covered by Oyler, and both peaceful and violent interfaith encounters, covered by Victoria Turner.

Instructors can also use epics as a window into the unique cultures that gave rise to them, using the essay by Sattar, for example, to introduce students to Hindu doctrine in the *Mahabharata*, discussing Maya cosmovision in *Popol Wuj* using the essay by Nathan Henne, and discussing Central Asian nomadic values in *Manas* using the essay by Roberta Micallef. Some contributors explore differing or even competing cultural codes and concepts within epics, such as the transition from a pre-Islamic Turkish ethos to an Islamic one in the early fourteenth-century *Book of Dede Korkut*, in the essay by Emrah Pelvanoğlu, and the upending of the warrior code by Buddhist-inspired nonattachment and insight into the impermanence of all things in *The Tale of the Heike*, in the contribution by Bialock. Other essays point to cultural blending, such as Johnson's discussion of the hero's need to acquire both Islamic *baraqah* (divine power) and traditional Mande *nyama* (occult power) in the West African epic of *Sun-Jata*.

Students may discover that epics—no matter how far back in time they originate or how unfamiliar their cultural context—present dilemmas that are perennial because they are inherent to human nature. Topics applicable across cultures and time periods include emotions and the quest for self-discovery, found in the essay by Luisanna Sardu; ethics, in the essays by Richman and Sattar; the celebration or interrogation of heroic values, in the essays by Akbari, Der Mugrdechian, Oswald, and Perkell; core human relationships and the nature of life, in Beck; strife, friendship, revenge, and compassion, in López-Ruiz; and the struggle to survive, in Hale. Contributors often contextualize these universal themes, for example, by asking how the opposition between good and evil may get channeled into an epic's theme of group identity formation. Some contributors focus on how epics reflect concerns that are especially relevant to our contemporary world, including social issues, in the essay by Beck, and aspects of identity, such as gender, race, body image, and socioeconomic class, in the essays by Akbari, Lotz, and Ortiz. A comparative approach, of course, does not mean downplaying the individuality of each text. In this vein, Henne offers instructors strategies to teach the Mesoamerican *Popol Wuj* by focusing on the unique worldviews that Maya literature can reveal and by avoiding apparent narrative parallels with Western epics that can undercut the real differences between these bodies of work.

Another topic addressed across several essays is authorial practice. Bialock, Hale, Johnson, and Frederick Turner devote special attention to performance, storytelling techniques, or the storyteller's essential but complex role. López-Ruiz delves into the markers of orality (such as formulas and epithets) in ancient written texts of the Mediterranean. Pelvanoğlu draws our attention to the importance of transmission history as well as to the representation of the oral milieu of the performer and the audience within the written text. Meaning is also manipulated through different rewritings and editorial choices. Nowhere, perhaps, is this clearer than in the centuries-long traditions of retelling the *Mahabharata* and the *Ramayana*. Sattar considers the extent to which versions of the *Mahabharata* (including retellings and adaptations such as films, plays, and even novels) may serve the instructor's goal to provide students with some sense of the vast epic narrative. Richman explores how retellings of the *Ramayana* from different perspectives (as related by devotees, women, and marginalized groups) and in various performance formats have reshaped the narrative tradition while keeping the epic alive and fluid.

Various contributors (e.g., Angelica Duran, Roberts, Seeber, and Strippoli) discuss the reception of an epic through various forms of adaptation, such as artworks, novels, comic books, operas, plays, films, television series, radio broadcasts, songs, and video games. Thomas A. DuBois explores the long-term cultural reception of the Finnish *Kalevala*, elements of which appear in frescoes, operas, symphonies, novels, movies, television series, games, and even tractor names. Other contributors turn to relevant films and television series for comparison, from Akira Kurosawa's classic film *The Seven Samurai* and its American remake, *The Magnificent Seven*, examined by Ross, to the *Star Wars* series, discussed in the essays by Hale, Johnson, and Reynolds.

Reception can also comprise the circumstances surrounding an epic narrative's emergence or reemergence and circulation in successive time periods and in different environments—including some of the darkest moments in world history. Henne contextualizes the K'iche' transcription (in turn based on an earlier hieroglyphic codex) and subsequent Spanish translation of the Maya *Popol Wuj* amid the colonization, marginalization, and genocide of Indigenous peoples in the Americas. Der Mugrdechian recalls how the centuries-old oral tradition of reciting *David of Sassoun* was ruptured by the Armenian genocide, which began in 1915, and how variants of the epic recited by survivors who escaped to the Republic of Armenia (later Soviet Armenia) became the basis for the first critical edition of the work. Micallef shows how the fate of the Turkic epic *Manas* has followed that of the Kyrgyz Republic, including the work's utilization to demonstrate the distinct origin of the Kyrgyz when the Kyrgyz Soviet Socialist Republic was created and the work's later suppression during the 1930s, when the Soviet regime censured Central Asian epics as "obstacles to building socialism" (Bennigsen 464).

Several essays include a consideration of epic as a genre. In some cases, epic is related to a number of other genres, namely, history (see the essay by Roberts), hagiography (see Grinberg), folktales and folk songs (see DuBois), chronicle (see Hale), and legend (see the essays by Micallef and Pelvanoğlu). Partly to further explore the epic genre's permeability, the volume includes works that are in dialogue with other genres, particularly romance and the historical novel. Sardu, for example, relates her experience of teaching Giulia Bigolina's Italian romance *Urania* in juxtaposition with Lodovico Ariosto's romance epic *Orlando Furioso*, which *Urania* sometimes creatively imitates.

Contributors likewise consider various theoretical and methodological approaches relevant to teaching the epic. Pelvanoğlu uses the scholarship of Walter J. Ong when reflecting on the textualization of oral epics from around the world. Grinberg references Joseph Campbell's monomyth as a tool to analyze heroic demeanor. Reynolds uses different critical tools depending on the aspect of the epic to be highlighted, using Otto Rank, Lord Raglan, and Campbell for classic analyses of the hero and the heroic journey and Milman Parry and Albert Lord for the basic concepts of oral literature and performance studies. Micallef references the nineteenth-century Kazakh ethnographer Chokhan Valikhanov's characterization of the Turkic epic *Manas*.

Some contributors share innovative strategies that combine interpretation of the primary texts with corollary activities. Grinberg, for example, outlines her active learning techniques in teaching epic youth narratives. Lotz discusses multimedia projects in which students use social media

12 Introduction

platforms to fashion online selves as a way to better understand identity creation and allegory in Spenser's *Faerie Queene*. Hamby encourages his secondary school students to participate in "epic engagement" through role-playing activities, "script-story" adaptations of the original epics, classroom games that re-create the action, and media resources. Beck uses animated video, graphic novels, large vinyl murals, an iPad reading app, and a digital classroom game to lead students into the world of the South Indian oral folk epic *The Legend of Ponnivala Nadu*.

The contributors offer many fruitful suggestions for comparative readings. As noted above, part 6 is dedicated to essays that discuss the juxtaposition of multiple epics. In Grinberg's course on world youth epics, for example, students compare classical epics such as *The Epic of Gilgamesh* and the *Ramayana* to infancy heroic narratives in the early Irish *Táin Bó Cúailnge* (*The Cattle Raid of Cooley*) and *Macgnímartha Finn* (*The Boyhood Deeds of Finn*), the medieval Franco-Italian *Geste Francor*, the medieval Arabic *Sirat al-amira Dhat al-Himma* (*The Tale of Princess Fatima, Warrior Woman*), the second-century Gnostic Infancy Gospel of Thomas, and Ashvaghosha's *Life of the Buddha*. Yet many essays outside part 6 likewise make connections across world epics and related works both within and beyond national literary traditions. Victoria Turner focuses on ideologies of intercultural encounters in three medieval French epics. López-Ruiz considers Homeric epics in dialogue with canonical texts from Mesopotamian, Hittite, and northwestern Semitic cultures, suggesting selections from *The Epic of Gilgamesh* and the Hebrew Bible for comparative analysis. Duran also draws from the Bible in her discussion of Milton's *Paradise Lost* before bringing in later works for comparison, including Ariosto's *Orlando Furioso*, Galileo's writings, and Bertolt Brecht's *Life of Galileo*. Ross looks ahead to Dante's *Divine Comedy* in discussing approaches to teaching Statius's *Thebaid*.

Finally, in a volume on world epics that are taught in English translation (and a few that are English-language works), it is befitting that some attention be devoted to the issue of translation. Grinberg discusses such topics as the difficulties that monolingualism causes in the undergraduate teaching of world literature; Ortiz considers how epic texts stage the obstacles in communicating across linguistic barriers; Akbari, Henne, and Sattar separately examine the challenge of translating concepts across languages; and Akbari also looks at the framing of the epic and its publication paraphernalia for English-language readers.

Courses

Teaching World Epics not only highlights the extraordinary wealth of the world's epic narrative traditions but also provides instructors with pedagogical tools and ideas to teach epics in a variety of courses. In addition to serving courses expressly dedicated to world epics, the volume is designed to be useful for more general comparative literature courses, courses designed by topic or theme, and courses in other areas, such as peace and conflict studies, transnational studies, women's studies, and religious studies.

Most of the contributors write with college students in mind, with the exception of Hamby, who teaches in a secondary school. A few contributors note the adaptability of their approaches outside the college classroom, whether for high school classes, as in the essay by Oswald, or for classes "ranging from the third grade up to and including undergraduate lectures and postgraduate and faculty seminars," in the essay by Beck. Regardless of the intended student body, the insights and strategies offered in this volume demonstrate that epic narratives are relevant, thought provoking, and potentially life changing across many different configurations.

To the extent possible, students should be encouraged to identify differences not only across epic traditions but also within them as a reminder that cultures are not monolithic. To this end, students might be invited to compare two epics within the same tradition, such as the *Ramayana* and the *Mahabharata*, from ancient India; the *Aeneid* and the *Thebaid*, from ancient Rome; or the *Nibelungenlied* (*Song of the Nibelungs*) and *Kudrun*, from medieval Germany. Time permitting, instructors could include different versions of a single epic to show how the same narrative may express quite distinct ideologies across time. As Richman discusses, this variation is the case not only in the oral tradition, where bards retell a story according to their own personal and political preferences or those of their audiences, but for written texts as well.

Whether an epic is thousands of years old or was composed yesterday, and whether it aims to capture the spirit of a people on the other side of the globe or in one's own homeland, it necessarily elicits different responses on the part of each reader. Discussing these texts in a classroom setting is a welcome occasion to acknowledge and explore different interpretations. Part of the educational experience, after all, is to understand how individuals from different cultures have expressed their most

14   Introduction

fervent values, deepest fears, and noblest aspirations—and to gain a greater awareness of one's own values, fears, and aspirations in the process.

Epics, moreover, offer an escape from everyday reality and a playground for the imagination while at the same time encouraging critical thinking and deep reflection on what it meant to be human in the past and what being human means in the present. Epic narratives may envision larger-than-life scenarios, but they recount real-life struggles and tough choices made in high-stakes situations to which we can all relate. This is perhaps why these stories still speak to us and our students today. Could avid fans of the television series *Game of Thrones* or players of the video game series *The Elder Scrolls* become equally engrossed in the eleventh-century Iranian epic *Shahnameh*? Our world can only become richer when we enter into the wealth of epic narratives that have captured the hearts, minds, and souls of readers and listeners from around the world and throughout the centuries.

Teaching World Epics, then, aims to encourage and support the teaching of epic narratives that have engaged, inspired, and provoked readers for centuries and even millennia and that await exploration by future generations across linguistic, religious, cultural, and national boundaries. New translations continue to demonstrate that there are more epics on earth than dreamt of by anglophone scholars just a few generations ago, and there has never been a better time to introduce students to this global (yet culture-specific) literary genre.

Notes

1. This statement, in turn, raises the issue of gender, as do all epics in one way or another, given their frequent reliance on martial activities from which women were excluded in most past societies (and, to a large extent, also today).

2. Ready points to prominent scholars who debate the possibility of distinguishing prose from poetry in any culture (86).

3. Lord notes that the South Slavic poems studied in *The Singer of Tales* were "comparatively short" (5). Scholars of African epics also make note of the relative brevity of those works; see Hale, Johnson, and F. Turner in this volume.

4. The scholarship of John Foley was instrumental in developing the field, as was the ongoing journal that he founded in 1980, *Oral Tradition.*

5. Some notable epics, such as the Haudenosaunee (Iroquois) founding epic *Kaianerekowa* (*The Great Law of Peace*), the East African epic of *Liyongo*, and the epic of *Köroğlu* from the Turco-Persian world and neighboring communities, have not been included in this volume because the lack of a viable English translation would make classroom use impractical.

6. In ordering the essays within each part, I was guided primarily by chronology but also took into account additional factors. In part 1, I opted for the geographic seamlessness that resulted from placing the *Iliad* essay directly prior to the contributions on Virgil and Statius and after those on the *Mahabharata* and the *Ramayana*, even though the *Iliad*'s textual composition predates the composition of the *Mahabharata* and the *Ramayana*.

Works Cited

Bachvarova, Mary R. *From Hittite to Homer: The Anatolian Background of Ancient Greek Epic.* Cambridge UP, 2020.

Beissinger, Margaret, et al., editors. *Epic Traditions in the Contemporary World: The Poetics of Community.* U of California P, 1999.

Bennigsen, Alexandre A. "The Crisis of the Turkic National Epics, 1951–1952: Local Nationalism or Internationalism." *Canadian Slavonic Papers / Revue canadienne des slavistes*, vol. 17, nos. 2–3, pp. 463–74.

Dabashi, Hamid. *The* Shahnameh: *The Persian Epic as World Literature.* Columbia UP, 2019.

Damrosch, David, editor. *Teaching World Literature.* Modern Language Association of America, 2009.

Dorson, Richard M. Introduction. *Heroic Epic and Saga: An Introduction to the World's Great Folk Epics*, edited by Felix J. Oinas, Indiana UP, 1978, pp. 1–6.

"Epic." *A Glossary of Literary Terms*, by M. H. Abrams and Geoffrey Galt Harpham, 11th ed., Cengage Learning, 2015, pp. 109–12.

Finnegan, Ruth. *Oral Poetry: Its Nature, Significance, and Social Context.* 1977. Wipf and Stock Publishers, 2018.

Foley, John M., editor. *A Companion to Ancient Epic.* Wiley-Blackwell, 2009.

Hale, Thomas A. "*A Siin de Mé*: Learning to Teach the African Oral Epic in African Literature Courses." *Women's Studies Quarterly*, vol. 25, no. 3, fall 1997, pp. 188–200.

Jensen, Minna Skafte. "Performance." Foley, pp. 45–54.

Lewis, C. S. *A Preface to* Paradise Lost. Oxford UP, 1961.

López-Ruiz, Carolina, editor. *Gods, Heroes, and Monsters: A Sourcebook of Greek, Roman, and Near Eastern Myths in Translation.* 2nd ed., Oxford UP, 2018.

———. *When the Gods Were Born: Greek Cosmogonies and the Near East.* Harvard UP, 2010.

Lord, Albert. *The Singer of Tales.* 1960. Edited by David F. Elmer, 3rd ed., Center for Hellenic Studies, 2019.

Martin, Richard P. "Epic as Genre." Foley, pp. 9–19.

Ready, Jonathan L. *Orality, Textuality, and the Homeric Epics: An Interdisciplinary Study of Oral Texts, Dictated Texts, and Wild Texts.* Oxford UP, 2019.

Turner, Frederick. *Epic: Form, Content, and History.* Transaction Publishers, 2012.

Part I

Epics from
the Ancient World

Arshia Sattar

Morality and Human Nature in the *Mahabharata*

The *Mahabharata*, one of the two great Indian epics, appeared first in Sanskrit and was compiled between the fifth century BCE and the second century CE. It is the longest poem in the world, running to 100,000 verses. It has hundreds of characters and thousands of stories. In its own culture and in others, it appears in stories and songs, in plays and sculptures, in contemporary retellings, and in metaphors and idioms in several languages.[1] Teachers are unlikely to ever read the entire text, they can never teach the whole of it, they will be compelled to leave out some of its most powerful moments and even episodes and stories that they love best, they will lose much of its meaning in translation and in different cultural and temporal contexts, and its characters and situations will frustrate students and teachers alike. Why teach it, then? Why proffer a diminished experience of a text that constantly points, for resolution and fulfillment, beyond what is being shared? The answer is really quite simple: We, as instructors, teach the *Mahabharata* because it is truly one of the greatest stories ever told. We teach it because we learn from it each time. We teach it because the moral questions it explores—about duty to others and responsibility to oneself, about the conflict between righteousness and justice, about war and sanctioned violence, about the desire for power and the quest for truth—are

19

20   *Mahabharata*

as important today as they were twenty-five centuries ago when these stories were first told.[2]

Despite the welter of myths, tales, and branching narratives, the central story of the *Mahabharata* is strong and clear. It concerns a ruling family and its disputed throne, claimed with equal conviction by two sets of royal cousins, the five Pandavas and the one hundred Kauravas. They grow up together with the same mentors and teachers, but the princes are bitter rivals from their childhood onward. Lust, greed, honor, betrayal, skill, and valor are catalyzed by boons, curses, acts of the gods, and fate as the enmity between the cousins hurtles inevitably toward a ghastly fratricidal war that signals the end of the world as we know it. Additionally, the *Mahabharata*'s narrative engines are fuelled by karma (the retributive force of one's past actions) and dharma (the elusive principle of righteous conduct). While karma and the supernatural forces that act on the lives of the characters determine what characters can do, dharma allows individuals to choose, to decide for themselves what is right and wrong. This conflict between determinism and free will lies at the heart of the Indian epics, and the *Mahabharata* places this problem front and center not only in the narrative arcs and actions of its characters but also in the philosophical discourses that it holds within itself.

When thinking about morality, about personal ethics, and about where collectives and individuals draw lines that cannot be crossed in terms of what happens here on earth as well as what could happen in the afterlife (or a next life), teachers and students can bring these issues into sharper focus by considering how they are handled by other cultures, what another ethos permits, and how a different set of mores is defined. A guided discussion around a text as rich and complex as the *Mahabharata* can lead class members to consider their own ethical norms in a new light. They can see where those norms come from and how they frame discourses and behavior. Teachers and students may realize that there are few, if any, moral absolutes and that ethics can often be separated from ideas of a good and perfect divine being.

Translations and Retellings

As with some other classics, the *Mahabharata* presents the additional problem of its enormous length—that is probably the first thing teachers have to negotiate in preparing to teach it. Fortunately, there are a few good abridged translations and many sincere retellings available in English, these latter of varying lengths and complexity. Whether using an abridged translation or a retelling, the reader is presented with only the central story of the *Mahabharata*, losing much of the other material, narrative and philosophical, that fills out the text. Teachers are likely to choose a retelling over an abridged translation because a retelling has already made the choices that teachers need to make—for clarity, brevity, and simplicity (to some extent). Because retellings differ so widely in emphasis and perspective, teachers can also choose a retelling that highlights the issues that they want to talk about, including war, ethics, and mythological narratives.

A retelling will, most likely, contain material that is not in the text. It might be something as ostensibly harmless as an imagined conversation, an expanded psychological moment that reveals motivation, or an extranarrative explanation for why something was done. Whatever the reasons for inserting material into the story, doing so is problematic. At the most obvious level, it prevents the reader from getting a sense of what the original text feels like, however dull or weighty parts of it might be. A translation, even an abridged one, will present the text as it is. It will carry with it the good and the bad, the magic that language is capable of as well as the moments when a passage drags on. A translator will tell you what the text wants to say, while a reteller is likely to have a perspective on the story and characters that they want to share. As such, even when teachers use a retelling that suits them, they should always support that with passages from a complete translation of the original text.

Despite my reservations about using a retelling as the primary classroom text, given the extraordinary length and complexity of the *Mahabharata* and what is available in English, I would suggest Carole Satyamurti's eloquent version, which is substantially close to the original. The language in this version is both precise and moving, and the extrapolations are few and contained despite the imaginative license that accrues to Satyamurti. The main story of the *Mahabharata* that she tells is clear and engaging. Her text is easily available and comes in at about seven hundred pages, so it is not meager and allows the reader to have some awareness of the heft of the original. Shorter retellings, for all their virtues, are not terribly satisfactory, and so I would suggest Chakravarthi V. Narasimhan's abridged translation as a reasonable second choice. For a full translation that can be referred to and excerpted as needed, J. A. B. van Buitenen's *Mahābhārata* volumes have no peer. Some of the later volumes of this translation remain in print, but should teachers decide to use material from sections of the original text that are unavailable in the Van Buitenen translation, the Kisari Mohan Ganguli translation, despite its archaic idiom, will suffice.

Whatever version of the *Mahabharata* teachers decide to assign, students will need a fairly detailed list of dramatis personae. Most versions come with a family tree of characters, but I have found a diagrammatic tree to not be quite enough. The names of the major characters in the *Mahabharata* are unfamiliar, they are mostly long and difficult to remember, and the critical relationships by blood and marriage between the characters are equally difficult to sort through, as they span generations. Some important connections are made through characters that we will not encounter in our abridged texts. As such, it is best for teachers to make their own list of characters as a handout. I have found that the most effective list is an alphabetical one with a brief thumbnail of each character's antecedents, role, and principal antagonist.[3]

Adaptations

Even when the course syllabus includes only a limited number of episodes from the *Mahabharata*, it is still useful for teachers to introduce students to the epic through an adaptation. Versions of the *Mahabharata* have appeared in Indian cinema and on television for decades: while some films place the story in the mythicohistorical past using agreed-on mise en scène conventions for visual stories located in the classical period, others transpose the story and its characters into a contemporary setting, often using political or wealthy families to play out the conflict over a common legacy.[4] *Raajneeti*, for example, is a sophisticated Bollywood film that transposes the *Mahabharata* onto contemporary Indian politics. Characters from the *Mahabharata* are easily identifiable in the film, and it is worth screening so that students can see how the *Mahabharata* is still used to understand the world in which we live. Should teachers use this or other film adaptations, they may have to parse the way Indian films tell their stories, alerting students to both cinematic and narrative conventions and practices that may be unfamiliar.

I have found the six-hour film version of Peter Brook's theatrical *Mahabharata*, with its international cast, to be invaluable. It is not without its problems, but those discomforts lead to animated and worthwhile discussions about representation, cultural ownership, and adaptation. In fact, the film's problems flag the boundaries for exactly what we are doing when we study a text from another culture and in a different time period.

For teachers working with students in India, adaptations in the form of dramatic scripts and novels work well in addition to films and television series. Some classical plays (such as those by the Sanskrit playwright Bhasa) depict smaller incidents in the story or elaborate well-known ones with different intent, for example, by making a traditionally villainous character heroic or by at least providing complex motivations for his actions.[5] Typically, Indian students have some knowledge of the *Mahabharata*, most often through stories they heard or read as children. They are, therefore, eager to engage with characters and their behavior and to discuss how and why they act as they do. However, Indian students are not often familiar with adaptations of the *Mahabharata*, and so their inclusion in a course is usually successful in generating a fuller understanding of the original text and the issues it places before us.

Teaching Approaches

As with any multivalent text, the *Mahabharata* fits into many classroom contexts. My great pleasure is to teach it as an epic—students relate enthusiastically to the genre, which seems familiar when they analyze its structural features and tropes. There are many known paths to follow as we open up the text—the warrior-prince hero, the usurped kingdom, the stolen wife, the exile and the journey filled with obstacles that must be overcome before the triumphal return, strange and magical companions and objects, and the great war. Students in the West often have some prior knowledge of an epic, and this brings us to the logical comparison that the *Mahabharata* offers with Homer's *Iliad*. Composed around the same time and part of a larger Indo-European universe that celebrates the heroism of warriors and may have given birth to the epic genre itself, the *Mahabharata* and the *Iliad* speak to each other across language and cultural specificity.[6] Characters, episodes, and relationships resemble one another and lead us to the same core questions: What is the price of war, and is it worth it? What does war do to those who fight and kill, what sense of moral righteousness does war bestow on them, and what happens to them when the war is over and the bloodlust has subsided? How do they think about their actions then, and how do we, untainted but often complicit, receive them when they return?

24   *Mahabharata*

The fact that the *Mahabharata* raises questions about war and violence that are profoundly relevant in the twenty-first century should reassure teachers that it has much else to say that will resonate with our current moment. Although the central event of the *Mahabharata* is the terrible fratricidal war, the road to it is marked by various complex moral choices that the key figures in the story must make. In Hinduism, the principle that underlies all moral action is the doctrine of dharma, a word impossible to translate into any other language partly because of its vast range of meanings and partly because, as the *Mahabharata* itself says, dharma is *sukshma*, or subtle (Van Buitenen 2: 149).[7] Unlike other moral codes, such as the biblical commandments, dharma does not present us with a template for what we should or should not do. On the contrary, it suggests that we need to make decisions for ourselves from the choices that lie before us. Often, we face many right choices (rather than one right and one obviously wrong way to act). These choices are not the same for us all: they depend on who we are and what stage of life we are in, and so dharma is not absolute, but as a principle it is eternal.

Dharma encompasses (but is not restricted to) duty, obligation, responsibility, righteousness, the good, the true, and the natural and the constructed laws by which society remains stable and by which the universe is regulated. Karma, which is the other principle of action, affects dharma, and vice versa. But, as mentioned earlier, while karma is about determined choices, dharma is about free will. The interaction of these two forces not only shapes the lives of humans and their relationships but also affects what happens to them after death. In this process, these principles of action shape a culture and a people.

The *Mahabharata*'s claim to being a text that explores the capacity for humans to be good is elevated by the fact that God appears in the world of humans as an actor in this story and provides a discourse about dharma and how an individual can be guided toward the right choice. The *Mahabharata* contains within it the *Bhagavad Gita* (loosely translated as the *Song of God*), wherein Krishna, an *avatara* (commonly translated as incarnation) of the great god Vishnu, instructs his dear friend and cousin Arjuna on how to live in the world and what the significance of his actions will be. The *Bhagavad Gita* is made all the more powerful by the fact that it uplifts the milieu of the epic, the war, into a metaphor for the moral dilemmas that we face in our everyday lives. On the morning of the battle between the cousins, Arjuna, the greatest warrior of his generation, breaks down in front of Krishna, whom he knows only as his human friend, and says that he cannot raise arms against his family, teachers, and elders. In short, he cannot kill the men with whom he has grown up, the men who made him who he is. He therefore refuses to fight. Krishna then goes on to explain that it is Arjuna's dharma, his duty as a warrior, to fight and that he will not be responsible for the death of the men that stand before him given that their souls are immortal (Patton). Krishna elaborates a doctrine of action that teaches individuals to act wherever and whenever without being attached to the fruits of their actions. Slowly, through the eighteen chapters of the *Bhagavad Gita*, this manifesto for right action is transformed into a theology of devotion and surrender. Krishna reveals himself to be God, the ultimate reality behind all that we see and do and the refuge of all beings. Arjuna is newly empowered to act and blows his mighty conch shell to signal the commencement of the war.

The *Mahabharata* does not end with the theophany at the heart of the *Bhagavad Gita* and Krishna's discourse on dharma, however. It goes on for many more books that contain, among other things, several other discourses on dharma and right action. Most of these are in the form of dialogues or conversations, and many of them arise from questions about specific situations, but they are almost never among equals. One of the participants in the conversation has the role of a wise teacher, leading the younger and usually troubled speaker toward a better understanding of how they might act.

My preference has always been to open up the conversation with students about morality and ethics through discussion of incidents and episodes rather than of the philosophical passages in the *Mahabharata*. Because dharma and the idea of God as manifested in Krishna and his actions are so staggeringly different from ideas that people outside the Hindu tradition are accustomed to, I find it more effective to use a pedagogy of showing rather than telling. This also allows students, who may have varied interests and academic specializations as well as diverse vocabularies, to refer to a character and an action when talking about moral or ethical problems in the text.

Several incidents in the main story of the *Mahabharata* can be used to think about ethics. If teachers use the *Gita* for this discussion, they can ask if there is ever such a thing as a righteous war or violence that can be justified, sanctioned even, in the service of a greater good. They can also ask if a morality separate from a perfect divine being or a set of categorical imperatives can be consistent and sustained. The catastrophic dice game where Yudhishthira loses everything and then stakes his wife to win back

26   *Mahabharata*

his kingdom is not only a scene of chilling drama but also allows us to think about the law (dharma) as an abstraction and about its effects on an individual, as when Draupadi confronts the elders after she has been humiliated in public (Van Buitenen 2: 124–55). The final conversation between Yudhishthira and Duryodhana, as the latter lies dying with his legs smashed (Narasimhan 170–76), will bring up questions about the spoils of war, however justified (or ordained) the war might have been, and about what the terms of victory and loss truly are. The climax of the story in heaven, where we are confronted with the effects of karma in the afterlife (Doniger 164–80), is also worth closer examination. Readers will be introduced to these scenes and the issues about conduct that they raise in any version of the text they read, but it would be best to supplement what they know with extracts from a complete translation.

In an early chapter, the *Mahabharata* says of itself that what is found here can be found elsewhere, but what is not here is nowhere else. Readers might be tempted to think that this is a boast about the work's encyclopedic scope, but I would suggest that the tall claim of containing all possibilities refers instead to the *Mahabharata*'s ferociously clear-eyed and unrelenting examination of human nature. The stories it tells are about humans in so many different situations: within a family, within society, within a marriage, in love, in hate, in anguish, and in exultation. We see humans in relation to God, and we see them search for truth, knowledge of the self, and tranquility in what lies beyond death. These are universal questions; they are in the *Mahabharata*, and they are everywhere else, in stories from around the world. We may not all have the same answers, but as humans surely we have the same questions. In a real sense, then, what is not in the *Mahabharata* is truly nowhere else.

Notes

1. See "*Mahabharata*" for a short summary of the story of the *Mahabharata*, a bibliography, and a list of other teaching resources.

2. As a modern comparison, Dan Taberski's *The Line*, a 2021 Apple Original series about a US Navy SEAL's trial for war crimes in Iraq, is a brilliant exploration of the ethics of war, the choices that fighting personnel are called on to make, and the psychological impact of combat on individuals and societies.

3. This is an example from my handout: "Arjuna: third of the Pandava brothers; born of Kunti by the king of the gods, Indra; best archer in the world; lover of many women and father of Abhimanyu; best friend of Krishna; hero of the *Bhagavad Gita*."

4. Most of the television series are available on various Internet platforms but tend to run either without subtitles or with subtitles of dubious quality. I have therefore refrained from listing them as resources.

5. Bhasa's *The Shattered Thigh* is particularly effective.

6. My preference is for Lombardo's translation of the *Iliad*, which is subtly slanted toward raising questions about the duties, obligations, and honor of a warrior as well as toward highlighting what war does to those who participate in the fighting and killing.

7. Van Buitenen translates *dharma* as "Law": "What a powerful man views as law in the world, that do others call the Law when Law is in question. I cannot answer the question decisively because the matter is subtle and mysterious as well as grave" (2: 149).

Works Cited

Bhasa. *The Shattered Thigh*. Translated by A. N. D. Haksar, Penguin Books, 2008.

Doniger, Wendy. *After the War: The Last Books of the* Mahabharata. Speaking Tiger, 2022.

Ganguli, Kisari Mohan, translator. *The* Mahabharata *of Krishna Dwaipayana Vyasa*. Andesite Press, India, 2017. 12 vols.

Lombardo, Stanley, translator. *The Iliad*. Hackett Publishing, 1997.

"*Mahabharata*." *World Epics*, edblogs.columbia.edu/worldepics/project/mahabharata/. Accessed 24 June 2022.

The Mahabharata. Directed by Peter Brook, Les Productions du 3ème Etage, 1989. English.

Narasimhan, Chakravarthi V., translator. *The* Mahābhārata: *An English Version Based on Selected Verses*. Columbia UP, 1997.

Patton, Laurie L., translator. *The Bhagavad Gita*. Penguin Books, 2008.

Raajneeti. Directed by Prakash Jha, Prakash Jha Productions, 2010. Hindi with subtitles.

Satyamurti, Carole, translator. *The Mahabharata*. W. W. Norton, 2020.

Van Buitenen, J. A. B., translator. *The Mahābhārata*. U of Chicago P, 1978–83. 3 vols.

Paula Richman

The Multivocal *Ramayana* Tradition of India

Teaching the *Ramayana* tradition in a world epics course presents unique challenges of scope but also offers an encounter with one of the most multivocal epic traditions in the world—one that began more than two millennia ago yet remains alive and visible in Indian culture today. The oldest extant telling of Rama's life from birth to death bears the title *Rāmāyana*, usually translated as *The Journey of Rama* and dated from around 250 BCE to 200 CE. Initially transmitted orally, the seven-book epic attributed to the sage Valmiki has achieved authoritative status in Hindu tradition because of its antiquity, composition in the sacred Sanskrit language, transmission by Brahmins, and circulation across much of the Indian subcontinent.

Valmiki's text portrays Rama's mission to be born on earth as a human to slay the monarch of the demons, Ravana, who performed such harsh asceticism that he won invincibility from deities and demons but considered it beneath his dignity to ask for protection from a mere mortal man. This "divine loophole" meant that only a human being could end the demon's tyrannous rule (Patel). After Ravana abducts Rama's wife, Sita, Rama enlists monkey allies and goes to war to rescue his wife. With Rama's unsurpassed strength, courage, and ability in archery, he slays Ravana and then

28

ascends the throne in Ayodhya. Valmiki represents Rama's reign as a golden age in which the hero's kingdom suffers neither natural disaster (e.g., famine or disease) nor social ill fortune (e.g., murder or theft) and his subjects contentedly perform their religiously prescribed duties.

Despite its privileged status among priests, kings, and poets, however, Valmiki's text is not the one that most Hindus knew in the past or know today.[1] With the exception of learned Brahmins immersed in Sanskritic culture, most Hindus know the retelling of the story that was composed in the literary or spoken language of their region and that, until quite recently, was hardly ever a word-for-word translation of Valmiki's text but instead an adaptation rooted in local customs and places. Moreover, until educational institutions began to expand in the twentieth century, most Hindus learned the epic either by hearing its regional retelling recited by those who knew it by heart or by seeing enactments of the story; thus, it was regional retellings that played pivotal roles in the epic's dissemination among most Hindus. Indeed, Indian literary tradition refers figuratively to "three hundred *Rāmāyaṇas*" as a way to articulate the richness of the *Ramayana* tradition (Ramanujan 22).

In a world epics course where the *Ramayana* tradition is allotted only two weeks, how can multiple retellings or renditions of the epic be taught? Just as a single course dealing with epics across the globe can— at best—introduce students to such epics, a unit on the *Ramayana* can only provide students with some examples of its multivocality. This essay furnishes instructors with resources and options for customizing a unit on the Indian *Ramayana* tradition to fit their overall goals in a world epics course.

This essay first shows how instructors can provide a foundation for understanding how the *Ramayana* tradition has encompassed diverse texts over time by familiarizing students with the epic's earliest overall narrative arc.[2] The essay then offers teachers some choices among types of retellings (devotional texts, women's retellings, retellings by marginalized groups, or performed enactments), episodes that can be selected for close analysis as case studies. The point is not to show how later retellings might deviate from Valmiki's text; such an approach would assume that Valmiki's is the only true version or that social norms represented in the text remain the same in India today as they were in ancient times. Instead, the readings offered here reveal how retellings reshape the narrative tradition, in accord with the historical context, region, genre, ideology, and social location of tellers and audiences, resulting in a narrative

30   *Ramayana*

tradition that remains fluid and alive. Finally, the essay suggests questions for discussion and debate.

The Overall Narrative Arc

Teachers preparing a unit on the *Ramayana* in a world epics course will find indispensable the seven-volume English translation (one volume for each of the epic's seven *kandas,* or books) of the critical edition *The* Rāmāyaṇa *of Vālmīki: An Epic of Ancient India,* translated from the Sanskrit by a team of scholars led by the general editor, Robert Goldman. Each volume includes introductory essays providing contextual information for that *kanda.*[3] The essays differ depending on what is foregrounded in that *kanda,* such as (but not limited to) historical, mythological, rhetorical, aesthetic, military, or sociological issues; these essays provide useful background that teachers can share with the class as needed.[4] Also useful in the back matter are glossaries of key Sanskrit words, proper nouns, and epithets, as well as explanations of weapons and lineages of demons.[5]

Which text below is best suited to familiarize students with the *Ramayana*'s overall narrative arc depends on the level of the course: advanced college seminar, introductory college course, or high school course. Also guiding the choice are the key epic themes emphasized by the instructor in the course, the course's role in department or graduation requirements, and the students' backgrounds.[6]

Readings of the Overall Narrative Arc

For a complete translation of the Sanskrit text that immerses advanced students of literature or graduate students, a paperback version of the translation by Goldman's team has been published by Princeton University Press, titled *The* Rāmāyaṇa *of Vālmīki: The Complete English Translation* (Goldman and Goldman). At about nine hundred pages, this text may be too long for all but the most advanced or diligent readers. One benefit of the translation is that it brings readers closest to the form, linguistic register, and poetics of the original Sanskrit. A thoughtfully abridged translation in paperback that conveys the spirit and liveliness of the original, *Vālmīki's* Rāmāyaṇa, translated by Arshia Sattar, is recommended. At 562 pages, it can work well if the *Ramayana* unit comes early in the course and the teacher requires students to read ahead.[7] For an introductory college course with just a few class meetings on the *Ramayana*, the summary by the master Indian storyteller R. K. Narayan engagingly recounts the main events and characters in the epic. Although Narayan retells the story as found in Kamban's *Irāmāvatāram*, composed around the twelfth century (see below), both Valmiki and Kamban essentially follow the same narrative arc, so Narayan's retelling also works to familiarize students with the *Ramayana*'s plot and prominent characters. High school teachers could consider assigning Ramayana: *Divine Loophole*, by the animator Sanjay Patel, a storyboard artist for Pixar Animation Studios; this version is suitable for students raised with graphic novels. The verbal material is a bit thin, but the visual creativity is quite engaging. The back matter illustrates the geography and types of characters in the epic (e.g., demons, monkeys, and humans).

No matter which one of these four texts is chosen, the focus of the class should be on the episodes listed in table 1. The Goldman team's seven-volume translation includes all the *kandas*. Sattar's translation of the final *kanda* is heavily abridged, but Sattar provides a full translation of it in a separate book, Uttara: *The Book of Answers*. Narayan deals with the final *kanda* in only three pages, while Patel omits it. Therefore, depending on

Table 1
Selected episodes from the *Ramayana*, listed by *kanda*

Kanda of Childhood	How Valmiki came to compose Rama's story. The bow contest and Rama's marriage to Sita.
Kanda of Ayodhya (the capital city)	Kaikeyi's boons redeemed, leading to Rama's exile in the forest. Bharata's refusal to rule except as regent.
Kanda of the Forest	Shurpanakha's offer and disfigurement. The golden deer's arrival and Ravana's abduction of Sita.
Kanda of Kishkindha (the monkey kingdom)	Rama meets Hanuman and Sugriva. The slaying of Vali.
Kanda of Beauty	Ravana threatens Sita. Hanuman brings Sita the ring of Rama.
Kanda of War	The slaying of Ravana. Sita's trial by fire. Rama's coronation.
Last *kanda*	*How Ravana won invincibility from gods and demons. *The beheading of Shambuka. *Sita's return to Mother Earth. Rama's return to the celestial world.

32   *Ramayana*

the choice of text, the instructor may need to summarize the episodes
starred in table 1 if they are used in the assignments discussed later in the
essay.

Case Studies

From this point onward, the instructor can customize the syllabus in ac-
cordance with the time allotted to teaching the *Ramayana* tradition, the
background of the students, and the pedagogical goals of the course.

Devotional Retellings

The two devotional retellings chosen for this section include three major
conceptual changes when compared to Valmiki's text. First, in different
regions of India, between the twelfth and the sixteenth centuries, Rama
was elevated to a major deity worshipped by his devotees. Usually, in devotional retellings he is viewed as an *avatara* (descent, incarnation) of Supreme Lord Vishnu, who has taken birth on earth out of compassion for
those who suffer greatly from Ravana's tyrannical rule. Second, Rama's
wife, Sita, is viewed as an *avatara* of Lakshmi, the goddess of good fortune and Lord Vishnu's heavenly consort. Third, a foe who dies at the
hand of Rama is said to attain salvation; as a result, that enemy is reborn
in heaven. Thus, devotional retellings serve to praise Rama's salvific deeds,
glorify his might, and show compassion for those who focus their minds
on him, whether as devotees or foes.

Kamban retells Rama's story from birth to the hero's coronation in
Irāmāvatāram (*The Descent of Rama*), in the South Indian language of
Tamil, in the twelfth century. In this first extant regional devotional retelling, Rama is portrayed as fully God on earth, despite choosing birth
as a human. Kamban's poetry is often compared to a necklace, with each
verse likened to a rare and precious gem. Teaching an excerpt from Kamban's only *kanda* currently translated into accessible English (Hart and
Heifetz) can pose difficulties because analyzing even a few verses requires
extensive course time, grounding in Tamil literary conventions, and linguistic analysis.[8] Instead, I suggest that students read David Shulman's article, which assesses the morality of the decision by Rama to contravene
his warrior dharma (code of conduct) when, while concealed behind a tree,
he slays the monkey king, Vali. Since the article incorporates translations
of key verses from Kamban's treatment of this episode, it immerses readers

in a narrative context while Shulman explores how Kamban depicts the relationship between God and the existence of evil, a question relevant to many epics.

Tulsidas retells the story of Rama in the sixteenth-century work *Rāmcaritmānas* (*The Lake of the Deeds of Rama*), written in Awadhi, a precursor to modern Hindi.[9] This work is the most well-known and widespread retelling of the *Ramayana* in India. Especially in north and central India, many devotees recite large parts of it by heart, and thousands of Indians have attended enactments inspired by the text. Such a production is called a *Ramlila* (a play about Rama).[10]

The initial recommended reading from the *Rāmcaritmānas*, one of its most beloved episodes, describes the first meeting between Sita and Rama. She and her female friends have come to the royal garden to pick flowers as offerings to the goddess Gauri, whom they will worship, asking that she bestow good husbands on them. Rama, his brother, and their guru have also come to visit the garden, which is famous for its beauty. When Rama and Sita catch sight of each other through the leafy trees, they immediately fall in love, although not a word is exchanged. When Sita goes to the shrine of Gauri, she requests Rama as a husband. Soon afterward, when Rama triumphs in the bow contest, he wins Sita as his bride (Lutgendorf 2: 101–67).[11] (In Valmiki's text, Rama and Sita never see each other until the bow contest.) The lovers' first encounter in the garden introduces a romantic element into the epic.

The next, brief excerpt reveals how Tulsidas has inserted a new incident into the epic that scholars interpret as a way to silence criticism of Rama for making Sita, after her rescue, undergo a fire ordeal to prove that she retained her fidelity to him during her captivity. This passage recounts how, when Rama and Sita were alone in their forest cottage during their exile, Rama requested that Sita enter their household fire. When she did so, a simulacrum of Sita emerged in her place; it is this illusory Sita whom Ravana abducts. Consequently, when the war ends and Rama has rescued the illusory Sita, he asks her to undergo a fire ordeal to test her chastity; when she enters the fire, the real Sita emerges. Through this substitution, Sita's reputation for purity remains unsullied by the touch of Ravana (Lutgendorf 5: 69–71).

The third excerpt comes from a part of the narrative that many Hindus recite in times of difficulty, illness, or hopelessness. In it, Hanuman uses his extraordinary power to jump across the sea to Lanka, where Sita

34   *Ramayana*

is kept captive by Ravana. Since Sita has refused to enter Ravana's palace, Hanuman finds her outside it in a grove, surrounded by female demons who guard and taunt her. Hanuman makes himself tiny and perches in a tree, where he witnesses Ravana threatening to kill Sita if she refuses to marry him by the deadline he has set. After he departs, Hanuman gives her Rama's ring and tells her that, within a short time, her husband will rescue her, restoring her hope that her trials will soon end (Lutgendorf 5: 219–35). Philip Lutgendorf's introductions help to contextualize the assigned episodes (2: vii–xi, 5: vii–xix).

Women's Retellings

Most documented women's retellings of the epic story appear in short songs that focus on one or a few incidents. Chandravati's Bengali ballad is a notable exception, since it begins with Sita's birth and ends with her return to her mother, the goddess Bhumi (Mother Earth). The next three readings deal with women's songs: one from South India, one from north India, and a comparative essay.

Chandravati, the daughter of a priest, composed the earliest extant, datable woman's retelling of Sita's story from Sita's birth to death, in the late sixteenth century. Evidence suggests that she knew both Sanskrit and Bengali; her ballad, like other women's songs from the region, is composed in an eastern rural dialect of Bengali. It includes an unusual birth story in which Sita is born in the form of an egg to Mandodari, the wife of Ravana. This ballad focuses on Sita's life, and the narrator expresses empathy with Sita's suffering due to her treatment by both Ravana and Rama (Bose and Bose 52–91; this edition includes useful annotations of the ballad). Teachers will appreciate Mandakranta Bose and Sarika Priyadarshini Bose's introduction to *A Woman's* Rāmāyaṇa (1–50), which contextualizes the ballad historically and in relation to genre, gender norms, and other folk ballads of the day.

Velcheru Narayana Rao has written an article based on published collections of anonymous songs sung by women in the language of Telugu in Andhra Pradesh, South India. Narayana Rao provides a survey of the songs' subject matter, explains when and how women sing the songs, summarizes some songs, and provides full translations of others. The songs focus on aspects of the life of Rama specific to his mother's experience (e.g., her morning sickness and her pain in birthing Rama) and aspects of Sita's life specific to her mother-in-law (e.g., the dowry Sita brought to her conjugal home).

Usha Nilsson analyzes *Ramayana* songs sung by female employers, contrasted with songs sung by their domestic employees (servants), and explains how singers learn the songs and how literate ones keep handwritten notebooks as memory aids. The songs are sung in Awadhi and Bhojpuri, dialects of modern Hindi. Nabaneeta Dev Sen provides a thematic survey of women's songs from various locations in India.[12]

Volga's "Reunion" is a modern short story that imagines Sita's life after Rama has banished her to the forest. In it she gives birth to twin sons and raises them in Valmiki's ashram and learns what happened to Shurpanakha, the female demon disfigured by Rama.

Tellings by Marginalized Groups in Modern India

The *Ramayana* texts of Valmiki, Kamban, and Tulsidas primarily focus on the actions of Kshatriyas (warriors and kings) and Brahmins (priests, teachers, and court advisers) mainly in Ayodhya. One exception to this focus appears in Valmiki's final *kanda*, which includes a short episode where Rama learns that his kingdom's order is under threat because a Shudra (a low-caste person) named Shambuka has adopted *tapas* (asceticism or penance) to gain religious liberation, a practice reserved by orthodox Hindu religious texts exclusively for the highest three castes. Brahmins and sages warn Rama to execute Shambuka immediately to restore order in the realm, and Rama does so. In the twentieth century, this previously little-known episode has been publicized and questioned in contemporary debates about the Hindu caste system. Shambuka's death has come to symbolize the fate of stigmatized groups of people who have been killed or maimed if they refuse to confine their behavior to rules imposed on them by those from upper castes. The first two selections in this section look at how modern writers have condemned, rejected, or altered the account of Shambuka's life (Richman, "Why"; Sherraden). Another exception to the *Ramayana*'s focus on high-caste characters is the episode in which Rama slays Vali while Rama conceals himself behind a tree, thereby contravening the warrior's code for a fair fight. In the last reading, Stuart Blackburn describes how a marginalized group of shadow puppeteers identify and memorialize Vali's death in a performance in Kerala, South India (79–94).

Performing Ramayanas in Modern India

For most of Indian history, the majority of Hindus watched enactments of the *Ramayana* rather than reading the story, so performance is pivotal

36   *Ramayana*

for understanding the epic's reception among Hindus. In a performance-focused course, one could substitute Anuradha Kapur's *Actors, Pilgrims, Kings and Gods: The "Ramlila" at Ramnagar* for the sources mentioned earlier to familiarize students with the overall arc of the epic. Kapur provides a fascinating day-by-day first-person account of a month-long *Ramlila* performed at Ramnagar and based on the *Rāmcaritmānas* (29–220).[13] If a short reading assignment about the *Ramlila* of Ramnagar is all that can fit into the course, Richard Schechner and Linda Hess provide an analysis of unique features of the performance. I look at Ravana as reinterpreted in South India, represented in two kinds of performance that present him sympathetically as an admirable or tragic figure, respectively (Richman, "Ravana"). K. V. Akshara analyzes *talamaddale*, a performance tradition in which a patron commissions two actors to perform; when the actors arrive at the venue, the patron assigns each to play a character from a particular episode. Then each must improvise dialogue with the other performer, trying to convince the audience that their interpretation of the episode is the most persuasive, drawing support from Hindu religious texts or contemporary life.

Issues and Questions

Below are some examples of questions about the *Ramayana* that are apt to resonate with students. They prompt students to consider and probe the motivations of characters and norms of society, especially when those norms differ from their own. The questions also emphasize how different versions of the *Ramayana* foreground different aspects of the narrative.

Valmiki's text. If the warrior code forbids a man to attack a woman in battle, is it honorable to attack a female demon? If one's religious preceptor orders one to perform a deed that seems immoral, may one deviate from obeying the advice of that guru? When should a leader stay within the limits of a so-called fair fight, and when, if ever, is assassination justified? When is going to war the right response to immoral behavior by an enemy? Which of Ravana's motivations are blameworthy and which are worthy of admiration? Is the fact that Ravana enjoys the pleasures of life necessarily a bad quality? When does pride in one's own accomplishments become arrogance? Is Rama's banishment of Sita after rescuing her from

Ravana a case of blaming the victim? When should rulers trust their own beliefs, and when should they yield to the will of the populace? When does maintaining order in society conflict with just rule?

Devotional retellings. What kind of changes in the *Ramayana* narrative tradition appear when a figure previously considered human—extraordinary but still human—gets elevated to the supreme deity? Why do deeds like Rama's killing of Vali become such a problem for a deity when they were less problematic for a human? If Rama is omniscient and supreme, does that trivialize his victories in war? How does the glorification of Rama's deeds in devotional retellings inflect the narrative? Is a devotional retelling still an epic, or is it a new genre? If Rama is the supreme deity, how does that change the way authors or performers represent Sita? Do you care about Ravana more or less if you know that after death he will go to heaven? Which characteristics of Ravana remind you of characters from science fiction? from comic books? from film noir?

Women's retellings. What differences did you find between Valmiki's narrative and Chandravati's ballad? How do you think different kinds of feminists would respond to the ballad? How did the fact that Chandravati does not include the disfigurement of Shurpanakha change your assessment of Rama's deeds, if it did? What was most striking about the choice of subject matter in Telugu women's songs? Which characters and themes predominate in those songs, and why do you think they predominate? Why do high-caste women dislike it when their female servants sing about Sita? Why do you think that both sets of women were silent during public *Ramayana* events? In the song that Nilsson has translated into English, how is the *dhagrin* (midwife) who delivers Prince Rama more powerful than King Dasharatha? In what ways is Dev Sen's analysis different from other readings about women's songs? In Volga's short story, which factors strengthen the ability of Sita and Shurpanakha to become friends when they meet again many years later in the forest?

Marginalized groups. Which features of retellings of Shambuka's story are shared in north and South India? In what ways are the two sets of retellings distinctive? How do different authors and playwrights shape Shambuka's motivations and effects in society? How are Shambuka's death and George Floyd's death similar or different?

38 *Ramayana*

Notes

1. Given that so much material is packed into a world epics course and that there is so little time, limiting the focus to Hindu *Ramayana*s is least confusing for students. (There are, however, a set of Jain versions of the epic and some Islamic retellings.) It is beyond the scope of this essay to include artistic representation of episodes from the *Ramayana*, which could be the subject of a course in itself.

2. For a concise synopsis of Valmiki's text, see Richman, "Introduction" 5–7.

3. The text of each volume is followed by an extensive set of annotations mainly targeted to Sanskrit specialists; see Goldman.

4. Some of the essays in volume 1 deal with technical issues of dating and interpolations, but from volume 2 onward each volume includes an essay that gives a synopsis of that *kanda*, keyed to each *sarga* (chapter), which teachers will find helpful if they want to assign additional readings.

5. Since epithets (and vocatives) in the text may be opaque to first-time readers, the glossary indicates whether an epithet refers to a character's ancestor, father, mother, or physical features. Rama is often called Kaakutstha, "descendant of King Kakutstha." Sita is often called Maithili, "she of Mithila kingdom," the region where she grew up. Ravana is also known as Dashagriva, "Ten-Necked One," because when he is angry, passionate, or arrogant, all ten of his heads become visible.

6. If one teaches a class filled with students of Indian heritage, some may already be familiar with the *Ramayana*, especially as represented by the Indian televised version or in comic books.

7. If needed, instructors could require less reading of the long war *kanda*.

8. Teachers who want to savor the sophisticated lyric poetry of Kamban can read Hart and Heifetz.

9. The names Rama (in Sanskrit) and Ram (in Hindi) refer to the same character.

10. In a Hindu devotional context, *lila* refers to divine action as a form of play or sport: when Rama is born on earth, he plays the divine role of saving the creatures on earth from Ravana's predations. *Lila* can also refer to a religious performance: the *Ramlila* is a play about Rama, in which an actor plays the role of Rama.

11. In the episode, King Janaka, Sita's father, has declared that only a warrior who can lift and string the huge bow of Lord Shiva will have the honor of marrying his daughter.

12. Paley's *Sita Sings the Blues* is an animated film in which various people of Indian heritage discuss Sita's life, accompanied by artwork from Indian court painters and shadow-puppet performances. The episodes in the epic are interspersed with incidents in the life of a young American artist whose boyfriend goes to work in India and breaks up with her in an email. The soundtrack features songs by Annette Hanshaw, an American blues singer. Whether shown in class or seen individually by students, the film provides an excellent starting point for class

discussion. Some Hindu groups have called for banning the film; others see it as yet one more retelling of the epic.

13. This *Ramlila* takes place in Banaras, Hinduism's most sacred pilgrimage site, and is the longest and most elaborate *Ramlila* in India.

Works Cited

Akshara, K. V. "Performing the Argument: Ramayana in Talamaddale." Richman and Bharucha, pp. 257–78.

Blackburn, Stuart. *Inside the Drama-House: Rāma Stories and Shadow Puppets in South India.* U of California P, 1996.

Bose, Mandakranta, and Sarika Priyadarshini Bose, translators. *A Woman's* Rāmāyaṇa: *Candrāvatī's Bengali Epic.* Routledge, 2004.

Dev Sen, Nabaneeta. "Lady Sings the Blues: When Women Retell the Ramayana." *Manushi*, no. 108, Sept.-Oct. 1998.

Goldman, Robert, general editor. *The* Rāmāyaṇa *of Vālmīki: An Epic of Ancient India.* Princeton UP, 1986–2017. 7 vols.

Goldman, Robert, and Sally J. Sutherland Goldman, translators. *The* Rāmāyaṇa *of Vālmīki: The Complete English Translation.* Princeton UP, 2021.

Hart, George L., and Hank Heifetz, translators. *The Forest Book of the* Rāmāyaṇa *of Kampan.* U of California P, 1988.

Kapur, Anuradha. *Actors, Pilgrims, Kings and Gods: The "Ramlila" at Ramnagar.* Seagull Books, 2006.

Lutgendorf, Philip, translator. *The Epic of Ram.* By Tulsidas, Murthy Classical Library of India / Harvard UP, 2016–22. 7 vols.

Narayan, R. K. *The* Ramayana: *A Shortened Modern Prose Version of the Indian Epic (Suggested by the Tamil Version of Kamban).* Penguin Books, 1972.

Narayana Rao, Velcheru. "A Ramayana of Their Own: Women's Oral Tradition in Telugu." Richman, *Many Rāmāyaṇas*, pp. 114–36.

Nilsson, Usha. "Grinding Millet but Singing of Sita: Power and Domination in Awadhi and Bhojpuri Women's Songs." *Questioning Ramayanas: A South Asian Tradition*, edited by Paula Richman, U of California P, 2001, pp. 137–58, 379–81.

Paley, Nina. *Sita Sings the Blues.* 2008. *YouTube*, uploaded by Golden Flicks, 2 May 2021, www.youtube.com/watch?v=SfbPtX0VoSA.

Patel, Sanjay. Ramayana: *Divine Loophole.* Chronicle Books, 2010.

Ramanujan, A. K. "Three Hundred *Rāmāyaṇas*: Five Examples and Three Thoughts on Translation." Richman, *Many Rāmāyaṇas*, pp. 22–49.

Richman, Paula. "Introduction: The Diversity of the *Ramayana* Tradition." Richman, *Many Rāmāyaṇas*, pp. 3–21.

———, editor. *Many Rāmāyaṇas: The Diversity of a Narrative Tradition in South Asia.* U of California P, 1991.

40   *Ramayana*

———. "Ravana Center Stage: *Origins of Ravana* and *King of Lanka*." Richman and Bharucha, pp. 97–122.

———. "Why Can't a Shudra Perform Asceticism? Shambuka in Three Modern South Indian Plays." *The* Ramayana *Revisited*, edited by Mandakranta Bose, Oxford UP, 2004, pp. 125–48.

Richman, Paula, and Rustom Bharucha, editors. *Performing the* Ramayana *Tradition: Enactments, Interpretations, and Arguments*. Oxford UP, 2021.

Sattar, Arshia, translator. Uttara*: The Book of Answers*. Penguin Books, 2016.

———, translator. *Vālmīki's* Rāmāyaṇa. Rowman and Littlefield, 2018.

Schechner, Richard, and Linda Hess. "The 'Ramlila' of Ramnagar." *The Drama Review*, vol. 21, no. 3, Sept. 1977, pp. 51–82.

Sherraden, Aaron. "Recasting Shambuka in Three Hindi Anti-caste Dramas." Richman and Bharucha, pp. 65–93.

Shulman, David. "Divine Order and Divine Evil in the Tamil Tale of Rama." *Journal of Asian Studies*, vol. 38, no. 4, Aug. 1979, 651–69.

Volga [Popuri Lalitha Kumari]. "Reunion." Translated by Krishna Rao Maddipati. Ramayana *Stories in Modern South India: An Anthology*, edited by Paula Richman, Indiana UP, 2008, pp. 91–98.

Carolina López-Ruiz

Understanding the World of Greek and Near Eastern Epics through Homer's *Iliad*

Homer's *Iliad* is still the classical epic par excellence in Western literature. Whether or not Alexander the Great really slept with a copy of the *Iliad* under his pillow (Plutarch 8,26), the ethos of Homer's heroes inspired audiences of all walks of life in antiquity as it does today. Yet the *Iliad* and *Odyssey* did not emerge in a literary vacuum. Roughly at the same time, around the late eighth or early seventh century BC, another Greek poet, Hesiod, composed shorter poems in the same epic verse, dactylic hexameters, about the birth of the world and the gods and their intergenerational struggles (*Theogony*) and about agricultural and moral advice (*Works and Days*, a poem within the genre of wisdom literature). These poems emerged from a long oral tradition of narrating myth and legend in verse, developed during the preceding centuries, probably since the Bronze Age, until alphabetic writing became widespread in the Aegean from around 750 BC onward, a technology that allowed for these poems to be preserved but that perhaps also affected their composition in some ways, as discussed below.

While Homer's and Hesiod's poems may be the earliest epics known in Europe, short written epics appeared much earlier in southern Mesopotamia among the Sumerians. They were probably composed in the context of the Ur III court of the twenty-first century BC, although they were preserved

41

42 Homer's *Iliad*

mostly by Babylonian scholars of the eighteenth century BC. Akkadian speakers of the second and early first millennia BC wrote long narrative poems about legendary figures, especially Gilgamesh, and about the creation of the world and the struggles among the gods. During the late Bronze Age the Hittites and Canaanites also produced epics on similar themes. All of these peoples exalted the victories of their respective storm gods (Marduk for the Babylonians, Ashur for the Assyrians, Teshub-Tarhun for the Hurrians and Hittites, and, for the Canaanites and Phoenicians, Baal, who was analogous to the Greek god Zeus), especially in creation myths in which the storm god defeats an entity, usually a dragon, representing chaos. On the later chronological end, Homeric motifs seemingly influenced some stories in the Hebrew Bible, discussed below, and provided the direct model for the Roman *Aeneid*, showing the persistence of epic themes within an eastern Mediterranean continuum of literary works, despite the different plots, characters, and culturally determined features in each case. The points in common that I briefly outline below illustrate how much Greek literature was influenced by nearby civilizations whose written epic traditions were much older.

Background and Composition of the *Iliad*

Homeric epics contain layers of storytelling and poetic skill transmitted through centuries. When the Greeks adopted alphabetic writing around 750 BC, poets composed longer epics that provided room for innovation and personal artistry, including allusions to other Greek epic poems and the creative adaptation of popular themes from Near Eastern epics. Just how much innovation over the previous oral traditions went into the *Iliad* and what the role of writing was in the process of composition of the Homeric poems as we have them are matters of much debate, and we know nothing about the author (or, perhaps, authors) of these poems except for their attribution to a poet of the name Homer (all these issues, and more, constitute the Homeric question).

Objects excavated from Mycenaean palaces and tombs of the late Bronze Age at sites mentioned by Homer (e.g., Troy, Mycenae, Tiryns) explain much of the culture that the *Iliad* and *Odyssey* commemorate. These epics feature high-walled citadels dominated by palaces, war chariots, full-body bronze armor, gold- and silver-studded and engraved swords, and other artifacts such as double-handled gold cups with doves on the rim or helmets covered with rows of boar tusks, elements that all match the second-millennium archaeological record and became part of a selective set of glorified memories of a distant era in Homer's time. The language of Homeric epic is also a kind of archaeological guide. Through centuries of oral epic tradition, the *Iliad* and *Odyssey* preserve a layer of archaic language (including word endings, phonetic phenomena, and entire terms) that philologists can use to tease out the influence of various Greek dialects and to study the development of the Greek language. For instance, Homer's diction retained the letter *digamma* (a sort of *w*), long lost in the spoken dialects he would have used; although the letter is not written in the preserved editions of these epics, the metrics of the verse reveal its presence. An example is the word for king used by Homer, *(w)anax* (ἄναξ), written *wana-ka* in Mycenaean Greek; the term is an archaism, as *basileus* (βασιλεύς) was the word for king in later Greek, while the *basileus* of the *Iliad* seems to be a chief, or in any case a lesser leader than the overlord, or *wanax*, the term for which was reserved especially for Agamemnon—*(w)ánax andrôn* (ἄναξ ἀνδρῶν; lord of men)—and occasionally gods.

The use of repeated adjectives and short phrases, called epithets and formulae, respectively, is essential to the *Iliad* and characterizes other world epics, including those of South Slavic bards. In fact, the study of Serbian formulaic oral epics in the 1920s was the basis for Milman Parry and Albert Lord's reading of Homeric epics as stemming from oral poetry (Parry). Epithets and formulae are part and parcel of this orally transmitted heritage and were essential to Homer's technique of composition. Descriptive word clusters such as "swift-footed Achilles," "Menelaos, son of Atreus," "well-balanced ships," "laughter-loving Aphrodite," and "the gods who possess Olympus" dressed the poem with an evocative epic veneer, but they were also a technical recourse for the oral poet, as memory aids that could be plugged into specific parts of the verse, which was made of six rhythmic units based on syllable length (e.g., "swift-footed Achilles" occupies exactly half of a verse). Homer also brought the action of the *Iliad* onto a universal plane through comparisons or similes drawing on scenes from the natural world and general human experience, whether comparing a woman's birthing pains to the pain and anger of a Greek hero, the shining spears of the packed soldiers to wavering wheat stalks under the sun, or Achilles's reaction at the sight of Patroklos's corpse to the reaction of a lion whose cubs have been stolen (the simile formula is "as when . . . so did . . .").

There is a popular perception that the *Iliad* narrates the entire Trojan War, but the poem's action is focused on a rather undefined and elastic

44   Homer's *Iliad*

short period of time in the last year of the war. The temporal allusions in the poem can add up to fifty-four days, while the narrated action zooms into just a few days, a small portion of the ten-year war. The *Iliad* assumes an audience familiar with the broader story of the Trojan War, including the mythical events leading up to and following the siege and capture of Troy. Homer masterfully alludes to but does not narrate this larger framework, allowing the audience to feel knowledgeable but still full of anticipation to see how famous characters, such as Agamemnon, Achilles, Hektor, Diomedes, and others (including the gods), act in specific circumstances. The *Iliad* opens by focusing our gaze on one character especially, Achilles, and his rage. He is a central presence even when he is absent, during much of the *Iliad*'s narrative. His withdrawal provides a tense plot arc while it opens room for other characters to take the spotlight. Through all this, the poet highlights the themes of strife, friendship, courage, revenge, and, in the end, compassion: in short, the existential troubles of the heroic human and his rapport with the gods. The Homeric heroes and themes were also the subject matter for classical Greek tragedy in the fifth century BC, when playwrights revisited and elaborated on them to highlight civic and moral issues that particularly concerned Athenians of the time.

In turn, the larger Trojan War story was narrated in a series of poems that have not been preserved except for random short quotations and much later summaries. These poems are known as the Epic Cycle. They covered events such as the Judgement of Paris and the kidnapping of Helen (the cause of the war), famous events during the war, and, on the other end of the *Iliad*, the death of Achilles, the sack of Troy, and the returns of various surviving heroes to Greece (the *Nostoi*, or *Returns*). The *Odyssey* is the only other extant archaic epic on the Trojan War theme, recounting the long and eventful return of Odysseus to Ithaca. It is also the only epic uniformly attributed to Homer in antiquity.

What the *Iliad* narrates, specifically, is the conflict between Achilles and Agamemnon and its consequences. From their falling out in book 1 until book 19, the epic focuses on the disastrous consequences of Achilles's pulling out of the battlefield. The death of Patroklos at Hektor's hands in book 16 marks the turning point: Achilles's desire to return to battle is aroused by the drive to avenge his beloved friend and assuage the pain of his loss with blood. The climax of the *Iliad* is this act of revenge, when Achilles kills Hektor, with the aid of Athena and the acquiescence of all-seeing Zeus (bk. 22). With the supreme Trojan warrior gone, the fate of

Troy is sealed, and the poem ends with what can be read as a nod as to how the final desolation of Troy will come (through the Trojan horse), as the city has lost Hektor, called "breaker of horses" in the very last words of the poem (Lattimore 24.804).

Most of the action described in the *Iliad* occurs during only three days of intense fighting. But the *Iliad*'s time becomes elastic through the brief description of multiple events, sometimes preceding or overlapping with the main Achilles-centered narrative (e.g., the plague sent by Apollo, Zeus's twelve-day visit to the Ethiopians, the days of truce to prepare Hektor's funeral, etc.). However the time covered in the poem is counted (usually fifty-one days), the *Iliad* makes an epic of twenty-four books or songs (15,693 verses) out of a single episode toward the end of a ten-year war. Moreover, Homer stretches our gaze into the past and the future by inserting passages that logically belong earlier in the story of the Trojan War. For instance, the catalogue of ships (2.494–759) describes all the naval contingents that went to Troy under the command of Agamemnon and Menelaos, king of Sparta and the offended husband of Helen; and in book 3, in the episode called the *teikhoskopia* (viewing from the walls), Helen and Priam look at the Greek forces from the walls of Troy, and Helen points out the most important leaders, while the armies prepare for the duel between Menelaos and Paris (also called Alexander). Looking in the opposite direction, toward the future, the recurrent allusions and premonitions of Achilles's death provide a tragic arc to the *Iliad*. The funeral of Patroklos, with its pyre, extravagant offerings, and athletic games (bk. 23), is clearly a prequel to the funeral of Achilles, which falls outside the *Iliad*'s narrative. Achilles's fate to die young at Troy, in exchange for glory, is foretold by his own mother, Thetis (1.414–18), and even by one of his semidivine horses (19.404–17).

Main Themes

At the center of the *Iliad* are the universal themes of human love, pride, and loss. But the gods seem chained to similar passions, including the grief (or anticipated grief) for mortal loved ones. Homer's gods are notoriously anthropomorphic, which provoked criticism from Greek intellectuals such as Plato. Whatever the effect that portrayal of the gods had on Homer's audience, the divine plane is the ultimate framework for the epics and inseparable from the fate of mortals, especially determined by the frequently invoked "will of Zeus" (Lattimore 1.5)

46   Homer's *Iliad*

Just as among Greeks and Trojans there are hierarchies and alliances (note that Homer calls the Greeks Argives, Achaeans, and Danaans, besides the subgroups led by the different leaders), so it is among the immortals. Set against a world of older gods (the Titans) and other minor nature deities (nymphs, divinized rivers, etc.), the Olympians are organized as a large family ruled by Zeus, who struggles to maintain an equilibrium in tension with his own desires and contested loyalties (e.g., to his wife Hera, his divine children, and his mortal offspring). The Trojan War becomes a proxy war for the gods, a stage on which they work out their tensions, and the gods, except for Zeus, align themselves to support either the Greeks (Poseidon, Athena, Hera, Thetis, Hermes, and Hephaistos) or the Trojans (Ares, Artemis, Apollo, and Aphrodite), each for their own reasons. In turn, the Olympian family dynamics are overlaid with the mechanisms of a political community, since the gods meet to debate issues in a council governed by Zeus, and he often acts as a revered judge. The counsel or assembly of the gods and heavenly hosts appears also in Near Eastern epics such as the Ugaritic (Canaanite) epics and in the Hebrew Bible, there among various slips that reveal Israel's polytheistic prehistory (e.g., in Ps. 82.1, 89.5–7; 1 Kings 22.19; Isa. 6).

How do these two planes, the human and the divine, intersect? As in historical communities, the *Iliad*'s characters interact with the gods in four possible ways: through offerings (including animal sacrifice), prayer (which follows particular formulae; see Lattimore 1.451–456), omens and oracles (often interpreted by specialists), and dreams in which messages are conveyed. Homer's listeners and readers, however, would have deduced that the *Iliad*'s characters were closer to the gods than they were. Many of the main heroes are demigods, that is, children of one god and one mortal, and the gods in the *Iliad* and *Odyssey* often directly interact with mortals (an epiphany), either in their true form (e.g., when jumping into a chariot to help in battle) or by deceitfully taking the form of a human.

All these encounters and interactions take place in four locations: the Greek camp by the seashore; the citadel of Troy; the plain between these two, where the battles and skirmishes happen; and the realm of Olympus from where the gods gaze on all this and occasionally intervene. The camp and the city encapsulate a basic contrast between the realms of nature and culture, a dichotomy that informs much of Greek mythology. The "strong-founded" city of Troy (4.33) contains houses, palaces, temples, ramparts, and gates and is filled with the civic and family life that the Greek camp lacks (the camp has palisades, beached boats, tents, captive concubines, and beach sacrifices). Eventually, the camp also becomes a besieged city, and the desolated, rugged battlefield provides a counterpoint to either human habitation. The two main heroes of the *Iliad*, Achilles and Hektor, also embody this dichotomy: Achilles's hubris, unrestrained rage, callousness, and self-centeredness (only moderated by the character's humbling toward the end of the *Iliad*) contrasts with the restrained, selfless, civic-minded character of Hektor; Achilles fights for a personal cause, and Hektor to protect his family and city, which makes him, for some, the real tragic hero of the *Iliad*.

Through minimal selection of books of the *Iliad* (see the appendix), we can follow the main turning points as well as themes that pertain not only to the *Iliad* but to the entire Trojan cycle. In book 1, for instance, the strife between Achilles and Agamemnon reminds us of what the entire war is about, a clash over an abduction, in this case not of Helen but of Achilles's war bride, Briseis, in exchange for Agamemnon's own war bride, Chryseis. The characters of Achilles and Agamemnon are fully painted in their proud and harsh exchange, while the gods' power is firmly established, not only that of Apollo (who sends the plague that devastates the camp) and Thetis (Achilles's mother, who begs Zeus to bring honor and glory to her offended son), but especially "the will of Zeus" (1.5).

Throughout the *Iliad*, but especially in book 5 (the *aristeia*, or exploits, of Diomedes), the anthropomorphic characterization of the gods is apparent, as is the unique relationship between the heroes and the gods. Diomedes is presented as "the best of the Achaeans" in Achilles's absence (5.103). The gods intervene wildly in battle, helping or fighting mortals of their choosing, causing chaos, and playing out their rivalries. While Athena and Ares (representing different aspects of war) stir up the battle, Aphrodite fights to save her son Aeneas but proves inadequate on the battlefield and is scolded by Diomedes and other gods, including Zeus himself. Most surprisingly, perhaps, Diomedes physically wounds Aphrodite on the wrist, and stories are told of other instances in which mortal heroes (Herakles mostly) wounded immortal gods, including Hades. We can see here the use of embedded myths within the narrative to illustrate a point: how Herakles previously wounded gods and sacked Troy, the background story of Aeneas's divine horses, and the story of Zeus and Ganymede. In short, book 5 shows the world of gods and mortals almost but not quite merging. Mortals might be a threat to the gods (Diomedes certainly is), but they are, in the end, not deathless like the gods.

48 Homer's *Iliad*

In book 9 we see the failed attempts to bring Achilles back to the Greeks' aid, when not even persuasive companions, such as Odysseus, Ajax, and Phoenix, can break through Achilles's stubborn position. The story of Meleager and the boar of Calydon is told as an example of someone who waited far too long to come to the rescue of his community and who was only stirred by his mother's imploring (9.529–99), but Achilles has not yet reached that personal tipping point in his heart. In this scene, Achilles reveals his alleged choice between two fates, a short but glorious life or a successful return to his home in exchange for oblivion (9.410–15).

Book 18 describes the desperate mourning and visceral rage of Achilles after the death of Patroklos, which spurs him to return to battle. Since Patroklos had been killed while wearing Achilles's armor, a new set of armor is now made by Hephaistos: the description of the shield of Achilles is priceless, as it seems to be engraved with scenes of community life in war and peace and is almost cinematographically described (18.478–608). Achilles now accepts his fate to die and be buried at Troy, but not before he obtains his revenge.

The fatal clash between Hektor and Achilles comes in book 22, in which Athena intervenes to help Achilles. Zeus judges between the two heroes, balancing their fates on his scales, and decides that it is Achilles's time to survive and Hektor's to die. The contrast between the brutal fight outside the walls and the chase of Hektor by Achilles, on the one hand, and the civilized city life inside, as well as the cold way in which Zeus decides Hektor's fate, makes the scene doubly tragic.

Only when Hektor's old, mournful father, Priam, comes down to Achilles's tent, risking his life to beseech Achilles to release his son's body, does Achilles become filled with compassion and set aside his rage. This scene in book 24 completes Achilles's character arc in the *Iliad* (from rage to sorrow to revenge to empathy), and the epic closes with a sense of reconciled community, especially in book 23 at the funeral games of Patroklos. Thus Homer closes the circle from the divisions among the Greeks in book 1, even as dark clouds loom over Greeks and Trojans alike.

Homer, *The Epic of Gilgamesh*, and Biblical Narratives

If there were a model for what a long heroic epic looked like before Homer in the early first millennium BC, that would have been *The Epic of Gilgamesh*. This mythologized story of a king of Uruk transcended Mesopotamian culture and was copied and translated into several Near Eastern languages. Unlike the *Iliad* and *Odyssey*, we can trace several written versions of *The Epic of Gilgamesh* through the centuries, going back to the Sumerians in the late third millennium BC. The most complete version we have (the Standard Babylonian Version) was redacted in Akkadian in the early first millennium BC.

Probably the same character as the king Bilgamesh of Uruk mentioned in the Sumerian king lists, the Gilgamesh of the epic is a demigod ("two-thirds of him was divine" [Dalley, *Epic*, tablet 1]) who is as intelligent, strong, and beautiful as he is arrogant. He makes a fast friendship with the wild man Enkidu, who balances his excesses, and with whom he fights monsters (Humbaba, the Bull of Heaven), but Enkidu's death—by the decree of the gods—comes too soon. Gilgamesh mourns Enkidu bitterly and sets out on a search for immortality, until he finds the survivor of the Flood, Utnapishtim (the Atrahasis of the Babylonian Flood epic), whose narration of the Flood makes Gilgamesh take the measure of his own mortality and return home to fulfill his kingly duties with new wisdom.

The most striking similarities between *The Epic of Gilgamesh* and the *Iliad* concentrate on the figures of Achilles and Gilgamesh (see the appendix for the recommended excerpts in *The Epic of Gilgamesh*). Achilles and Gilgamesh are both sons of a goddess; they both possess extraordinary strength and valor but are too arrogant; their beloved friends (Patroklos and Enkidu, respectively) die, and the heroes bitterly mourn for them; and this loss marks a turning point in both stories, which leads the heroes on different journeys: Achilles returns to battle and seeks revenge and glory, whereas Gilgamesh wanders in the wilderness in search of immortality. It is through their separate encounters with an older man (Priam and Utnapishtim, respectively) that both heroes acquire a humbling acceptance of their mortal condition. There are many other similarities, such as how the heroes mourn their friends (*Il.* 18, 19; *Epic of Gilgamesh*, tablet 8): their hypermasculinity gives way to the gestures of female mourners, they are likened to brides and to lionesses deprived of their cubs, and neither of them bury their friend for a long time, until worms take over the body (or are feared to do so). Moreover, in both stories the highest gods (Zeus and Enlil, respectively) weigh the fate of the heroes (against Hektor's and Enkidu's fates) at some point and decide that Achilles and Gilgamesh will not die there and then (*Il.* 22; *Gilgamesh*, tablet 7). The episode in the *Iliad*, book 5, in which Diomedes, acting as a surrogate for Achilles, wounds Aphrodite, and she complains to her parents up on Olympus, is often compared with Gilgamesh's rejection and insulting of

50   Homer's *Iliad*

Ishtar (the Mesopotamian love goddess) in tablet 5, whereupon she sends the Bull of Heaven after Gilgamesh as punishment. In different ways, *The Epic of Gilgamesh* also finds echoes in the *Odyssey*: both Gilgamesh and Odysseus fight against semidivine monsters (Humbaba and the Cyclops, respectively) and travel, with their different purposes, to the underworld or the Beyond. The theme of a descent to the underworld, or *katabasis* (literally Greek for "descent"), appears first in Mesopotamian epics and subsequently in Homer's works and then in Virgil's *Aeneid* and Dante's *Divine Comedy.*

In a sense, the *Iliad* and the *Odyssey* capture different sides of the Mesopotamian classic epic, one emphasizing the themes of hubris, loss, and the spiritual journey to accept death, the other emphasizing the monster slaying and physical journey to return home. The opening lines of these epics (which served as titles in the Near East, as in the traditional Hebrew names of the books of the Hebrew Bible) suggest their theme: the *Iliad* begins, "The rage, sing, O goddess, of Achilles, the son of Peleus" (Powell, *Il.* 1.1), and the *Odyssey* begins, "Sing to me of the resourceful man, O Muse, who wandered / far" (Powell, *Od.* 1.1–2). The Standard Babylonian Version of *The Epic of Gilgamesh*, on the other hand, opens, "[H]e who saw the deep, the country's foundations . . . was wise in all matters" (George tablet 1). These openings reverberate much later in the *Aeneid*'s first line, "Arms and the man I sing of Troy" (Ahl 1.1). The *Aeneid*'s hero, Aeneas, ties together characteristics and adventures from both Achilles and Odysseus, forever joining the most ancient tropes of the Trojan epics to Italy and its foundation myths.

Not all eastern Mediterranean cultures took to the genre of epic. In ancient Egypt, for instance, mythology is reflected in religious hymns, funerary texts, and a few prose narratives closer to the future genre of the novel, which contain allusions to the story world involving the gods, but no written epic poems were developed. The Hebrew Bible also contains no epic poetry. But the Israelites adapted mythological themes from the broader Near Eastern milieu, such as the Flood narrative from Mesopotamia and themes that once belonged to the Canaanite storm god Baal (who was the subject of an epic written at Ugarit in the second millennium BC). The influential themes from Gilgamesh's epic and even aspects of the Homeric world permeated some biblical stories that probably took their final form after Homer's epics were circulating broadly. Thus, the world of demigods seems to be evoked in the idea of the semidivine race of Nephilim born as the "sons of god" and mortal women ("heroes that were of old, warriors of renown" [*New Oxford Annotated Bible* Gen. 6.2, 4; see also Job]). In addition, the passionate and tragic friendship of David and Jonathan, the latter of whom is mourned bitterly (2 Sam. 1.23–27), follows the narrative pattern that would have been widely known from the epic pairs Gilgamesh-Enkidu and Achilles-Patroklos. The episode of David and Goliath (1 Sam. 17) seems to channel some Homeric influence as well, not only in the single combat, akin to those in the *Iliad*, but also in the details of Goliath's full bronze armor, presented as unusual and echoing the Homeric panoply. This image was attached to Goliath precisely because he was one of the Philistines, who were of foreign origin (likely from the Aegean), and the image's effect was to exalt David's unexpected victory, as David was armed only with a sling and the favor of his god.

Appendix: Recommended Classroom Materials

Suggested Excerpts and Translations

Homer's *Iliad*, books 1, 5, 9, 18, 22, and 24 (Lattimore; Powell)
The Epic of Gilgamesh, tablets 1, 2, 7, and 11 (Dalley, *Epic*; George)
Other Near Eastern texts, including biblical passages, as desired (see, e.g., Dalley, *Myths*; Hoffner; López-Ruiz; Parker)

Discussion Questions

Note how in *Iliad*, book 5, Athena helps Diomedes, while Aphrodite, Ares, and Apollo help Aeneas. What are their motivations? Is divine intervention similar or different in Gilgamesh's story?

Discuss the theme of friendship in the *Iliad* and *The Epic of Gilgamesh*. What are other motives driving the heroes' actions?

How does the concept of *hybris* (excessive arrogance, sometimes with violent manifestations or tragic consequences) apply to Achilles, Gilgamesh, and other characters in the stories? Does *hybris* have explanatory value in our society?

Which of Achilles's two possible fates is better? Does our society value glory and fame in the same way as Achilles does?

Notice how Athena and Ares are described in the *Iliad* (e.g., bk. 5): which different aspects of war and violence do they represent?

Find instances in book 5 of the *Iliad* where Homer remarks on the physical characteristics of the gods and discuss what you find interesting about them. More generally, what might be the effect (for Homer's audience and for you) of the anthropomorphic depiction of the gods?

Notice the crude descriptions of battle and death in the *Iliad* (e.g., bk. 5); compare these descriptions with treatments of violence in modern literature and media.

Does the dichotomy between nature and culture in the *Iliad* have the same importance in modern fiction?

52   Homer's *Iliad*

The *Iliad*'s plot revolves around objectified women such as Helen, Chryseis, and
Briseis. Discuss their lack of agency and power and find female characters
(e.g., among the gods) that do not fit the pattern.

The Trojan enemies are supposed to be non-Greeks, but are they represented
any differently than the Greeks in terms of language, religion, or customs?
What does this representation mean for the Greeks' view of others?

Further Reading

For the relationship between epic and Greek myth, see Graf (especially 57–78).
For the composition of the epic and its historical background (e.g., Mycenaean
civilization, Troy, the Homeric question, the development of the Greek alphabet),
see Powell 1–20; West 3–77. For structure and internal resonances in the *Iliad*,
see Heiden. For Hektor and the issue of nature and culture, see Redfield, and for
the Greek hero in Homer and beyond, see Nagy. For Achilles's motivations, see
Wilson; Scodel. For comparisons between Achilles and Gilgamesh, see Currie;
Clarke; and, involving also biblical heroes, Smith. On the Nephilim and other
biblical themes of Homeric resonance, see Doak; Smith. For comparison of the
Iliad with biblical and Ugaritic (Canaanite) epics, see Louden. Brief introductions to ancient Mediterranean myths, including epics, are also in López-Ruiz.

Works Cited

Ahl, Frederick, translator. *Aeneid*. By Virgil, Oxford UP, 2007.

Clarke, Michael. *Achilles beside Gilgamesh: Mortality and Wisdom in Early Epic
Poetry*. Cambridge UP, 2019.

Currie, Bruno. *Homer's Allusive Art*. Oxford UP, 2016.

Dalley, Stephanie. *The Epic of Giglamesh*. Standard Babylonian Version. Dalley,
Myths, pp. 39–135.

———. *Myths from Mesopotamia: Creation, the Flood*, Gilgamesh, *and Others*.
2nd rev. ed., Oxford UP, 2000.

Doak, Brian R. *The Last of the Rephaim: Conquest and Cataclysm in the Heroic
Ages of Ancient Israel*. Ilex Foundation, 2013.

George, Andrew R., translator. *The Epic of Gilgamesh*. 2nd rev. ed., Penguin
Books, 2003.

Graf, Fritz. *Greek Mythology: An Introduction*. Johns Hopkins UP, 1993.

Heiden, Bruce. *Homer's Cosmic Fabrication: Choice and Design in the* Iliad.
Oxford UP, 2008.

Hoffner, Harry A., Jr. *Hittite Myths*. 2nd ed., Society of Biblical Literature,
1998.

Lattimore, Richmond, translator. *The* Iliad *of Homer*. 1951. U of Chicago P,
2011.

López-Ruiz, Carolina, editor. *Gods, Heroes, and Monsters: A Sourcebook of Greek,
Roman, and Near Eastern Myths in Translation*. 2nd rev. ed., Oxford UP, 2018.

Louden, B. *The* Iliad: *Structure, Myth, and Meaning.* Johns Hopkins UP, 2006.

Nagy, Gregory. *The Greek Hero in Twenty-Four Hours.* Harvard UP, 2013.

The New Oxford Annotated Bible. Edited by Michael D. Coogan, New Revised Standard Version, 5th ed., Oxford UP, 2010.

Parker, Simon B., editor. *Ugaritic Narrative Poetry.* Society of Biblical Literature, 1997.

Parry, Milman. *The Making of Homeric Verse: The Collected Papers of Milman Parry.* Edited by Adam Parry, Oxford UP, 1971.

Plutarch. "Alexander." *Greek Lives: A Selection of Nine Greek Lives,* translated by Robin Waterfield, Oxford UP, 1998, pp. 306–81.

Powell, Barry B., translator. *The Iliad.* Oxford UP, 2014.

———, translator. *The Odyssey.* Oxford UP, 2015.

Redfield, James. *Nature and Culture in the* Iliad: *The Tragedy of Hector.* Expanded ed., Duke UP, 1994.

Scodel, Ruth. *Epic Facework: Self-Representation and Social Interaction in Homer.* Classical Press of Wales, 2008.

Smith, Mark S. *Poetic Heroes: The Literary Commemorations of Warriors and Warrior Culture in the Early Biblical World.* William B. Eerdmans, 2014.

West, Martin L. *The Making of the* Iliad: *Disquisition and Analytical Commentary.* Oxford UP, 2011.

Wilson, Donna F. *Ransom, Revenge, and Heroic Identity in the* Iliad. Cambridge UP, 2002.

Christine G. Perkell

Ambiguity in Virgil's *Aeneid*

The *Aeneid* of Virgil introduces a figure new to heroic epic, Aeneas, the selfless hero dedicated to his mission on behalf of others. Aeneas is called on by visions and divine signs to lead his family, in the first instance, and soon other followers from fallen Troy to their destined new home. Eventually, it is further revealed to Aeneas that the destined site is to be found in Italy and will, in the far future, become imperial Rome. Aeneas does not seek out this mission, but neither does he refuse it. Aeneas's other-directed heroic purpose transcends his own lifetime by many centuries (as the ancients determined) and is still seen by many as a model of the highest form of heroism.

In the poem's first half (bks. 1–6) Aeneas sails the Mediterranean in search of his fated destination; in the second half (bks. 7–12) he fights to settle his people there. In books 1–6 Aeneas's faith in his mission is tested by wrong turns, failures, and losses; in books 7–12 Aeneas's humanity and the ethical limitations of *pietas* are tested. *Pietas* is the Romans' traditional cultural imperative. *Pietas* (whence the English words *pity* and *piety*) refers to the Romans' performance of what is owed to their fatherland (*patria*), their family, and their gods. The moral limitations of *pietas*, as Aeneas understands it, are tested by his eventual victory and achieved power, which constitute moral hazards for the formerly vanquished Trojans, now the ruling victors.[1] Shipwrecked on the shores of Carthage, Aeneas introduces himself to the first "person" (his goddess mother, Venus, in disguise as a young Tyrian girl) he encounters as *pius Aeneas* (dutiful Aeneas). *Pius* is his self-defining epithet, epitomized in his carrying his lame father on his shoulders out of burning Troy as he holds his young son by the hand. In the poem's last lines Aeneas kills Turnus, the leader of the Italian forces ranged against him (Virgil 12.919–52). In the course of the poem, then, Aeneas moves from defender to aggressor, from defeated to victorious, from Trojan fugitive to Roman founder, from wishing he had died in Troy (in his first speech in the poem) to killing a man, Turnus, in infuriated vengeful rage (his last speech [12.945–49]). The meaning of the *Aeneid* as a whole, to the degree that it is a function of Aeneas's experience, inheres in this trajectory. Aeneas accomplishes his mission, certainly; but some scholars and readers suggest that, in winning the Italian war as he does, killing the suppliant Turnus (on his knees, hands extended), who has conceded defeat before his people, relinquished his claim to Lavinia, and asked (albeit unforthrightly) to be spared, Aeneas compromises the moral authority that might otherwise justify the losses he inflicts in pursuing his *pietas*-driven mission. Thus Virgil both heroizes and problematizes *pietas*. Just as Homer puts the heroic code into question in the *Iliad* (Redfield; Silk 96–97),[2] so Virgil, it may be argued, puts *pietas* into question by not concealing the sometime opposition between *pietas* and a more universal humanity.

The climactic testing of Aeneas occurs in the poem's last lines when he hesitates before killing the wounded (but not mortally) and suppliant Turnus. The recognized textual model for the killing of Turnus is *Iliad* book 22 (significantly, not the poem's end), wherein Achilles fatally wounds Hector with his spear cast. Hector, dying, asks for burial, which Achilles savagely refuses (at this juncture in the story). By making Turnus not *fatally* wounded, Virgil allows the whole poem to come down to this question for Aeneas: whether to spare or kill Turnus. For Virgil's contemporary readers, the killing of Turnus marks the success of Aeneas's mission and the foundation of the Roman people and their empire. Some, however, reading the poem today (and likely even then), question whether Aeneas's *furor* (he kills Turnus with "terrifying *furor* and anger" [Virgil 12.946]),

56 Virgil's *Aeneid*

or anyone's *furor* (unreasoning, unreasoned, vengeful, violent rage), can ever be seen as a good or as contained by *imperium* (empire, rule), reason, or Augustus. (This summary of the scene simplifies the layers of moral complexity that bedevil critics.)

From 29 until 19 BCE, when he died, Virgil worked on the *Aeneid*. The ancient *Life of Virgil* says Virgil planned to spend three years in Greece revising the poem and then turn to philosophy, but he caught a fever and died in Brundisium (Brindisi). The *Life* tells us, further, that during his illness he asked his executor, Varius, to burn the poem. This request, the *Life* says, was countermanded by Augustus himself, who ordered that the poem be published virtually as it was (Donatus). Many readers, stunned by the brutal, abrupt ending of the poem, starkly *un*interpreted by the epic narrator or any character, would like to believe that Virgil would have changed it if he had lived.

Despite the poem's long fame and canonical status, the meaning of the entire *Aeneid*—its worldview and political and moral import—is currently contested by Virgil scholars. Is the poem comic (i.e., life-affirming, a story in which the hero ends up well) on the Odyssean model or instead tragic on the Iliadic model? Does it support or oppose Augustus's imperial project? Is Aeneas, in his movement from defeat to victory, morally edified or undone? In current scholarly debates, the first view belongs to the so-called optimistic, pro-Augustan reading of the poem (largely by European scholars), and the second to the pessimistic, anti-Augustan Harvard school reading (largely by American scholars), which coincided with many Americans' questioning of the United States' role in the Vietnam War during the 1960s.[3] Current scholarship fixes on the final scene and its interpretive challenges, where both Turnus's and Aeneas's last words are dissected as to their sincerity and intention.

The *Aeneid* in the Classroom

Given that the most basic meaning of the *Aeneid* is still contested, as is the authenticity of the all-important ending, the best approach, I believe, is for instructors to read consequential passages together with students, posing questions and responding to those of the students. For instructors who can spend six classes on the *Aeneid*, I would suggest scheduling a whole class each for books 1, 2 (Aeneas's narrative of the fall of Troy), 4 (Aeneas's desertion of Dido followed by her suicide), and 6 (Aeneas's visit to the underworld to consult the shade of his father); one class for books

8 and 10 (Latins and Trojans at war, deaths of major characters); and a final class for book 12, concluding with discussion of the whole poem from the perspective of the end point.

Concurrent with the first reading assignment, instructors could aid student comprehension by posting a brief plot summary of the whole poem and a list of dates important for the poem's action (e.g., Julius Caesar's crossing of the Rubicon; Caesar's assassination by Brutus; and the battles of Pharsalus, Philippi, and Actium, this last battle completing the defeat of Antony and Cleopatra by Octavian, Caesar's heir, soon to be given the title Augustus by the Roman senate). Many translations of the *Aeneid* contain such aids for students. Instructors may also help students think about the issues in advance of class discussion by pointing out interpretive problems (e.g., inconsistencies or gaps) that characterize Virgil's verses. Was it stormy the night when Palinurus fell off the ship at the end of book 5? Why does the Golden Bough not come easily when Aeneas tries to pluck it in book 6? How could Aeneas have seen or known about some of the events he recounts to Dido in book 2? Since the poem is characterized by such puzzles, we must consider that these are integral to Virgil's poetics and therefore are best treated by interrogation instead of normalization.[4] Good questions to pose or post in advance are genuinely open, with more than one reading or answer possible. A well-composed question gets at key interpretive issues and triggers students' desire to contribute to discussion. This method can succeed in both small and large classes. I also assign readings of important interpretive articles for students to explicate and critique. This practice gives students the opportunity to see models of how such scholarship is done and to encounter approaches other than mine.

Throughout the epic, Virgil's purposes emerge most clearly when readers can recognize and appreciate his strategy of allusion, which functions significantly not as mere imitation but as contestation or irony. The contribution to meaning made by Virgil's allusions to the Homeric poems cannot be overstated.[5] Virgil alludes to many other texts as well, but, as Joseph Farrell puts it, the *Odyssey* and *Iliad* are the "polar coordinates" of the *Aeneid* (194). The *Aeneid* features several characters who appear in the *Iliad* and *Odyssey*, seven or so centuries earlier than Virgil's lifetime. Virgil's Aeneas, however, shares little with the Iliadic character Aineias (whose name is here transliterated from the Greek) or with Homer's Achilles or Odysseus, although Aeneas sometimes speaks their words. In this case, the differences in context and import illuminate differences between

58   Virgil's *Aeneid*

the characters' purposes and values. Students should therefore ideally have read the *Iliad* and the *Odyssey* previously in the course or should be assigned specific episodes in conjunction with the alluding passages in the *Aeneid*. Short passages, like the proems, as well as whole episodes can be profitably compared and contrasted with their Homeric models. For example, in *Odyssey* books 9–12 Odysseus tells to the Phaeacians the famous events of his wanderings (e.g., his encounters with the Cyclops, Calypso, and the lotus eaters). These books can be contrasted to *Aeneid* books 2–3, where Aeneas tells his story from Troy's fall to his shipwreck on the beach of Dido's Carthage.[6] How do the goals of Odysseus and Aeneas as narrators of their tales differ? What explains the different responses of the listening audience in each case? (When Aeneas concludes his tale, Dido wants to marry him. When Odysseus concludes his tale, the Phaeacians make haste to send him off home.) Similarly, the passage in *Odyssey* book 11, where Odysseus in Hades learns the secret of homecoming (i.e., not to eat the cattle of the sun) from the seer Tiresias (Homer, *Od.* 11.104–14), can be contrasted with Aeneas's underworld encounter with the spirit of his father, Anchises, who foretells to Aeneas the feats of great (and some bad) Romans up to Virgil's own lifetime. Aeneas also learns from Anchises what we might call the secret of empire: the purpose of deploying force and who should be spared and who not (Virgil 6.851–53).[7] How do these different kinds of knowledge (the secret of homecoming versus the secret of empire) reflect the values implicitly put into question and those implicitly endorsed in the two poems?[8]

For the final class on *Aeneid* 12, students will want to have read *Iliad* book 22 (where Achilles pursues and kills Hector) and *Iliad* book 24 (the reconciliation of Achilles and Priam, the ransom of Hector's body, and Hector's funeral). Despite the tragedies that the *Iliad* portrays, the weight of sorrow is lightened for characters and readers by the affirmation of the value of Hector's life through the series of preparations for and carrying out of Hector's funeral ceremony (Homer, *Il.* 24.420–804). Even though the Trojan Hector is formally the antagonist in the poem, the Greek Homeric narrator treats him with sympathy throughout. James Redfield writes persuasively about the significance of ceremony to give form and meaning to human lives. The funeral ceremony confers a "definite social status" or "form" on the dead person (175), who thus retains his human value. Hector's life still matters. In this light, Redfield might say that funeral is the purification of death, as culture is of nature, or as cooked is of raw. It would appear that Virgil understood all this. Given the full sequence of ceremonies with which the *Iliad* ends, we are surely to see the close of the *Aeneid*, by contrast, as emphatically raw, unillumined by any insight or interpretation on the part of Aeneas or the epic narrator. Readers are stranded, alone with their thoughts. Is Virgil implying that the elevated ending of the *Iliad* is a vain dream? that in reality the unreasoning madness of *furor* will always threaten and overcome even those who strive for reason and control? If the story of Virgil's asking on his deathbed for his manuscript of the *Aeneid* to be destroyed is true, perhaps it is because he did not want to leave Augustus and later readers with such a dark vision. The madness of Rome's civil wars that killed so many during the first four decades of Virgil's life surely contributed to the despair that arguably colors the end of the *Aeneid*. Virgil could not know that the Roman Empire would endure for more than four hundred years after his death and that two hundred of those years would in retrospect be called the *Pax Romana*, the Roman peace.

Sample Presentation of Features and Themes in Book 1

My classes are very much text-based. Before class I upload on the large electronic whiteboard the passages important for discussion, along with discussion questions. I can toggle between them as desired. The questions come from my decades of reading, thinking, and posing questions to students about the texts of Homer and Virgil. I keep track of questions that have been productive for discussion. Below I offer examples of discussion points and questions for book 1 of the *Aeneid* (see Perkell).

The first book of the poem deploys elements that are characteristic of Homeric epic and that, therefore, have become traditional for the epic genre: proem, speech, episode, simile, prophecy, ekphrasis, and a female character or two at odds in some way with male purposes. In the famous first line of the *Aeneid* (*arma virumque cano*, literally, "arms and a man I sing"), Virgil is understood to be alluding to the subjects and first words of the *Iliad* and *Odyssey*, war and man respectively: "My song is of war and a man" (Virgil). I call students' attention to the three first lines and ask for comments from them on how the *Aeneid* proem recalls but expands, corrects, or contests each Homeric beginning. What is the narrator implying about himself as a Roman poet constructing the Roman hero and Roman story in open competition with the most famous poet, heroes, and stories of ancient Greece?

In the first speech of the *Aeneid*, Juno, patron goddess of Carthage and supporter of the Greeks at Troy, explains the causes of her *furor* and

60   Virgil's *Aeneid*

her hatred of the Trojans, who, despite her hostility, are making their way to Italy (Virgil 1.12–133). I ask students how her motives are characterized, what it would mean for human beings if she represents the nature of a god. Are the enmity between Rome and Carthage and the total destruction of the latter in the Punic Wars explained by Juno's *furor*?

The first episode of the poem includes characterization of *furor*, *imperium*, and *pietas*. Juno wants to drown the Trojans. She asks Aeolus, god of the winds, to make a big storm. He does. Aeneas fears drowning. He loses ships and men (Virgil 1.50–179). The raging goddess Juno harasses the Trojans over land and sea. I ask students if Juno elicits from them any sympathy for her felt slights. Is she in some sense the real hero?

In the poem's first simile, the raging, furious crowd is calmed by the man of *auctoritas* (moral authority) and service (Virgil 1.148–53), just as the storm winds will be dispelled by Neptune, god of the sea. I ask students what is being implied about this idealized Roman man of *auctoritas*, who needs no force to command the raging crowd. On the divine level, Neptune, in calming the winds, threatens them with unspeakable punishment. Is force necessary after all? Viktor Pöschl is excellent in his introduction on *furor* and the oppositions implicit in this episode: Neptune/Juno, Aeneas/Dido, Rome/Carthage, male/female, storm/calm, and reason/*furor* (13–33). These oppositions are, however, significantly modified in the poem's course.

In his first speech in the poem, Aeneas, fearing death by drowning and losing faith in the mission, says he wishes he had died in Troy (Virgil 1.92–101). I ask students, Is that how readers expect a hero to talk? What is the effect or possible meaning of characterizing Aeneas in this way? Is he sympathetic or contemptible in his weakness? In his second speech, when Aeneas is shipwrecked on the beach in Carthage, he pretends courage and faith for his men (Virgil 1.197–207). Both these speeches have Odyssean models (Homer, *Od.* 5.306–12 and 12.208–12). I put them all up on the whiteboard and elicit from the students what character differences emerge between Odysseus and Aeneas. From the comparison we derive a reading that illuminates both characters. Aeneas, the Roman hero, who will not—like Odysseus—lose all his men in completing his mission, will become both less and more of a hero than Odysseus.

In the poem's first prophecy, Jupiter prophesies empire without end for the Romans, masters of the world, wearers of the toga. He misrepresents Rome's history by eliding the killing of Remus by his brother Romulus

(Virgil 1.279–82). Civil war plagues the Romans from the very start of the city. What kind of a supreme god conceals true things?

In the first instance of ekphrasis in the poem, Aeneas sees representations of scenes from the Trojan War on the walls of Juno's temple in Carthage (Virgil 1.453–93). He recognizes himself, Priam, the sons of Atreus, Achilles, and troops of both sides fleeing. He interprets the images as showing pity for the Trojans and for *lacrimae rerum* (literally, the "tears of things"): "The world weeps" (Virgil 1.462). This is likely a misreading, as the temple is Juno's and would presumably show images celebratory of Juno's victory at Troy. Juno wants to kill Trojans, not pity them.[9] Aeneas does not attend to context, nor does he read to the all-important end of the story told in the frieze. I ask students, Will we as *Aeneid* readers misread the *Aeneid* itself by forgetting context or not reading to the end? Although book 12 of the *Aeneid* gets much scholarly attention these days, this is a relatively new development.

I have taught the *Aeneid* in advanced Latin courses, where it is the only text; I have taught it in conjunction with the *Divine Comedy*; most often I have taught it in a course on epic where our goal is to trace the polemical relationships of later epic poets to their predecessors. What constitutes heroism is continually contested and redefined in these works for new historical and cultural circumstances.

Notes

1. See Pöschl 40 for a more detailed definition of *pietas*.

2. Redfield and Silk, separately, read Achilles as challenging the heroic code when he withdraws from the war, stating that his life is worth more than all the goods he would win from staying to fight gloriously in Troy. Silk writes, "The greatest literature is wont to subvert the dominant ideological categories that it purports to, and does indeed, also embody. Thanks to Achilles, the *Iliad* does just that" (84).

3. Johnson describes the two schools. Galinsky, Stahl, and Pöschl are examples of optimistic readers, and Putnam, Parry, and Boyle of pessimistic readers.

4. Fish makes this argument. See also O'Hara on reading inconsistencies in the *Aeneid* and other Roman epics.

5. Clausen shows how the differences between Aeneas and Odysseus are illuminated by a comparison of their speeches that begin with the same line ("three and four times blessed are those who died in Troy" [Clausen 76]) but that continue

62   Virgil's *Aeneid*

their thought to different purpose. As Clausen argues, difference is the meaning of the allusion. See Pöschl for a different understanding.

6. Most proposes that Odysseus's underlying purpose in his tale to the Phaeacians is to teach them not to eat or detain their guests. One might ask students what Aeneas's underlying purpose is in how and what he tells Dido of his past and whether his motivations are all on the surface. Ahl argues that Aeneas can plausibly be read as withholding or fabricating events in his narration of Troy's last night.

7. "You, Roman, remember your own arts: to rule the world with law, impose your ways on peace, grant the conquered clemency and crush the proud in war" (Virgil 6.851–53).

8. See the discussion in Shadi Bartsch's introduction (Virgil xliv–xlvii).

9. Horsfall was the first to note that Aeneas must be misreading the meaning of the pictures, as, given the setting (Juno's temple), they are likely intended to be celebrations of Juno's (Hera's) and the Greeks' victory over the Trojans, not sympathy for the Trojans, whom Juno hated.

Works Cited

Ahl, Frederick. "Homer, Vergil, and Complex Narrative Structures in Latin Epic: An Essay." *Illinois Classical Studies*, vol. 14, 1989, pp. 1–31.

Boyle, Anthony J. "The Canonic Text: Virgil's *Aeneid*." *Roman Epic*, edited by Boyle, Routledge, 1991, pp. 79–107.

Clausen, Wendell V. "An Interpretation of the *Aeneid*." *Harvard Studies in Classical Philology*, vol. 68, 1964, pp. 139–47.

Donatus, Aelius. *Life of Virgil*. Translated by David Scott Wilson-Okamura, 2014, www.virgil.org/vitae/a-donatus.htm.

Farrell, Joseph. *Juno's* Aeneid*: A Battle for Heroic Identity*. Princeton UP, 2021.

Fish, Stanley. "Reading the *Variorum*." *Critical Inquiry*, vol. 2, 1976, pp. 465–85.

Galinsky, Karl. "The Anger of Aeneas." *American Journal of Philology*, vol. 109, 1988, pp. 321–48.

Homer. *The* Iliad *of Homer*. Translated by Richmond Lattimore, U of Chicago P, 1951.

———. *Odyssey*. Translated by Richmond Lattimore, HarperCollins, 1967.

Horsfall, Nicholas. "Dido in the Light of History." *Proceedings of the Virgilian Society*, vol. 13, 1973–74, pp. 1–13.

Johnson, W. R. *Darkness Visible: A Study in Vergil's* Aeneid. U of California P, 1976.

Most, Glenn G. "The Structure and Function of Odysseus' *Apologoi*." *Transactions of the American Philological Association*, vol. 119, 1989, pp. 15–30.

O'Hara, James J. *Inconsistency in Roman Epic*. Cambridge UP, 2007.

Parry, Adam. "The Two Voices of Virgil's *Aeneid*." *Arion*, vol. 2, 1963, pp. 66–80.

Perkell, Christine G. "An Epic Program." *Reading Vergil's* Aeneid: *An Interpretive Guide*, edited by Perkell, U of Oklahoma P, 1999, pp. 29–49.

Pöschl, Viktor. *The Art of Vergil: Image and Symbol in the* Aeneid. Translated by Gerda Seligson, U of Michigan P, 1962.

Putnam, Michael C. J. *The Humanness of Heroes: Studies in the Conclusion of Virgil's* Aeneid. Amsterdam UP, 2011.

Redfield, James. *Nature and Culture in the* Iliad: *The Tragedy of Hector*. Chicago UP, 1975.

Silk, M. S. *Homer: The* Iliad. Cambridge UP, 2004.

Stahl, Hans-Peter, editor. *Vergil's* Aeneid: *Augustan Epic and Political Context*. Duckworth, 1998.

Virgil. *The Aeneid*. Translated by Shadi Bartsch, Random House, 2021.

Charles S. Ross

Bad Boys to the Rescue in Statius's *Thebaid*

Statius's *Thebaid* (*Seven against Thebes*), completed in 92 AD, takes as its topic the attempt of Polynices, one of two sons of Oedipus, to gather an army in the city of Argos and force his way back into his home city of Thebes after his brother, Eteocles, refuses to give up his rule after one year, as the two had agreed. In a manner similar to how many modern computer games offer a series of combats between figures with special powers—the ability to spin, morph, throw gold coins, or fire ray guns—the epic is structured mainly as a series of vain assaults by seven heroes, each of whom has some individual quality (less technically advanced than those of modern superheroes) that makes their performances unique and allows them to live or die in a way appropriate to their particular power.

Although the *Thebaid* may be taught, and certainly should be read, as a work of art—"[m]uch of the charm of Statius depends on his deliberate departure from heroic tension, his quest of graceful and romantic variation" (Lewis, *Allegory* 56)—an equally rewarding method of teaching is comparative: first, as a step in the development of Western literature and thought from Plato to Dante's *Divine Comedy*, and second, as a commentary on the cultures in which were produced the post–World War II

Japanese movie *The Seven Samurai* and its American Western remake, *The Magnificent Seven*.

Ancient Greek Intertexts

The city of Thebes plays an important role in Greek mythology. The name *Thebes* (Θῆβαι) is plural, as is *Athens*. When Θῆβαι is combined with the Greek suffix -δε, denoting movement toward, it produces the title *Thebaid*. The movement alluded to is that of an army from Argos, the seven against Thebes, marching to take over the city. Despite the epic's Greek subject, as a Roman citizen Statius wrote in Latin, modeling his poem on the work of Virgil, especially the *Aeneid*. The lengthy dedication (Statius 1.19–40) to the emperor Vespasian mimics a similar passage praising the emperor Augustus in the *Georgics* (Virgil 29–30; 1.24–42). Many other borrowings may be found in the introduction to my translation (Statius xiv–xvi). These can be the basis for individual class assignments.

Another good exercise is to look at how Statius fashioned the history of Thebes from his main source, Ovid's *Metamorphoses*, published in 8 AD, a Roman retelling of Greek mythology that gives special attention to the trials of women. After Jove assumes the shape of a bull to carry away Europa (2.833–75), Ovid temporarily shifts the poem away from a meditation on sex and society to the inevitable civil strife that accompanies the gathering of people into cities, as Europa's brother, Cadmus, must fight the men who grow from the dragon's teeth he sows in the land to which Jove has taken his sister (3.1–137). Later, King Pentheus faces the unruly women who worship Cadmus's grandson Bacchus, the guardian of Thebes (bk. 4). Patron of the vine and drunkenness, the cause of irrationality in his devotees, Statius's Bacchus similarly stirs the women of Lemnos to kill all their men as an experiment (5.85–235). At first, female modesty is admired (2.226–35), but in the end, the Theban women, led by Antigone, heroically tend the dead and enlist the help of Theseus to save Thebes, suggesting that Statius knew that good behavior could hide deep passions.

In Greek myth, the Theban war preceded the Trojan War, and it is worth an effort to explore the places where Homer mentions it. In the *Iliad*, Diomedes is identified as the son of Tydeus, one of Statius's seven against Thebes (6.235). In the *Odyssey*, Melampus recalls that Amphiaraus, another of the seven, died at Thebes because his wife was bribed by a gift (15.245–249), the fatal necklace of Harmonia that Eripsyle craves (Statius

66   Statius's *Thebaid*

2.262–307). The contrast between Troy, and Thebes is also significant. Although both wars are motivated by revenge for injustice, Homer's Greeks fight to recover Helen of Troy, whereas Statius's Polynices is merely ambitious. The truancy of Achilles delays the Grecian victory, just as a series of delays devised by Statius keep the Argives commanded by King Adrastus and Polynices from reaching Thebes for the first half of the *Thebaid*. Homer never mentions plunder as a goal for the Greeks, but Troy is a wealthy city. By contrast, Statius specifically says that Thebes is a poor city: "The brothers went to war for power alone; / they fought to win a kingdom that had nothing" (1.150–51).

It is also useful to set Statius's story in the context of Greek drama. The *Thebaid* takes place after the events portrayed by Sophocles in *Oedipus Rex* but before the action of *Antigone*, the second play in Sophocles's Theban trilogy. As the *Thebaid* starts, Oedipus is alive, though blind. Because he believes his sons have mistreated him, he curses them. In Aeschylus's play *Seven against Thebes*, Eteocles mentions the "curse / Of Oedipus my father, mighty in revenge" (90), which dooms him to fight his brother. In *The Phoenician Women*, another Greek tragedy, Euripides has Jocasta, Oedipus's wife and the mother of their warring sons, explain that her sons agreed to alternate rule because they were terrified by the curses of their father, who felt mistreated when they locked him away. Later in this play, Jocasta journeys to stop Polynices from invading Thebes, but she fails. In the *Thebaid* she berates Eteocles before his final duel, with similar results (Statius 10.315–53).

Statius and the *Thebaid* in Dante's *Divine Comedy*

Most of our students first encounter Statius when he shows up as a character in Dante's *Purgatory*. C. S. Lewis lists a number of elements in the *Thebaid* that might have led Dante to believe, or invent, the idea that Statius was a Christian and therefore eligible for purgatory—the appearance of a Jupiter less like the cruel Zeus of classical literature and more like a monotheistic creator; the descent of the allegorical figure of Virtue, like grace, to Menoeceus, whose suicide saves Thebes; the modesty of the maidens Argia and Deipsyle before their future husbands; the demonic behavior of gods like Apollo; and the role of the allegorical figures Piety and Clemency in addition to Virtue ("Dante's Statius"). But Lewis does not pay much attention to what Dante's Statius says about the issue that some students find troubling, and that is the nature of the soul, the necessary element for an afterlife.

What Dante's Statius has to say about the soul follows his meeting with the pilgrim Dante and his guide Virgil. There has been an earthquake as Dante and Virgil navigate the fifth terrace of Purgatory, where the avaricious and the prodigal dwell, and Virgil asks a shade they encounter why the earth should shake, when otherwise the mountain of Purgatory at this elevation is free from perturbations. The shade explains that the mountain trembles when a soul feels itself cleansed and rises of its own will to the next level (*Purg.* 21.58–60). Till then the soul longs for punishment, to do penance according to divine justice (21.64–66). The shade who speaks (soon to be identified as Statius) has just graduated from the fifth terrace, according to this standard. Dante is happy for him because "joy / is greater when we quench a greater thirst" (21.73–74).

Four cantos after Statius explains that souls judge themselves, the nature of the soul resurfaces when Dante, looking at the lustful on the seventh terrace, asks Statius how these shades can seem so emaciated when they have no need to eat (*Purg.* 25.20–21). Souls are perhaps like mirrors, Virgil suggests (25.26), and he asks Statius to explain further. Statius rambles on about the body, blood, seeds, sponges, and other items gleaned from Aristotle. Parental blood intermingles at conception, for example, and the soul is like a plant at first but attains perfection when the Prime Mover breathes new spirit and self-consciousness into it. Physically, it's all difficult to understand until we realize that Dante's *Divine Comedy* is not visually representational (Freccero 210), just as the physical fighting in the *Thebaid* is less important than what motivates it. The point is that feelings and desires shape the soul (*Purg.* 25.31–108). To put it in other words, it is like a person washing a prized car on a Saturday afternoon. The car may look spotless to someone else, but that proud owner is out there anyway, buffing it up, because it is not yet clean *enough*. In the same way, no one else but you knows if your mirror is dirty, because your conscience tells you so. Characters like Statius's Capaneus and Tydeus never learn this lesson.

From Dante's Statius, then, we learn that the only thing that holds souls back in Purgatory is the longing to do penance. It's an idea that goes back to Plato's *Gorgias*, where Socrates argues that it is worse to do wrong than suffer wrong. In that dialogue, Socrates takes on Callicles, who argues that might makes right and that the stronger and superior person is happier than a weak person, however wise the weakling might be. Against this commonly held, Nietzschean position, Socrates argues

68   Statius's *Thebaid*

that a self-controlled soul is better than a chaotic one. He claims that it is better "to suffer what is unjust than to do it" (813; 469c), "something so radical that his hearers think it has to be a joke," as one modern commentator observes (Goldstein 142).

Not really having convinced anyone that there is ultimate justice, Socrates ends the dialogue by resorting to a fable about how Zeus arranged that his sons Minos, Rhadamanthus, and Aeacus would judge men after they die, looking not at their bodies—because wicked souls can hide in "handsome bodies" and bring "many false witnesses to testify that they have lived just lives" (Plato 866; 523c)—but at their souls, for when the soul "has been stripped naked of the body," nothing can disguise any "distortion and ugliness due to license and luxury, arrogance and incontinence in its actions" (867; 525a). Socrates concludes by saying that this account is just "an old wives' tale," and he is not surprised if someone feels "contempt for it" (868; 527a).

Plato's admittedly creaky myth of justice—along with similar accounts in the *Republic* and the *Phaedo*—nonetheless greatly influenced Western thinking. For most of us, suffering evil means suffering physically, as when under the control of a tyrant, but for Socrates evil is a moral term, and to do evil means to endure the shame of doing wrong. Dante found exactly this lesson in Statius's epic. He explains that "[t]he sense of shame is the fear of being disgraced for a fault that has been committed. From this fear springs repentance for the fault, which consists of a bitterness that acts as a constraint against renewing the fault"; he then cites Statius, who, in Dante's words, describes how "when Polynices was asked by King Adrastus about his origin, he hesitated before speaking for shame of the fault he had committed against his father, and also of the faults of his father Oedipus, for they seemed to abide in the shame of the son" (*Convivio* 4.25.10; see also Statius 1.466–68).

Shame implies that we believe right and wrong exist—Augustine says even a thief prefers not to be stolen from (*Confessions* 2.4.9)—and Dante found in the *Thebaid* an example of the emotional release that penitence offers. When Dante meets Beatrice, she forces him to say whether he repents. At first Dante cannot answer, but finally, in a faint voice, he says he is sorry and weeps (*Purg.* 31.7–36). We can say that Dante's tears show not only repentance but also joy, because previously Dante compares his joy at meeting Guido Guinizzelli to the reunion of Statius's Hypsipyle with the two sons she had borne to Jason and had lost years before; they suddenly appear and console her as she faces the rage of Lycurgus, the father of a baby who died in her care (Dante, *Purg.* 26.91–99; Statius 5.710–30), and she weeps for joy.

Hypsipyle is the character from the *Thebaid* that Dante mentions more than any other. She is first referred to as a victim of Jason, one of the seducers lashed by demons in the larger circle of fraud in hell. Dante's Virgil refers to how Hypsipyle deceived the women of Lemnos to save her father, before she was abandoned by Jason (*Inf.* 18.82–99; Statius 5.28–498). Later she is described as "the woman who showed Langia" (*Purg.* 22.112), a passage that alludes to the episode where she saves the Argive army from thirst by leading it to water. Statius's description of soldiers dying of thirst in turn recalls the trope of thirsting for salvation that Jesus uses when he speaks to the Samaritan woman (Statius 4.649–851; *Bible Hub* John 4.5–15 and Matt. 5.6; Dante, *Purg.* 21.1–3).

In contrast to Hypsipyle, Capaneus, Polynices, and Ugolino never question themselves in the *Thebaid* (Nohrnberg 82). Like Achilles in the *Iliad*, they fight knowing or strongly suspecting that they are fated to die. Capaneus hurls defiance at the gods, until Zeus kills him with a thunderbolt (Statius 10.827–939). He is the giant that Dante notices among the blasphemers who lie on fiery sands, disdaining the gods, however many lightning bolts hit him (*Inf.* 14.43–72) as he flits back and forth over the fine line between debilitating pride and strength of purpose.

Similar relentless behavior occurs when the bodies of Polynices and Eteocles are burned on the same funeral pyre. The flames that arise from the dead brothers battle each other, so strong was their hatred in life (Statius 12.420–46). Dante transfers this image into the forked flames of Ulysses and Diomedes that Dante the pilgrim sees in the circle of fraudulent counselors (*Inf.* 26.52–57). The question for class discussion is whether either Polynices or Ulysses deserves to be condemned or whether both should be praised for standing up for themselves in adversity. Tydeus, too, is relentless, but at what point does his behavior become demonic? Demons were traditionally deceivers and liars; they were thought to be good jugglers, able to move objects faster than we can see. Statius's Tydeus is no liar; he cannot hide his disgust when Eteocles rejects his embassy of peace (2.368–481). But he moves like a demon. In his final scene, we never see him eat the head of Melanippus, whose spear has killed him (8.716–67). Dante, however, pictures Ugolino gnawing the head of the man who imprisoned him—"no differently had Tydeus gnawed the temples / of Menalippus [sic]" (*Inf.* 32.124–32).

70   Statius's *Thebaid*

There are things left unsaid in the *Thebaid* because Statius was an economical poet. In this passage, he shows only Athena's reaction to Tydeus's cannibalism, not Tydeus's gnawing. The goddess recoils at the sight of a gory face before she flies away to mystic fires and cleansing waters (8.758–67). We must imagine the rest for ourselves, just as it helps in the classroom to understand what must have motivated Dante to have Statius articulate the message that the soul is not an object or something you see but a feeling that informs the will—and the willful, like Tydeus, who calls for the head of Melanippus.

I make sure to include the cantos that refer to Statius when Dante is on my syllabus, just as when my syllabus calls for a shortened version of Statius's epic I choose the portions most relevant for the *Divine Comedy* (Statius 1, 2, 8.655–end, 10, and 12.416–end).

The Seven Samurai **and** The Magnificent Seven

The *Thebaid* is not only relevant for a reading of ancient Greek literature and Dante's medieval poem but also has something to tell us today about power untethered from right and wrong (Ahl 2904). Perhaps the most effective way to teach Statius's epic from this perspective is to compare it to Akira Kurosawa's *The Seven Samurai* and John Sturgis's *The Magnificent Seven*. Both movies are structured like the *Thebaid*. We get to know each hero's personality through a preliminary vignette, then the character either dies or survives in a way intimately connected to his overreaching personality. The artist's trick is to individualize the seven warriors in strange and quirky ways.

It's therefore an effective classroom project to line up Statius's characters against the movie versions. James Coburn's character, for example, may be compared to Statius's Capaneus. I like to show the scene of Coburn's knife-throwing prowess in *The Magnificent Seven* (30:49–35:10). The horses and catchy music keep a class entertained enough to watch Coburn demonstrate in a duel that his switchblade kills faster than a Colt .45. I then show the source of Coburn's character, the samurai sword master in Kurosawa's film (*Seven Samurai* 46:00–50:00) whose calm concentration similarly defeats his more aggressive opponent. Both scenes are guaranteed to hold the attention of a class, but showing Sturgis's version first familiarizes students with the subject matter and makes it easier for them to engage with Kurosawa's film, which has subtitles and is in black and white.

After this comparison the class can debate further equivalences. Statius's Tydeus is a little guy, for example, but impossibly strong, loyal, and mean when you get him on a bad day. For some, he's definitely the character played by Steve McQueen in *The Magnificent Seven*. Again, the formal leader of the seven in Statius's poem is Adrastus, king of Argos, whose daughter marries Polynices. He is the only one who survives the attack on Thebes, probably because his heart is in the right place, which is exactly how Yul Brynner, who plays the leader of the magnificent seven, describes his character's role in an interview on the DVD version of the film: "He's a dirty bum. There are only two clean things about him: his gun and his soul" ("Guns" 9:30). Kinbei Shimada is similarly worn out but upright as the chief samurai in *The Seven Samurai*. Polynices, the aristocratic, sulking son of Oedipus, is the equivalent of Robert Vaughn's dude character in *The Magnificent Seven*. I would pair the prophet Amphiaraus with the Brad Dexter character who mistakenly thinks there's gold in Mexico, since he's so sure of the future.

Hippomedon, who drowns fighting a river (Statius 9.196–546), is an elemental giant, too strong for his own good, and so must die when he undertakes an impossible task, like Charles Bronson's wood chopper in *The Magnificent Seven* and his nameless Japanese equivalent in *The Seven Samurai*. The overly attractive young warrior Parthenopaeus (Statius 9.683–910) is a handsome young man in both movies, not yet a veteran gun fighter or samurai, and therefore ready to marry and settle down in the aftermath of the violence.

It is surprising that in his Christian epic Dante does not mention Menoeceus, who offers his life after Tiresias calls for a sacrificial lamb to save Thebes (Statius 10.589–790). Prompted by the allegorical figure of Virtue, who descends from Heaven to inspire him, Menoeceus says that he is "prodigal" of his life (10.766) and throws himself from a tower. The equivalent of such sacrifice in the two films may be, respectively, the Mexican and Japanese farmers who die fighting to defend their villages from bandits. Like Tydeus, Capaneus, Hippomedon, and the others, these local people suspect they will die but press forward nonetheless.

For Statius, humans are self-destructive and prone to anger; Kurosawa's film is close in mood and horror to Statius's vision. Filming in the wake of Japan's defeat in World War II, the Japanese filmmaker understood what it meant to live in the wake of the grim victories that established an imperial state. It is so easy to go awry. Some of this mood lingers

72 Statius's *Thebaid*

in *The Magnificent Seven*. Although it sanitizes Mexican peasant life ("Guns" 20:30–21:17) in contrast to Kurosawa's realism, it also hints at a ruthlessness beneath the surface of American power, whose wielders can be uneducated, unsteady, and liable to new problems as well as old emotions. The fighters in the film succeed, yet they are oddly troubled by their profession. They long to hang up their guns and find stability, a family, and a place to settle.

By showing the brutal attrition of the Theban war and the ensuing pacification of the city by the mythical Athenian Theseus, Statius may have provided Rome with an image of its own success and the cost of that success (Zeitlin 148). A good question for a final essay exam, based on the comparisons I have suggested, is therefore to discuss how an epic conflict configured as a response to injustice might matter to anyone living in a time of real or perceived tyranny.

Works Cited

Aeschylus. *Seven against Thebes*. Prometheus Bound, The Suppliants, Seven against Thebes, The Persians, translated by Philip Bellacott, Penguin Books, 1961, pp. 88–121.

Ahl, Frederick M. "Statius' *Thebaid*: A Reconsideration." *Augstieg und Niedergang der rhomischen Welt*, vol. 32, 1986, pp. 2803–912.

Aristotle. *On the Soul*. On the Soul *and Other Psychological Works*, translated by Fred D. Miller, Oxford World's Classics, 2018, pp. 1–69.

Augustine. *Confessions*. Translated by Henry Chadwick, Oxford UP, 1991.

Bible Hub. 2022, biblehub.com.

Dante Alighieri. *Convivio*. *Princeton Dante Project*, 2000, dante.princeton.edu/pdp/convivio.html.

———. *Inferno*. Translated by Allen Mandelbaum, U of California P, 1980.

———. *Purgatorio*. Translated by Allen Mandelbaum, U of California P, 1982.

Euripides. *Phoenician Women*. Translated by Peter Burian and Brian Swann, Oxford UP, 1981.

Freccero, John. *The Poetics of Conversion*. Harvard UP, 1986.

Goldstein, Rebecca Newberger. *Plato at the Googleplex*. Random House, 2015.

"Guns for Hire: The Making of *The Magnificent Seven*." Directed by Louis Heaton, 2000. *Magnificent Seven*.

Homer. *Iliad*. Translated by Alexander Pope, CreateSpace, 2012.

———. *Odyssey*. Translated by Allen Mandelbaum, Bantam Classics, 1990.

Lewis, C. S. *The Allegory of Love: A Study in Medieval Tradition*. 1936. Oxford UP, 1958.

———. "Dante's Statius." *Medium Ævum*, vol. 25, 1956, pp. 133–39.

The Magnificent Seven. Directed by John Sturgis, United Artists, 1960. DVD.

Nohrnberg, James. "The *Inferno.*" *Homer to Brecht: The European Epic and Dramatic Traditions,* edited by Michael Seidel and Edward Mendelson, Yale UP, 1977, pp. 76–104.

Ovid. *Metamorphoses.* Translated by Allen Mandelbaum, Harcourt Brace, 1993.

Plato. *Gorgias. Plato: Complete Works,* translated by Donald J. Zehl, edited by John M. Cooper, Hackett, 1997, pp. 791–869.

The Seven Samurai. Directed by Akira Kurosawa, Toho, 1954. Japanese with English subtitles.

Statius, Publius Paninius. *The Thebaid: Seven against Thebes.* Translated by Charles Stanley Ross, John Hopkins UP, 2004.

Virgil. *Georgics. P. Vergili Maronis opera,* edited by R. A. B. Mynors, Oxford UP / Clarendon Press, 1969, pp. 29–101.

Zeitlin, Froma I. "Thebes: Theater of Self and Society in Athenian Drama." *Nothing to Do with Dionysos? Athenian Drama in Its Social Context,* edited by John J. Winkler and Zeitlin, Princeton UP, 1990, pp. 130–67.

Part II

Epics from the Tenth
to the Fifteenth Century

Victoria Turner

Ideologies of Intercultural Encounter in Three Epics of Medieval France

As the most famous of Old French epic texts, or chansons de geste, *The Song of Roland* has long stood as the gateway text for non-French speakers interested in French epic literature. In its earliest French version it narrates a battle between Christian (Frankish) and Muslim (here called Saracen or pagan) forces high in the Pyrenees at Rencesvals pass. Following conquests in Spain, Charlemagne (or Charles) and his army are returning to France when the Christian rearguard led by Charlemagne's nephew, Roland, is ambushed because Roland's stepfather, Ganelon, has conspired with the Saracen ruler Marsile. Roland and his elite companions are overcome, and, after his martyr-like death, the second part of the text describes how Charlemagne and the main army defeat the Saracens, who are now led by Emperor Baligant. The text ends with the trial, then punishment, of the traitor and the summoning by the angel Gabriel of a weary Charlemagne to further conflict elsewhere in his empire. This version of the epic is known as the Oxford *Roland* because its earliest and sole witness is Bodleian Library's manuscript Digby 23. Composed around the end of the eleventh century, it coincides with the First Crusade and, on the surface at least, seems to promote binary religious oppositions: its eponymous hero famously claims that "pagans are wrong and Christians

78   Epics of Medieval France

are right" (*Song*, line 1015), while the offensive rhetoric and extreme violence require clear trigger warnings in today's classrooms. It is therefore easy to see why students, when first confronted with this text, might take its hero's assertion at face value and focus on ideological absolutes: good versus evil, Christian versus Saracen, West versus East. Furthermore, in survey modules, whether part of comparative literature or modern languages courses, it can be especially difficult to provide sufficient contextual discussion to frame such a charged text or the curricular space to unpack the rhetorical layering present. The excellent volume *Approaches to Teaching the* Song of Roland gives a range of study episodes along with a survey of techniques, contexts, and critical approaches (Kibler and Morgan), and it is not my intention here to repeat this work but rather to explore how a recent translation of *The Song of Roland*, by Simon Gaunt and Karen Pratt in their Oxford World Classics series book, The Song of Roland *and Other Poems of Charlemagne*, constitutes a particularly valuable volume for comparative courses. By uniting the well-known Oxford text of *The Song of Roland* with one of the few extant Occitan epics, *Daurel and Beton*, and the curious *Charlemagne's Journey to Jerusalem and Constantinople*, this collection presents epics that not only remind us of medieval France's linguistic diversity but also span the medieval Mediterranean from the Pyrenees to Cairo and Constantinople. In what follows I set out how this collection might be used to explore the connectivity of the medieval world and reveal different, if often complementary, ideological agendas to nuance the Oxford text's place within grand narratives of Christian-Muslim encounter and East-West antagonism associated particularly with epics of the crusading period. As the translators note, "The *Roland*, despite its crusading zeal, may well have offered audiences matter for debate" (Gaunt and Pratt xvii).

I have taught *The Song of Roland* both within a comparative literature survey course on good and evil and in specialist final-year French modules in the context of contact and exchange between communities and have found the modular framing of this epic to be key: the syllabi choices we make as educators are political acts in themselves, and conversely, leading students to *The Song of Roland* through a conceptual binarism can challenge its antagonistic staging and encourage students to acknowledge their own assumptions both about the period and about the long history of Christian-Muslim interaction. I begin my lecture series by asking students what qualities they expect from a hero and a villain. While this is a superficial exercise, the list produced can serve as a useful touchstone during the class—a visual aid allowing me to challenge the binary thinking peppering the surface of the text: the Saracen lord Blancandrin, for example, is a wise, brave, and loyal vassal to Marsile, while the Christian nobleman Ganelon is a traitor; the debates between Roland and his companion, Oliver, about blowing the horn or "oliphant" to summon help (e.g., line 1059) reveal Roland's hubris and concern for reputation. As Oliver comments, "Your brand of bravery, Roland, has been our ruin!" (line 1731). Simple though this exercise may be, it begins to reveal the cracks in the binary logic of the poem and in its situatedness, nuancing the clash-of-civilizations rhetoric found in any cursory reading of *The Song of Roland* by showing how Roland's own ideological outlook is far from uncontested by those around him. Placing *The Song of Roland* alongside the two other epics in Gaunt and Pratt's volume then allows me to move class discussion beyond intratextual features and to dislocate this binary logic still further by showing how geography and space not only frame the encounters that take place in each text but also reflect and produce the ideologies that surround them.[1]

"France the Fair": Imagined Geographies and Collective Identities in *The Song of Roland*

In contrast to nineteenth-century studies claiming *The Song of Roland* as a national epic and expression of incipient French identity, most recent scholarship on this epic has problematized the ideological work enacted by the text (Gaunt and Pratt xii). In particular, recent scholarly approaches to *The Song of Roland* have highlighted how the text's geographic framing is central to the construction of ideologies of nation and community. Sharon Kinoshita situates the work in relation to the system of *parias* that existed in medieval Iberia—tribute monies exchanged between Christian and Muslim rulers. She notes that "the *Roland* works to produce 'Frank' as a new collective identity, recoding Roland's *feudal* intransigence as a clash of civilizations based on *religious* difference" (*Medieval Boundaries* 16). Lynn Ramey uses *The Song of Roland*'s status as "a quintessentially border epic" in a more abstract sense, showing how a teaching approach informed by postcolonial theory—border pedagogy—can address points of encounter between genders and cultures: in the "contested space" of *The Song of Roland*, caught, as it is, in a geographic border zone, "the tale that emerges is a master narrative, bending to the ideological imperatives of the stronger force, the French army" (232). One such ideological

80   Epics of Medieval France

imperative is the need to produce collective identities among the forces concerned, and exploring how the text works to root these identities in geography as much as in religion, for instance, can nuance the reading of its binary oppositions and the framing of religious warfare. Three key episodes to explore in this light are the opening scenes positioning the forces of Charlemagne and those of Marsile (the council scenes), Roland's death, and the representation of Charlemagne's and Baligant's forces.

It is no wonder that we find the intercultural encounters of *The Song of Roland*, a narrative centered on acts of territorial invasion and military conquest, to be mediated by the representation of spaces and geographies. From the opening *laisse* (or stanza) of the poem, the reader is situated in Spain and told that "as far as the sea [Charles] conquered this haughty land" (line 3), so that his military campaign seems directed at territory rather than peoples or faiths. The Saracens, initially at least, similarly fear losing "resplendent Spain" (59) rather than the denigration of their faith or forced conversion. Roland, we learn, "disputes the ownership of all lands" (394), and his primary role seems to be to expand Charles's territory (401). Many of Marsile's Saracen nobles have names that evoke places shrouded in darkness—gloomy valleys and black mountains: Valdabrun, Escremiz of Val-Terne, Chernuble of Muneigre (see Bancourt). Space establishes more than difference, however, since the opening council scenes also show both Charlemagne and Marsile seated in an orchard in the shade of a pine tree, a mirroring effect that frames their shared social organization. Rootedness in the land, it seems, is a shared preoccupation for the two forces, while it is also their desire for the possession and control of land that divides them.

Another key episode to consider in this context is the scene of Roland's death. When Roland finally summons aid from Charlemagne's main army, he blows the oliphant so hard that he bursts his temples. As he feels his end approaching, he walks toward Spain (*laisse* 168), desiring to die facing enemy lands (174). The description of his death further emphasizes his role in territorial conquests as he addresses his sword, Durendal, and notes, "[W]ith you I have won so many battles in the field / and have conquered so many vast lands" (lines 2306–07), a statement repeated twice in the next two stanzas. He continues in *laisse* 172 to list the lands conquered for Charles and to express his fear that France will suffer humiliation if the sword should fall into pagan hands, despite the fact that France as the unified political and geographic entity we know today did not exist in this period, when it was instead formed of regional power centers. In this respect, Roland's France is fragmented—a series of conquered realms—yet also unified as an imagined geography of collective suffering. This imagined geography echoes earlier associations in the text between Roland's individual deeds and the nature or status of France: Roland is concerned, for instance, that his decision to summon help will put his reputation at risk and thus negatively affect "fair France" (line 1064), while "the universal grief for the death of Roland" (1437) is marked by the lashing storm back in France. In some ways, it is Roland himself who produces a geographically collective identity for the Franks.

While the Franks are united by and in the figure of Roland, a geographically rooted collective identity remains an ideal that must be constructed throughout the narrative, and the Franks are consistently marked by plurality of origin, if not of faith. When Charlemagne assembles his forces for battle against Baligant, the companies are noted for their equipment or valour and determined by geographic provenance: Frenchmen, Bavarians, Germans, Normans, Bretons, and Poitevins and soldiers from the Auvergne, Flanders, Frisia, Lorraine, and Burgundy (*laisses* 217–27). In contrast, Baligant's forces are mainly formed of fictitious groups, some of which are allotted supposedly geographic origins and some of which are said to originate from places whose names, like the names of the barons, have negative connotations, such as Malprose (*mal* meaning "bad") and Val-Peneuse (*peneuse* meaning "painful"). The listing of these fantastical places, worthy of Lewis Carroll's sonorous wordplay, leaves most of the Saracen forces entirely identified by their geographic origins, as if the sound alone of each word or its connotative power conveyed their qualities.

Allies Abroad: Escaping to Cairo in *Daurel and Beton*

The second text in Gaunt and Pratt's volume is drawn from the small corpus of epics written in Occitan—the language of southern France. *Daurel and Beton* was composed around the late twelfth and early thirteenth centuries and, in contrast to both *The Song of Roland* and *Charlemagne's Journey*, about which much ink has been spilled, it remains relatively unstudied, having mainly attracted attention for its representation of knightly friendship and betrayal, the theme of sacrifice, and the figure of the minstrel. It narrates how a vassal, Guy, betrays the friendship of his lord, Duke Bovis of Antona, and kills him during a boar hunt to claim for himself Bovis's wife, Ermenjart, and wealth. Guy also desires to kill Bovis's son,

82   Epics of Medieval France

Beton, but the child is rescued by Bovis's faithful jongleur, Daurel. After sacrificing his own son in Beton's place, Daurel escapes with the noble infant to foreign lands where Beton is then raised, becoming a favorite of the emir of Babylon (Cairo). Beton is set to marry the emir's daughter but wishes first to return to France; he does this, takes vengeance on Guy, and is about to turn his anger on Charlemagne for having forced his mother (Ermenjart) to marry Guy when the text cuts off. The period of intercultural encounter in this work is therefore pivotal to the narrative, and while it has mostly been discussed for the unusual attention paid to the child's development, its depiction of Christian-Saracen relations reveals different ideological currents from those in *Charlemagne's Journey* and *The Song of Roland*.

In *Daurel and Beton* the emir and his court essentially serve as a place of refuge for a Christian child and the minstrel who has rescued him from traitors at home. This motif appears in numerous chansons de geste (for instance, *Aye d'Avignon* [*Aye of Avignon*]) where the foreignness of a pagan court and its disconnection from the Frankish realm make it attractive. The detailed description of Beton's growing up and display of noble, courtly behavior assumes that cultural norms of generosity, courtly love, and prowess and pastimes such as jousting are common to both the emir's court and the text's audience: radical similarity is the name of the game here, rather than processes of othering. In a sense, geographic othering is the only real form of distancing that takes place, along with the use of the honorific *emir*—although even this term is mostly replaced in the text by *king*, as if to further downplay the sense of cultural difference. We are clearly reminded that this is a Saracen court when the emir's daughter promises to convert to Christianity to marry Beton, fulfilling the Saracen princess trope common to chansons de geste. However, the Saracen society portrayed in the text elicits no sense of alienation in Daurel and bestows no obvious foreignness on Beton: there is no mention of his ability to speak *Sarrasinois* (a term frequently used in Old French epics to denote the language of the Saracens), merely one reference to the training he receives from a Saracen arms master (lines 1583–99). Cairo is therefore imagined as a space to learn and perfect combat abilities in an example of the topos *translatio studii et imperii*—the idea that knowledge and power are appropriated and transferred from East to West: here, Beton is able to return to France a fully trained and well-provisioned knight.

Like the Eastern Christian realm of King Hugo in *Charlemagne's Journey*, the Muslim territory of the emir in *Daurel and Beton* represents a land of peace and prosperity under good kingship, but unlike Hugo's realm, the emir's utopia is contrasted with the treachery and weakness the protagonist finds at home, both in his family and in his overlord. As is common to many chansons de geste, cultural capture occurs in this text through love and marriage, since the Saracen princess is converted to Christianity, married to a Frankish knight, and removed from her homeland by the end of the narrative.[2] However, *Daurel and Beton* also reveals the workings of a further, complementary kind of desire for the other that uses utopian ideology to locate allies abroad who can intervene deus ex machina style. This intercultural encounter highlights and rectifies the failings of the Christian community at home and, in Beton's promised marriage to the emir's converted daughter, also provides the protagonist with a future inheritance and territorial expansion. Writing in relation to medieval utopic texts, Michael Uebel notes how such works developed in response to perceived differences between cultures: "The inception of utopia in the twelfth century is tied to the cultural and psychological work of imagining Western self and Oriental other in dialectical relation" (5). In my teaching, I situate this fantasy of finding benevolent support from afar in relation to the figure of Prester John and thus open up class discussion to include western Christendom's relationships with other parts of the medieval world, showing how there are multiple medieval Easts that perform varied ideological work. Prester John was a supposed Christian ruler residing beyond western Christendom, located in India and later in Africa; in texts such as the *Letter of Prester John*, written around 1160, Western writers tell how he would one day arrive as an ally against Muslim forces. In *Daurel and Beton*, however, the benevolent foreigner is not Christian but Saracen and apparently remains so: while the end of the text is missing, there is no mention of the conversion of the king, queen, and their people when the princess Erimena is betrothed to Beton—and, interestingly, her own conversion is specifically linked to Beton's need to "take her with [him] to Poitiers" (line 1862). While a possible closing scene of mass conversion cannot be ruled out, Cairo, it seems, may well have retained its Saracen yet utopic status: after defeating Guy, rather than returning to Cairo, Beton summons Erimena to France, where they marry and "live happily ever after" (2086). In essence, the text ends with a coalition between a Saracen emir and a Frankish nobleman against Emperor Charlemagne, so that Muslim power is appropriated and brought to France, rather than destroyed, and used against *The Song of Roland*'s defender of Christendom, Charlemagne himself.

84   Epics of Medieval France

Seeking Superiority: Material Culture and *Charlemagne's Journey to Jerusalem and Constantinople*

Charlemagne's Journey to Jerusalem and Constantinople is a short tale of 870 alexandrines in assonanced *laisses* narrating the fictitious journey of Emperor Charlemagne first to Jerusalem then to Constantinople with what Philip Bennett has described as "a promiscuous mixing" of heroes from different medieval French epic text cycles ("Origins" 62). It also details the supposed transfer, or *translatio*, of relics from Jerusalem to the important Parisian abbey of Saint Denis. Its events occur before those of *The Song of Roland* and have been much discussed for their comedic feel, intertextual references, and genre (Trotter 76). However, the narrative is also framed from the start as a kind of quest: when Charlemagne's wife mentions that she has heard tell of a king who wears his crown better and "is richer than you in possessions, gold, and money," Charlemagne declares, "I shall go to find a king of whom I have heard reports," and later informs his men that "never shall I return home until I have found him" (*Charlemagne's Journey*, lines 27, 72, 199). In contrast to the narrative of *The Song of Roland*, then, here is not a rhetoric of conquest or defeat but of seeking, and the very purpose of the journey is to stage an intercultural encounter: one based, significantly, around material comparison.

This is a slippery text to teach because of the lack of consensus regarding dating (estimates for its composition range from the eleventh to the thirteenth century), the limited contextual and production information (its sole manuscript went missing in the late nineteenth century), and the resulting difficulties in judging aspects of tone or questions of parody. For instance, the extent to which *Charlemagne's Journey* links to the Second Crusade, led by Louis VII, is uncertain, and a discussion of parody and humor in the text is restricted when it is unclear who or what is the target. Nonetheless, the text is a valuable teaching counterpart to *The Song of Roland* because it shows intercultural encounters as materially conditioned rather than focused on the battlefield. As revealed in the references to Greece, Constantinople, Persia, Cappadocia, and Antioch when the queen names King Hugo the Strong as Charles's potential rival, the medieval world was interconnected. In my teaching, I use this interconnectivity to explore how binary thinking about East-West relations is constructed, to underline the circulation of material culture, and to discuss ideologies of cultural appropriation. I direct students' attention to the two main eastern stages: Jerusalem and Constantinople.

The Road to Jerusalem

In *Charlemagne's Journey* material culture troubles the status of the Franks as pilgrims and travelers rather than warriors from the offset of their journey. The text's translators, Gaunt and Pratt, note how the gold- and silver-laden camels taken as provisions echo the Saracen gifts sent to Charlemagne in *The Song of Roland* (Gaunt and Pratt xxii); the emphasis on pilgrim staffs and scrips and the specific rejection of military equipment encourage us not to read the Franks as armed pilgrims (essentially, crusaders), yet this emphasis and rejection jar with Charles's references to companies of thousands of men (*Charlemagne's Journey*, lines 95 and 98).[3] Is the poet poking fun at these would-be pilgrims who cannot escape the mindset of crusaders, or critiquing the lack of true religious intent behind crusading missions in general? The preparations for this journey present a good moment to discuss with students how crusaders are often referred to as pilgrims in medieval sources despite the relative absence of the idea of crusade as pilgrimage from the chansons de geste. Charles's relationship to Christianity is also problematized through his ignorant and undeserving behavior in Jerusalem, where he is lavished with precious relics to aggrandize France rather than the Christian faith (Gaunt and Pratt xxii–xxiii). He irreverently sits in the thirteenth seat in the Church of the Pater Noster, and the comedy of this scene is extended when a passing Jew converts to Christianity after having taken Charles for "God Himself" (*Charlemagne's Journey*, line 139). Furthermore, the church Charles builds in Jerusalem enables mercantile exchanges, not meaningful engagements with Christianity. It seems significant too that the patriarch of Jerusalem's offer of unlimited wealth to the parting emperor precedes the patriarch's instruction "to slaughter Saracens, who so despise us" (227), that Charles promises in return to go to Spain, and that the comment from the narrator on this is a reference to Rencesvals: "there died Roland and the twelve peers with him" (232). Is this episode a hint, perhaps, that such ventures are driven as much by financial transactions as by Christian ideologies? After all, the central element of the Jerusalem episode concerns detailed descriptions of relics that "possess great power" (186) bestowed on Charles by the patriarch. As Glyn S. Burgess suggests, "[R]elics take the place of weapons"

86   Epics of Medieval France

so that divine agency works through material objects rather than military skill (xxii).

The Wonders of Constantinople

Given that Constantinople was often perceived as an ideal city by medieval writers, as highlighted by Rima Devereaux, it is no surprise that the city serves as a crucible for the rivalry between Charlemagne and King Hugo in *Charlemagne's Journey*. As was the case in Jerusalem, no siege or defeat on the field of battle is necessary; rather, the Constantinople episode locates the superiority of the Byzantine ruler, and its ultimate overturning, in material culture. For example, both Kinoshita and Devereaux have noted the significance of Hugo's palace as a site of cultural contact. For Devereaux, the "utopian power" of Constantinople is situated in the revolving palace of Emperor Hugo (55). For Kinoshita, the palace reveals the contrasts between a feudal Europe and tributary, imperial Mediterranean, disrupting grand narratives that suggest that knowledge and power migrated from East to West ("*Voyage*" 258), the *translatio studii et imperii* topos mentioned above. In my teaching I therefore use this palace as a focal point for framing the use of this topos in medieval writings, asking students to reflect on just what is brought from East to West (and vice versa) and how we might map this text differently through the networks revealed.

While material culture is used as an expression of power in *Charlemagne's Journey*, it also provides traces of Mediterranean trade that convey alternative narratives of intercultural encounter and challenge the reading of this text along a linear East-West axis. E. Jane Burns has shown how *Charlemagne's Journey* constructs the East as an economic rival of the West where silk is "a vibrant commercial commodity and a key diplomatic currency: a mark of both mercantile success and political power" (138). Drawing attention to the presence of such a commodity and contextualizing its significance in this period reveal lines of connectivity that differ from those forged by crusading and pilgrimage. In seminars, I discuss with students how silk could function more broadly as a conventional marker of foreign (especially Saracen or pagan) wealth to be contrasted with Christian piety (Burns 140–41) and how material culture was used by medieval writers to exoticize the East more generally—even other Christians such as the orthodox community of Constantinople (Moore). I have found that such themes also lend themselves well to comparisons in chronologically broad survey courses, given the further entrenchment of such attitudes in, for instance, later European travel narratives. The trade of silk across the medieval Mediterranean "critiques strict confessional divides" (Burns 143) since it reminds us that commerce connects: in *Charlemagne's Journey*, silk is both traded at Charles's Jerusalem church and worn by Hugo and his Byzantine court. The superior status of the Franks is thus framed by their surroundings but mediated by materials: silk effaces lines of difference, while relics assert yet also undercut the Franks' power. The relics carried by the Franks facilitate their journey from Jerusalem to Constantinople and enable them to fulfill their foolish boasts and thus to triumph over Hugo and, by extension, the East, with no military intervention. Yet the comedic exaggeration of their power along the way also undercuts this. Margaret Burrell sees the clash of literary tone here between the heroic and satiric as creating the feeling of a "world upside down" (50), seen too when the Franks initially encounter king Hugo tending his fields atop a golden plough (*Charlemagne's Journey*, line 283). Whatever the purpose, the humor of *Charlemagne's Journey* surely disorients the reader and thus any attempt to form the ideological agendas at work into absolutes.

Charlemagne's Journey helps to show students how cultural violence can be enacted on and through materials as much as on and through bodies. Kinoshita notes the parallel in this respect between the vocabulary used to describe the destruction of Hugo's palace and, in *The Song of Roland*, the violence enacted on bodies, which are both "fendu" ("split" or "broken in two") by the Western Christian forces ("*Voyage*" 265). Even if not all crusade-related interactions in these epics are about bloodshed, there are still complex ideologies of annihilation, appropriation, and cultural capture at work. While Gaunt and Pratt primarily combine these three French epics to show the ambiguous medieval representation of Charlemagne, studying this trilogy of works also gives students an important awareness of the varied ideological agendas not just in *The Song of Roland* but across a range of intercultural encounters in the different texts. Together, these epics show how spaces and geographies could be used by medieval writers to produce identity and community but also how such writers destabilize these ideologies, prompting reflections on wider processes of nation and community building. Approaching medieval French epics through this literary mappemonde thus encourages students to read the heroes of *The Song of Roland* against those in other medieval contact zones, mapping the narrow pass of Rencesvals in relation to a broader world of contact, travel, and exchange.

88   Epics of Medieval France

Notes

1. See the appendix for sample discussion questions.

2. See Kinoshita, *Medieval Boundaries*; Bennett, "Storming."

3. See Trotter 88 for references to crusaders as pilgrims in the chansons de geste.

Appendix: Sample Discussion Questions

Compare the representation of material objects in *Charlemagne's Journey to Jerusalem and Constantinople* with that in *The Song of Roland*. How do those objects circulate? What do they tell us about the different cultures concerned?

What are the ideologies or key systems of ideas and ideals in each text? To what extent are ideologies of intercultural encounter always based on violence?

Discuss how the ideology of cultural appropriation is represented in one of the texts. Who or what is appropriated, and by whom?

Works Cited

Bancourt, Paul. *Les Musulmans dans les chansons de geste du cycle du roi.* Université de Provence, 1982. 2 vols.

Bennett, Philip E. "Origins of the French Epic: *The Song of Roland* and Other French Epics." Kibler and Morgan, pp. 57–66.

———. "The Storming of the Other World, the Enamoured Muslim Princess and the Evolution of the Legend of Guillaume d'Orange." *Guillaume d'Orange and the Chanson de Geste*, edited by Wolfgang van Emden and Bennett, U of Reading, 1984, pp. 1–14.

Burgess, Glyn S. Introduction. *Le Pèlerinage de Charlemagne*, edited and translated by Burgess, Société Rencesvals, 1998, pp. ix–lvii.

Burns, E. Jane. *Sea of Silk: A Textile Geography of Women's Work in Medieval French Literature.* U of Pennsylvania P, 2009.

Burrell, Margaret. "The *Voyage of Charlemagne*: Cultural Transmission or Cultural Transgression?" *Parergon*, vol. 7, 1989, pp. 47–53.

Charlemagne's Journey to Jerusalem and Constantinople. Gaunt and Pratt, pp. 197–224.

Daurel and Beton. Gaunt and Pratt, pp. 135–96.

Devereaux, Rima. *Constantinople and the West in Medieval French Literature.* D. S. Brewer, 2012.

Gaunt, Simon, and Karen Pratt, translators. The Song of Roland *and Other Poems of Charlemagne.* Oxford UP, 2016.

Kibler, William W., and Leslie Zarker Morgan, editors. *Approaches to Teaching the* Song of Roland. Modern Language Association of America, 2006.

Kinoshita, Sharon. *Medieval Boundaries: Rethinking Difference in Old French Literature*. U of Pennsylvania P, 2006.

———. "*Le voyage de Charlemagne*: Mediterranean Palaces in the Medieval French Imaginary." *Olifant*, vol. 25, nos. 1–2, 2006, pp. 255–70.

Moore, Megan. *Exchanges in Exoticism: Cross-Cultural Marriage and the Making of the Mediterranean in Old French Romance*. U of Toronto P, 2014.

Ramey, Lynn T. "The Death of Aude and the Conversion of Bramimonde: Border Pedagogy and Medieval Feminist Criticism." Kibler and Morgan, pp. 232–38.

The Song of Roland. Gaunt and Pratt, pp. 3–134.

Trotter, D. A. *Medieval French Literature and the Crusades (1100–1300)*. Droz, 1987.

Uebel, Michael. *Ecstatic Transformation: On the Uses of Alterity in the Middle Ages*. Palgrave Macmillan, 2005.

Katherine Oswald

The Calculated Heroism
of the *Poema de mio Cid*

Weeping, the banished warrior contemplates his deserted hometown as he prepares to leave for exile: "De los sos ojos tan fuerte mientre llorando / tornava la cabeça y estava los catando" ("With the tears flowing so freely from his eyes / he turned his head and gazed upon them"; *Poema*, lines 1–2; *Poem of My Cid*, lines 1–2).[1] These, the first preserved verses of the *Poema de mio Cid*, present a striking image of the hero protagonist, Rodrigo Díaz de Vivar, affectionately known as *mio Cid* ("my Cid"), as he gazes on the emptiness of his hometown. While the missing first folio of the manuscript renders these opening verses coincidental, it is fitting that the audience's initial image of the hero is one in which he is deep in thought, as this is the first of numerous cases in which Rodrigo pauses instead of acting hastily. Among the pantheon of world epic heroes, and more particularly, among Spanish epic heroes, the Cid stands out for his moderation as he works tirelessly in the name of honor, establishing himself as an ideal vassal and lord. This connection between the hero's measuredness and his honor is one lens through which students can approach the *Poema de mio Cid*, and it offers the opportunity for focused analyses over short units of study. Keeping this lens in mind, the present essay is meant to facilitate the incorporation of the *Poema de mio Cid* in a comparative course, offering an introduction to the hero and the poem, guidance as far as the selection of translations and passages, and recommendations of activities to supplement traditional discussion techniques.

Rodrigo Díaz, the Cid, was likely born in Vivar around 1043 (Fletcher 107). *El Cid* (the Cid) is an unofficial title gained in his later years, which stems from the Arabic *sayyid* and can be translated as *señor* or lord (3). He came from an aristocratic family and was placed in the household of King Fernando I's eldest son, Sancho (later King Sancho II), when he was about fourteen, serving Sancho in battle by 1063 (108, 111). Upon Sancho's assassination in 1072, the Cid became the vassal of the slain king's brother, Alfonso VI, with whom he fell out of favor on more than one occasion (116, 118–20). He was banished by Alfonso in 1081, during which time he served the Muslim ruler of Zaragoza, and, after recovering Alfonso's favor, was banished a second time in 1089 (125). After numerous military campaigns in the Levante in the 1090s, he besieged Valencia in 1093, which surrendered in 1094 (163–64). He held the city—though not unchallenged—until his death in 1099. His wife, Jimena, remained there until 1102, at which point the city was evacuated after a lengthy siege by Almoravid forces (186). Jimena, who would live at least another decade, returned Rodrigo's body to Castile, where it was reinterred at the monastery of Cardeña (187).

On a personal level, Rodrigo married Jimena in 1074 or 1075 (Fletcher 123). They had three children who survived to adulthood: Cristina, María, and Diego, though the order of their births is unknown. Cristina married Ramiro, the grandson of King García III of Navarre, and María married Ramón Berenguer III of Barcelona; little is known about Diego, who does not feature in the *Poema de mio Cid*. Rodrigo's daughters, called Elvira and Sol in the poem, are central figures of the second half of the work.

The tremendous successes (and challenges) experienced by Rodrigo have led to many retellings of his life and deeds. The *Poema de mio Cid* is one of the earliest surviving retellings and relates the exploits of a mature hero.[2] Before considering the poem itself, however, it is important for me to note its place within the Spanish epic tradition and, more broadly, the place of the latter within the context of world epics. One of the distinguishing characteristics of the Spanish epic tradition is the dearth of poems that have been preserved in writing: only three texts survive, and the *Poema de mio Cid* is the earliest and by far the most intact. The other two poems that have survived in writing are *Las mocedades de Rodrigo* (*The Youthful*

92   *Poema de mio Cid*

Deeds of Rodrigo, the Cid), a fourteenth-century poem that recounts Rodrigo's youthful exploits, and *Roncesvalles,* a thirteenth-century work of which only one hundred verses survive. This small number of preserved *cantares de gesta* (epic poems) greatly distinguishes the Spanish epic tradition from many other medieval epic traditions, particularly the French. In a comparison of the corpora of Iberian and French epic poems, the former consists of only the three aforementioned works, totaling more or less five thousand verses, while the latter consists of more than one hundred poems and one million verses (Deyermond, *Historia* 68). A silver lining, however, is the preservation of many additional Spanish epic legends in other media, such as medieval chronicles and episodic ballad poems (Deyermond, *"Cantar"* 11).[3]

The work now known as the *Poema de mio Cid* or *Cantar de mio Cid* survives in one fourteenth-century manuscript. The manuscript itself is incomplete, missing four folios, including the first (Montaner 465). While there is uncertainty surrounding the nature of the *Poema de mio Cid*'s initial formation (oral or written),[4] the text that we have was likely composed in the final years of the twelfth century or the beginning of the thirteenth (*Poema* 18; *Poem of the Cid* 16), as the final three lines provide the terminus ante quem: "Quien escrivio este libro ¡del Dios paraiso, amen! / Per Abbat le escrivio en el mes de mayo / en era de mill e .cc xlv años" ("May God grant his paradise to the man who wrote this book! Amen. / Per Abbat wrote it down, in the month of May, / in the year 1207"; *Poema,* lines 3731–33; *Poem of My Cid,* lines 3731–33).[5] The use of *escrivir*—to write—in the colophon refers to the act of copying, as opposed to composing. As such, Per Abbat was likely a scribe who copied an extant poem in the year 1207. It is unknown who composed the work that Per Abbat copied, but the juridical and ecclesiastical presence in the *Poema de mio Cid* suggests that the writer would have been a learned poet, perhaps a lawyer, notary, or cleric (Deyermond, *"Cantar"* 17–19). The central theme of the *Poema de mio Cid* is honor, as the hero journeys to recover and maintain both his public and personal honor, and this goal guides his decisions and actions (27). A further discussion of the primary themes in the *Poema de mio Cid* and their incorporation in units of study dedicated to the poem can be found in the final paragraphs of this essay.

English speakers are fortunate to be able to select from numerous verse and prose translations of the *Poema de mio Cid.* Peter Such and John Hodgkinson's *The Poem of My Cid* is an excellent verse translation that maintains the important characteristics of orality that appear frequently throughout the work. Whether the *Poema de mio Cid* was originally composed orally or in writing, the element of orality (be it from composition or recitation) is undeniable: the poetic voice frequently addresses the audience (e.g., in lines 307, 572, 1127) and incorporates formulaic language such as epic epithets (e.g., in lines 41, 65, 734–42) and, as Such and Hodgkinson describe in their introduction (*Poem of My Cid* 26), pair phrases or binary expressions that constitute half-line units (e.g., in lines 17, 149, 1242). Such and Hodgkinson's introduction is noteworthy for being detailed yet accessible. Finally, the entire text of this edition is available through *JSTOR*. In the following paragraphs I outline three textual approaches to teaching the *Poema de mio Cid*.

Given the *Poema de mio Cid*'s importance within the Spanish literary corpus, many valuable resources are available beyond Such and Hodgkinson's translation. *The Poem of the Cid*, translated in prose by Rita Hamilton and Janet Perry and introduced (1–19) and glossed by the preeminent Cid scholar Ian Michael, is an excellent resource for those looking to teach a prose version. Matthew Bailey's *Cantar de mio Cid / Poem of My Cid* (miocid.wlu.edu) is a phenomenal electronic resource that will allow students to listen to a modern reading of the poem. The reading itself is in Spanish, with both Spanish and English subtitles available. In addition to the opportunity to hear the poem, Bailey has included an in-depth commentary in English that would undoubtedly enrich students' reading. Also translated and commented on by Bailey is an overview of the *Cantar de mio Cid* housed at the website *Open Iberia/América*. Bailey gives a concise introduction followed by facing translations of several central passages and his commentary. As I discuss below, this resource provides a solid foundation for a one-day unit of study.

The next practical question concerns the specific passages to include in a unit dedicated to the *Poema de mio Cid*. I begin with suggestions for a two-week unit, then discuss one-week and one-day options. I do so with a university schedule in mind, though any of the three approaches could be adapted to a high school framework. For a two-week unit, I recommend that students read the entire work. What makes this work particularly challenging for students of Spanish is navigating the Old Spanish; that is not an issue when students read the poem in translation, and in my experience teaching this text in English, such students do not struggle with comprehension.[6] Instead, students reading the work in translation have

94   *Poema de mio Cid*

struggled with two fundamental issues. The first is distinguishing fact from fiction. The *Poema de mio Cid* reads like a biography and is generally plausible enough that students interpret it as a work of historiography, which it is not. Second, students often make sweeping generalizations about the Middle Ages and, more specifically, medieval Iberia. These challenges can be faced head-on through a thorough introduction to the textual history and cultural context of the poem. As such, table 1 presents two sample text divisions for a two-week unit of study, assuming two class meetings per week.

Table 1
Sample text divisions

Division 1	Division 2
Day 1: Introduction and lines 1–64	Day 1: Introduction and lines 1–64
Day 2: Remainder of *cantar* (canto) 1 (65–1084)	Day 2: Remainder of *cantar* 1; *cantar* 2 (1085–656)
Day 3: *Cantar* 2	Day 3: Remainder of *cantar* 2 (1657–2277); *cantar* 3
Day 4: *Cantar* 3	Day 4: Synthesis

Considering the introductory materials available, sections 1 through 6 of Such and Hodgkinson's introduction (*Poem of My Cid* 1–24) will prove especially useful to students as they contextualize the *Poema de mio Cid* and its composition. The assigned lines of the poem provide only a brief introduction to our hero in a lesson otherwise devoted to foundational background. Beyond the first day, the level of the class might dictate the approach to the textual divisions. For upper-level students accustomed to a heavier reading load, the second sample text division could lead to higher-order analyses, as the sample includes a class session dedicated to considering the work as a whole, as opposed to each individual *cantar*. For first-year students who might still be acclimating to university reading yet are ambitious enough to tackle the entire poem, the first sample text division, dedicating one day to each *cantar*, is likely preferable.

To read the *Poema de mio Cid* in a one-week unit of study, consider the following selections:

Day 1: Introduction, sections 1–5; *cantar* 1, lines 1–925
Day 2: *cantar* 2, lines 1170–262, 1568–745, 1831–2155; *cantar* 3, lines 2278–557, 2697–916, 3060–507

As with the two-week plan, day 1 here includes an in-depth introduction to the text. Along with the introduction is almost the entire first *cantar*. Because the Cid experiences numerous pivotal moments in his journey during the first *cantar*, it is useful to read it as a cohesive unit, as opposed to reading individual episodes. Modern readers enter the poem in medias res: the Cid's public honor is at its absolute lowest point as he abandons Vivar only to find himself wholly rejected in Burgos. After making preparations for exile, including his deceit to gain the necessary start-up funds and his heartbreaking goodbye with his wife and children, he quickly begins to recover his honor through conquests and victories, both as aggressor and defender. The spoils from his defensive victory are significant enough to merit his first appeal to Alfonso VI for pardon.

To read both *cantar* 2 and *cantar* 3 in one day requires significant textual excerpting. The episodes selected from *cantar* 2 include the siege and surrender of Valencia and subsequent defense of the city; the arrival of the Cid's wife and daughters in Valencia; the battle against Yusuf, emir of Morocco; the third meeting with Alfonso, in which the king agrees to pardon his vassal and proposes that the Cid's daughters marry the *infantes* (nobles) of Carrión; and Alfonso and Rodrigo's reunion. The episodes selected from *cantar* 3 include the famous lion episode, the battle with Búcar of Morocco, the plan hatched by the *infantes* to seek revenge for their humiliation suffered in the two preceding episodes, their assault of their wives (the Cid's daughters) and the Cid's decision to seek legal justice, and the ensuing scenes in the courts. Notably absent from the episodes are the duels that result from the Cid's third petition in the courts. While the duels are noteworthy and further distinguish the Cid and his vassals from their adversaries, he himself does not participate. Furthermore, the scenes in the courts are central to his characterization, highlighting his measuredness.

A third textual approach to teaching the *Poema de mio Cid* is a one-day unit of study. For such a lesson, Bailey's introduction and selected translations and commentaries offer a cohesive overview of the work. This selection of episodes shines a light on the different facets of the hero: husband, father, vassal, lord, and conqueror. To supplement Bailey's selection, verses 1–64 (the Cid's departure from Vivar and rejection in Burgos) and 3060–507 (the courts) offer the opportunity for extended consideration of the hero's character. Since a one-day approach inevitably limits the range of conversation, a thematic approach centered, for example, on the question of honor could prove useful to students.

96   *Poema de mio Cid*

As mentioned above, the primary theme of the *Poema de mio Cid* is honor, and more specifically the journey of the hero to recover first his public honor (lost upon his exile) and then his private honor (lost upon the assault and abandonment of his daughters by the *infantes* of Carrión). Honor is, therefore, the driving force behind Rodrigo's actions, leading to calculated decisions at every turn. While the historical Cid was known, at times, to take rash action (Fletcher 130–32), the hero of the poem is profoundly characterized by his measuredness, as such a quality is central to his honor and, therefore, to establishing him as the ideal vassal and lord. The most salient example is the Cid's decision to operate through the judicial system after the assault of his daughters by their husbands. Every decision that he makes in this scenario elevates his own honor while systematically dismantling that of his adversaries. To consider other examples (though by no means an exhaustive list), the hero's calculating nature can be seen in his strategic battle plans (lines 435–85, 553–793), his treatment of the conquered (616–22), and his payment and personal treatment of his vassals (437–42, 512–14); in the latter two examples, there is a direct correlation between his moderation and his honor. Even his appeals to Alfonso reflect his restraint: the king rejects the Cid's first appeal for pardon on the grounds that not enough time has passed; consequently, his second appeal does not include a request for his own pardon, but only the request that his family be allowed to join him in Valencia. It is only after the massive victory against Yusuf's troops that the hero decides that he has the grounds to seek his own pardon, though his vassals who meet with Alfonso still do so indirectly. The relationship between the hero's honor and level-headedness can provide ample fodder for classroom discussions and activities. As a supplement to traditional discussion techniques, appeals to students' creative thinking can lead to critical analyses of the themes in question. The following are only a few examples of countless opportunities for student engagement with the poem.

Given the broad context of world epics, graphic organizers are useful tools to guide students in a comparison of the Cid to other heroes studied. A chronologically and contextually relevant example would be a comparison of the Cid with the Roland depicted in the *Chanson de Roland* (*Song of Roland*). The composition of the Oxford manuscript of the *Chanson de Roland* around 1100 occurred only a century before the composition of the *Poema de mio Cid*. In terms of context, Rodrigo and Roland both battle Muslim adversaries in the Iberian Peninsula, though their motives and attitudes leave much room for comparison and analysis by the students.

Regarding the *Poema de mio Cid* in isolation, students are consistently surprised (and even slightly annoyed) that the hero does not seek private vengeance after his daughters are attacked by their husbands. Preparing and holding mock debates between the Cid and his vassals regarding the merits of public justice versus private vengeance allows the students to delve into and analyze the Cid's frame of mind, considering not only the reasons behind his actions but also the consequences as they relate to his and the *infantes'* honor and how those consequences elevate him even further as an ideal vassal and lord. There are several ways to approach such an activity. One option is to divide the class in two groups—one representing the Cid and one representing his vassals—and have each group prepare their argument. After a given amount of time, the groups converge, and each student then partners with someone from the other group. The pairs are given time to debate privately, after which a whole-class discussion highlights the key points of each side, analyzing the rationale and consequences of Rodrigo's decision.

Another option is to appeal to students' use of social media, which can provide a manner for students to creatively dissect the material. Creating vlog posts from the perspective of Alfonso VI as he reacts to Rodrigo's first appeal for pardon allows students to experience and analyze the rocky relationship between king and former vassal from a new perspective. Writing a series of *Twitter* reactions to the lion episode from the perspective of multiple figures (such as the *infantes* of Carrión, the Cid himself, one of his vassals, and one of his daughters) allows students to consider the episode from different angles, using individual responses and the consequences thereof as a method of characterization. Beyond the tweets themselves, crafting creative yet relevant *Twitter* handles for the figures of the *Poema de mio Cid* also requires that students engage in character analyses, so that the handles aptly represent the individuals selected. Through such activities, students can approach the material from different perspectives, leading, ideally, to fruitful discussions of this unique epic poem.

I have had the joy of teaching the *Poema de mio Cid* in Spanish and English, in fragments and its entirety, and through a variety of contextual lenses. Students sympathize with both the exiled hero and those he conquers; they are surprised and, at times, irritated by his moderation; and, overall, they appreciate the journey that the Cid, in his quest for honor, experiences. It is my hope that this essay facilitates the incorporation and enjoyment of the *Poema de mio Cid* in comparative classes at any level.

98   *Poema de mio Cid*

Notes

1. Throughout this essay, I refer to the edition of the *Poema de mio Cid* edited by Smith. I use *The Poem of My Cid*, translated by Such and Hodgkinson, only to cite the poem in English. Such and Hodgkinson's volume is a facing translation, which uses Smith's Spanish edition as its base. As such, line references can refer to either the Spanish or English versions, since Such and Hodgkinson maintain the same line divisions as Smith.

2. For more on Latin and Arabic accounts that predate the *Poema de mio Cid*, see Fletcher 92–99.

3. For a discussion of the possible relationship between the *Poema de mio Cid* and the ballad tradition, see Wright.

4. For an overview of theories regarding the formation of the Spanish epic tradition, see Faulhaber.

5. The manuscript references "en era de mill e .cc xlv años" (*Poema*, line 3733), or 1245 in the era of Julius Caesar, a dating system thirty-eight years ahead of the Christian era (*Poem of the Cid* 242n).

6. This is, of course, presupposing that the students are native or near-native speakers of English. For students for whom English is their second (or additional) language, I would not foresee comprehension challenges beyond those expected for their individual levels of English.

Works Cited

Bailey, Matthew. "*Cantar de mio Cid.*" *Open Iberia/América*, 17 Sept. 2020, openiberiaamerica.hcommons.org/2020/09/17/cantar-de-mio-cid-ca-1200/.

Chanson de Roland. Edited by Luis Cortés, translated by Paulette Gabaudan, Librairie Nizet, 1994.

Deyermond, Alan. *El "Cantar de mío Cid" y la épica medieval española*. Sirmio, 1987.

———, editor. *Historia de la literatura española: La Edad Media*. 21st ed., Editorial Ariel, 2008.

Faulhaber, Charles B. "Neo-traditionalism, Formulism, Individualism, and Recent Studies on the Spanish Epic." *Romance Philology*, vol. 30, 1976, pp. 83–101.

Fletcher, Richard. *The Quest for El Cid*. Alfred A. Knopf, 1989.

Las mocedades de Rodrigo. Edited by Leonardo Funes, Tamesis, 2004.

Montaner, Alberto. Estudios y anexos. *Cantar de mio Cid*, Galaxia Gutenberg, Círculo de Lectores, 2011, pp. 221–1178.

Poema de mio Cid. Edited by Colin Smith, 26th ed., Cátedra, 2008.

The Poem of My Cid. Translated by Peter Such and John Hodgkinson, Liverpool UP, 1987. Aris & Phillips Hispanic Classics. *JSTOR*, www.jstor.org/stable/j.ctv16zjx36.

The Poem of the Cid. Translated by Rita Hamilton and Janet Perry, Penguin Books, 1984.

Roncesvalles. Épica medieval española, edited by Carlos Alvar and Manuel Alvar, Cátedra, 1997, pp. 166–70.

Wright, Roger. "Hispanic Epic and Ballad." *Medieval Oral Literature,* edited by Karl Reichl, De Gruyter, 2012, pp. 411–27.

Stefan Seeber

The *Nibelungenlied*: Otherworld, Court, and Doom in the Classroom

The *Nibelungenlied* (*Song of the Nibelungs*) is one of the undisputed classics of world literature, and its history of adaptation and reception is as fascinating (e.g., Wagner's four-opera cycle; see Cusack) as it is terrifying (especially in the Third Reich; see Hoffmann). The popularity of this classic and the general familiarity of the story in art and scholarship are both a curse and a blessing because they make it necessary for teachers to distinguish the text as a work in its own right against the material tradition. In addition, the overabundance of research on the *Nibelungenlied* makes it difficult for students to get an overview of the major approaches to analyzing the text.

My purpose here is not to present the well-known text and its tradition; this information is readily available from the commentaries and introductions that accompany English translations of the *Nibelungenlied*. Rather, I want to suggest possibilities for using the *Nibelungenlied* as a world classic in the classroom. My essay provides possible reading assignments, shows starting points for a closer look at key parts of the poem, and offers a concluding section on major works of research.

100

Three paperback editions of the *Nibelungenlied* in English translation are easily available and can be used for teaching: Arthur Hatto's translation is the oldest but is still readable and offers nearly one hundred pages of accompanying information on the song's form, plot, and major characters and on the saga tradition. The newer edition by Cyril Edwards has less accompanying text but includes an extended commentary. The latest edition, by William Whobrey, offers a contemporary translation (see Schneider) and relies on recent research for its introduction. Whobrey also includes a translation of the *Klage* (*Lament*), the poem that in almost all *Nibelungenlied* codices concludes the text. Although all three paperback editions are suitable for study of the *Nibelungenlied*, Whobrey's edition is the most accessible, and Hatto's continues to be widely used.

To help students get started, instructors can assign a short film: Sommer's World Literature series (which is in high demand by German students and has also won a prestigious Grimme Online Award) has produced an English summary of the *Nibelungenlied*, narrated by game characters, which is available on *YouTube* (*Song*). The playful video does not replace the students' own examination of the text but can be the starting point for studying the *Nibelungenlied*, as it is easy to watch at home. Students should be given a worksheet in advance listing the names of the main characters and providing information about the structure of the *Nibelungenlied*, such as the central themes of love, betrayal and the use of ruses, and violence and the characterization of men and women in the two parts of the poem. The end of the video also problematizes the status of the song as a national epic in Germany (see See). Instructors can ask students whether the video is justified in explicitly depicting the poem's violence, especially violence against women. In addition, students can reflect on the effectiveness of the didactic reduction that Sommer's World Literature offers, and at the end of the course unit they can come back to the video and debate its depiction of the epic on the basis of their own reading and better knowledge.

Following the introductory video, instructors can focus on the basic outline of facts regarding the poem's authorship, its time of origin, and its tradition: every classic, for all its supratemporal significance, is a child of its time and of the conditions under which it was created. Even the first stanza's first line—"Uns ist in alten maeren wunders vil geseit" ("We have been told in ancient tales many marvels"; Schulze; Hatto 17)—displays the status of the *Nibelungenlied* as a hybrid of written text and oral transmission. Using the digitized manuscript C ("'Nibelungenlied' und 'Klage'"),

102   *Nibelungenlied*

instructors can give students a glimpse of medieval manuscript culture and how texts were produced (and also how hard it is for modern readers to decipher the writing).

The line quoted above also alludes to the *Nibelungenlied* author's anonymity (Wunderlich): the poem presents the narrator as the mouthpiece of a tradition that goes back to the time of early medieval tales. This kind of storytelling was unusual at the time when the *Nibelungenlied* was presumably written: around 1200, courtly narratives dominated in Middle High German epic poetry, and their authors identified themselves by name in their work. The *Nibelungenlied*, on the other hand, uses a stanzaic form that was already obsolete by 1200; its way of writing goes back to Germanic alliterative verse and puts special emphasis on the last line of each stanza. These final lines often offer premonitions of future events and of doom, starting with the prophecy in the second stanza: "dar umbe muosen degene vil verliesen den lîp" ("causing many knights to lose their lives"; Schulze; Hatto 17). When read aloud, "degene" and "lîp," as final words of the two halves of the long verse, are emphasized as the main points of the argument. The unusual sentence structure additionally reinforces the impression of a hermetic narrative style, which does not follow the customs of Arthurian poetry.

Michael Curschmann called this particular language of the *Nibelungenlied* "Nibelungisch" ("Nibelungish"; 94; my trans.) because it does not follow the conventions of a written narrative, but it also does not display a conceptionally oral discourse.[1] As always in poems from the Middle Ages, there is a semantics of form, and this artificial language points to the special position of the *Nibelungenlied* between old heroic poetry and the contemporary Arthurian epic. The division of the poem into a total of thirty-nine chapters or adventures (*Aventiuren*) of varying length also belongs in this context. It can be assumed that the *Nibelungenlied* was only recited in parts, possibly with musical accompaniment. The late Eberhard Kummer has given an impression of how such a musically accompanied recital might have sounded, and playing an excerpt of the performance in class could help students understand how poetic texts were presented in the Middle Ages (*Aventiure*).

The *Nibelungenlied* tells its story by combining legends about the Burgundians and about the king Etzel (i.e., Attila the Hun). It is not a historic account but rather an artificial blending of materials from the Dark Ages into one story that transposes the old heroes into a courtly setting. The connection difficulties that arise can be exemplified by the hero, Siegfried.

Chapter 2 paints the picture of a courtier-knight who possesses all possible advantages: he is an excellent fighter (stanza 19) and is good-looking, he knows how to behave (stanza 22), and he is generally well liked. The knighting of Siegfried is described in detail in the poem (stanzas 27–40). But as soon as he sets out in chapter 3 to woo the beautiful Kriemhild at the court of Worms, his behavior becomes erratic, at least from a courtly point of view. Once at Kriemhild's court, he wants to fight her brother, King Gunther, in a duel. This chapter is relatively extensive, but it is worthwhile as a first reading for students.

In chapter 3, various elements become apparent that exemplify the outline of the entire *Nibelungenlied*. Siegfried is a mythical hero of unimaginable power and at the same time a courtly, well-bred knight. As a courtly knight he woos Kriemhild, and as a mythical hero he wants to fight Gunther. These two modes of behavior stand unreconciled, and therefore Siegfried is a split figure. The poem outsources the account of Siegfried's heroic deeds to Hagen. This Burgundian warrior tells about the immeasurable treasure of the Nibelungs. The Nibelungs are referred to as mythical kings, but ownership of the treasure allows first Siegfried and later Gunther and his men to become Nibelungs as well—*Nibelung* is a designation of honor for heroes in the poem. Hagen also recounts Siegfried's bath in the dragon's blood and tells the court about Siegfried's sword and cloak of invisibility. The cloak will later be used to betray Brünhild, and Kriemhild will use the sword to kill Hagen in the final chapter of the poem. Like Siegfried, Hagen is a figure not fully absorbed into the courtly sphere. He has mythical powers and knows about Siegfried's prowess, which is potentially dangerous to the court. The beginning of the poem thus indicates that Hagen will play an important role in the second part of the *Nibelungenlied*. The court is the place where things happen, but not only courtly things happen at court. There is also a threat of violence that will eventually break out. The role of women in the poem is limited. Women have to endure and accept their fate in the first part of the *Nibelungenlied*. In chapter 3, Kriemhild is the woman Siegfried desires, but she is not supposed to speak or show herself to him. Instead, she is the object of negotiation between men. Chapter 3 also gives exemplary insight into the poem's mode of narration. The narrator reports like a chronicler of events, predicting the looming evil and giving considerable space to the characters' dialogues.

Already at the start of the poem, the two spheres of the heroic and the courtly come into conflict. It becomes obvious that they cannot coexist

104 *Nibelungenlied*

peacefully and that one of them has to dominate the other. In the beginning, as is shown in chapter 3, the court seems to overpower and integrate the heroic sphere. But over the course of the epic, the heroic sphere metastasizes insidiously and eventually takes over the court and its values. Jan-Dirk Müller has described this process, in his foundational work *Rules for the Endgame*, as a gambling away of the courtly alternative: the heroic sphere is initially suppressed when Siegfried and then Brünhild are incorporated into the court, but later it breaks free and, unchecked, eventually destroys the courtly sphere. Central landmarks of this gambling away are found in chapter 7, when Siegfried uses his mythic powers to support Gunther's hopeless efforts to win Brünhild, and in chapter 10, when Brünhild is overpowered by Siegfried and raped by Gunther. Brünhild is not aware of her betrayal by Siegfried, and tensions arise from the ensuing misapprehension. Since bridal quests in Middle High German epics usually bring together the best fighter and the most beautiful woman, Brünhild considers her husband the best knight and Siegfried's superior, when in fact Gunther depends on Siegfried's help. The men's secret cannot be kept for long, and in chapter 14 the two wives fight about their respective husbands' prowess and political superiority.

Reading excerpts from these chapters allows students to sharpen their view of the role of women in the *Nibelungenlied* and to juxtapose Brünhild with Kriemhild. For this purpose, it is useful to look at the fight between Gunther and Brünhild on Isenstein, in Brünhild's realm, from chapter 7, when Gunther is fighting for Brünhild's hand and is about to lose the battle (see Starkey). Stanzas 429 to 464 show how Siegfried comes to Gunther's help and overcomes the mighty opponent using his cloak of invisibility. This action undermines one central rule of courtship, which prescribes that the best should win the fairest. Here the best knight helps a weaker suitor in his courtship, and the social order is fundamentally disturbed.

Stanzas 646 to 680 in chapter 10 describe how Siegfried helps Gunther to force the unwilling bride Brünhild to sleep with him. In addition to using the cloak of invisibility again to overcome Brünhild, Siegfried steals her ring and belt (which in medieval imagery signify her virginity) before handing her over to Gunther. This theft blurs the lines between what the audience knows to have happened and the outward appearance Siegfried displays, as the stolen goods suggest that he took Brünhild's virginity. Working with excerpts from chapters 7 and 10, students can uncover the following: Like Siegfried, Brünhild is an exorbitant figure; she has special powers and lives as a queen in her own realm. Gunther can win her only by trickery, and he needs Siegfried's help. In the tension between the courtly and heroic spheres, cunning and discord flourish, sowing the seeds for the downfall of the Nibelungs' world. Women in the *Nibelungenlied* are defined by their relationships to men: Gunther wants Brünhild as his wife, and Siegfried helps him achieve this, in exchange for being allowed to marry Kriemhild. When viewed against the background of modern gender theories, the rape of Brünhild also exemplifies that women in the *Nibelungenlied* have no voices of their own. In the second part of the poem, Kriemhild tries to break through this suppression through revenge. Walter Haug has therefore proposed ascribing her traits to an individually shaped, protomodern figure (25, 326–38). The main point, however, is that Brünhild is silenced, while Kriemhild develops a negative identity by actively turning away from courtly ethics.[2]

The first part of the *Nibelungenlied* ends with Siegfried's death. Students do not need to read this passage; the 1845 painting by Julius Schnorr von Carolsfeld can serve as a starting point for discussion. The painting's forest scene shows Hagen, a bearded villain with a crazy stare, as he stabs Siegfried in the back. Portrayed as an angel, the hero Siegfried has laid down his weapons to drink from a spring. Gunther and his brothers stand in the background as Hagen's accomplices. Even though the Burgundians planned Siegfried's death jointly, Hagen is still singled out as the murderer. The painting sums up both Hagen's traitorous intent and the group dynamic that makes all the Burgundian characters sympathizers with his deed. Siegfried is innocent, unsuspecting, and vulnerable and thus falls prey to the eagle Hagen, as was foreshadowed in Kriemhild's dream in chapter 1: "In disen hôhen êren troumte Kriemhilde, / wie si zuge einen valken, starc, schoen und wilde, / den ir zwêne aren erkrummen. daz si daz muoste sehen, / ir enkunde in dirre werlde leider nimmer geschehen" ("Kriemhild dreamt she reared a falcon, strong, handsome and wild, but that two eagles rent it while she perforce looked on, the most grievous thing that could ever befall her"; Schulze, stanza 11, lines 1–4; Hatto 18).

The second part of the *Nibelungenlied*, which comprises chapters 20 to 39, offers several passages that are worth a closer look. If the class places a special emphasis on the portrayal of women, then students should discuss Kriemhild's intentions for revenge for her murdered husband, whose killers, especially Hagen, never take responsibility for their actions and, in addition to killing Siegfried, take the Nibelung treasure from Kriemhild. These aspects are foregrounded in chapter 23. This chapter shows that

106 *Nibelungenlied*

Kriemhild's loyalty is to her first husband (Siegfried), not to her second (Etzel). She uses her second husband to initiate her revenge. Etzel is a weak figure in the *Nibelungenlied* and is portrayed as inferior to his wife. Kriemhild is evaluated negatively for the first time in the text in this chapter; the narrator thinks that the devil, the "ubele vâlant" ("the foul fiend"; Schulze, stanza 1391, line 1; Hatto 177), guides her in her plans for revenge. This demonization of the woman who takes matters into her own hands and disobeys the courtly rules pervades the rest of the epic. The downfall of the Nibelungs is initiated by Kriemhild through her revenge, as foretold in the second stanza of the poem.

Students can also consider the dynamics of male alliances in this part of the poem, a good example of which is Hagen's bond with Rüdiger of Bechelaren, the margrave of Etzel. This bond leads the two heroes to refuse to fight against each other. This episode is treated in detail in chapter 37, which also lends itself to more intensive consideration because of the emotions portrayed. Rüdiger stands between the lines of conflict as Etzel's subject, but he is also a friend to the Nibelungs, as the Burgundians are called in the second part of the poem. When he enters the battle on Kriemhild's side, Rüdiger does so only after he has shown at length his courtly disposition toward Hagen and the Burgundians. His change of behavior is described inchoatively as "ertoben" ("going berserk"; Schulze, stanza 2203, line 2; Hatto 272) and as "des muotes ertobete," which Hatto paraphrases as "[t]he noble Margrave's fighting blood was up" and which Edwards translates more explicitly as "[h]e went berserk" (199).

The last chapter (chapter 39) should be read, at least in excerpts, to show the murders of Hagen and Kriemhild. Hundeshagen's fourteenth-century manuscript illustrates both the war scenes and the end of the poem. The burning hall in which the Nibelungs fight and the last conversation between Hagen and Kriemhild (during which she holds Gunther's severed head in one hand and Siegfried's sword in the other, ready to execute Hagen) can function as the basis for a discussion of how the female figure is displayed and how violence is staged in both illustrations and the text.[3] In particular, Kriemhild's scandalous self-empowerment can be observed in the illustration of her last conversation with Hagen ("Kriemhilds letzter Wortwechsel"). She is about to kill Hagen, who awaits his death with bowed head, but also present is Hildebrand, who in turn will kill Kriemhild shortly after Hagen's murder. The illustrator thus shows a woman who has overstepped her boundaries and taken up a weapon (which does not befit women in medieval culture) but also makes it abundantly clear that justice will be served by Hildebrand, the man in the front center of the picture.

Although the short text sections discussed in this essay do not fully capture the *Nibelungenlied*, they provide insights into the various themes that are important for a general understanding of the epic. Further topics that could be explored in class include the manuscript tradition and the different versions of the story displayed in the most important manuscripts: C, B ("St. Gall Nibelung Manuscript B"), and A ("Nibelungenlied und die Klage"). The fact that the text belongs to the realm of fiction as well as to that of history shows the difficult nature of this medieval courtly epic, whose narrator is portrayed as an evaluative chronicler of events. The *Nibelungenlied* consequently does not meet modern demands for coherence and psychology in fiction. This becomes abundantly clear to students when they trace the characters of Siegfried, Brünhild, and Kriemhild and their respective roles in the plot. The *Nibelungenlied* is therefore a double narrative. On the one hand, it tells of the downfall that is unalterably approaching; on the other hand, it shows the actors forgoing all possibilities of averting the disaster. Even time and space are bent to the inevitable destruction, and, like a great black hole, the hall at Etzel's castle draws in all elements of the narration and lets them culminate in the extinction of all the main characters.

Students may be asked to consider why the ending is so abrupt. The narrator openly admits to not knowing (or not caring) what "sider da geschach" ("happened after this"; Schulze, stanza 2376, line 1; Hatto 291). The narration is fulfilled once the narrator has finished the report about those characters who were destined to die; those who live on are not of interest (stanza 2374, line 1). The task of offering the narrative of mourning and explaining the catastrophe is taken over by the poem *Klage*, which is appended to the *Nibelungenlied* in almost all manuscripts. In rhyming couplets, which were a more modern literary form in the thirteenth century, the *Klage* reports how the news of the catastrophe spreads and how the mourners resume their lives. The downfall is not final; there is hope in the Christian Middle Ages beyond the end of the *Nibelungenlied* (see Henkel).

The study of the *Nibelungenlied* as a world epic is, on the whole, a twofold task: on the one hand, it is about understanding the poem as an artifact of (and in) its time. On the other hand, the poem allows readers to form their own opinions, and every era shapes its own image of the Nibelungs. After its modern rediscovery in the eighteenth century, the song

108 *Nibelungenlied*

was celebrated as the German *Iliad*. Wagner retold the story as a Nordic myth and initiated a "Teutonenkult" ("Teutonic cult"; Müller, *Nibelungenlied* 183; my trans.), and Fritz Lang's cinematic adaptation made the *Nibelungenlied* accessible to broader audiences as a cultural phenomenon in the Weimar Republic,[4] before Nazi war propaganda used the fall of the Nibelungs as a heroic example for the Germans. Indeed, in 1943, Hermann Göring proclaimed Nibelung loyalty as a motto after Stalingrad (Krüger). Only recently, through films and also comic dramatizations (Schmidt), has the epic been reinterpreted and read in new ways. The *Nibelungenlied* now stands as the inspiration for a medievalism that is postnationalist and mainly interested in medieval cultural assets. The poem's status as a UNESCO world heritage document, gained in 2009, honors its importance ("Heldengeschichten"), and the ongoing retellings, interpretations, and scholarly attention prove that, like so many world epics, the *Nibelungenlied* is still very much alive.

Notes

1. See Ready 2 for more on orality and textuality in epic poetry.

2. As Albrecht Classen points out in his essay on *Kudrun* in this volume, the silencing of women is not a given in medieval epics—Kudrun is a mighty figure who uses speech and tactics to pursue her political goals, and she is displayed as a self-determining character throughout the poem, which was possibly composed as a poetic counterargument to the *Nibelungenlied*.

3. For an image of the burning hall, see "Nibelungenlied: Hundeshagenscher Kodex."

4. See Levin 97, which refers to Lang's anti-Hollywood stance and display of supposed German superiority over American film production.

Works Cited

Aventiure (Das Nibelungenlied*). YouTube*, uploaded by Eberhard Kummer, 14 May 2014, www.youtube.com/watch?v=c4PcPR4hf6Y.

Curschmann, Michael. "*Nibelungenlied* und *Nibelungenklage*: Über Mündlichkeit und Schriftlichkeit im Prozeß der Episierung." *Deutsche Literatur im Mittelalter: Kontakte und Perspektiven: Hugo Kuhn zum Gedenken*, edited by Christoph Cormeau, Metzler, 1979, pp. 85–119.

Cusack, Carole M. "Richard Wagner's *Der Ring des Nibelungen*: Medieval, Pagan, Modern." *Relegere: Studies in Religion and Reception*, vol. 3, no. 2, 2013, pp. 329–52, https://doi.org/10.11157/rsrr3-2-584.

Edwards, Cyril, translator. *The Nibelungenlied*. Oxford UP, 2010.

Hatto, Arthur E., translator. *The* Nibelungenlied: *A New Translation*. Penguin Books, 1965.

Haug, Walter. *Strukturen als Schlüssel zur Welt: Kleine Schriften zur Erzählliteratur des Mittelalters*. Niemeyer, 1989.

"Heldengeschichten des Mittelalters." *UNESCO*, www.unesco.de/kultur-und-natur/weltdokumentenerbe/weltdokumentenerbe-deutschland/nibelungenlied. Accessed 25 Aug. 2022.

Henkel, Nikolaus. "'Nibelungenlied' und 'Klage': Überlegungen zum Nibelungenverständnis um 1200." *Mittelalterliche Literatur im Spannungsfeld von Hof und Kloster*, edited by Nigel F. Palmer and Hans-Jochen Schiewer, Niemeyer, 1999, pp. 73–98.

Hoffmann, Werner. "The Reception of the *Nibelungenlied* in the Twentieth Century." *A Companion to the* Nibelungenlied, edited by Winder McConnell, Camden House, 1998, pp. 127–52.

"Kriemhilds letzter Wortwechsel mit Hagen, Handschriftenabteilung Hundeshagenscher Kodex." *Wikimedia Commons*, commons.wikimedia.org/wiki/File:Kriemhilds_letzter_Wortwechsel_mit_Hagen_Handschriftenabteilung_Hundeshagenscher_Kodex.jpeg. Accessed 25 Aug. 2022.

Krüger, Peter. "Etzels Halle und Stalingrad: Die Rede Görings vom 30. 1. 1943." *Die Nibelungen: Sage-Epos-Mythos*, edited by Joachim Heinzle, Reichert, 2003, pp. 375–405.

Levin, David J. *Richard Wagner, Fritz Lang, and the Nibelungen*. Princeton UP, 1998. Princeton Studies in Opera.

Müller, Jan-Dirk. *Das Nibelungenlied*. Schmidt, 2009. Klassiker-Lektüren 5.

———. *Rules for the Endgame: The World of the* Nibelungenlied. Translated by William T. Whobrey, Johns Hopkins UP, 2007.

"Nibelungenlied: Hundeshagenscher Kodex." *Wikimedia Commons*, commons.wikimedia.org/wiki/Category:Hundeshagenscher_Kodex?uselang=de#/media/File:Der_Saalbrand_Hundeshagenscher_Kodex.jpeg. Accessed 25 Aug. 2022.

"Das Nibelungenlied und die Klage (Leithandschrift A)." *Münchener DigitalisierungsZentrum*, daten.digitale-sammlungen.de/~db/0003/bsb00035316/images/.

"'Nibelungenlied' und 'Klage.'" *Badische Landesbibliothek*, 2003, digital.blb-karlsruhe.de/737536.

Ready, Jonathan. *Orality, Textuality, and the Homeric Epics: An Interdisciplinary Study of Oral Texts, Dictated Texts, and Wild Texts*. Oxford UP, 1998.

Schmidt, Klaus M. "Die Wormser Nibelungen von Moritz Rinke und Dieter Wedel." *The* Nibelungenlied: *Genesis, Interpretation, Reception (Kalamazoo Papers 1997–2005)*, edited by Sibylle Jefferis, Kümmerle, 2006, pp. 213–34. Göppinger Arbeiten zur Germanistik 735.

Schneider, Christian. "Review of Whobrey, *The Nibelungenlied*." *Speculum*, vol. 95, no. 1, 2020, pp. 306–07.

110 *Nibelungenlied*

Schnorr von Carolsfeld, Julius. *Siegfrieds Tod. Wikimedia Commons,* commons
.wikimedia.org/wiki/File:Siegfrieds_Tod.jpg. Accessed 8 Dec. 2022.

Schulze, Ursula. *Das* Nibelungenlied*: Mittelhochdeutsch/Neuhochdeutsch, nach
der Handschrift.* B. Reclam, 2010.

See, Klaus von. "Das *Nibelungenlied*—ein Nationalepos?" *Die Nibelungen:
Sage-Epos-Mythos,* edited by Joachim Heinzle, Reichert, 2003, pp. 309–43.

The Song of the Nibelungs to Go. YouTube, uploaded by Sommer's World
Literature to go, 6 July 2016, www.youtube.com/watch?v=Wn2t7pT_29E.

Starkey, Kathryn. "Brunhild's Smile: Emotion and the Politics of Gender in the
Nibelungenlied." *Codierungen von Emotionen im Mittelalter,* edited by
C. Stephen Jaeger and Ingrid Kasten, De Gruyter, 2003, pp. 159–73.

"St. Gall Nibelung Manuscript B with the Nibelungenlied (The Song of the
Nibelungs) and 'Klage' (Lament), 'Parzival' and 'Willehalm' by Wolfram von
Eschenbach, and Stricker's 'Karl der Grosse' (Charlemagne)." *E-codices,*
10 Aug. 2015, www.e-codices.unifr.ch/en/list/one/csg/0857.

Whobrey, William T. *The* Nibelungenlied *with the* Klage. Hackett, 2018.

Wunderlich, Werner. "The Authorship of the *Nibelungenlied.*" *A Companion to
the* Nibelungenlied, edited by Winder McConnell, Camden House, 1998,
pp. 251–77.

Albrecht Classen

The Middle High German *Kudrun*: A Female Protagonist's Action to End Male Violence

Many readers familiar with European heroic epics assume that the genre has certain stable features regardless of the time period or geographic location in which these works were composed (Konstan and Raaflaub). Students in a survey course on world epics might expect to encounter a series of prominent heroes who fight against superior opposing forces and whose own superhuman strength and abilities help them in the end to overcome an enemy and restore the good. It would not be unusual for students to imagine the hero, typically male, losing his life in that process and thereby gaining supreme honor. Close readings of many of the better known European epic poems, however, tend to reveal quite different perspectives regarding the heroes' character and intelligence. Even within the medieval European epic genre, the development of narrative events and the emergence of new types of protagonists can trouble our modern understanding even further (Classen, "Downfall").

In Middle High German literature, there are a good number of heroic epics that are fairly easily defined and qualified. But there are also various texts that are included in that genre though the genre's traditional criteria do not seem to apply to them, such as in the case of the confusing and perhaps simply poorly composed *Der Wunderer*, written around 1500

112   *Kudrun*

(see Classen, "*Wunderer*"). Most interesting is the poem *Kudrun*, written between 1220 and 1250, which has survived in only one late manuscript, a miscellany known as the Ambraser Heldenbuch, from between 1504 and 1514. The poem uses a rather unusual structure, being divided into four major parts, each of which represents a new generation. While the initial three generations are devoted to heroism based on violence, in the fourth generation there is the rather unexpected switch to a new set of ideals when the eponymous heroine decides that her society's entire political and military structure requires a profound reform (McConnell xix).

The Ambraser Heldenbuch, today housed in the Austrian National Library in Vienna, represents a most unusual case in medieval literature, perhaps only paralleled by the Auchinleck Manuscript, from the late fourteenth century, which is held by the National Library of Scotland and is another fascinating but also puzzling miscellany (Fein). Named after the Ambras Castle outside of Innsbruck, Austria, the Ambraser Heldenbuch was copied down by the Bozen toll official Hans Ried between 1504 and 1516 and contains twenty-five Middle High German texts, some of which are unique.[1] Ried had been charged with this task by the Habsburg emperor Maximilian I, who endeavored to secure his own memory in posterity through architectural projects, sculptures (e.g., in the Hofkirche in Innsbruck), paintings, and literature (several quasi-autobiographical works), as well as through this huge collection of heroic, courtly, didactic, and entertaining verse narratives (Müller; Klarer). Despite the title of this collection, which I translate as "Book of Heroic Epics," its content defies its straightforward categorization and offers numerous opportunities for students to explore the collection from a variety of perspectives, gain a better understanding of various literary genres, and grasp the character of medieval miscellanies (*Kudrun* [Gibbs and Johnson] xiii).

Kudrun has since been discussed, edited, and translated numerous times, which makes teaching this Middle High German text in an English-language class considerably easier. Its thirty-two chapters can be covered in two to three weeks. The latest critical edition was published by Karl Stackmann; Marion E. Gibbs and Sidney M. Johnson have prepared an excellent modern translation into English, as has Winder McConnell. Both translations, however, resort to prose, whereas the original was composed in four-line stanzas, in contrast to the traditional rhymed couplets of the courtly romance (*Kudrun* [Gibbs and Johnson] xxxiv–xxxv). Older translations, certainly not to be dismissed, such as by Emma Letherbrow (Gudrun: *A Story*), Mary Pickering Nichols (Gudrun: *A Mediaeval Epic*), and

George P. Upton (*Gudrun*), are now freely available online. *Kudrun* has also been translated into French, Italian, Spanish, Dutch, and Russian.

Kudrun constitutes a significant contribution to thirteenth-century German literature, and its survival in a sixteenth-century manuscript means that readers can scrutinize its unique features to gain deeper insights into the paradigm shift from the Middle Ages to the early modern age (Classen, *Paradigm Shifts*). Indeed, *Kudrun* proves to be an intriguing counterexample to the traditional heroic epic; the poem's narrative is influenced deeply by military principles and practices but eventually replaces them with more diplomatic strategies that make the establishment of peace possible. The appearance of major female figures who wrestle the metaphorical sword out of the hands of some of the most martial male warriors (such as Wate), insisting that new social norms need to be implemented, invites a critical discussion with students about contrasting value systems in the poem.

How, then, might instructors approach teaching this unique Middle High German heroic epic in an English-language literature context? When students examine *Kudrun*, gender issues emerge front and center, beginning with the practice of marriage itself since in each successive generation wives are regularly conquered forcefully by their would-be husbands (in a tradition known as the bridal quest). Why does the text ultimately assign agency in ending this cycle of violence to a woman? Does this assignment imply a connection between gender and mediation aimed at conflict resolution? It might be useful for instructors to reference Ann Marie Rasmussen's more general reflection on the role of female networks in medieval German literature: "Women mediate between competing kinship systems, yet at the same time they have a powerful interest in asserting their understanding of what those kindred networks represent" (Rasmussen 100). Attention to women and family could also center on the highly meaningful mother-daughter relationship, a bond that appears as a significant theme in a variety of medieval texts (Rasmussen). Further, the episode in *Kudrun* in which the infant Hagen is abducted by a griffin as food for its young ones and in which especially his father responds emotionally to this tragic loss provides students with an opportunity to examine the issue of childhood in the Middle Ages (Classen, *Childhood*).

Students may be invited to focus more closely on the distinctive character traits that make Kudrun an effective peace weaver, as she has been called (Vollmann-Profe; see also Classen, "Heuristic Value"). Although Kudrun is unable to prevent her abduction, once she is committed to her

114   *Kudrun*

future husband, Herwic, she never wavers in resisting all attempts by her kidnapper, Hartmut, to sway her in his favor or to force her by imposing slave work on her. Moreover, as much as she is treated as a captive, Kudrun never loses her dignity, and even the lowly work of doing the family's laundry does nothing to undermine her strong sense of independence, honor, and royalty. Once the enemy has been defeated—both of Hartmut's parents are killed in the fighting—Kudrun gains her own agency and determines the political stage at home. At the same time, instructors might note that attempts to recognize here specifically Christian ideals have mostly failed (Siebert 49–51).

Kudrun may also be compared with other female characters who emerge as the almost dominant figures throughout the epic. Ute, for example, a Norwegian princess later identified as Scottish, proves to be the really influential person in her marriage to the mighty king Sigebant of Ireland. Right from the outset she teaches him how to perform properly as a ruler, pay respects to his knights and guests, and provide them with honor and gifts. When the couple's young son Hagen is abducted by a griffin, Sigebant breaks down in tears, while his wife responds in a resolute and self-disciplined fashion that saves their royal reputation. After young Hagen has survived the attack by the griffin, he finds refuge with three princesses: one from Portugal, another from Iserland (possibly Iceland), and the third, Hilde, from India, whose presence in this text raises interesting geographic and racial issues.

Kudrun is actually connected to the Indian princess through plot twists as well as genealogy. Once Hagen has grown up, he marries Hilde, and they have a daughter whom they also call Hilde. The younger Hilde is later abducted by the Danish king Hetel, who receives significant help from his mighty liege man Wate of Stormarn. Hagen pursues and engages Hetel in battle until they decide, exhausted, to strike up an alliance and let Hetel marry the young woman. The couple's daughter is Kudrun, who in turn is wooed by three princes. King Herwic of Sealand wins out over the other two, but during the waiting period of their engagement, Hartmut of Normandy abducts Kudrun, setting into motion events that will bring the cycle of abductions to a close.

Students may, conversely, read the work through the lens of its male warriors and rulers—in terms of their relationships to each other as well as to the women in their lives. Although the narrator gives much respect to military might, the male warriors often only respond to and do not take charge of their country's politics. Indeed, those who assume the role of military leaders—such as Hagen, who fights a griffin and later pursues the kidnappers of his daughter—do not necessarily prove to be superior political leaders. Hagen's father, Sigeband, leaves a negative impression because of his weakness, and Hartmut's father, Ludwig, though a mighty warrior, fails to help his son find the right marriage partner and ultimately dies as punishment for having taken Kudrun prisoner. The women in the poem, by contrast, assume a consistently more active role, especially in the case of Hilde after her daughter Kudrun's abduction and her husband's death. Hilde, in fact, emerges as the driving force to liberate Kudrun and operates as the decisive figure in the long-term effort to achieve that goal.

Whether the poem's attention to strong female characters allows us to recognize behind the anonymous poet a woman remains a fascinating speculation, but we have no firm evidence for that idea (McConnell 96–98). However, the narrator definitely contrasts the bloody clashes between the warriors (especially Hagen and later Wate) with the efforts by the female rulers (Hilde and Kudrun) to pursue diplomatic measures through which the endless warfare can be substituted by marriage arrangements among the former enemies (Schmitt 249–57).

Yet it would be inaccurate to conclude that peace wins out over war in the poem simply because a woman's innovative policy replaces martial heroism. The final diplomatic resolution would not have been possible if Kudrun had not been liberated thanks to military force. The Normans, under the leadership of Ludwig, had killed Kudrun's father and many of his men when they had tried to free her during the battle on the so-called Wülpensand (the name of an island). But Kudrun was not liberated for several more years, until her brother Ortwin had grown up and was ready to resume the conflict with all his might and with the full support of his mother and other allies. *Kudrun* offers us, in other words, a fantastic opportunity to explore archetypal conflicts involving gender, power structures, dynastic interests, marital arrangements, and generational conflicts (for parallel cases in Old English literature, see Eshleman).

There are plenty of opportunities for instructors to assign students to study individual figures in the poem, such as Hagen, Wate, Hartmut, and Hilde, who need to be analyzed closely in terms of their characters, abilities, social functions, and performance. Studying gender roles and their relativization would also offer many valuable perspectives, as would studying the awareness of foreign countries and cultures as reflected in the poem. Attention to warriors and kings could bring the discussion to the issue of peace versus war, a central concern in the contributions of philosophers,

116   *Kudrun*

theologians, poets, and artists from the Middle Ages to today (Classen and Margolis). Additionally, students may be asked to report on references in the poem to monsters and typically medieval wonders (Lecouteux; Tuczay).

Kudrun can be assigned in conjunction with selections from its most relevant parallel or reference text, the *Nibelungenlied*. This famous Middle High German epic poem can be found on the reading list of many seminars on medieval heroic epics or medieval literature more broadly because of the universal and monumental themes it explores—heroism, gender relations, the relationship between humans and the otherworld, betrayal, murder, prophecy, revenge, and mutual slaughter in war (Classen, "Glory"). The *Nibelungenlied* concludes with a veritable Armageddon, after virtually all its heroes, including Queen Kriemhild, have been killed except for King Attila and his two warriors, Dietrich and Hildebrand (who originate from a different Germanic tribe). The poem is followed, at least in most manuscripts—either by itself or in combination with other texts, as in the Ambraser Heldenbuch—by a lament on the devastating consequences of the events triggered by Siegfried; then by his murderer, Hagen; and finally by the avenger, Siegfried's wife, Kriemhild. Referred to as *The Lament of the Nibelungen*, this reflection replaces the heroic code with a much more emotional, culturally sophisticated, and perhaps already somewhat courtly concept. Thus, the *Nibelungen* tradition already contains a radical critique of the traditional warrior mentality.

Reading *Kudrun* in tandem with selections from the *Nibelungenlied* would put into relief the different endings as well as the distinct female characters in the two works. As noted above, *Kudrun* continues for much of its length to promote the traditional ideals of male heroism that defends the family against intruders, but in the last section the poem features a female protagonist who intervenes to prevent further slaughter. In this way, a military ethos is replaced with a marriage policy that compels former enemies to accept each other as more or less equal partners and to undertake open negotiations. The most striking comparison would be between Kriemhild, who brings devastation to the Burgundians and the Huns, and Kudrun, who prevents the fighting from getting out of hand, establishes peaceful relationships, and creates marriage bonds.

Students may discuss the extent to which *Kudrun* might serve as a critical response to the themes of the *Nibelungenlied*. As Barbara Siebert has demonstrated, the *Kudrun* poet was fully aware of the rich tradition of Middle High German literature and drew from a variety of sources even while *Kudrun* does not copy the heroic model. Some scholars have argued that *Kudrun* is indeed a contrafacture to the *Nibelungenlied* (Millet 238–52), especially because in the latter epic poem Kriemhild, Siegfried's widow and then the new wife of the Hunnish ruler Attila, endeavors with all her might, even at the cost of her own child's life, to avenge Siegfried's death by getting the entire Burgundian army (and finally also the murderer, Hagen) killed. Kriemhild herself is then cut down, leaving behind nothing but a field of corpses, both friend and foe. Kudrun, by contrast, sustains her suffering with patience and heroic grandeur, even when she is bitterly humiliated by her would-be mother-in-law, Gerlind, who forces her to wash clothing in the sea (hence the somewhat questionable argument by Huber that it might have been composed at the court of Rügen on the Baltic Sea instead of at a Bavarian-Austrian court). Nor does Kudrun allow her emotions to rule her once her brother and future husband have arrived together with their troops to liberate her.

Attention to *Kudrun*'s archetypal projection can allow instructors to discuss the epic in relation to any number of other medieval works. Generational conflict, for example, which in *Kudrun* takes the form of the hostile tensions between the captive Kudrun and her presumed future mother-in-law, Gerlind, can be found in texts of many genres written at many different times, whether we think of the pan-European *Apollonius of Tyre*, Geoffrey Chaucer's *The Man of Law's Tale*, or the anonymous *Mai und Beaflor* (*Mai and Beaflor*). Later fairy tales, such as those recorded by the Brothers Grimm, often copy the same model and thus perpetuate the universal or archetypal generational conflict outlined here. *Kudrun* serves equally well in comparative analyses with other works, such as *Beowulf*, with its strong female characters, or the *Poema de mio Cid*, in which the hero reestablishes his status and honor through much fighting, but in which diplomacy, the use of legal means, and the pursuit of honor in political terms matter much more. To further interrogate notions of genre, students may compare *Kudrun* to adventure stories in the vein of *Duke Ernst* and *King Rother*, written between 1170 and 1200, or any number of courtly romances.

Although little appreciated during the time of its composition, *Kudrun* now proves to be a valuable item on the reading lists for many comparative literature classes dedicated to the premodern world. Its combination of fantasy, heroism, bloody warfare, political cabal, kidnapping, military strategizing, and peace weaving can productively contribute to a more nuanced discussion in a course on medieval literature or world epics. Studying this

118   *Kudrun*

so-called heroic epic invites a much broader approach to cultural, ideo-logical, political, literary-historical, and art-historical investigations and builds significant bridges between the high and late Middle Ages and nineteenth-century political and cultural history. In addition, consider-ation of the creation of the massive Ambraser Heldenbuch manuscript in the early sixteenth century and its preservation throughout the centuries, especially the care it received in the early nineteenth century as an iconic document for Habsburg Austria, leads to meaningful questions concern-ing modern forms of identity and the grounding of modern culture in the medieval past (see "Ambras Castle").

Note

1. In 1806 the Ambraser Heldenbuch was transferred to the Kunsthisto-risches Museum in Vienna ("Ambraser Heldenbuch"). For a complete transcrip-tion, see *Ambraser Heldenbuch*.

Works Cited

"Ambras Castle in Innsbruck." *Tyrol*, 2022, www.tyrol.com/things-to-do/attractions/all-attractions/a-ambras-castle.

"Ambraser Heldenbuch." *Wikipedia*, 24 July 2022, en.wikipedia.org/wiki/Ambraser_Heldenbuch.

Ambraser Heldenbuch: Gesamttranskription mit Manuskriptbild. Edited by Mario Klarer, De Gruyter, 2021. 11 vols. *De Gruyter*, www.degruyter.com/serial/ahg-b/html.

Classen, Albrecht, editor. *Childhood in the Middle Ages and the Renaissance: The Results of a Paradigm Shift in the History of Mentality.* De Gruyter, 2005.

———. "The Downfall of a Hero: Siegfried's Self-Destruction and the End of Heroism in the *Nibelungenlied*." *German Studies Review*, vol. 26, no. 2, 2003, pp. 295–314.

———. "The Glory and End of the Heroic World in the *Nibelungenlied*." *601 CE to 1450 CE*, edited by Christine Chism, Wiley-Blackwell, 2019, pp. 1243–54. Vol 2 of *A Companion to World Literature*, Ken Seigneurie, general editor.

———. "The Heuristic Value of German Literature: The Eternal Plea for the Relevance of Medieval and Early Modern Literature from a Practical/Pedagogical Perspective." *Literature and Aesthetics*, vol. 28, no. 1, 2018, pp. 157–92, openjournals.library.sydney.edu.au/index.php/LA/article/view/12602/11573.

———, editor. *Paradigm Shifts during the Global Middle Ages and the Renais-sance.* Brepols, 2019.

Albrecht Classen 119

———. "*Der Wunderer*: Hybridität, Erzähllogik und narrative Fragmentierung in der Literatur des deutschen Spätmittelalters." *Wirkendes Wort*, vol. 66, no. 3, 2016, pp. 371–84.

Classen, Albrecht, and Nadia Margolis, editors. *War and Peace: Critical Issues in European Societies and Literature, 800–1800*. De Gruyter, 2011.

Eshleman, Lori. "Weavers of Peace, Weavers of War." *Peace and Negotiation: Strategies for Coexistence in the Middle Ages and the Renaissance*, edited by Diane Wolfthal, Brepols, 2000, pp. 15–37.

Fein, Susanna. *The Auchinleck Manuscript: New Perspectives*. York Medieval Press / Boydell and Brewer, 2016.

Gudrun. Translated by George P. Upton, A. C. McClurg, 1906. *Internet Archive*, archive.org/details/gudrun00schm/page/n5/mode/2up.

Gudrun: *A Mediaeval Epic*. Translated by Mary Pickering Nichols, Houghton, Mifflin, 1889. *Internet Archive*, archive.org/details/gudrunmediaevale00 nichiala/page/n5/mode/2up.

Gudrun: *A Story of the North Sea*. Translated by Emma Letherbrow, Edmonston and Douglas, 1863. *Internet Archive*, archive.org/details/gudrunstoryofnor 00leth/page/n9/mode/2up.

Huber, Eduard. "Die Kudrun um 1300: Eine Untersuchung." *Zeitschrift für deutsche Philologie*, vol. 100, 1981, pp. 357–80.

Klarer, Mario, editor. *Kaiser Maximilian I und das Ambraser Heldenbuch*. Böhlau, 2019.

Konstan, David, and Kurt A. Raaflaub, editors. *Epic and History*. Blackwell, 2010.

Kudrun. Translated by Marion E. Gibbs and Sidney M. Johnson, Garland, 1992.

Kudrun. Translated by Winder McConnell, Medieval Texts and Translations, 1992.

Kudrun. Edited by Karl Stackmann, Max Niemeyer Verlag, 2000.

The Lament of the Nibelungen (Div Chlage). Translated by Winder McConnell, Camden House, 1994.

Lecouteux, Claude. "Die Sage vom Magnetberg." *Burgen, Länder, Orte*, edited by Ulrich Müller and Werner Wunderlich, UVK Verlagsgesellschaft, 2008, pp. 529–39.

McConnell, Winder, editor. *The Epic of* Kudrun: *A Critical Commentary*. Kümmerle, 1988.

Millet, Victor. *Germanische Heldendichtung im Mittelalter: Eine Einführung*. De Gruyter, 2008.

Müller, Jan-Dirk. *Gedechtnus: Literatur und Hofgesellschaft um Maximilian I*. Wilhelm Fink, 1982.

Rasmussen, Ann Marie. *Mothers and Daughters in Medieval German Literature*. Syracuse UP, 1997.

Schmitt, Kerstin. *Poetik der Montage: Figurenkonzeption und Intertextualität in der "Kudrun."* Erich Schmidt Verlag, 2002.

120 *Kudrun*

Siebert, Barbara. *Rezeption und Produktion: Bezugssysteme in der "Kudrun."* Kümmerle, 1988.

Tuczay, Christa A. "Motifs in 'The Arabian Nights' and in Ancient and Medieval European Literature: A Comparison." *Folklore*, vol. 116, no. 3, 2006, pp. 272–91.

Vollmann-Profe, Gisela. "Kudrun-eine kühle Heldin: Überlegungen zu einer problematischen Gestalt." *Blütezeit: Festschrift für L. Peter Johson zum 70: Geburtstag*, edited by Mark Chinca et al., Max Niemeyer Verlag, 2000, pp. 231–44.

Der Wunderer. Edited by Florian Kragl, De Gruyter, 2015.

Emrah Pelvanoğlu

Epic Tales, Ethics Codes, and Evidence of Legitimacy: The Intriguing Case of *The Book of Dede Korkut*

Conventional wisdom has it that epics are tall tales of extraordinary deeds performed in a time beyond living memory by heroes with supernatural abilities and that these tales are long-cherished in a given culture. Minstrels performed these stories orally in their respective environments. Some of these ancient stories were put into written form, which enabled them to reach their manifold readers to this day. From this perspective, the process from the oral to the written form is often regarded as natural or inevitable and therefore tends to be overlooked. While the written form prolongs the life of an epic and helps it to endure, it also in a sense denaturalizes it by removing it from the context in which it emerged.

In *Orality and Literacy*, Walter J. Ong draws our attention to this startling paradox: "The deadness of the text, its removal from the living human life-world, its visual fixity, assures its endurance and its potential for being resurrected into limitless living contexts by a vast number of living readers" (80). When considering the emergence (and the resurrection) of epics around the world, I argue that Ong's paradox can be useful as well as intriguing to teachers and their students. This paradox illustrates that the textualization of epics such as the *Iliad*, *Manas*, or *The Book of Dede Korkut*, from the early emergence of their written substrata by

122   *The Book of Dede Korkut*

anonymous compilers to their current published forms, is also the death of their once authentic existence. Nonetheless, thanks to the written versions of these epics, we can now appreciate them universally as part of the cultural heritage of humanity.

In this regard, *The Book of Dede Korkut*, the written form of the epic tales of the Oghuz tribes, invites students to consider the importance of transmission history. The tales and legends circulating in the oral environment of the ancient Oghuz Turks were written down as a response to the legitimacy crises of various dynasties and political groups in different eras and contexts. This textualization led to the reproduction of related texts that are bonded in complicated but traceable ways. *Oghuzname* became the generic name for this textual network and for the texts within it, which include different poetic forms such as declamations, epic tales, legends, and genealogies. The oldest known *Oghuzname* dates to the thirteenth or fourteenth century, and the most recent one to around the nineteenth century. *The Book of Dede Korkut* is the best known of the *Oghuznames*.

There are currently two English translations of *The Book of Dede Korkut* available in paperback: the first by Faruk Sümer, Ahmet Uysal, and Warren Walker, and the second by Geoffrey Lewis. The translators of both editions sketch the same historical background in their introductions, yet they offer different hypotheses regarding the time period in which the stories took written form. The consensus is that the initial narratives that served as the source for these epic tales concerned the lives of the Oghuz tribes between the Jaxartes and Oxus Rivers, the region into which they migrated from the East in the ninth and tenth centuries. During this period, the Oghuz tribes, whose members began to convert to Islam en masse, started a political and religious struggle with their northern pagan neighbors, the Kipchak Turks. According to Sümer and colleagues, the descriptions of the Kipchaks and accounts of the deeds of their leaders could have been evidenced in a lost written variant of *The Book of Dede Korkut*, which would have formed the work's substratum (xi). On the other hand, according to the more cautious Lewis, the phrase "in the days of the Oghuz," which appears in the third and sixth tales, reveals that these epics had taken written form at a time when Oghuz Turks (who came to identify themselves as Turkmen) no longer considered themselves Oghuz (9). Indeed, there is no evidence that the substratum of the present *Book of Dede Korkut* appeared before the thirteenth century, and many scholars propose that the substratum of these epic tales first took written form in the fourteenth or fifteenth century.

Broadly speaking, the *Oghuznames* can be considered in three categories, though their distinctions are not always absolute: Oghuz Khan narratives, epic tales compiled in *The Book of Dede Korkut*, and proverbs and declamations.

Oghuz Khan Narratives

Derived from the pre-Islamic, pagan milieu of Turkic people and composed orally, Oghuz Khan narratives include the life, conquests, and descendants of Oghuz (also called Oghuz Khan, Oghuz Khagan, Oghuz Aqa, or Oghuz Ata), who is the legendary ancestor of the Oghuz tribes. The Oghuz Khan narratives also represent the etiologic myth explaining the formation of the Oghuz tribes, which we can see in *The Book of Dede Korkut*. As İlker Evrim Binbaş has noted, the most important written text concerning these narratives is the book *Jāmi'u't-tawārikh* (*The Compendium of Chronicles*), which the Ilkhanid (Mongolian-Persian state) historian Rashiduddin Fazlullah composed in Persian in the period 1300–10 CE. The chapter in *The Compendium of Chronicles* titled "The History of Oghuz" (Thackston 27–35) starts with an introduction that connects Oghuz and his family genealogically and topographically to Japheth, one of the three sons of Noah. It then narrates the conversion, conquest, and etiology narratives of Oghuz Khan.

Born as a monotheist (but not a Muslim), according to "The History of Oghuz," Oghuz Khan converts his mother and then his wife, but his monotheism creates a great rift between him and his father, Qara Khan, and his uncles. Thereupon, Oghuz kills his father and two of his uncles and then conquers the whole world. We encounter the figure of Dede Korkut, under the name Korkut Ata, for the first time in "The History of Oghuz." The wise Korkut Ata—who lives 295 years, serves as a consultant to a number of Oghuz supreme leaders, and is sent as a messenger to the prophet Muhammad—is different from the shaman-wali-bard character in the tribal milieu of *The Book of Dede Korkut*.

Apart from Rashiduddin's "History of Oghuz," there is a significant yet mysterious legend of Oghuz Khan that gives an early history of the Oghuz narratives, which was translated into English by Balázs Danka. This text was written in a vertical Uyghur script in an eastern Turkic dialect by

124   *The Book of Dede Korkut*

an anonymous compiler. A unique but incomplete manuscript of this narrative dating back to the thirteenth or fourteenth century was found in the city of Turpan (in today's China). While the Turpan manuscript does not contain the theme of conversion to monotheism that is present in "The History of Oghuz," it focuses on many miraculous episodes such as the ones in which Oghuz's wives descend from the sky and in which a male wolf takes on an important role in the expedition to Urum (the Roman or Byzantine Empire). The written forms of both Oghuz Khan narratives were likely to have been produced as a direct consequence of Genghis Khan's invasions and the new order brought by the successor states across Eurasia after the conqueror's death in 1227. Since the Turpan manuscript does not include the conversion theme, it is likely to be more related to the pagan, oral milieu of the Oghuz Turks and thus more authentic. On the other hand, the conversion theme that appears in "The History of Oghuz," added by a known author who could choose and adapt various oral and literary sources, was required by his holistic perspective and agenda.

History of *The Book of Dede Korkut*

One can say that the epic stories that make up *The Book of Dede Korkut*, starting from the substratum text, were given written form as a result of the ongoing legitimacy crises following the Mongol invasion. In this sense, the historical context for *The Book of Dede Korkut* goes back to the Battle of Ankara in 1402, in which the forces of the Timurid Empire under Timor defeated the Ottomans. Sultan Bayezid I was captured by Timur, who made Bayezid's sons his vassals after the battle. According to Beatrice Forbes Manz, Timur envisioned the restoration of the Mongol Empire of Genghis Khan: "In his formal correspondence he continued throughout his life to portray himself as the restorer of Chinggisid rights. He justified his Iranian, Mamluk and Ottoman campaigns as a re-imposition of legitimate Mongol control over lands taken by usurpers" (25). The Ottomans remained as vassals of the Timurid Empire until the reign of Mehmet II, known as the Conqueror, and Timurid oppression led to the resurrection of the Oghuz legacy once again.

The first and most voluminous manuscript (manuscript D) of the substratum of *The Book of Dede Korkut* was found in the Saxon State and University Library in Dresden. Heinrich Fredrich von Diez, the Prussian ambassador to Istanbul during the reign of Sultan Selim III, made a defective copy of the manuscript for the Berlin State Library. Diez, who introduced manuscript D with his 1815 article "Der neuentdeckte oghuzische Cyklop verglichen mit dem Homerischen" ("The Newly Discovered Oghuz Cyclops Compared with the Homeric"; 399–457), put the German translation of the eighth tale, "The Story of How Basat Killed Goggle-Eye," at the end of his article. He also compares the Cyclops in Homer's *Odyssey* with the one-eyed giant in the eighth tale and claims that the Cyclops in Homer is derived from "the Cyclops of Oghuz." This curiosity of Diez undoubtedly fit the early-nineteenth-century Romantic understanding of history.

In the beginning of the twentieth century, the Ottoman ruling elite or men of letters experienced another transformation as the Ottoman Empire struggled to survive in the face of international and domestic challenges. Already at the end of the nineteenth century, numerous intellectuals, military officers, and civilian bureaucrats had rejected Ottomanism and instead embraced Turkish nationalism. During World War I, Ottoman intellectuals searched for national authority by establishing institutional channels like Âsâr-ı İslâmiyye ve Milliyye Tedkik Encümeni (Commission of the Investigation of Islamic and National Monuments). Formed by the ministry of education in 1915, the commission published *Milli Tetebbular Mecmuası* (*Journal of National Research*), a highly ranked semi-academic journal, as well as *Divan-ı Lügat-it Türk* (*Glossary of Turkish Languages*), a compendium compiled in the eleventh century, and the commission summoned the photographs of the Diez copy of the Dresden manuscript from the ally capital Berlin. *Divan-ı Lügat-it Türk* provided a fresh approach to Turkish history and philology in the context of high culture since it had an authenticated author, Mahmud of Kasghar, and a manuscript in the form of a bound book.

In 1916, Kilisli Rifat, who supervised the publication of *Divan-ı Lügat-it Türk*, also published for the first time *The Book of Dede Korkut* in book form. But responses to *The Book of Dede Korkut* were insignificant and quite late compared to those for *Divan-ı Lügat-it Türk*, probably because the literati mostly regarded *The Book of Dede Korkut* as a compilation of fairy tales and because the information about these epic tales was already in circulation in folkloric milieus.

In 1950, Ettore Rossi discovered a second manuscript (manuscript V) at the Vatican Library, which he published in facsimile; in his edition he included an Italian translation of the text. Manuscript D was not reprinted until Muharrem Ergin's variorum edition appeared in two volumes, the

126 *The Book of Dede Korkut*

text itself in 1955 and the index and grammar in 1963. Misled by his quest for a singular, perfect original, Ergin made the mistake of taking manuscript V as an imperfect and incomplete version of manuscript D. In 1964, he published his one-volume critical edition of *The Book of Dede Korkut* (*Dede Korkut Kitabı*). In 2001, Semih Tezcan and Hendrik Boeschoten published the V and D manuscripts together for the first time. In 2018, a new manuscript of *The Book of the Dede Korkut* (manuscript G) was discovered in the northern Iranian city of Gümbed. The work is an eighteenth-century Qajar-period copy of a sixteenth-century substratum text called the Turkmen Sahra or the Gümbed manuscript. Including twenty-seven declamations and two tales, manuscript G has a relatively short text compared to manuscripts D and V, and it was published (with its text, facsimile, index, and grammar) by a group of PhD students in 2019. In 2020 Youssef Azemoun translated the two tales and one of the declamations of manuscript G into English. One of the tales provides information about how Salur Kazan acquired his name.

Comparative Analysis of "The Story of How Salur Kazan's House Was Pillaged" and the *Iliad*

In many ways, we can consider Salur Kazan the main protagonist of *The Book of Dede Korkut*. As the son-in-law of the Great Khan Bayındır, who almost always remains in the background, Kazan takes charge of the social and political affairs of the Oghuz tribes. Here, I present a comparative analysis of one of the epic stories on Salur Kazan and of the *Iliad*. Following Diez's footsteps, I believe this comparative analysis will help teachers and students to comprehend these epic stories in a broader notion of epics and orality and give them the opportunity to have fruitful class discussions.

Long before its elements were collected and written down, like the *Oghuznames* in *The Book of Dede Korkut*, the great epic *Iliad* was recited in an oral milieu. That is why students should read these stories with a different attitude than that used for reading anything that was composed by a literate mind. To help students comprehend and appreciate the authenticity of these epic stories, instructors may appeal to the psychodynamics of orality, which is explained in Ong's book.

Explaining the similarities in the representations of the protagonists in both epics would be a good starting point. Achilles, one of the best-known heroes of world literature, the son of the sea goddess Thetis, is the most brutal and skillful of warriors. Salur Kazan, the son-in-law of Bayındır, is a red-blooded warlord who is the "prop of forsaken warriors" (Lewis 42) and rules over all Oghuz. As Ong states, in primary oral cultures memory works with such "heavy characters" who perform monumental deeds and participate in memorable activities. This use of memory is related not only to the agonistic, aristocratic lifestyle of heroic traditions but also to the needs of the oral poetic processes that Ong calls "noetic economy": "Colorless personalities cannot survive oral mnemonics" (68). This is why the amazing Karajuk, who is not a bey or a khan but only a shepherd, remains one of the most memorable characters in the *Book of Dede Korkut*.

This brings us to the usage of epithets and formulaic expressions in both epics. In the *Iliad*, Achilles is constantly referred to with epithets like the "son of Peleus" or "swift runner" (Homer 1.582, 1.142). In the opening phrases of "The Story of How Salur Kazan's House Was Pillaged," Kazan is introduced as the "son of Ulash Khan," "hope of the wretched and the helpless," "luck of the teeming Oghuz," and the "prop of forsaken warriors" (Lewis 82). In both epics these kinds of formulaic expressions are not limited to protagonists. Almost every character is presented with their typical characteristics and deeds, such as Burla Hatun "the Tall" (43)—Salur Kazan's wife—or in the *Iliad*, Odysseus "the great tactician" (Homer 2.202). According to Ong this serves the narrative preferences of oral folk literature, which is "aggregative rather than analytic" (38). Although these stock expressions give a heavy load of epithets and formulaic baggage to oral compositions that "high literacy rejects as cumbersome and tiresomely redundant" (42), they are much closer to the human lifeworld. Unlike the abstract, neutral world of lists or indexes, these oral expressions are directly derived from concrete human conditions. As in the famous catalog in the second book of the *Iliad*, primary oral cultures tend to accommodate their lists in narrative form. Thus in the *Iliad* a catalog stretching over four hundred lines, which compiles the names of ship captains and the regions they ruled, is fashioned as human action (Ong 42):

> Then men who lived in Aspledon, Orchomenos of the Minyans,
> fighters led by Ascalaphus and Ialmenus, sons of Ares
> whom Astyoche bore in Actor son of Azeus' halls
> when the shy young girl, climbing into the upper rooms,
> made love with the god of war in secret, shared his strength.
> In her two sons' command sailed thirty long curved ships.
>
> (Homer 2.601–06; 116)

128   *The Book of Dede Korkut*

Another catalog, which functions very much like the *Iliad*'s catalog of ships, is located at the end of "The Story of How Salur Kazan's House Was Pillaged." Salur Kazan chases and then ambushes the "six hundred infidels" that took his son, wife, and mother, with the aid of Karajuk the Shepherd (Lewis 44). Despite being just two people, our larger-than-life characters manage to surprise the enemy army, but the Shökli Melik, the enemy's king, refuses to free Salur Kazan's old mother. At that moment, Oghuz nobles who had heard of the disaster arrive, and the narrator-minstrel catalogs nine of them, describing their kinship, appearance, and heroic deeds:

> At that moment they arrived. Let us see, my Khan, who they were who arrived. Kara Gone galloped up, he whom the Almighty set at the narrows of the Black Valley, the coverlet of whose cradle was of black bull-hide, who when he was angered made black rock into ashes, whose moustaches were knotted seven times at the back of his neck, that dragon of heroes, the brother of Prince Kazan. "Wield your sword, brother Kazan!" said he, "Here I am!" (55)

Apart from these examples, one can also notice other structural similarities in the psychodynamics of orality in *The Book of Dede Korkut*, the *Iliad*, and other oral-derived epics. Among these are the qualities of being "additive rather than subordinative," "redundant or copius," "conservative or traditionalist," and "empathetic or participatory rather than objectively distanced" (Ong 36, 39, 40, 45). Keeping these almost universal features of oral epics in mind, teachers and students may compare the diverse spectrum of epics they read irrespective of their cultural milieus or similarities and differences in content.

Declamations and Proverbs

Students should be encouraged to pay attention to the special place of declamations and proverbs in the *Oghuzname* network since these elements frame the tribal ethics and succinctly state themes addressed in the tales themselves. Not only do the three known manuscripts of *The Book of Dede Korkut* each contain a chapter of declamations and proverbs, but these elements can be found in all the epic tales in the variants of *The Book of Dede Korkut*. Apart from *The Book of Dede Korkut* manuscripts, many other *Oghuznames* also have chapters of different lengths dedicated to declamations and proverbs, and two seventeenth-century manuscripts (referred to as the Berlin and St. Petersburg manuscripts) consist entirely of these orally composed aphorisms.

The declamations reveal the intense and dynamic relationship between the written forms of *Oghuznames* and orality. Although the textual network of *Oghuznames* started to interact with literary sources after the fourteenth century, *Oghuznames* continued to have vestiges of orality and to be nourished by the declamation and storytelling traditions of nomadic Oghuz or Turkmen tribes. These declamations—which have lines ending in a refrain or rhyming words, form partial plotlines, and consist of wisdom clichés that reflect tribal ethics and that guide the Turkmens—are mostly attributed to Dede Korkut, who is pronounced "the consummate soothsayer of the Oghuz" in *The Book of Dede Korkut* (Lewis 190).

Both English translations include the chapter of declamations and proverbs found at the beginning of the V and D manuscripts, albeit with a different placement.[1] The first declamation in this chapter is a prophecy about the sovereignty of the Ottoman dynasty: "In time to come the sovereignty will again light on the Kayi and none shall take it from their hands until time stops and the resurrection dawns" (Lewis 190). This oracular declamation, which reorients the text through the Ottoman political agenda of the Murad II era, is then reinforced by the assertion that Dede Korkut "said many more words like this." As Lewis notes, we encounter the name of Korkut Ata nowhere else in the book except for this opening paragraph (211). This fact is enough to read the opening declamation as a later interpolation; moreover, the historical context I mentioned above also gives us enough data to interpret the declamation that way.

Apart from the opening paragraph, the declamations in this chapter consist of five separable parts, and transitions between them are provided by the phrase "let us see, my Khan, what [Dede Kortkut] declaimed" (Lewis 190, 192). While the first four parts are attributed to Dede Korkut himself, the fifth, about women, begins with the phrase "The bard speaks, from the tongue of Dede Korkut" (193). The declamations begin by praising the omnipotence of God. The natural order, shaped by God's will, works with divine and earthly boundaries and absolute rules that will never change unless God wants them to. The bard, whose audience is primarily the Oghuz nobles, both legitimizes and absolutizes the patriarchal tribal order by imbuing it with divine rules and boundaries: "The lake cannot be a hill, the son-in-law cannot be a son. . . . [T]hough you dress a captive girl in a robe she does not become a lady. . . . Worn cotton does not become cloth; the old enemy does not become a friend" (191). Even when

130   *The Book of Dede Korkut*

one lives according to these absolute limits, following the rules that perpetuate the natural order cannot provide assurance of good fortune and prosperity. Because nothing is certain in the face of luck, wealth should not be accumulated but distributed. As put in the declamations, "[w]hen a man has wealth as massive as the black mountain, he piles it up and gathers it in and seeks more, but he can eat no more than his portion. . . . [I]f a man does not spend his wealth, his fame will not go forth. . . . What should the son do if his father dies and no wealth remains? But what profit in a father's wealth if there be no luck on his head?" (190–91).

Students may be invited to imagine circumstances under which the Oghuz tribes would develop an ethics of sharing resources and holding large feasts instead of accumulating wealth. Further context can be found in the second and twelfth tales. The latter narrates the Oghuz civil war. Oghuz nobles customarily pillage the tent of Salur Kazan once every three years. When, however, the inner Oghuz nobles carry out the plunder without waiting for the outer Oghuz nobles to arrive, the latter group gets offended and rebels against the inner Oghuz. In the second tale, Salur Kazan goes hunting with the Oghuz nobles after a feast that he held for them. Learning of Salur Kazan's absence, the infidels raid and plunder his house, stealing all his wealth and abducting his family. Unfortunate events like these occur in other tales of *The Book of Dede Korkut* as well. Because foes are always wide-awake, the epic's protagonists cannot always prevent such misfortunes.

Class discussion on the declamations and proverbs may also center around the hero figure in *The Book of Dede Korkut*. It is the ultimate burden of the noble hero not to compromise his heroic attitude. For it, he will sacrifice his life if necessary, and he will be worthy of his fame. This attitude of the hero is necessary both for the protection of the tribal society and for its restoration after a possible threat. As Michael E. Meeker states, "[H]eroic feats are of value only as acts of self-sacrifice that lead to the emotional reunion of family and society" (398). And just as praiseworthy actions enhance the well-being and reputation of one's family, the reverse is also true. This sentiment is expressed in the following declamation: "Better that the loutish son who does not maintain the good name of his father should never come down from his father's loins; if he falls into his mother's womb, better that he be not born. Best is the fortunate son when he maintains his father's good name" (Lewis 191–92).

The bard is another figure who merits close attention when reading the declamations. After a series of aphorisms regarding natural order, such as "the fox knows the scents of seven valleys" and "the mother knows who sired the son," the focus turns to the bard's position in tribal society: "The bard roams from land to land, from prince to prince, carrying his arm-long lute; the bard knows the generous man and the stingy man" (192). Students could discuss such statements in the context of the third tale (59–87), in which the protagonist Bamsı Beyrek encounters a bard on his way back from a sixteen-year captivity. Like Odysseus returning home in the *Odyssey*, this traveler seeks to hide his identity, and he therefore exchanges his horse for the bard's lute. The way that the Oghuz nobles treat Beyrek while he is clothed in bardic garb also shows that, as entertainers, bards were not at all respected in Oghuz society. Instructors may want to explore with students the difference between this anonymous bard figure, who may represent one of the possible compilers of *The Book of Dede Korkut*, and the legendary figure of Dede Korkut, who in the tales has the power of soothsaying, wisdom, and casting miracles.

Students studying *The Book of Dede Korkut* should take into account that these tales are part of a larger textual network. This will make it easier for them to contextualize the important themes, references, and metaphors in the stories. In addition, instructors may juxtapose these tales with epics from other territories and time periods that have gone through similar textualization processes and can explore with students whether these other works have undergone similar legitimacy crises. *The Book of Dede Korkut*, with its intriguing textual history throughout different eras, cultures, and regions, can provide alternative perspectives in comparative epic studies to help readers reconsider dichotomies such as East and West, ancient and modern, or orality and literacy.

Notes

Special thanks to Samet Onur, Tekin Atmaca, and Veysel Şimşek for their feedback on an earlier draft of this essay.

1. While Sümer et al. fashion the chapter as a prologue (3–8), Lewis moves it to the end of his translation and titles it "The Wisdom of Dede Korkut" (190–94).

Works Cited

Azemoun, Youssef. "The New Dädä Qorqut Tales from the Recently-Found Third Manuscript of *The Book of Dädä Qorqut*." *Journal of Old Turkic Studies*, vol. 4, no. 1, 2020, pp. 16–27.

132   *The Book of Dede Korkut*

Binbaş, İlker Evrim. "Oğhuz Khan Narratives." *Encylopedia Iranica*, iranicaonline
.org/articles/oguz-khan-narratives.

Danka, Balázs. *The Pre-Islamic Oğuz-nämä: A Philological and Linguistic
Analysis.* 2016. U of Szeged, PhD dissertation. *SZTE*, doktori.bibl.u-szeged
.hu/id/eprint/3179/1/danka_disszertacio_06_20.pdf.

Diez, Heinrich Friedrich von. *Denkwürdigkeiten von Asien.* Berlin, 1815.

Ergin, Muharrem, editor. *Dede Korkut Kitabı: Metin-Sözlük.* Türk Kültürünü
Araştırma Enstitüsü, 1964.

Forbes Manz, Beatrice. "Temür and the Problem of a Conqueror's Legacy."
Journal of the Royal Asiatic Society, vol. 8, Apr. 1998, p. 25.

Homer. *The Iliad.* Translated by Robert Fagles, Penguin Classics, 1990.

Lewis, Geoffrey, translator. *The Book of Dede Korkut.* Penguin Classics, 1974.

Meeker, Michael E. "The Dede Korkut Ethics." *International Journal of Middle
East Studies*, vol. 24, 1992, pp. 395–417.

Ong, Walter J. *Orality and Literacy: The Technologizing of the Word.* Routledge,
2005.

Rifat, Kilisli Muallim [Bilge], editor. *Kitab-ı Dede Korkud Alâ lisan-i taife-i
Oğuzân.* Matbaa-i Amire, 1916.

Rossi, Ettore, editor. *Il Kitab-i Dede Qorqut.* Vatican Apostolic Library, 1952.

Sümer, Faruk, et al., translators. *The Book of Dede Korkut: A Turkish Epic.* U of
Texas P, 1972.

Tezcan, Semih, and Hendrik Boeschoten, editors. *Dede Korkut Oğuznameleri.*
Yapı Kredi Yayınları, 2001.

Thackston, Wheeler M, translator. *Rashiduddin Fazlullah's* Jāmiʻuʼt-tawārīkh:
Compendium of Chronicles: *A History of the Mongols.* Harvard U, 1998.

David T. Bialock, Elizabeth Oyler, and Roberta Strippoli

A Buddhist Perspective on War, Exile, and Women in *The Tale of the Heike*

Chronologically, *The Tale of the Heike* takes shape and achieves a mature form over the course of the thirteenth and fourteenth centuries, or what is sometimes referred to as the Japanese medieval period. This time frame is significant because it positions the *Heike* in a well-developed tradition of court literature already hundreds of years old, setting it apart from epics like the *Iliad, Beowulf, The Song of Roland*, and the *Nibelungenlied*, which were all regarded as having been composed at the putative start of their respective literary traditions. The same medieval period also saw the expansion of Buddhist doctrine into the Japanese popular sphere. What further sets the *Heike* apart from most world epics, then, is the Buddhism that infuses the work. This essay aims to help instructors guide students through a discussion of how Buddhism colored the treatment of courtly, martial, and placatory themes, exile and political geography, and women and salvation. The intersection of Buddhist values with these themes offers students endless possibilities for comparative work in a course on world epics, and the episodes discussed in this essay can be read in the space of a one-to-two-week teaching unit.[1] Further resources on the tale and its context can also be assigned.[2]

134 *The Tale of the Heike*

Courtly, Martial, and Placatory Themes (David T. Bialock)

The Tale of the Heike's combination of *ikusagatari* (battle narrative) with elements of a refined court literature is one of its distinguishing characteristics as an epic narration. Another feature of the tale is the incorporation of Buddhist prayer and elements of Buddhist sermonizing that sometimes frame its battle episodes. How these elements of a courtly, Buddhist, and more purely martial tradition of battle narrative separate or combine from episode to episode is another of the intriguing features of the tale as epic literature. In this opening section, I look at the interweaving of battle narratives with courtly and religious themes across several episodes, including three of the most celebrated examples of warrior *saigo* (last moments) in chapter 9: "The Death of Etchū no Zenji" (312–13), "The Death of Tadanori" (313–14), and "The Death of Atsumori" (315–17).

Students reading *The Tale of the Heike* for the first time are often struck by the absence of graphic violence in the battle portions of the narrative. Unlike the *Iliad* and many other traditions of battle epic, the *Heike* contains little in the way of gory descriptions of battlefield slaughter or battle wounds. While dozens of warriors are slain in vividly narrated battles, the deaths are nearly always noted in a spare, matter-of-fact style that avoids explicit mention of bloodshed or gruesome details. This absence of blood and gore is often matched by descriptive embellishments that substitute aesthetic effects for the expected violence. When hundreds of warriors fall to their watery deaths after the planks of a bridge are surreptitiously removed, the narrator observes, "The undulating suits of armor, with their green, flame-red, and dark red lacings, resembled the colored leaves from Mount Kaminabi, when in late autumn they enter the Tatsuta River on gales from the peaks and linger, trapped, where the flow is impeded" (156). Here, the violent action is dissipated in the poetic associations of autumn leaves floating down the Tatsuta River, a common seasonal trope in the tradition of court poetry. The same image is echoed later in a passage that describes the sea after a long battle in chapter 11: "Littered with abandoned red pennants and discarded red badges, the surface of the sea resembled the Tatsuta River strewn with storm-scattered autumn leaves; the white waves approaching the shore were tinged a pinkish hue" (381). Here the color patterning, with the repetition of red and white waves tinged with a "pinkish hue," is about as close as we get to an explicit mention of blood in the entire tale, and even here the impression is oblique and aestheticized. All the more remarkable, then, is that this passage sums up the aftermath of the battle of Dan no Ura, the violent and destructive sea battle that definitively destroyed the Heike warrior clan.

Poetic embellishment, however, is not always the echo or lingering trace of battle violence; it can also be a prelude to a heroic action or a battle: "As was to have been expected at the start of the Second Month, there were places where lingering patches of snow dappled the peaks like blossoms, and others where the warriors heard warblers in the valleys and made their way through thick haze . . ." (304–05). In this long passage from "The Old Horse," of which only a portion is quoted, the imagery of dappled snow, warblers, mossy paths, and the elegant confusion of plum blossoms for snowflakes derives from the lexicon of seasonal court poetry and sets the mood for what will develop into one of the most famous battle exploits in the *Heike*, the Minamoto warrior Yoshitsune's daring assault from the cliff against the Heike in chapter 9.

If the imagery of drowned warriors cast adrift like floating maple leaves and other narrative ornaments infuse *Heike* battle exploits with evocative overtones, these images can also stand in stark contrast to the warrior's quest for fame and battle rewards that forms the centerpiece of many battle narratives in the tale. Along with the standard motifs of dressing the warrior, the warrior grappling with the enemy, and the boasts and challenges voiced during the fight, the central theme of many of the battle narratives is the warrior's act of *nanori* (self-naming) on the battlefield. One of the more dramatic instances occurs in "The Death of Etchū no Zenji" in the ninth chapter. To summarize, the Heike retainer Moritoshi, strong enough to haul a sixty- or seventy-man ship, marks out and grapples down the equally impressive Genji warrior Noritsuna, "renowned in the Eight Provinces for his great strength" (312). Pinned down and unable to get hold of his dagger, Noritsuna challenges Moritoshi with the following words: "Did you hear me announce my name? A man who kills an enemy does not perform a great exploit unless he takes the head after identifying himself and requiring the other to do the same. What will you gain by taking an anonymous head?" Taunted in this fashion, Moritoshi announces his name and then requests the same of Noritsuna. At this point, the wily Noritsuna manages to trick Moritoshi into setting him free and then takes advantage of another Genji warrior's arrival on the scene. "Presently, a warrior attired in a suit of armor with black leather lacing came galloping toward them on a whitish horse." The arrival of a third warrior during a grappling scene functions as a virtual theme in Japanese battle narratives, serving to

136 *The Tale of the Heike*

intensify the drama, and here it is given even greater weight by the brief description of the enemy warrior dressed in black and mounted on his white horse. With Moritoshi now off his guard, Noritsuna recovers, snatches Moritoshi's dagger, and then the narrator, in an expansion of the standard formulaic phrase "took his head," tells how Noritsuna "plunged the weapon into his flesh three times, hilt, fist, and all," highlighting Noritsuna's ferocity. The episode concludes with a long boast by Noritsuna, further emphasizing his ferocity (313).

If the death of Etchū no Zenji provides us with an example of a raw, unvarnished battle narrative in the *Heike*, with its standard themes of self-naming, grappling, and challenging the enemy and with its formulaic variations on the theme of dressing the warrior and the death blow, then the two celebrated episodes that follow, "The Death of Tadanori" and "The Death of Atsumori," exemplify the tale's unique fusion of battle narratives with aesthetic embellishment and Buddhist motifs that began our discussion. In both episodes, standard themes and formulas of battle narrative are modified to great effect. Each episode begins with an elaborate expansion of the theme of dressing the warrior, beautifying the soon-to-be-slain Heike warriors Tadanori and Atsumori from the start. With the Genji warriors having marked out their enemies, grappling matches and challenges to the Heike warriors to identify themselves follow, but in both cases the Heike warrior refuses to name himself. The slaying of the two Heike warriors is drawn out to highlight their submission and resignation in the face of inevitable death. Tadanori, with his arm lopped off, pauses to recite invocations to the Buddha for his salvation. The supine Atsumori, "so handsome that the Genji warrior Kumagae no Jirō Naozane could not find a place to strike," provokes a paroxysm of compassion in Naozane: "His senses reeled, his wits forsook him, and he was scarcely conscious of his surroundings." In both cases, the disclosure of the slain warrior's identity is brought about by the discovery of an emblem of the warrior's artistic accomplishments: a poem in Tadanori's arrow quiver, and a flute tucked away in a brocade bag at Atsumori's waist. The narrator concludes the account of Atsumori's death with this observation about the effect the discovery of the flute has on Naozane: "It is deeply moving that music, a profane entertainment, should have led a warrior to the religious life." The *hosshin* (Buddhist conversion) of the enemy warrior Naozane is even more striking in the light of his fierce pursuit of fame and rewards that was highlighted only a few episodes earlier in "The First and Second Attacker," where in a crescendo of increasingly lengthy *nanori* Naozane identifies himself three times (305–08).

After examining several of the key motifs, themes, and rhetorical techniques of *Heike* battle narratives, including the contrast between the hybrid form of the Tadanori and Atsumori episodes and the more purely martial ethos of Etchū no Zenji's death scene, instructors may guide students through a discussion of the larger implications of these kaleidoscopic shifts in style, tone, and atmosphere. On the one hand, it is clear that many of the battle narratives have been refracted through a sensibility conditioned by the court aesthetic. The poetic embellishment of battle narratives and the magnification of individual warriors through descriptions of their gorgeous attire, as in the examples of Tadanori, Atsumori, and others in the tale, pull the warrior into the orbit of an earlier tradition of court literature and all its associated prestige. One has only to think of the exquisite descriptions of court costumes in the earlier Heian masterpieces of court literature like *The Pillow Book* and *The Tale of Genji* to feel this kinship in narrative tone. On the other hand, in the more purely martial battle narrations, which may have developed independently of the court tradition, these same techniques of magnification, or *auxesis*, to use the Greek term, can be understood as serving the warrior's preoccupation with fame and material rewards.

In a practical sense, glorious deeds and severed heads translated into land for the winner in battle, and the magnification of those violent acts by the reciter assured the warrior's fame and that of his lineage. Yet poetry is also a way one may seek to win glory within the court tradition. In an earlier episode in *The Tale of the Heike*, "Tadanori's Flight from the Capital," narrated in chapter 7, Tadanori stops off at the home of his poetry teacher, Shunzei, to leave with him some of his poems (246–47). His hope is that Shunzei will include one of his poems in the imperial poetry collection that he is editing. As it turned out, one of the historical Tadanori's poems did in fact appear in *The Collection for a Thousand Years*, edited by Shunzei, but, in an echo of Tadanori's nameless death on the battlefield, it was listed as anonymous.

Finally, students should consider how Buddhist values color the martial narratives in the *Heike*. Episodes like Tadanori's and Atsumori's death scenes, in addition to celebrating the warriors' association with the elegant arts of poetry and music, also signal the efficacy of Buddhist doctrine. Like advertisements, these scenes inform the medieval listener that if even warriors, whose profession is killing, can be saved and achieve

138   *The Tale of the Heike*

enlightenment, so can you. This salvific function even relates to the performative aspect of the *Heike* through the blind itinerant reciters who had custodianship of certain texts, including the version of the *Heike* that has been translated into English. The *biwa hōshi*, priests who recited the tale to the accompaniment of a *biwa* (lute-like instrument), also performed the ritual function of placating the dead. In the light of this fact, we can surmise that at some point the *nanori* theme and the theme of the warrior's attire broke away from battle narrative and became independent themes, tending more to serve the ritualistic or Buddhist concerns of the reciters, whose functions included both placating the spirits of dead warriors and celebrating and memorializing the deeds of warriors in general. In Tadanori's and Atsumori's refusal to name themselves, coupled with the aesthetic heightening of the scenes, we can clearly discern the placation function. To elaborate, the motif of ritual placation in battle narrative suggests a process whereby stories about slain warriors either became linked to local cultic practices and agricultural rites or spontaneously arose in response to the baleful effects of pestilence, crop failure, and drought. Initially, the voice of the dead warrior may have been mediated by a local shaman or spirit medium, in which case the refusal to name and the subsequent identification would reflect stages of the shaman's possession trance in which the unappeased spirit's reluctance or inability to reveal itself was followed by disclosure and placation. Once such episodes were incorporated into the *Heike*, the *biwa hōshi* took over the placating and naming function. This explanation is borne out by the version of Atsumori's death scene in the Engyōbon *Heike*, a variant intended to be read in addition to being recited, where Naozane asks Atsumori to disclose his identity so he can be rewarded with Atsumori's estates. This version stays much closer to the ethos of raw battle narrative. In the standard version of the *Heike*, especially in episodes like those centered on Atsumori and Tadanori, the battle narrative has been transformed and subverted from eristic to irenic ends.

Exile and Political Geography (Elizabeth Oyler)

In narrating the Genpei War, *The Tale of the Heike* addresses a moment that in the eyes of later generations represented a profound shift in the political and cultural landscapes of Japan. Even though the imperial family and the bureaucratic structures of government remained intact in the ancient capital of Heian-kyō (Kyoto), the war's conclusion witnessed the establishment of Japan's first shogunate, an office overseeing warrior

David T. Bialock, Elizabeth Oyler, and Roberta Strippoli 139

affairs, by the war's victor, Minamoto no Yoritomo, in the distant seaside hamlet of Kamakura, in the eastern provinces to which he had been exiled as a young man. The war brought to conclusion a series of struggles between the Heike clan, under the hegemon Kiyomori, and Yoritomo's Genji clan, and one important role the *Heike* fills is in narrating the Genji victory as a restoration of order after decades of disorder, a political manifestation of the Buddhist idea that all human affairs move in cycles, but with each cycle humanity moves further from the time of the historical Buddha and into *mappō*, the latter days of Buddhist law.

In describing this new reality, the compilers of the *Heike*, as we saw with the battle scenes discussed above, drew from classical poetic and literary conventions. Prominent among these was the trope of the exiled nobleman, a feature of many of early Japan's best-known literary works. This section explores how banishment as a literary motif shapes the *Heike*, as well as how the motif is subtly transformed in the *Heike*'s narrative of geopolitical rearrangement brought about by a karmic response to the rise of a bad ruler. First, I focus on how exile functions as a motif throughout the work to illustrate the folly of the proud and selfish Heike clan, and then I turn to the narrative of one Heike general, Shigehira, to examine how his capture and execution at the war's end refigure the motif of exile in the work. The reworking of this theme and the very configurations of political space as a result of war provide one window through which the *Heike* can be considered in relation to other epics considered in this volume that are framed by different cultural norms.

In literature from Japan's classical age, the political realm is configured as a set of concentric circles radiating out from the capital city of Heian-kyō. The most severe punishment for an aristocrat was banishment, and throughout the four centuries preceding the Genpei War the experience of banishment proved rich terrain in art: the exile of a young nobleman appears prominently in the influential *Tales of Ise* and *Tale of Genji*, in which a hero's cultural value is manifested in how fully he weaves images of local landscapes into poetry that also expresses his longing for home. Through such narratives and countless poems, the hinterlands to which noblemen were expelled were lyrically integrated into the realm, even though they were simultaneously maintained at a distance from the country's center, whose vitality as the source of political and literary meaning simultaneously they affirmed.

The Tale of the Heike at once rests on and reconfigures this motif. Banishments of the Heike clan's enemies, all competent men punished simply

140 *The Tale of the Heike*

for the threat they were perceived to represent, fill the narrative's early chapters. Individually, these stories are personal tragedies, and some even receive extended narrative treatment, but the tale further uses them as portents. Each expulsion drains the capital city of traditional markers of power, leaving it weakened and vulnerable. That some of the banished die in exile compounds the situation, as a death in exile, like a death on the battlefield, could be cause for destructive posthumous rancor.

These individual banishments are signs of a world in disarray, and they give the shape of banishment to Kiyomori's capricious decision, in chapter 4, to relocate the emperor and the court from Kyoto to the hereditary Heike stronghold at Fukuhara (near modern-day Kobe) as Kiyomori struggles to place distance between himself and the powerful temples of Nara, whose soldier-monks represent a threat to his power. The removal of the markers of power (in the person of the emperor and his imperial regalia) from the traditional capital is an even clearer portent of the war to come. For the courtiers forced to follow the emperor to Fukuhara, the move feels like a banishment. That the site lies near Suma, a strand along the inland sea made famous as the site of a self-imposed exile by the hero of *The Tale of Genji*, only underlines this characterization. When the new locale is abandoned a mere five months later, and Heian-kyō is restored as the capital, the displaced courtiers "abandoned everything without a backward glance, obsessed with the idea of returning home" (193).

The idea of a world drained of meaning by a series of individual and collective banishments thus frames *The Tale of the Heike*, and the remaining chapters focus on the most important expulsion from the capital, that of the Heike clan members themselves, who flee as Yoritomo's partisans encroach (in chapter 7). The numerous lyrical episodes that linger over Heike farewells to friends as the clan members depart—Tadanori's farewell is especially prominent among them (246–47)—again evoke the motif of poeticized exile, but now it is juxtaposed with the return of Yoritomo's clan, which had been banished from the capital twenty years earlier. But this return is unusual. Whereas the Heike will spend the rest of the war in exilic wandering until they meet their final defeat in the battle of Dan no Ura at the realm's western edge, a trajectory following the traditional arc of a banishment narrative, the end of the war finds the Genji, by contrast, settled in Kamakura rather than Heian-kyō, which they in effect claim as a political center. The meaning of Kamakaura-as-center is expressed most clearly in the story of another Heike clan member, the general Shigehira, Kiyomori's fifth son.

Like his Heike relatives, Shigehira was a powerful courtier before the Heike clan's fall, as well as being specially favored by his parents. His fate changes dramatically in the opening salvos of the war, however, when he is sent by his father to the ancient capital city of Nara to suppress soldier-monks who had been complicit in an unsuccessful coup d'état. The punitive force engages the monks in a hard day's fighting, and, as the sun sets on the battle, Shigehira orders his men to light a fire, which, fanned by a violent wind, spreads to the major temples of Nara, leveling them and killing all who had found shelter from the day's fighting within them (194–96). This is a horrific act of murder and desecration, and all save Kiyomori see it as yet another sign of disorder in the realm.

The narrative of the burning of Nara is a turning point in the tale. The episode closes chapter 5, marking the last moment in which the Heike clan members are still firmly in control of the capital city. By chapter 7, Kiyomori has died, and Yoritomo's allies are encroaching from the north. Shigehira is captured at the battle of Ichinotani, in the same mop-up that results in the deaths of Atsumori and Tadanori (314–15). His capture marks the beginning of a complicated exilic journey for him that is intimately connected with the fate of the realm.

Shigehira is first paraded through the streets of the capital as a prisoner in an exposed carriage, the visible object of derision and sometimes pity in the city where he so recently would have been protected from the gaze of commoners. What marks a newness in the geography of exile in his story really begins here: rather than being judged and punished in the imperial capital, he is sent to Kamakura to be questioned by Yoritomo. His travels to Kamakura cleave to the lyrical pattern of exilic wandering: the narrative is delivered in the lilting meter of poetry and song, and it quotes older poems as it describes his passage through the unfamiliar eastern landscape. Shigehira is inspired to compose poems in the same vein (335–38).

Although the narrator earlier condemns Shigehira for his sin of burning the Nara temples, as he travels east, he is increasingly cast as a romantic hero and a tragic victim of fate. When he arrives at Kamakura, he takes full responsibility for his crimes and stoically prepares to meet his end. Yoritomo and his warriors are deeply moved by his gentility. Yoritomo remarks, "I had always thought of the Heike as out of their depth in everything except warfare, but I stood and listened all night long while Shigehira played the lute and chanted. He is a man of the utmost cultivation" (340–41). Nevertheless, Yoritomo condemns him to be executed in Nara, the site of his crimes (397–400).

142   *The Tale of the Heike*

In his appreciation for Shigehira's skill as a musician, Yoritomo claims a level of sophistication generally associated with the central elite, and in reversing Shigehira's journey—Yoritomo sends him back to the central provinces for punishment—he imbues the peripheral locale of Kamakura with meaning usually reserved for the political center. This is a significant if subtle shift: Yoritomo's return from exile is political and cultural but does not involve physical movement. Instead he claims for Kamakura the kinds of meaning that until now had been reserved for Heian-kyō. The proud Heike clan members have reaped the karmic return for their pride, and although order is restored, this shift registers also the slipping away from the ideals of the past and further into the latter and lesser days of Buddhist law.

In his travel to Kamakura, Shigehira laments in a poem that "[h]ome, even / does not inspire longing . . . since the capital will not be / my final dwelling" (336). While his despair is conventional, there is a new kind of truth revealed in his melancholy verse: the world has shifted such that the capital that had been the home base for centuries of classical exiles was fast disappearing, and the rise of Kamakura as a power center would forever alter the political and cultural landscapes.

Women and Salvation (Roberta Strippoli)

Although *The Tale of the Heike* is focused primarily on the actions of men, it features a surprisingly large number of female characters, some of whom are central to the plot and essential to the expression of the profound meanings of the *Heike* as a whole. Some of these women are seen making quick decisions and performing memorable actions: for instance, Tomoe, the brave warrior at the service of Kiso Yoshinaka, who promptly decapitates an enemy when asked to leave the battlefield, as a homage to her master or maybe to show him and us one more time how skilled she is (292). Or Lady Dainagon-no-suke, wife of the Heike commander Shigehira, who, after her husband's execution, collects his body, demands the restitution of his severed head from the Nara monks, and cremates the recomposed remains (400). Or the Nun of the Second Rank, matriarch of the Heike clan, who commits suicide in the final battle of the Genpei War, taking her young grandson, Emperor Antoku, with her as she jumps into the sea (378).

Within the variety of roles they serve in the tale, women are featured strongly as survivors and custodians of memory. Most notable among these is the Imperial Lady Kenreimon'in, the last survivor of the Heike clan and the mother of the drowned Antoku. Having become a Buddhist nun at the end of the war, she alone bears the burden of preserving the memory of its events, making sense of history, and praying for the deliverance of family members who encountered violent deaths in the war (426–38). Her role is extremely important, even more so if, as suggested earlier, the pacification of the souls of the Genpei War dead is one of the central purposes of the *Heike*.

This section focuses on Giō and Hotoke, two performers who were the lovers of the Heike leader Kiyomori (30–37). The episode that tells their story appears in chapter 1 of *The Tale of the Heike* and helps characterize Kiyomori as a selfish man who lacks empathy and who acts impulsively—an inadequate patron and lover, and ultimately a bad leader who will be responsible for the fall of his clan.

Giō and Hotoke are not seen decapitating enemies or committing suicide by drowning, but they are nonetheless unforgettable, to the point that their story has influenced theatrical plays (such as Noh and Kabuki), visual arts (such as manuscript illustration and woodblock printing), and cultural heritage (for example, the multiple memorial sites of Giō and Hotoke that exist around Japan). This influence is made more interesting by the fact that these are literary characters who might not be based on real people. The reverberations of this story in multiple aspects of Japanese culture give us a sense of the great impact that *The Tale of the Heike* had in the centuries after its composition and continues to have today.

On the one hand, the Giō-Hotoke episode provides an idea of the hard life and difficult choices facing women of the past, who largely depended on men. On the other hand, it forcefully brings to focus the Buddhist concepts at the center of the *Heike*. The most important of these is impermanence: all things, good and bad, including power and privilege, will eventually come to an end. Another concept is salvation, understood to mean a good rebirth, possibly on a lotus throne in the special paradise set up by Amida Buddha for those who have faith in him. Being reborn in Amida's Pure Land is the ultimate goal for most characters in the *Heike*, as well as in medieval and early modern Japanese literature in general.

As the story opens, the singer-dancer Giō and her family, her mother and a sister, enjoy Kiyomori's patronage. They are provided with a house and monthly allowance and are envied by everyone. One day a young and stunningly beautiful performer called Hotoke shows up at the residence Kiyomori shares with Giō, asking to audition to be considered for patronage. This sets in motion a series of events that will result in Giō's expulsion from the house, to be replaced by the new girl. Giō also has to withstand

144 *The Tale of the Heike*

humiliation by Kiyomori when summoned back to her former residence months later to perform for the couple. She considers committing suicide but resolves to become a Buddhist nun instead, moving to a hut on the outskirts of Heian-kyō with her mother and sister. There they can live in peace, invoking the name of Amida Buddha. Three months later, in the middle of the night, someone knocks at their door. The women are terrified, as they imagine it could be a malevolent spirit interfering with their spiritual quest. However, the visitor is none other than Hotoke, who has escaped from Kiyomori's residence and become a nun herself. She has exchanged the privilege of being the favorite woman of Japan's most powerful man with the humble but spiritually elevated life of someone who spends her days praying for salvation. The four women will be reborn in Amida Buddha's paradise, as the narrator tells us at the end of the episode (37).

Another central theme of this story, intertwined with impermanence and salvation, is the relationship between the two women, which is one of solidarity rather than rivalry. Giō intercedes for Hotoke when she arrives at the Heike leader's residence—Kiyomori does not even want to meet her, as she has come without an invitation. Giō explains that showing up uninvited is a common practice among dancers and that the young girl deserves to be given the opportunity to perform at least once. Hotoke understands that she has received help and is horrified when she is told that she will replace Giō, her benefactor, in Kiyomori's house and heart. But there is nothing she can do about it because Kiyomori will not listen to her remonstrations.

Poems are featured prominently in works of Japanese narrative (whether read or performed), including in *The Tale of the Heike*, and this episode is no exception. Forced to leave, Giō visits her room one more time and writes this poem on a sliding panel:

> Since both are grasses
> of the field, how may either
> be spared by autumn—
> the young shoot blossoming forth
> and the herb fading from view? (33)

This is a poem about impermanence, and a beautiful one, bringing up the image of grasses of the field that are destined to disappear, regardless of how fresh they are, simply because nothing lasts forever. Of course, coming from the abandoned lover Giō, the poem can also be interpreted as showing some resentment toward the "young shoot," the woman who has turned out to be the cause of her ruin. Here Giō might be seeing impermanence not just as something to prompt one to abandon worldly desires and focus on religion but as something that makes her feel better, since her rival too will one day be discarded. In fact, this poem will later help Hotoke to deeply understand impermanence and will inspire her to escape from Kiyomori's residence, become a Buddhist nun, and concentrate on what is important, her future rebirth. When Hotoke shows up at Giō's hut and the women resolve to live together as nuns, both of them feel relieved. Before that moment, resentment was keeping Giō from fully focusing on salvation, as her mind kept going to Hotoke enjoying the elevated status she herself had before. Seeing Hotoke's shaved head, she is able to renounce her feelings of resentment and invoke the name of Amida Buddha with a pure heart.

Hotoke is finally free from Kiyomori's whims. In addition to almost certainly securing rebirth in Amida's paradise, becoming a nun is possibly the only way these women have to remove themselves from the influence of such a powerful and despotic man. Now that Giō and Hotoke are nuns, Kiyomori (or any other patron) cannot visit their hut, summon them, or interfere with them in any way. It is interesting to note that although women in *The Tale of the Heike* are considered dependent on men all their lives (on their fathers, then their husbands, then their sons) and are generally less trained in Buddhist doctrine, they are the ones who understand impermanence best and are able to take proper action.

Kiyomori, on the other hand, has no understanding of impermanence and seems to believe that his leadership and power will last forever. Although in the past he took vows as a Buddhist novice, he does not live a Buddhist life and prefers to stick to his evil ways. On his deathbed, he tells his family not to build sacred buildings or offer services on his behalf. Instead, he requests that his enemy, the Genji leader Yoritomo, be captured and decapitated and that Yoritomo's head be hung in front of his grave (211).

Notes

1. The episodes from *The Tale of the Heike* discussed in this essay, and cited throughout in Helen McCullough's translation, are as follows: "Giō" (30–37), "The Burning of Nara" (194–96), "The Death of Etchū no Zenji" (312–13), "The Death of Tadanori" (313–14), "The Death of Atsumori" (315–17), "The Capture of Shigehira" (314–15), "The Journey down the Eastern Road" (335–38), and "The Execution of Shigehira" (397–400).

146   *The Tale of the Heike*

2. *The Tale of the Heike* has been translated into English several times. In addition to the translation used here, we suggest Royall Tyler's translation, which emphasizes the recitational form of the tale. For concise overviews of the development and reception of the *Heike*, see Bialock, "Tales" 295–305, focusing on the *Heike*'s evolution as a genre, and "Nation" 151–78 (especially 170–76), addressing how the *Heike* came to be cast as a Japanese national epic. Instructors interested in fuller treatments of the *Heike* might consult Bialock, *Eccentric Spaces*; Oyler; and Selinger. For a complete discussion of the story of Giō and Hotoke and its influence on subsequent literary and theatrical genres, see Strippoli, *Dancer*. Oyler and Watson includes translations and studies of stories from the *Heike* adapted to the Noh stage. For the stories of several women appearing in the *Heike*, see Strippoli, "Between the Court."

Works Cited

Bialock, David T. *Eccentric Spaces, Hidden Histories: Narrative, Ritual, and Royal Authority from the "Chronicles of Japan" to "The Tale of the Heike."* Stanford UP, 2007.

———. "Nation and Epic: *The Tale of the Heike* as Modern Classic." *Inventing the Classics: Modernity, National Identity, and Japanese Literature*, edited by Haruo Shirane and Tomi Suzuki, Stanford UP, 2000, pp. 151–78.

———. "The Tales of the Heike." *The Cambridge History of Japanese Literature*, edited by Haruo Shirane et al., Cambridge UP, 2016, pp. 295–305.

Oyler, Elizabeth. *Swords, Oaths, and Prophetic Visions: Authoring Warrior Rule in Medieval Japan*. U of Hawai'i P, 2006.

Oyler, Elizabeth, and Michael Watson, editors. *Like Clouds or Mists: Studies and Translations of Nō Plays of the Genpei War*. Cornell UP, 2013. Cornell East Asia Series 159.

Selinger, Vyjayanthi R. *Authorizing the Shogunate: Ritual and Material Symbolism in the Literary Construction of Warrior Order*. Brill, 2013.

Strippoli, Roberta. "Between the Court and the Battlefield: Samurai Women in *The Tale of the Heike*." *Revista Cerrados*, vol. 25, no. 44, 2017, pp. 30–42.

———. *Dancer, Nun, Ghost, Goddess: Giō and Hotoke in Traditional Japanese Literature, Theater, and Cultural Heritage*. Brill, 2018.

The Tale of the Heike. Translated by Helen C. McCullough, Stanford UP, 1988.

The Tale of the Heike. Translated by Royall Tyler, Penguin Books, 2012.

Moss Roberts

Three Kingdoms: Division, Unification, and National Identity from the Han Dynasty to Today

The long and complex narrative called *Sanguozhi yanyi* (*Three Kingdoms*) is a semifictional Ming dynasty work based on dynastic records—*Sanguozhi* (三國志) in Chinese—compiled more than a millennium earlier in the late third century by Chen Shou. Its historicity is registered in the Chinese title of the novel since *zhi* means historical records (though commonly the title is shortened to *Sanguo yanyi*). There is no simple solution to translating the genre *yanyi* (演義), however. The conventional term *romance* puts too much emphasis on the fictional aspect and insufficient emphasis on the historical. Given that the Chinese generally say the novel is seven parts history and three parts fiction, I use the term *historical novel*; however, *semifictional epic drama* is among the other choices since many plays from the preceding Yuan (Mongol) dynasty significantly influenced the novel's author. The words *yanyi*, however, could more literally be translated as "expanding on or elaborating on the moral significance or inner meanings of the story." There is a further complication with respect to the title: the words *sanguo* can mean political power (*guo*) divided three (*san*) ways as well as three kingdoms.

The novel's author is said to be Luo Guanzhong, about whom little is known. The first published edition, discovered only in the twentieth

148   *Three Kingdoms*

century, dates from 1522 but has a preface dated 1494. How much earlier it was composed and circulated in manuscript form is an open question. Early in the Qing (Manchu) dynasty, in the mid-1660s, a slightly revised edition was published, and that is the one universally read and acclaimed in China, Japan, Korea, and Vietnam, as well as translated into many Western languages.[1]

As suggested by the novel's opening—"The empire long divided, must unite; long united, must divide"—*Three Kingdoms* relates the conflict between the traditional centralized authority of the Han dynasty that had reigned for over four centuries and the three regional authorities that eventually replaced it: in the north, Wei under the Cao family; in the south, Wu (the Southland) under the Sun family; and in the west, Shu (the Riverlands) under the Liu family. As in many other epics, state formation and state dissolution set the background while memorable larger-than-life figures dominate the foreground and provide dramatic action. Virgil's *Aeneid*, for example, narrates the ruin of Troy while foreshadowing Aeneas's founding of Rome and suggests an analogy between Aeneas and Rome's refounder Augustus, Virgil's patron.

Three Kingdoms begins during the reign of the Han dynasty's last ruler, the child emperor Liu Xie, whose title is Han Xiandi (Emperor Xian of the Han). He reigned from 189 to 220. Western readers may recall the warning in Ecclesiastes 10.16: "Woe to thee, O land, when thy king is a child" (*Bible*). Since 206 BC, the Liu clan had ruled the Han, China's longest and mightiest dynasty and the name of China's majority ethnic group. The first two-thirds of the novel (chs. 1–80) track the breakdown of Han dynastic rule over three decades before its formal end in AD 220, which coincided with the start of the three kingdoms period, which lasted from 220 to 280. The novel ends in 280 when the newly established Jin dynasty (which displaced Wei in 266) conquers the south and forms a united empire (ch. 120). *Three Kingdoms* thus allocates twice as much space to the first three decades (eighty chs.) as it does to the last six (forty chs.). Presumably, the author's main interest is more in the dissolution of the Han dynasty (as an object lesson of dissipated power?) than in the three kingdoms sequel.

The first chapter introduces the protagonists in the ensuing power struggles and presents the work's dominant political themes. A peasant rebellion under the leadership of the so-called Yellow Scarves targets local officials appointed by the Han court. This episode, which historically occurred around 184 AD, reflects peasant unrest in China during much of the second century due to flood, famine, rent, and labor exploitation. The government—with child emperors on the throne since 105 and thus dominated by eunuchs and relatives of the emperors' wives or mothers—was ineffective at suppressing the rebels. Lacking the will and resources to cope with the Yellow Scarves, the royal court issues a general call for reinforcements. In response, three strangers—the warriors Liu Bei, Lord Guan, and Zhang Fei—meet in a peach garden and form a brotherhood, virtually plighting their troth, as the peach is a symbol of marital fidelity. Their vow of mutual commitment and loyalty—to live and die, one for all and all for one—hangs over the first two-thirds of the narrative. The sworn brothers' solidarity contrasts with the ominous inversion of gender and seniority hierarchies at the Han court and the intrafamilial betrayals in some regional ruling families. But can a symbolic brotherhood rule an empire? And can it transfer power to a new generation to sustain an ailing dynasty?

To begin to understand the novel's moral universe, students should know that three of its prominent characters are associated with what is known as the three teachings (*teaching* [*jiao*] being the closest word in Chinese to *religion*): Confucianism, Daoism, and Buddhism. The strong, virtuous, senior Liu Bei, one of the warriors seeking to restore authoritative dynastic rule, is an ideal Confucian leader. Like Confucius, however, he will ultimately fail to reach his goal. Kongming (the name means "wise as Confucius"), who reluctantly comes out of seclusion to serve as advisor to the virtuous Liu Bei, is a Daoist devotee. Kongming never rides a horse as the other warriors do; rather, he rides in a carriage, symbolizing civilian rule and political intellect. Lord Guan (Guan Gong), one of Liu Bei's sworn brothers, is a mighty warrior who undergoes a posthumous conversion to Buddhism after Sun Quan, the ruler of Wu, executes him. The career of this third figure—which is ninety percent fictional—is one of the guidelines of the narrative. The reader who knows what Lord Guan is doing at any given moment should be able to avoid getting lost in the novel's plots and subplots.

Another character students should pay attention to is Cao Cao, a morally ambiguous figure who becomes a larger-than-life villain as the work progresses. Cao Cao enters the narrative—as does his primary antagonist, Liu Bei—in the context of the Yellow Scarves rebellion (ch. 1). He emerges from the ranks of the military ostensibly as a protector of the emperor. In an attempt to strengthen the court and pull the empire together, Cao Cao gets rid of the male relatives of the emperor's consorts and the court

150 *Three Kingdoms*

eunuchs, some of whom colluded with the rebels. At first he promotes Liu Bei and his sworn brothers to reward them for their military successes against the Yellow Scarves, but he soon comes to see Liu Bei as a dangerous rival. When Cao Cao's ambitions become evident (chs. 20–21), Liu Bei contends with him for the throne. As Cao Cao's thoughts turn to usurpation, students might profitably compare his desire for power with that of Shakespeare's Macbeth. How does this protector of the failing royal court under the child emperor Liu Xie become a would-be usurper?

Students may be asked to further probe the distinction between regent and emperor when discussing Cao Cao. What prevents him from simply declaring himself the supreme political authority? Although he would like to found his own dynasty to replace the hapless court, Cao Cao rules as a regent to preserve a semblance of central Han authority under a figurehead emperor who can legitimatize Cao Cao's commands, decrees, and campaigns. Cao Cao could not declare himself emperor without destroying his image as a regent, a role that in China and Japan necessitates deference to the throne and restraint in seeking power. This limit to Cao Cao's ambition enables Liu Bei to challenge the Cao clan for the Han throne while Cao Cao prepares the way for a son to assume power.

Any reading assignment for *Three Kingdoms* should include a memorable female character who stands as a counterpoint to the violent male power struggles that take center stage. When I was in China I was often asked which character or characters I consider most important or heroic. Since I was expected to name one of the abovementioned characters, my questioners were usually taken aback when I said Diao Chan. This teenage songstress, the adopted daughter of a high minister, is one of several characters who subvert the conventional expectations of the warrior-heroic code. Her action is to seduce and thereby undo the villainous Dong Zhuo (chs. 8 and 9). This unscrupulous warrior, a precursor of Cao Cao, had taken the nine-year-old emperor hostage. Later he eluded Liu Bei, Lord Guan, and Zhang Fei in armed combat. Diao Chan's success in foiling Dong Zhuo a few chapters after the sworn brothers' failure to take him down gives an antiheroic tone to the rest of the narrative by suggesting the limits of male heroic prowess as a force shaping history.

Students may go on to consider if there are other ways in which the work dramatically or symbolically undermines male battlefield heroism as the ultimate *aristeia* (the heroic culmination of a warrior's career, such as Aeneas's victory over Turnus or Achilles's over Hector). Any discussion of this question should address the final failure of the Liu Bei–Kongming project. Does Liu Bei's inability to restore the Han court's authority and the throne's prospects of stable continuity undermine the institution of emperorship? Why is it that neither the brotherhood nor the traditional dynasty proves capable of restoring authoritative unifying rule? From this perspective, *Three Kingdoms* may be likened to a Shakespearean problem play that leaves the audience with foreboding because of the problematic manner in which it ends.

In addition to assigning chapters 1, about the Yellow Scarves rebellion (5–13); 8–9, about Diao Chan (62–76); 20–21, about Cao Cao (156–69); and 120, the ending (925–36), instructors could ask students to read chapters 43–65 (328–502), the central chapters encompassing the Battle of Red Cliffs, the turning point of the narrative. Cao Cao amasses a huge army to invade the south, which enjoys some protection from the mighty Yangzi River. Liu Bei, now recognized as Cao Cao's main foe and rival, is sheltered in the neighboring province of Jingzhou with his two sworn brothers. He has also been joined there by the gifted diplomat and military strategist Kongming. In chapters 43–44, Kongming realizes that his lord, Liu Bei, is doomed if the ruler of the southern kingdom of Wu, Sun Quan, surrenders to Cao Cao. Wielding all his powers of persuasion, Kongming succeeds in convincing Sun Quan to resist the northern army and ally with Liu Bei instead. This section thus offers another opportunity for an instructor to show how the work underscores the limits of sheer battlefield prowess by emphasizing Kongming's skill in argumentation and his tactical ingenuity. Kongming next uses an agent to persuade Cao Cao to link his ships before they cross the Yangzi and land on the southern shore. He then mounts a platform and speaks to nature in Daoist terms to invoke a wind that will drive boats loaded with inflammable material into Cao Cao's linked fleet on the far side of the river. This ruse enables Kongming to set Cao Cao's whole fleet on fire, thereby deterring the invasion. There is no *aristeia* in *Three Kingdoms*, nor are there any gods to protect the novel's heroes.

Cao Cao's defeat in this battle marks the end of his drive to bring the semiautonomous south back under Han imperial authority, and he subsequently escapes to the north (chs. 47–51). Kongming, in the meantime, tells Liu Bei that he must leave Jingzhou and establish his own kingdom (Shu) in the west; this is the third kingdom (ch. 65). Once there, Liu Bei and Kongming start planning jointly with the south an invasion of the north. Thus, the Battle of Red Cliffs not only leads to the founding of the three kingdoms (Wei in the north, Shu in the west, and Wu in

152   *Three Kingdoms*

the south) but lays the groundwork for the end of the Han dynasty a dozen years later in 220. In a real sense, then, all subsequent events stem from the outcome of this battle.[2] Students can compare this episode to a historical account of the battle in chapter 6 of *Imperial Warlord*, Rafe de Crespigny's biography of Cao Cao (241–86).

In a course devoted to world epics, *Three Kingdoms* may be studied in juxtaposition with *The Tale of the Heike* (*Heike monogatari*). This Japanese epic covers the transition from the late Heian period of child emperors (with the inevitable influence of their male relatives on the distaff side) to the masculine-militarist phase of Japanese history, the shogunate, and the transfer of the capital from Heian-kyō (Kyoto) to Kamakura. In this light, students may consider Cao Cao as a Chinese version of a shogun. Reading the two works side by side offers an opportunity to raise many questions. For example, why is the time line of the Chinese epic so long (almost a century) compared to the time line of the Japanese epic (less than a decade)? Why is the style of *Three Kingdoms* formal and official, while that of the Heike tale is informal, almost like a personal diary? How might Cao Cao be compared to the Heike (or Taira) leader Kiyomori, who fails to dominate the emperor and eventually undergoes divine punishment? Why in the end does the Japanese epic take no sides between the two clans fighting to dominate the court, while *Three Kingdoms* makes Liu Bei a potential ideal emperor and Cao Cao a villain? Students should also discuss the two distinct endings: *Three Kingdoms* concludes with a military conquest, while *The Tale of the Heike* ends with an elegiac reflection, a sort of Noh drama, on the events by two important survivors, a retired emperor and his daughter-in-law. Finally, how is the Japanese *monogatari* (tale) different from the Chinese *yanyi* (historical novel) in terms of genre?

Another fruitful juxtaposition is with selections from the fourteenth-century Chinese *Outlaws of the Marsh* (*Shuihu zhuan*, also translated as *Water Margin*). This lengthy novel treats with sympathy a protracted rebellion at the time of the transition from the northern to the southern Song dynasty, detailing the exploits of the rebels, the evils of the royal court, and the negotiations between the two, ending in the last thirty chapters with the rebels turning around to serve the court by doing battle against other rebels—a recruitment policy called *zhao an* (summoned for pacification operations). Comparing how *Three Kingdoms* treats the Han rebels, *Outlaws of the Marsh* the Song rebels, and *The Tale of the Heike* the Heike usurpers would be a useful approach to examine the political messages of these respective epic narratives.

An examination of *Three Kingdoms* can also be combined with an exploration of recent Chinese history, for example the Communist-Nationalist civil war in the twentieth century. From the perspective of the sixteenth and seventeenth centuries, by which time the Han dynasty seemed a model to emulate, the recurring pattern of Chinese history over the millennia was for periods of unity to alternate with periods of disunity, their transitions often marked by civil war. This pattern continued into the twentieth century after the fall of the Qing dynasty in 1911–12 and the birth of a republic when north and south divided and Japan invaded, creating in the northeast the independent kingdom of Manchuria. Reunification came in 1949 when the Communist Party took power and drove their Nationalist rivals to Taiwan. China has remained unified (if not completely) ever since. Anxiety over territorial integrity may explain China's high level of concern not only vis-à-vis Taiwan but also vis-à-vis Tibet, Xinjiang, and Hong Kong.

Another way to approach *Three Kingdoms* in a university course in the United States is to ask students to seek commonalities and differences between the novel's characters and memorable figures in early American history. Students should be able to recognize and discuss the novel's parallels with the political conflicts that Thomas Jefferson had with Alexander Hamilton and John Adams. In the first case, Hamilton advocated strong central authority in opposition to Jefferson's plan to protect regional autonomy through a more limited federal government with less executive power. In the second case, John Adams of Massachusetts represented a pro-English faction that sought a continuation of the English parliamentary tradition stronger than the monarch, whereas Jefferson, a fierce advocate of the French Revolution, argued for government by men of virtue. This idea of the virtuous ruler is a key concept in *Three Kingdoms*, and the term *de* (virtue) is even part of the Confucian Liu Bei's style name (Xuande). Additional components of late-eighteenth-century American history that offer apt parallels for discussion include impersonal issues such as the Articles of Confederation versus the Constitution, state legislatures versus Congress, King George III versus the colonists fighting for independence from England, and military leadership (e.g., George Washington's) versus hereditary rule. In *Three Kingdoms* we find a centrifugal rather than a centripetal dynamic as in the American case, the breaking down rather than the fortifying of central control.

Finally, students could be asked to think about how the opening verses in *Three Kingdoms* may serve as a foreshadowing of the entire narrative:

154 *Three Kingdoms*

"On and on the Great River rolls, racing east / Of proud and gallant heroes its white-tops leave no trace" (3). It will be helpful to know that in Chinese culture white is the color of mourning, and water represents the female principle, based on metaphors in the Daoist classic *Dao De Jing*. While *de* is masculine, the Dao, representing both nature and time, is the universal mother of all ten thousand things that move through time from birth to death in unending cycles. These connotations may allow for a final reflection on the role of gender as well as the three teachings (Daoism, Confucianism, and Buddhism) in a work that devotes so much attention to conflict among male warriors.

In China, *Three Kingdoms* has had an enduring appeal into the twenty-first century and is likewise popular in Korea (still divided) and Vietnam (recently reunited). In the United States, however, the work to date has had a small readership outside of classrooms devoted to Chinese history or literature. In addition to the topics discussed above, students might compare the work to any other heroic epics assigned in the course. What, if anything, makes *Three Kingdoms* distinct from works of heroic poetry other than the fact that it is in prose rather than verse? In this context, students can use the work in a conversation about distinguishing epic from romance and the novel. Selections from Christine Reitz and Simone Finkmann's *Stuctures of Epic Poetry* may be assigned to ground the discussion on genre, time permitting.

Notes

1. My own translation was jointly published in 1991 by the University of California Press and the Foreign Languages Press in Beijing as a complete version with an afterword and numerous footnotes, many of which indicate variations with respect to the 1522 Ming dynasty version. A revised version of this complete translation was printed in two volumes by the University of California Press in 2004; see Three Kingdoms. The same press also published an abridged classroom version without the footnotes that has been reprinted several times, most recently in 2020.

2. For a more detailed summary of the entire plot, see Roberts and navigate to the summary tab in the resources section.

Works Cited

The Bible. King James Version. *Bible Gateway*, www.biblegateway.com/versions/King-James-Version-KJV-Bible/#booklist.

De Crespigny, Rafe. *Imperial Warlord: A Biography of Cao Cao, 155–220 AD*. Brill, 2010.

Outlaws of the Marsh. Translated by Sidney Shapiro, Indiana UP, 1993.

Reitz, Christine, and Simone Finkmann, editors. *Structures of Epic Poetry: Foundations, Configuration, Continuity.* De Gruyter, 2019. 4 vols.

Roberts, Moss. "*Three Kingdoms (Sanguo yanyi).*" *World Epics,* edblogs .columbia.edu/worldepics/project/three-kingdoms/. Accessed 15 Sept. 2022.

The Tale of the Heike. Translated by Helen McCullough, Stanford UP, 1990.

Three Kingdoms: *A Historical Novel.* Translated by Moss Roberts, U of California P, 2004. 2 vols.

Part III

Literary Epics of
the Sixteenth and
Seventeenth Centuries

Luisanna Sardu

Epic Poems and Emotions: Anger in Ariosto's *Orlando Furioso* and Bigolina's *Urania*

"What does literature teach us about emotions?" asks Patrick Hogan in his influential study on the representation of emotions in world literature.[1] Hogan aimed to bring attention to the cognitive value of literature of the past and present to understand and interpret emotions in society. His research advanced the study of emotions as an interdisciplinary subject, pushing beyond the traditional reading of a text. I have used his approach to introduce students to the world of Italian epic poems through the lens of emotions, encouraging engaged debate and discussion about the historical context within which each work was written, analyzing how emotions were understood at the time, and asking how the texts can be understood today.

"Since Love Made Me a Dweller of the Woods": When Nature and Man Began Their Conversation is the title of the course I designed and taught for a European-literature-masterpiece program.[2] Starting with Petrarch, I invited students to reflect on literature from a different perspective: as a reservoir of interlaced emotions that describe human experiences. In particular, students explored how the emotions of the characters are developed, how their actions are affected by one another's emotions, and whether and how

160   Anger

emotions enter into a conversation with ethics. These analyses provided students with a novel way to analyze Italian epic poems.

The course focused particularly on the emotion of anger and the ways in which it was depicted and experienced by different characters in different texts. To do this, I assigned readings from texts by a man and a woman, respectively—Ludovico Ariosto's *Orlando Furioso* (*Orlando's Frenzy*), published in 1532, and Giulia Bigolina's *Urania*, written around 1552, the first known example of fiction written in Italian by a woman. Although *Urania* reuses episodes from *Orlando Furioso*, it breaks with some of the traditional elements in the canon of epic works written by men.[3] Anger, and in particular the overcoming of anger, is portrayed differently by the two authors. Most strikingly, while Ariosto orchestrates a trip to the moon (canto 34), Bigolina chooses instead to conquer anger with a Neoplatonic kiss (160).

Using a comparative approach, students analyzed the cognitive processes of the characters and investigated how a male and a female author of the early modern era portrayed anger. Moreover, students could compare these distinct portrayals of anger with their contemporary experiences. The goal was to help students better understand anger through the prism of these texts and their contextual nuances. By comparing and contrasting views of anger in these works, students could understand how these portrayals may continue to influence societal perceptions of gender and anger.

I designed the course for undergraduate students with diverse major courses of study. Some students were pursuing an Italian minor, but most were majoring in English, history, computer science, or nursing, and most knew nothing about either *Orlando Furioso* or *Urania*. One of the first challenges was to render these works familiar through popular entertainment, using works such as *The Lord of the Rings*, *Game of Thrones*, and *Harry Potter*, among others. These globally successful narratives have generated new conversations on topics such as social-class discrimination, misogyny, power, justice, and vengeance and their significance for both male and female characters. Indeed, all the students had read, viewed, or heard of at least one of these contemporary sagas. Unsurprisingly, the mere existence of these stories and the narrative frames they provide aided the reading of Ariosto's and Bigolina's work, as students were primed for debates about gender, cross-dressing, diversity, and politics within the context of the epic saga. Reading *Orlando Furioso* and *Urania* was, for many students, an opportunity to explore earlier narratives containing these types of stories, topics, and debates.

Although I encouraged students to read the entirety of *Orlando Furioso* and stressed the influence of Ariosto's work on William Shakespeare, Edmund Spenser, and John Milton, among others, students' class assignments contained only selections from cantos 1 (the protasis, Angelica's escape [stanzas 10–81]), 4 (Atlante's castle [7–45]), 11 (Olimpia [54–80]), 19 (Angelica and Medoro [16–40]), 23 (Orlando's madness [101–35]), 31 and 33 (Bradamante's jealousy [4–7, 1–109]), and 34 (Astolfo's journey to the moon [5–92]). These cantos demonstrate the range and patterns of the characters' emotions, which for this contribution I limit to selected stanzas from canto 23. The success of *Orlando Furioso* in England and North America has led to many English translations (e.g., by John Harington, Guido Waldman, Allan Gilbert, and David Slavitt). I selected Barbara Reynolds's translation because Reynolds beautifully reproduces Ariosto's rhymes and the humor of the original poem. The translation lends itself well to a class discussion about anger that can be covered in two weeks. Furthermore, Reynolds provides an elucidating introduction to Ariosto's work, its origins, and its influence on English literature, which students found helpful in familiarizing them with the history and culture of Ariosto's time.

While students encountered difficulties reading in verse when studying *Orlando Furioso*, one of my students considered *Urania*'s prose narrative to be "a jump back to modernity." *Urania*'s modern narrative form, in fact, paved the path to women's prose writing of the later 1600s and anticipated protofeminist discourses, something that prompted students to reflect on and compare the representation of female characters in Ariosto's and Bigolina's works. I assigned Valeria Finucci's translation of *Urania* because it achieves a natural flow that invites an uninterrupted reading (Bigolina). Furthermore, the edition is part of the University of Chicago Press series The Other Voice in Early Modern Europe and presents an excellent overview of the history and philosophy surrounding misogyny during Bigolina's time. It is also an insightful introduction to the study of other early modern women authors. For *Urania*, students were assigned the sections "Dedicatory Epistle" (73–84), "Questions of Love" (95–106), "The Love Triangle" (142–52), and "Return to Salerno" (156–74). In addition, to compare Ariosto's and Bigolina's depictions of anger, I focused on *Urania*'s wild woman's story (150–51) and on Urania's kissing of the wild woman (160–61).

Alongside the primary sources, students were assigned critical readings that they presented on during the semester and used in their final

162 Anger

project. Some of the recommended scholarship included Albert Ascoli's *Ariosto's Bitter Harmony*, Giuseppe Mazzotta's "Power and Play in the *Orlando Furioso*," Deanna Shemek's "That Elusive Object of Desire," Valeria Finucci's *The Lady Vanishes*, Virginia Cox's *Women's Writing in Italy*, and William Reddy's chapter "What Are Emotions?" in *The Navigation of Feeling* (1–138). Because the analysis of emotions in the medieval and early modern periods is deeply indebted to the writings of Aristotle and Plato on the subject, I also referred to their definitions of anger.[4] For Aristotle and Plato, the process of feeling anger begins with the evaluation of what or who caused it, continues with the perception of the individual experience of pain or pleasure, and culminates in the contemplation of a vendetta. The steps through which anger unfolds reveal a rich cognitive web relevant to the analysis and understanding of, for example, how Orlando's disbelief turns into rage and how Urania's grief is disguised as anger.

Early modern authors, in striving to better understand human nature, also grappled with the tension between the new and emerging philosophies—such as Renaissance Galenism and Neoplatonism. Because the physical manifestation of emotions was understood as the excess or lack of humors by many Renaissance Galenists, I explained the theory of the humors (black bile, yellow bile, blood, and phlegm) by asking my students to think of the focus that modern society places on the idea of balance—a balanced diet, a balanced lifestyle, and so on. Renaissance Galenists discussed the four bodily liquids that, they believed, controlled our emotions. Whenever there is too much (or too little) of one of those four bodily liquids, we can feel gloomy, irritable, passionate, or apathetic.[5]

Approaching Ariosto's and Bigolina's texts comparatively, despite their different narrative styles, led students to connect the portrayals of the characters and the expression of their emotions. The anger of both Orlando and Urania is triggered by their respective beloveds' abandonment but also, and more importantly, by a sense of betrayal and injustice, as well as by the realization that the object of their desire preferred someone else. Students found this aspect of the two narratives a particularly relatable and intriguing way to trace the different stages of anger.

In canto 23 of *Orlando Furioso*, the paladin Orlando learns of Angelica's encounter with Medoro by reading about their love story carved on every tree and rock, which initially tortures his mind with disbelief (stanzas 101–03). When he is eventually convinced of the offense, Orlando becomes so *furioso* (furious) and destructive that he not only "slashe[s] the offending rock, . . . the cave, the trees, each bole or stem or stock" but also wreaks havoc on any animals and humans in his path (stanza 130). Orlando himself acknowledges the process of losing his sense of self through his anger, declaring, "I am not he, I am not he I seem. / He who Orlando was is dead and gone" (stanza 128). Students, especially psychology majors, were intrigued by Orlando's loss of identity and consequent inability to control his rage.

I used *Google Arts and Culture* to show my students visual depictions of Orlando's *furia* (fury) by Gustave Doré and Arnold Böcklin (both titled *Orlando furioso*), which helped students understand the violence of the paladin's action. Students also noted how the depictions by Ariosto, Doré, and Böcklin contrast with depictions of women's anger in art and literature, going back as far as antiquity. Since Medusa's head is considered by many as the most representative classical depiction of women's anger, after summarizing Ovid's version of the Medusa myth from his *Metamorphoses*, I also showed students Michelangelo Caravaggio's *Medusa*, Paul Rubens's *Head of Medusa*, and Böcklin's *Medusa*. The contrasting visions of Orlando's violent actions and Medusa's horrific head allowed students to see the ancient root of perceptions of women's anger as not only murderous and unjust but also monstrous.[6]

The way in which Orlando's jealousy and anger unfold—ultimately leading to the loss of the paladin's identity—served as a useful introduction to Urania's journey to self-discovery. This latter process starts when Urania compares herself to Clorina, the woman with whom her beloved Fabio betrayed her. In a letter to Fabio, Urania states, "I know that you love another woman more beautiful than me—for I do not regard you as being so blind that I could believe you abandoned me for another woman less beautiful—but I am certain that she is no more virtuous than I am" (Bigolina 87). Urania evaluates herself and Clorina, concluding that her intellectual virtues are superior to Clorina's physical ones. This assessment recalls the jealousy Orlando feels when comparing himself to the lower-ranked Medoro, though the key distinction is that, unlike Urania, he is not able to affirm his superiority.

Students discussed how each character experiences anger differently. Orlando flies into irrational rage, while Urania rationalizes her grief and anger by engaging in conversation with anyone she meets during her escape. She discusses the pain caused by love and men's misogyny with the men and women she encounters during her journey, who urge her "to narrate her disgrace" (121). As a result, a sense of balance between mind and body seems almost restored in her. Urania's ability to rationalize

164   Anger

her emotions aloud will allow her to rebuild her own identity. It is Urania's eventual encounter and kiss with the wild woman, a unique character who represents the body, that will allow the protagonist's final reckoning with her fractured self and therefore make her whole again.

But who is the wild woman, and what is Bigolina telling us with the creation of this innovative character? Students wondered if she represents Urania's *furiosa*, her angry other half. The wild woman is filled with hatred and rage because her companion, the wild man, has been killed (150). Because the wild woman thinks that the perpetrator is a woman, she develops a violent aversion to the female sex and an increased sexual appetite for men. Such a portrayal of female rage and sexuality recalls the classical figures of not only Medusa but also the Furies in Aeschylus's *Oresteia*, Clytemnestra, and Medea, to name a few: all tragic figures who are still used as symbols of women's irrational and unjust anger.

Comparing Orlando's fury with the wild woman's rage provided students with several possible ways to understand anger. First, students discussed how Orlando's ultimate loss of balance (sanity) was a result of divine punishment for having abandoned his duty as a paladin for the love of a pagan woman. In this light, Orlando's transgression and demise appear as a moral and religious lesson. In fact, the epic hero will be able to restore his balance only thanks to Astolfo's divinely orchestrated journey to the moon (canto 34). Students then noted how, by contrast, Bigolina's creation of the wild woman does not serve to moralize or to suggest that anger is related to sin. Rather, Bigolina suggests that women should use their intellect and confront challenges—to kiss the metaphorical wild woman and be made whole again. Indeed, in *Urania*, the wild woman represents Urania's irrational physical anger that needs to be tamed. By dominating her wild part, Urania will prevail, free Fabio, and return to her city and a civilized version of herself.

Disguised as Fabio, Urania is able to approach and deceive the wild woman, circumventing the latter's hatred of other women. Their kiss serves as a balm for them both. It brings together two halves of a whole, restoring Urania's identity. Urania achieves her Aristotelian vendetta, reestablishing the balance between mind and body that she lost because of the injustice of Fabio's betrayal.[7] Students appreciated the complexity of this resolution, especially when it was contrasted to Orlando's madness and deus ex machina recovery. While Bigolina's wild woman strongly alludes to Orlando's beastly transformation, Urania's kiss offers a human way to restore balance between mind and body, without harming others. Relative to the female characters in Ariosto's work, Urania carries a broader significance for narratives of female vendettas and jealousy. Thanks to this resolution, students found that Bigolina's narrative ultimately refutes the stereotype of irrational and unjustifiable female anger handed down from classical literature and philosophy.[8]

To further cement their understanding, students were encouraged to use Christopher Nissen's *Kissing the Wild Woman*, which they found to be a valuable text, particularly where Nissen states that the *femina selvatica* (wild woman) and the wild man play self-reflexive roles in literature (189). Additionally, Roger Bartra's *Wild Men in the Looking Glass* helped students understand the juxtaposition of the wild and civilized man. In this work Bartra states that "the wild man was created to answer the questions of civilized man" (204) and that "the medieval wild man lives in a state of incivility and misery, and through contrast has permitted the figure of civilized man to shine intensely" (144).

Why is the comparative study of emotions in *Orlando Furioso* and *Urania* relevant in our contemporary world? The history of emotions allows us to study how anger, grief, and jealousy were experienced and expressed in past literature. As Barbara Rosenwein and Riccardo Cristiani have stated, this focus "looks at what has changed and what ties together [emotions'] past and present" (10). Ariosto's and Bigolina's different expressions of anger, grief, and jealousy invite modern readers to consider their own experiences dealing with disappointment and injustice and to reflect on why women's anger is often still perceived as disproportionate by society. By comparing Urania's response to that of Orlando, students encounter a positive female model in early modern literature that demonstrates why talking about one's own anger is important to reestablish a mental and physical balance.

To conclude the semester and offer a visual performance of anger and jealousy in action, I introduced two modern examples showing how anger continues to play a role in societal understandings of gender. I invited my students to watch John Osbourne's play *Look Back in Anger* and *Twelve Angry Women*, Sherman Sergel's adaptation of Reginal Rose's *Twelve Angry Men* (Rose).[9] In *Look Back in Anger*, Jimmy Porter, the main character, is described by his wife, Allison, as "a knight in shining armor" and represents the angry generation of his time, cheated out of economic and social stability (Osbourne 43:10). His anger is also directed at the emotionally cold upper class, represented by Allison. *Twelve Angry Women* extolls the virtues of women's anger and highlights the importance of stating

166 Anger

one's mind. Future iterations of this class could further examine women's anger, vengeance, and quest for justice by including works such as *Circe*, by Madeline Miller, and episodes from the television series *The Handmaid's Tale*, adapted from Margaret Atwood's classic novel of the same name.

Interestingly, to students, anger is a necessary emotion, one that "sensitizes us to injustice and motivates us to uphold justice" (Callard). Anger, however, should never be excessive and deadly—like Orlando's violent physical outbursts. Rather, individuals should learn to rationalize the emotion, communicate it, and talk about it, as Urania does before pacifying her angry other half.

Notes

1. Hogan's study about the value of literature paved the way to a cognitive science of emotions and considers how emotions are produced, experienced, and enacted in works by Shakespeare, Li Ch'ing-Chao, and the contemporary Nigerian author Wole Soyinka. Hogan's work is particularly relevant to understand the relations between emotional response and ethical judgment.

2. The first part of the course title is a verse from poem 237 of Petrarch's *Canzoniere*.

3. Among the most familiar refashioned episodes is Emilia's infatuation with Urania when she is disguised as Fabio (Bigolina 121–22), which mirrors Fiordispina's longing for the armored Bradamante in *Orlando Furioso* (canto 25, stanza 29).

4. In *Rhetoric*, Aristotle states, "Let anger be [defined as] a desire accompanied by pain for perceived revenge caused by perceived slight, of the sort directed against oneself or one's own, the slight being undeserved" (1378a31–33). Plato treats anger in several dialogues. In *Republic*, Plato defines anger in connection with the passion of the soul, borrowing the word *thumos* from Homer. For Plato, *thumos* is spiritedness and "unreasoning anger" (*alogistos thumoumeno* [441c]). He defines anger in relation to pleasure and pain in the *Philebus*. Along with envy and jealousy, anger is a condition "in which we should find a mixture of the two elements [pleasure and pain]." (50c). Finally, in *Laws*, anger is explained in terms of motivation of human actions, specifically as "an uncontrollable rage" (869a). For further readings and explanations about emotions in ancient Greece, see Konstan.

5. For further readings and examples of Galen's theory of humors and influence on history and literature, which students may find helpful, see "History."

6. For a visual and geographic approach to Ariosto's work, it was also effective to have students use the *Orlando Furioso Atlas*. This website, moreover, offers a link to information on Italian women writers, thus offering a valuable tool for students who want to compare Bigolina's work with that of other women authors.

7. Aristotle's idea of revenge is connected to the meaning of justice. He argues that since anger is caused by "perceived injustice" (1378a31), revenge is motivated by a desire to rectify this injustice or undeserved slight.

8. On the perception of women's anger in antiquity, see Konstan's explanation that women of all social classes were not allowed to show anger at their fathers and husbands, and if they did so, they were accused of being weak and lacking self-control (41–76).

9. During spring 2012, students had an opportunity to see Sam Gold's rendition of *Look Back in Anger* on Broadway, starring Matthew Rhys as Jimmy Porter, the main angry character. However, students could also watch the 1989 movie on DVD, available in the university library (Osbourne).

Works Cited

Ariosto, Ludovico. *Orlando Furioso.* Translated by Barbara Reynolds, Penguin Books, 2006. 2 vols.

Aristotle. *Aristotle: Rhetoric.* Edited by Edward Meredith Cope and John Edwin Sandys, Cambridge UP, 2010.

Ascoli, Albert Russell. *Ariosto's Bitter Harmony: Crisis and Evasion in the Italian Renaissance.* Princeton UP, 1987.

Bartra, Roger. *Wild Men in the Looking Glass: The Mythic Origins of European Otherness.* U of Michigan P, 1994.

Bigolina, Giulia. *Urania: A Romance.* Translated by Valeria Finucci, U of Chicago P, 2005.

Callard, Agnes. "The Philosophy of Anger." *Boston Review,* 16 Apr. 2020, bostonreview.net/forum/agnes-callard-philosophy-anger.

Cox, Virginia. *Women's Writing in Italy, 1400–1650.* Johns Hopkins UP, 2008.

Finucci, Valeria. *The Lady Vanishes: Subjectivity and Representation in Castiglione and Ariosto.* Stanford UP, 1992.

"History of Medicine." *National Library of Medicine,* www.nlm.nih.gov/hmd/index.html. Accessed 16 Sept. 2022.

Hogan, Patrick C. *What Literature Teaches Us about Emotion.* Cambridge UP, 2014.

Konstan, David. *The Emotions of the Ancient Greeks: Studies in Aristotle and Classical Literature.* U of Toronto P, 2006.

Mazzotta, Giuseppe. "Power and Play in the *Orlando Furioso.*" *The Play of the Self,* edited by Ronald Bogue and Mihai Spariosu, State U of New York P, 1994, pp. 183–202.

Miller, Madeline. *Circe.* Back Bay Books, 2018.

Nissen, Christopher. *Kissing the Wild Woman: Art, Beauty, and the Reformation of the Italian Prose Romance in Giulia Bigolina's Urania.* U of Toronto P, 2011.

Osbourne, John. *Look Back in Anger.* Directed by Judi Dench, Shock DVD, 2013.

168 Anger

Petrarch. *The Canzoniere; or, Rerum Vulgarium Fragmenta.* Translated by Mark Musa, Indiana UP, 1999.

Plato. *Laws.* Translated by Robert Mayhew, bk. 10, Clarendon Press / Oxford UP, 2008.

———. *Philebus.* Translated by Dorothea Frede, Hackett Publishing, 1993.

———. *Republic. Great Dialogues of Plato,* translated by W. H. D. Rouse, Signet Classics, 2015, pp. 287–327.

Reddy, William M. *The Navigation of Feeling: A Framework for the History of Emotions.* Cambridge UP, 2001.

Rose, Reginald. *Twelve Angry Women: A Play in Three Acts.* Adapted by Sherman L. Sergel, Dramatic Publishing, 1984.

Rosenwein, Barbara H., and Riccardo Cristiani. *What Is the History of Emotions?* Politi Press, 2018.

Shemek, Deanna. "That Elusive Object of Desire: Angelica in the *Orlando Furioso.*" *Annali d'Italianistica,* vol. 7, 1989, pp. 116–41.

Jason Lotz

Teaching Spenser's *Faerie Queene* through Allegory and Digital Rhetoric

Given its complexity and vastness, Edmund Spenser's *Faerie Queene* can be daunting to teach. Straightforward comparisons to other literary works tend to skim one or two basic similarities off the surface of the epic. Style and genre connect it to Ovid's *Metamorphoses* and continental epic romance, and allegiance to the monarchy and indeed the poet's ambitions align it with Virgil's *Aeneid*, while its considerations of nobility and virtue as well as the contest between art and nature put it in conversation with Shakespeare's *King Lear* and Baldassare Castiglione's *Courtier*. This ready ability to be networked with other texts makes *The Faerie Queene* ideal for a variety of literature survey courses, but the challenge is to keep the poem from being relegated to secondary readings for context and to ensure that it is appreciated on its own merit. One way to preserve the poem's integrity in a course of study limited to excerpts is to focus on the crucial contribution Spenser's allegory makes to Western conceptions of self-fashioning and, more precisely, on how the allegorical move from immaterial to material underpins social mobility in both the early modern period and the Internet age.

170 Spenser's *Faerie Queene*

Reading in Context: Textbooks and Reading Selections

Because of *The Faerie Queene*'s indebtedness to both English and world literature, any thorough study of the poem requires comparison with a host of other works. As a result, for a survey course, many instructors will opt for an all-in-one anthology. Although the tenth edition of *The Norton Anthology of English Literature*, with its inclusion of complementary texts that support comparative studies across periods and genres, works well for a survey of English literature, its limited excerpts, especially designed by its editor, Stephen Greenblatt, to illustrate his theory of power and self-fashioning, significantly narrow the thematic teaching options. Regrettably, W. W. Norton's world literature collections completely ignore Spenser, missing out on the many possible comparisons between *The Faerie Queene* and continental romance. While not always a sensible option for an undergraduate survey course, my uncontested favorite *Faerie Queene* textbook is the revised second edition by Pearson, edited by A. C. Hamilton. Hamilton, who also edited the extremely useful *Spenser Encyclopedia*, offers supplementary annotations that are somehow comprehensive without being overwhelming and focused without losing a respect for diverse scholarly perspectives.

The *Faerie Queene* is not episodic in the form of Ovid's *Metamorphoses* or a collection like Chaucer's *Canterbury Tales*, but its combination of characters and plots still lends itself to the format of a literature survey, the various components of which might be arranged by genre, theme, or historical period. Selected episodes allow students to see Spenser's allegory at work and provide enough text to connect the work to its precedents and heirs. However, Spenser's allegory operates both locally and holistically, making sense within each episode but also contributing to the poem's overall allegorical puzzle. Unlike Homeric epics that derive continuity from the problems facing a single protagonist, *The Faerie Queene* relies on the overarching concept of its allegory to maintain its wholeness. Accordingly, we can understand an excerpt from book 3 without knowing the full plot of book 1, but we will likely miss out on the whole vision of the allegory without at least some references to an array of episodes.

Book 1 ("of Holiness") offers the most efficient and straightforward accounting of Spenser's allegory. It offers also, arguably, the simplest form of allegory within the poem and the easiest to understand on its own. Students can easily identify the allegorical core of holiness as union with the one true faith (Una) and its correlates of battling pride, avoiding lust and despair, and, eventually, defeating the heresy of the Catholic Church (a dragon called Error). Book 1 establishes the basis of both the mechanics of Spenserian allegory and the doctrine of its moral lesson. In that way, it orients the entire work by establishing the central node from which the allegory and its objective branch.

The tree metaphor implied here may be helpful for introducing the structure of the poem to students. Holiness comes first in the poem because, in their departure from Catholicism, Protestants emphasized salvation (by grace through faith) as the first step toward sanctification; one cannot transform one's character or cultivate virtue without first aligning with the one true faith (allegorized as Una in bk. 1). With the tree metaphor, we can see holiness as the trunk on which all other virtues depend. As the allegory of the Christian English courtier progresses, the doctrinal rigidity gives way to more complex and diverse manifestations of virtues that are at once more contextual and showier; thus, courtesy constitutes the last and most visible, perhaps flowery, of the six virtues.

A number of complementary texts make it easy enough to situate *The Faerie Queene* relative to other works (by genre) and among sociocultural energies of its time (by themes): for a British literature survey, *The Norton Anthology of English Literature* is maybe the most convenient textbook for comparative study. I have students read the Prologue from *The Canterbury Tales* (Chaucer 261–80) and then, in groups, sketch each character, following Chaucer's detailed descriptions of appearance and costume. These visual representations highlight the way dress and appearance mark status, setting up an analogy to allegory in *The Faerie Queene*. Students also read Thomas Hoby's English translation of Castiglione's *Courtier* (the chapter on grace [176–78] makes sense of Spenser's stated purpose to "fashion a gentleman or noble person" [*Faerie Queene* 714]) and Philip Sidney's *Defense of Poesy* (whose opening analogy to horsemanship pairs directly with *The Faerie Queene* 2.4.7–9, and Sidney's dictum that poets create images to "teach and delight" provides a contemporary, corresponding theory for Spenser's use of allegory [*Defense* 553]). Selections from the sonnet sequences demonstrate the traditions of courtly love (a miniature version of Spenser's adoration of Elizabeth and another example of poetry extending the reputation of its subject).[1] *King Lear* is directly related to Spenser's own version of Leyr and his three daughters (*Faerie Queene* 2.10.27–32). Spenser includes it in the middle of his allegory of temperance, and both poem and play benefit from a comparative analysis tracking the theme of art versus nature, especially in Guyon's dealings with Phaedria's

172 Spenser's *Faerie Queene*

Isle of Mirth (2.6), Acrasia's Bower of Bliss (2.12), and Edmund's "Nature, art my goddess" speech (Shakespeare, *Lr.* 1.2.1, 1.2.1–22). Alternatively, when I teach Shakespeare's *Hamlet* instead of *Lear*, Hamlet's "unweeded garden" speech (1.2.135, 1.2.129–158) corresponds with *The Faerie Queene*'s garden episodes (Spenser, *Faerie Queen* 2.6, 2.12, and 3.6) and a consideration of nature, art, and nobility. For a class devoted to issues of colonialism or other institutionalized injustices, I assign portions of book 5 along with Spenser's *A View of the Present State of Ireland*. While a survey class rarely has time to reach into book 7 of *The Faerie Queene*, the "Cantos of Mutabilitie," a major-authors course or special topics course on epic romance can find rich parallels between the unfinished book 7 and Ovid's *Metamorphoses*. Finally, *The Faerie Queene* also sets up John Milton's *Paradise Lost* generically and thematically. Both poems aim to be English and Protestant, both concern the relationship between systemic government and self-government, and both rely heavily on allusions in order to take their respective places within the epic and romance traditions.

The Function of Allegory: Power of Fiction, Fiction of Power

In addition to interpreting the intricate allegory of *The Faerie Queene*, I also want students to understand what allegory accomplishes outside the poem. How allegory works is only the first step to understanding what allegory does in society. Drawing on other examples of allegory gives us more access to its practical dimensions. This discursive, or cross-pollinating, approach eases some of the pressure students may feel when tackling Spenser's challenging trifecta of old-fashioned English, ornate poetry, and complex allegory. Not all examples are equally helpful, however. Some students will have read George Orwell's *Animal Farm*, which can confuse more than clarify Spenserian allegory if students expect to find one-to-one substitutions for each character. Another more recent point of comparison is the Pixar animated film *Inside Out*, which depicts a child's coming-of-age as a drama carried out by five personified emotions. This film gets us a little closer to Spenser's allegory of the virtues and can help students understand allegory as a way of seeing; by thinking of one's emotions or virtues as persons with wills and motives, one organizes the mind and takes authorship of one's experience.[2] *Inside Out* perfectly maps onto C. S. Lewis's definition of allegory in *Allegory of Love*: "start with an immaterial fact, such as the passions . . . then invent *visibilia* to express them" (44–45).

Following this definition of allegory, I then draw attention to the ways students regularly perform allegories in their social interactions. Online, they invent *"visibilia"* in the form of images, associations, and behaviors to stage their ideas of themselves; they project fictions that work toward various ends.[3] Often these ends come about as a surprise, which is one of the perils of social media and one of the justifications for promoting digital literacy. When students realize their identities operate allegorically, this realization not only gives them a new perspective of *The Faerie Queene* but also engenders a greater respect for their own roles in shaping the world.

Underlying the course objectives to develop students' reasoning, appreciation for the humanities and arts, and communication skills, my philosophical goal is to cultivate citizenship. I want students to see their own literacy as a means of making the world rather than merely consuming it. Whether they are composing text messages, posting to social media, studying literature, or writing essays, they are gathering, moving, and organizing language through which the world is accessed and shaped. In *The Faerie Queene*, and particularly in its relationship to Queen Elizabeth I and her efforts to maintain her sovereignty, we find a rich and complex schematic for constructing the early modern world that conveniently parallels the demands of the Internet age.

Spenser operated within a culture that increasingly saw virtue as performative and, by extension, character as not only outwardly measurable but perhaps outwardly constitutive—that is, faking it was quite near to making it. Thomas Hoby's widely read English translation of Castiglione's *Courtier*, an elemental constituent of the Italian Renaissance, raised the question of nobility—is it purely inherent or could it be learned? Spenser straddles this debate in a letter to Walter Raleigh by claiming that the purpose of his poem is "to fashion a gentleman or noble person in virtuous and gentle discipline" (*Faerie Queene* 714, 713–19) while also reserving certain noble graces that are, as he puts in *The Faerie Queene*, "[p]roper to gentle blood" (2.4.8). But in Elizabeth herself, the social implications of performance and appearance become most prominent; to combat the challenges to her rule, Elizabeth presented herself as an allegory of England, of the power inherent in the position attached only incidentally to her physically female body. This move to embody the abstraction of English sovereignty established a highly visible precedent for crossing class or gender barriers by dressing up in abstracted virtues. Be reifying her sovereignty as a thing separated from her sex, Elizabeth implemented the allegorical means of self-fashioning within her own court.[4]

174   Spenser's *Faerie Queene*

Given the duality of their Internet and physical lives, students are apt to recognize in the crafting of an idealized Faerie Land rhetorical moves similar to those that govern success in the digital world. Crucially, however, even though many students are habitual consumers of social media, few of them may have figured out how to integrate their online and offline lives, let alone mobilize their digital practices to meet their personal or professional goals. Pairing our analysis of *The Faerie Queene* with a cultivation of digital literacy illuminates the correlation between the selves we want and the bodies we inhabit, providing a practical basis for discussions of gender, race, body image, and socioeconomic class.

In *The Allegory of Love*, Lewis claims that *The Faerie Queene* is "not like life, but the experience of reading it is like living" (358). In that sense, the allegorical nature of the poem is practical; Faerie Land is a gymnasium of the mind, in which the virtues—more than being contemplated—can be practiced. In *The Faerie Queene*, Spenser creates a literary world in which one's character and identity are subjected only to imagination. This assertion is not the same as saying that Spenser writes a story making himself out to be a knight or gentleman; he goes much further than that: through the fiction, Spenser cultivates the virtues of nobility without being a noble. Thanks to the coincidence of Elizabeth's own means of establishing power, what happens in Faerie Land does not stay in Faerie Land; what happens in the allegory matters in the real world.

Through allegory, *The Faerie Queene* carves out a fictional space in which ideals take bodily form so that bodies in the real world can be treated ideally. Such is the promise, though not the reality, of the Internet, and the rhetoric required to understand the one (allegory) applies in parallel to the other (the Internet). Both require effort, responsibility, and savvy; both fall prey to abuse and misconception.

Imitation, Nature, and Art

One of the ongoing criticisms of social media concerns the prevalence of false images; from overly curated pictures of cuisine to photoshopped skin complexions, standards of realness and authenticity are as much a part of the social contract today as they were when Sidney defended the poet's use of fiction. Digital literacy begins when students can see that these so-called lies on social media (as in any fiction) follow rules contracted by purpose, audience, and context. Nearly every student in the classroom has a story about someone's exaggerated or misleading online profile, and such stories provide an opportunity for engaging the theme of nature versus art, which shows up in a variety of early modern texts. While our discussion may begin with the basic complaint against fake online profiles, our objective is to get beyond the binary judgment of real or fake so that we can see how images, statements, and associations convey meaning that in turn contributes to the shape of the world and one's place in it. This discussion supports an analysis of Spenser's own confrontation of art and nature, which shows up throughout the writer's allegory but especially in the garden scenes (*Faerie Queene* 2.6, 2.12, 3.6). Spenser complicates the apparent opposition and—like his contemporary Sidney, who advocates for poetic license in beautifying nature—sees that civilization demands the marriage of art and nature. The difference between the temptation of the Bower of Bliss, which must be destroyed by the knight of Temperance, and the celebrated delights of the Garden of Adonis is not that one is fake (or made by magic) and the other is natural but rather that one ends in excess and ego and the other in harmony and love. The end makes the imitation, or the art, good or bad.

To solidify the parallels of early modern and current, online self-fashioning, I ask students to think about what it means to be a citizen today and compare that to Spenser's idealized noble person. Here are some sample discussion questions that can be modified for essay prompts, small-group-generated discussions, or multimedia projects:

How did the six virtues allegorized in *The Faerie Queene* equip one for success in early modern England? What virtues are essential for citizenship today? How do the virtues allegorized in the poem manifest differently today?

Describe and justify the appearance of Red Cross Knight; how might his appearance be changed for today's society?[5]

How does Spenser weave the virtues together so that the completeness of the noble person depends as much on the coherence of each virtue as on the mastery of any individual virtue?

Choose any two of the six virtues and explain their interdependence.

After Spenser invokes the classical muses at the beginning of *The Faerie Queene*, he also asks for the attention and inspiration of Queen Elizabeth: "And raise my thoughts too humble and too vile, / To think of that glorious type of thine" (1.4.6–7). What does this invocation suggest about the importance of role models, inspirational public figures, or heads of state?

176 Spenser's *Faerie Queene*

For a more creative assignment, I borrow from the popular social media trend #TheTellMeChallenge, in which users post videos or tweets asking their friends to reveal something about themselves without literal declarations. For example, one might begin the challenge by saying in a post, "Tell me you're lonely without telling me you're lonely," to which someone might respond with a video of them talking to a volleyball with a painted face. While not precisely allegory, the exercise requires creativity, abstraction, and a grasp of subtext, and it helps students move away from too literal interpretations of the text. I might ask them, for example, to tell me what courtesy is without telling me what courtesy is; after seeing what they come up with, we compare their expressions to excerpts from *The Faerie Queene*.

Images of Women

Spenser's attention to gender owes much to Elizabeth, and any study of his so-called feminism should begin by tracing his debt to her. Arguably, *The Faerie Queene* is an artifact of her legacy; as such, the poem continues to resonate as an emblem of female empowerment. Few characters in English literature impose a more formidable model of leadership than Britomart. Our introduction to her in book 3 sees her knock Guyon, the principal knight of book 2, off his horse, and her ensuing adventures only seal her reputation as a warrior. At the beginning of the second canto of book 3, Spenser directly addresses the genesis of the character, blaming men for the underrepresentation of women in accounts of war:

> Here haue I cause, in men iust blame to find,
> That in their proper praise too partiall bee,
> And not indifferent to woman kind,
> To whom no share in armes and cheualree,
> They doe impart, ne maken memoree
> Of their braue gestes and prowess martiall;
> Scarse doe they spare to one or two or three,
> Rowme in their writtes; yet the same writing small
> Does all their deedes deface, and dims their glories all. (3.2.1–9)

Spenser continues into the next stanza, arguing that men make laws specifically to exclude women from authority. He is defending the plausibility of his poem and praising Elizabeth, but the passage is often cited as evidence of the poet's feminism. Book 3 goes on to display the fierce, undaunted Britomart as perhaps the most memorable and remarkable of the poem's characters.

Britomart's narrative arc—like many of the other plotlines in the poem—remains unresolved. Through a vision in a looking glass, she learns she is destined to marry Arthegall, a man she will eventually meet in book 4, when they end up on opposite sides of a battle. They pledge themselves to each other before separating to pursue their individual quests and leaving their pending marriage to a distant future outside the poem. Britomart is a not-so-veiled allusion to Queen Elizabeth, whose unmarried status allowed her to preserve an ungendered majesty and sovereignty that would have been compromised by the union of her physical body. Britomart, still unattached to Arthegall, combats men (usually in disguise), saves men, and, more generally, accomplishes tasks that men fail at.[6] Perhaps the most prominent of these episodes occurs at the end of book 3 when Britomart saves Amoret from the House of Busirane. When Scudamore, Amoret's lover and would-be savior, cannot pass through the fires guarding Busirane's fortress, Britomart steps in. Being the embodiment of chaste love, she is able to pass through the flames (perhaps of erotic desire) while Scudamore's too lusty attempts leave him helpless against Busirane's magic (3.11.21–27).

Here we remember that Britomart's prowess exists within an allegory. While Britomart remains a feminist symbol, class discussions benefit from a consideration of her role within the idealized composition of a virtuous person. To frame the issue with contemporary social concerns, I ask my students to compare Spenser's association of women and chastity to public images of women today: Why does Spenser allegorize chastity as a woman (Britomart)? How does the allegory compare to representations of women on social media or in advertisements? Are women more likely than men to be paired with certain products or activities in these representations?

There is no substitution for reading the whole poem. In his introduction, A. C. Hamilton describes his own deep study of *The Faerie Queene*: "I read until I had the sense of standing at the centre of a whirling universe of words each in its proper order and related to all the others, its meanings constantly unfolding from within until the poem is seen to contain all literature, and all knowledge needed to guide one's personal and social life" (Spenser, *Faerie Queene* 18, 1–20). No undergraduate or graduate survey could possibly hope to recreate such an immersive experience of Spenser's poem, but the best miniature sketches trace as many threads of

178   Spenser's *Faerie Queene*

the web as possible, giving students a sense of their cultural proximity to the richness and complexity of the allegory.

Notes

1. I assign Shakespeare's sonnets 18, 19, and 130 (Sonnets 724, 725, 736); Spenser's *Amoretti* sonnets 1, 34 (487), 54, and 75 (488, 490); and Sidney's *Astrophil and Stella* sonnets 1, 5, and 49 (586–87, 587–88, 595).

2. Barrett outlines a similar strategy for developing and refining one's emotional intelligence. She argues that the more nuanced and detailed one's emotional conceptions are, the more control one has over experiences. These concepts become what she calls "a toolbox for a meaningful life" (176), which might easily be a descriptor of Spenser's allegory.

3. One simple manifestation of this form of allegory appears on platforms such as *Instagram*. A photo of curated cuisine is often less about the food and more about the projected character of the person behind the image. Addressing the subtext is the first step; students quickly realize that a picture of a purportedly exotic dish means "I am the kind of person who eats this," which can be further interpreted as "I am an adventurous person." In a kind of reverse-engineering move, students take the image and trace it back to the desired abstract virtue. When they can see behind the image in this way, we can begin to draw parallels to Spenser's imagining of chastity as a formidable warrior who can walk through flames of sexual desire without being burned (see *Faerie Queene* 3.11.21–27).

4. For a scholarly account of the relationship between power and image in this context, instructors could assign Greenblatt, *Renaissance Self-Fashioning* 162–67.

5. This question is a simplified version of the previous one, designed for classes that might read only book 1.

6. For a class focused on Spenser's treatment of women, I recommend the following selections: the appearance of Belphoebe (*Faerie Queene* 2.3.21–42), Gloriana's beauty of mind (2.9.3–4), Alma as ruler of passions (2.11.1–2), the introduction to Britomart and the prophecy regarding Arthegall and their descendants (3.1–3), Belphoebe as a healer (3.5), the birth of Belphoebe and Amoret (3.6), Britomart saving Amoret (3.11–12), Britomart winning a tournament (4.4), the meeting of Britomart and Arthegall (4.6), Belphoebe saving Amoret (4.7), and the allegory of womanhood (4.10).

Works Cited

Barrett, Lisa Feldman. *How Emotions Are Made.* Houghton Mifflin Harcourt, 2017.

Castiglione, Baldassare. *The Courtier.* Translated by Thomas Hoby. Greenblatt, *Norton Anthology*, vol. B, pp. 176–92.

Chaucer, Geoffrey. *The Canterbury Tales.* Greenblatt, *Norton Anthology*, vol. A, pp. 256–360.

Greenblatt, Stephen, editor. *The Norton Anthology of English Literature.* 10th ed., vol. A, W. W. Norton, 2019.

———, editor. *The Norton Anthology of English Literature.* 10th ed., vol. B, W. W. Norton, 2019.

———. *Renaissance Self-Fashioning: From More to Shakespeare.* 1980. U of Chicago P, 2005.

Hamilton, A. C., editor. *The Spenser Encyclopedia.* U of Toronto P, 1997.

Inside Out. Directed by Pete Docter and Ronnie del Carmen, Pixar / Disney, 2015.

Lewis, C. S. *The Allegory of Love.* Oxford UP, 1958.

Shakespeare, William. *Hamlet.* Edited by Constance Jordan, Pearson, 2005.

———. *King Lear.* Edited by Claire McEachern, Pearson, 2005.

———. Sonnets. Greenblatt, *Norton Anthology,* vol. B, pp. 722–38.

Sidney, Philip. *Astrophil and Stella.* Greenblatt, *Norton Anthology,* vol. B, pp. 586–603

———. *The Defense of Poesy.* Greenblatt, *Norton Anthology,* vol. B, pp. 546–85.

Spenser, Edmund. *Amoretti.* Greenblatt, *Norton Anthology,* vol. B, pp. 486–91.

———. *The Faerie Queene.* Edited by A. C. Hamilton, revised 2nd ed., Pearson, 2007.

———. *A View of the Present State of Ireland. Renascence Editions,* Jan. 1997, www.luminarium.org/renascence-editions/veue1.html.

Joseph M. Ortiz

New World Epics: Camões's *Os Lusíadas*, Ercilla's *La Araucana*, and Villagrá's *Historia de la Nueva México*

Teaching early modern epic poetry at the undergraduate level has not grown easier for me over the last twenty years. The challenges that Renaissance epics pose for my students—their complex form and language, presumption of classical learning, and sheer length—compete with the other demands of students' literature classes. In addition, the relevance of these poems is not always clear: epic's apparent fealty to outdated political, class, and gender models can make the genre seem less useful for students who are committed to a progressive educational program. Partly in response to these challenges, I regularly include a unit on New World epics in my undergraduate and graduate courses on epic literature. In particular, I assign excerpts from English translations of Luís Vaz de Camões's *Os Lusíadas* (*The Lusiads*), from 1572; Alonso de Ercilla y Zúñiga's *La Araucana* (*The Araucaniad*), from 1569; and Gaspar Pérez de Villagrá's *Historia de la Nueva México* (*History of New Mexico*), from 1610.[1] Teaching these works, I have been able to make my courses on epic poetry more comparative, giving my students exposure to more linguistic and national traditions. More importantly, studying New World epics allows my students to explore more fully the epic genre's investment in discourses of colonialism, Orientalism, and race. In the case of Villagrá's poem, my students are also able to see their own location (El Paso) through the narrative and ideological lens of the genre.

Editions

A perennial challenge of teaching New World epics in English literature classes is the relative scarcity of high-quality, widely available translations. Unlike the classical Greek and Latin epics (by Homer, Virgil, and Ovid) and the Italian Renaissance epics (e.g., by Ludovico Ariosto and Torquato Tasso), the New World epics I teach are each represented by only one or two translations still in print, and these are of varying quality and usefulness. The most accessible and affordable of the three poems is Camões's *Os Lusíadas,* which is available in two English translations, both in paperback: William C. Atkinson's 1975 prose translation and Landeg White's 1997 verse translation. The White translation is the more useful of the two since, in addition to preserving Camões's eight-line stanzas, it includes maps, a bibliography, and substantial explanatory notes. Ercilla's *La Araucana* is represented by a single edition, the 1945 translation by Charles Maxwell Lancaster and Paul Thomas Manchester, reprinted in 2014. This version also preserves the eight-line stanza form, though without any glosses or explanatory notes. The lack of paratextual aids is a significant drawback, since the literalness of the translation often results in an awkward style that is not easy to read. The most impressive modern edition of the three is the 1992 verse translation of Villagrá's *Historia de la Nueva México* by Miguel Encinias, Alfred Rodríguez, and Joseph P. Sánchez. This version includes a substantive introduction, a historical overview, maps, illustrations, and a copious index. Most importantly, the edition provides side-by-side Spanish and English texts, with annotations for both, making it extremely useful for English, Spanish, and bilingual readers. The only drawbacks of this beautifully produced book are its cost and size: it is only available in hardcover, and its large pages make scanning and photocopying slightly difficult.

Approach and Suggested Selections

In both of the classes where I teach New World epics, I begin with a complete reading of Virgil's *Aeneid.* This allows me to introduce many of the

182 New World Epics

epic conventions that the later poets imitate and transform, including the *translatio imperii*, the notion that great empires naturally progress westward (or northwestward) over time. I explain to my students that in the early modern period this idea is accompanied by the *translatio studii*, the notion that the center of humanist learning likewise travels westward. This two-pronged theory of westward movement is especially poignant for Spanish and Portuguese writers, who often experienced an inferiority complex when comparing their humanist writers to those in Italy and France. Indeed, all three New World poets allude to this national sense of belatedness, and they compensate by asserting that their own national superiority is in exploration and military conquest.[2] For example, Camões boasts that Portugal is on a par with the Roman and Macedonian Empires at the same time that he laments the fact that his country lacks "men of culture" (*Lusíads* [White], canto 5, stanza 95).

I emphasize the notion of *translatio imperii* since it represents an ideology that was consciously used by New World epic poets—with varying degrees of success—to authorize their respective countries' imperial campaigns. In other words, *translatio imperii* makes colonial conquest appear natural and predetermined. Within this framework, I focus on three rhetorical strategies that these epics use to construct and reinforce an imperial ideology: a mapping of the world, a construction of racial difference, and a recording of linguistic difference. The New World poets employ all three strategies as a means of bolstering their imperial and poetic authority.

Typically, I spend about two weeks on New World epics, and so necessarily I assign selections from each poem. (The entire *Os Lusíadas* could reasonably be read in an advanced undergraduate class in a week, but the other two are much longer.) The following set of common selections fits easily into a two-week unit: Camões, *Os Lusíadas*, cantos 1, 5, 7, and 9–10; Ercilla, *La Araucana*, cantos 1 and 31–33; and Villagrá, *Historia de la Nueva México*, cantos 1–2, 12–18, and 33–34. I provide short synopses of the unassigned cantos so that students can get a sense of the larger narratives, though for the most part the excerpted cantos are fairly easy to follow on their own. I spend more time on Villagrá, partly because his poem is the most immediately relevant to my students in El Paso but also because he is the most interested in the problem of communication between Spanish colonists and indigenous Americans.

Camões's *Os Lusíadas*

Camões provides a good introduction to New World epics, since he explicitly evokes the sense of competition that is conventional in the genre; he also shows clearly the connection between poetic and imperial ambition. In the long, invocational passage that begins *Os Lusíadas*, Camões interweaves the achievements of historical Portuguese figures with the stature of his own poem:

> It would take Homer's lyre to commend
> Sufficiently Egas Moniz and Fuas Roupinho;
> For France's twelve peers, I give you
> The twelve of England led by Magriço,
> And likewise Vasco da Gama, whose genius
> Snatched renown from wandering Aeneas.
> (*Lusíads* [White], canto 1, stanza 12)

At first the competition seems to be with Homer and Virgil, but a closer reading of the stanza suggests that it has as much to do with Portuguese rivalries with France, England, and Italy. (As White notes in his edition of the poem, even today *Magriço*, a nickname for Álvaro Gonçalves Coutinho, is used as a rallying cry for Portugal's football team [Camões, *Lusíads* (White) 246].) Camões's reference to a "wandering Aeneas" is likewise a loaded term. My lessons on the *Aeneid* earlier in the semester incorporate David Quint's discussion of epic wandering (laid out in the first two chapters of his *Epic and Empire*), so by the time we get to Camões's poem my students are quick to pick up the implications of a wandering hero—that is, a hero who is distracted from political or spiritual duties. Camões shows here that he has no qualms about suggesting the superiority of his epic subject to Virgil's. Unlike Virgil's Aeneas, Camões implies, Vasco da Gama will not be distracted from his imperial mission to find an ocean route to India.

Camões's poem is especially useful for showing how a particular geographic mapping of the world can help to construct an emerging racial ideology. As the poem follows da Gama's journey around the African continent, it orients the reader so that the apparent extremities of the populated world coincide with peoples who are different from the Portuguese in religion, morals, cultural habits, technological advancement, and skin color. A stunning example of this narrative strategy appears in canto 5, when da Gama's men land in Saint Helena Bay near Cape Town:

184   New World Epics

We found we had long ago left behind
The southern Tropic of Capricorn,
Being between it and the Antarctic,
That least-known region of the world.
At this, my companions returning,
I saw a stranger with a black skin
They had captured, making his sweet harvest
Of honey from the wild bees in the forest.

He looked thunderstruck, like a man
Never placed in such an extreme;
He could not understand us, nor we him
Who seemed wilder than Polyphemus.
I began by showing him pure gold
The supreme metal of civilization,
Then fine silverware and hot condiment:
Nothing stirred in the brute the least excitement.
                    (*Lusíads* [White] 5.27–28)

As Quint has pointed out, this episode is based on an incident that actually took place during da Gama's campaign (116). It is thus instructive that Camões takes pains to connect da Gama's meeting with the Khoikhoi, an indigenous people in South Africa, to the Portuguese technologies in astronomy and geography (two stanzas earlier Camões refers to da Gama's use of the astrolabe). In this way the episode efficiently combines the issues of mapping, racial difference, and linguistic difference that I focus on in my unit on New World epics. Reading this passage aloud in class, I remind my students that Polyphemus is the name of the one-eyed Cyclops that threatens Odysseus in Homer's *Odyssey* and Aeneas's men in the *Aeneid*. I also point out that the European term for the Khoikhoi people (at least through the end of the twentieth century) was *Hottentot*, a word that also came to be used more generally to characterize African peoples as savage and barbaric. Camões's classical allusion to Polyphemus, "bruto Polifemo" in the original ("crude Polyphemus"; *Os Lusíadas* 5.28; my trans.), likewise reinforces an ideology that is both racializing and racist, insofar as it represents the Khoikhoi as ethnically different from the Portuguese and marks them as inferior and uncivilized. At this point I pose two larger questions to my students: Why is it so important for Camões and other New World epic poets to construct a racialized other in their versions of the *translatio imperii*, especially given that such racialization is largely absent from the *Aeneid*? And why does the episode with the Khoik-hoi appear almost at the exact center of the *Os Lusíadas*?

Ercilla's *La Araucana*

Given the sprawling nature of Ercilla's *La Araucana* and the fact that the only available English translation is not student-friendly, I generally spend less time on this poem than on the other two New World epics. However, I emphasize that Ercilla is a uniquely important figure for Spain's relation to *translatio imperii* and *translatio studii*. He received a solid humanist education at the royal court in Valladolid, and he was well acquainted with other leading Spanish humanists (López-Chávez 70). In addition, unlike Camões, Ercilla actually participated in the imperial campaign he wrote about: in this case, the Spanish military campaign in Chile from 1556 to 1563, which involved the violent suppression of Araucanian Indians. In the prologue to *La Araucana*, Ercilla writes that he was so struck by the bravery of the Araucanians that he was compelled to write an "authentic history" of them (4). I point out that Ercilla's claim to historicity has been the target of much criticism by modern readers, not least because he clearly uses poetic conventions in representing the conflict between Spaniards and Araucanians. This point leads naturally to some important discussion questions in class: Are history and poetry inherently incompatible, or even opposed to each other? What is gained or lost by using the conventions of epic to tell the story of a foreign people? Is it possible for a Spanish colonizer like Ercilla, however sympathetic to the Araucanians, to relate their history in any kind of truthful way? More often than not my students come to the conclusion that, while Ercilla's decision to write the history of the Araucanians in epic form may make them more legible or relatable to a European reader, the project ultimately amounts to an imposition of a European narrative onto indigenous peoples.

In terms of reading, I typically assign cantos 31 through 33, a fairly self-contained section in the poem that recounts a failed raid by a group of Araucanians (a revision of the nighttime raid in *Aeneid*, book 9); the story of Lauca, an Araucanian woman who has lost her husband; and Ercilla's revision of Virgil's account of Dido. It is in this part of the poem that Ercilla expresses most explicitly his ambivalence about his participation in the imperial project, repulsed as he is by the "havoc and excesses" of Spanish soldiers (canto 32 line 5). The meeting with Lauca prompts him

186   New World Epics

to expound on the "loyal faith of Indian women," whom he compares to "chaste Elissa Dido" (32.43). When one of his fellow soldiers accuses him of misreading Virgil, Ercilla angrily responds that Virgil's depiction of Dido is "opinionated slander" (32.45), pointing out that the historical Dido lived over a century after the fall of Troy. He then spends the next canto and a half giving the so-called true history of Dido, focusing on her persecution by her brother Pygmalion and suitor Yarbas. In this version of the story, Dido's suicide is a noble, self-sacrificial act that saves her city of Carthage, not the desperate last resort of a lovesick woman. This episode forms part of Ercilla's stated agenda to recover the histories of strong and noble women—histories that have been erased or distorted because of the chauvinism of male writers like Virgil.

In discussing these cantos, I ask my students whether Ercilla's representation of the Chilean campaign and of ancient history succeeds in producing an effective critique of empire—either of the Spanish treatment of the Araucanians or of the ideological (Virgilian) foundations of empire—as is sometimes claimed (Quint 159; Moore 47). Some students feel that Ercilla's sympathy with Araucanian women and Dido does indeed constitute such a critique, though others also suspect that Ercilla is not condemning colonialism per se. Instead, they suggest, he may be warning the Spanish against the use of excessive force, or he may be showing that the Spanish are better imperial rulers than their Roman (Italian) counterparts. He may also be thinking about his own literary reputation: from this perspective, Ercilla's recuperation of Dido is as much an attempt to compete with Virgil as it is an effort to set the historical record straight. This skepticism over Ercilla's motives is heightened when I tell my students that a similar revision of Virgil's Dido was made by Petrarch two hundred years earlier, when he attempted to write an epic poem of his own (*Africa*). In a class where we had previously read Ariosto's epic, a student also pointed out that Ercilla's defense of women in history sounds an awful lot like the one in *Orlando Furioso*.

Villagrá's *Historia de la Nueva México*

In my unit on New World epics, I devote more time to Villagrá's poem than to those by Camões or Ercilla, in part because the places that Villagrá describes are immediately recognizable to many of my students here in the American Southwest. In addition, the *Historia de la Nueva México* allows us to complicate the issues raised by the earlier two poems. Another reason for emphasizing Villagrá's poem has been its unique—and recently contested—place in literary history. Although educated at the University of Salamanca (like Ercilla), Villagrá was a Creole born in New Spain, and he participated in the New Mexico campaign led by Don Juan de Oñate. Thus, while some modern Spanish literary critics include the *Historia de la Nueva México* in the canon of early modern European or Spanish epics, some American critics make a case for the poem as American literature (Pérez-Linggi). Indeed, one of my colleagues in my department teaches the poem in his early American literature classes. This problem of classification gives my students an opportunity to talk about, and problematize, definitions of European and American literature, as well as Mexican American and Chicano literatures, and it often leads to broader discussions about canonization and disciplinary boundaries.

Like the other two epics, the *Historia de la Nueva México* also takes pains to map the world, though with a somewhat different aim. Whereas Camões and Ercilla emphasize the remoteness of the colonial regions, Villagrá makes a surprising case for the familiarity of New Mexico. In canto 1, after establishing Oñate as the Spanish Aeneas (and implying that he himself is the Spanish Virgil), Villagrá places the expedition in the area that is now El Paso, in a way that demonstrates his mastery of geographic and astronomical knowledge:

> Beneath the Arctic Pole, in height
> Some thirty-three degrees, which the same
> Are, we know, of sainted Jerusalem,
> Not without mystery and marvel great,
> Are spread, extended, sown, and overflow
> Some nations barbarous, remote
> From the bosom of the Church, where
> The longest day of all the year contains and has
> Some fourteen hours and a half when it arrives,
> The furious sun, at the rising of Cancer,
> Through whose zenith he doth usually pass
> The image of Andromeda and Perseus,
> Whose constellation always influences
> The quality of Venus and Mercury. (canto 1, lines 49–62)

Most of my students (many of whom grew up in El Paso) are surprised to learn that El Paso has almost the exact same latitude as Jerusalem. Villagrá uses this convenient geographic coincidence to reinforce the missionary, Christianizing purpose of the expedition but also to make

188   New World Epics

New Mexico appear more familiar to his Spanish readers. He may do this partly because of the fact that he was from New Spain, and so his tracing of ancient Mexican ruins may have seemed analogous to the search for ancient ruins in Europe. In any case, the effect is that the Spanish campaign in New Mexico appears to be something that Europeans have done before.

Villagrá's tendency to domesticate the New World also influences the writer's representation of indigenous Americans. Like Camões and Ercilla, Villagrá represents the American Indians as racially and linguistically different from the Spanish—but not as incomprehensible. Two of his frequent terms for the Indians are *alárabes* (Arabs) and *moros* (Moors), which cast them as the other but also (from the Spanish perspective) as familiar (see 1.52). Villagrá's reasons for doing this are manifold. For one thing, by equating Indians with Moors, he suggests that the Spanish conquest of New Mexico will be a replay of Spain's expulsion of the Moors. In fact, in canto 16 Villagrá records a performance of a *Moros y Cristianos* (Moors and Christians) play, a type of drama that had been ritualized in Spain as a way of commemorating the Reconquista. Moreover, by casting Indians as Moors, Villagrá also suggests a method for comprehending indigenous languages. In the sixteenth century, European humanists had turned their attention to the study of Arabic, even producing translations of the Qur'an. Villagrá suggests that a similar humanistic expertise will be needed for Spanish interests in the New World (while he frequently puts on display his own humanist credentials). Thus, while he often reminds his reader of the strangeness of indigenous speech, he points out the presence of translators in the poem. It is not a coincidence that the first indigenous persons named in the poem, Milco and Mompil, are those with whom the Spaniards are able to communicate (12.416–64).

Inevitably our class discussion centers on the final cantos (30–34) of the *Historia de la Nueva México*, in which Villagrá recounts the Battle of Acoma. This was a brutal conflict that ended with the utter destruction of Acoma Pueblo and the mutilation of the surviving Acoman men. The violence enacted by Oñate's soldiers in this case was one of a string of incidents that ultimately led to Oñate's removal as governor of New Mexico, and the Battle of Acoma remains to this day a subject of debate in the region (including over how to name it). It is thus all the more surprising that Oñate is almost entirely absent in the last cantos of the *Historia de la Nueva México*, an exclusion that some critics have read as a sign of Villagrá's ambivalence about the Spanish campaign. Instead of focusing on his Spanish Aeneas, Villagrá instead ends the poem with the figures of Tempal and

Cotumbo, two Acomans who deliver a searing curse to the Spaniards before committing suicide in order to avoid conversion to Christianity. The strangeness of the poem's ending prompts my students to ask: Whose history is Villagrá attempting to record at the end of the poem? If an epic poem is understood as a kind of literary monument, then who is ultimately being monumentalized here?

A few years ago when teaching the *Historia de la Nueva México*, I found that the questions of colonialism and monumentalization had an especially immediate relevance for my students at the University of Texas, El Paso. At that time the El Paso International Airport had just installed a large, conspicuous statue of Oñate in front of the airport, a move that had sparked vigorous local debates over Oñate's legacy and the appropriateness of monuments to Spanish colonizers (these debates were concurrent with those in other parts of the country over Confederate statues). Ultimately the statue was renamed but not removed. My students were passionately invested in the issue, and our reading of the *Historia de la Nueva México* enabled them to situate the debates over the Oñate statue within the larger context of cultural monuments and colonial historiography. While Villagrá's epic, like those of Camões and Ercilla, contains disturbing and offensive representations of indigenous peoples, my students for the most part do not respond by suggesting that we ignore these complex works. Rather, studying these poems has given my students purchase in addressing historical inequities, and it gives them a unique entry point into debates about the legacy of colonialism that have been taking place for centuries—and that continue to take place today.

Notes

1. Although *Os Lusíadas* is not technically a New World epic, since it takes place in Africa and India, it was an important model for many New World epics and is regularly studied alongside them. A more accurate, though less wieldy, term for these poems by Camões, Ercilla, and Villagrá would be *early modern imperial epics*.

2. This gesture is itself an imitation of the *Aeneid*: in book 6, the spirit of Anchises tells Aeneas that, while the Greeks will retain superiority in the arts, the Romans are destined for imperial supremacy (Virgil 6.847–53).

Works Cited

Camões, Luís Vaz de. *Os Lusíadas*. Edited by Frank Pierce, Oxford UP, 1973.

——. *The Lusiads*. Translated by William C. Atkinson, Penguin Books, 1975.

190   New World Epics

——. *The Lusíads*. Translated by Landeg White, Oxford UP, 1997.

Ercilla y Zúñiga, Alonso de. *The Araucaniad*. 1945. Translated by Charles Maxwell Lancaster and Paul Thomas Manchester, Vanderbilt UP, 2014.

López-Chávez, Celia. *Epics of Empire and Frontier: Alonso de Ercilla and Gaspar de Villagrá as Spanish Colonial Chroniclers*. U of Oklahoma P, 2016.

Moore, Cyrus. *Love, War, and Classical Tradition in the Early Modern Transatlantic World: Alonso de Ercilla and Edmund Spenser*. ACMRS Press, 2014.

Pérez-Linggi, Sandra. "Gaspar Pérez de Villagrá: 'Criollo' or Chicano in the Southwest?" *Hispania*, vol. 88, no. 4, Dec. 2005, pp. 666–76.

Quint, David. *Epic and Empire: Politics and Generic Form from Virgil to Milton*. Princeton UP, 1993.

Villagrá, Gaspar Pérez de. *Historia de la Nueva México, 1610*. Translated by Miguel Encinias et al., U of New Mexico P, 1992.

Virgil. *Aeneid*. Translated by Allen Mandelbaum, Bantam Classic, 2004.

Angelica A. Duran

"Thou Hast Seen One World Begin and End": Worldmaking with *Paradise Lost*

Representations of acts of creation or worldmaking are particularly rich touchstones for teaching John Milton's *Paradise Lost*.[1] After all, this early modern English epic was created during the first era in which human agents traveled the whole circuit of the earth and grappled with new conceptual realities. This context perhaps accounts for the epic's 128 uses of "world" and "worlds."[2] Further, Milton's choice to center the epic narrative on the founding of humanity in "the world" (*PL* 1.3) rather than of the writer's native England results in an absorbing set of textual loci to build a "vast design," as one of the epic's earliest readers, the poet and politician Andrew Marvell, well recognized (line 3).[3]

The "vast" yet immediately relevant topic of worldmaking—or critical thinking—can spur instructors and students to examine collaboratively the worldmaking required of all cohesive long narratives, particularly epic ones. Through discussion, research, and minor or major writing assignments within a one-to-two-week teaching unit, students can acquire content knowledge and practice interpretative skills and methodologies through Milton's epic world of allusions.[4] Equally important, instructors can define the value and strategies—or, in twenty-first-century academic parlance, outcomes and methodologies—of the unit as they tap into the

192 *Paradise Lost*

excitement, destabilization, and possibilities of Milton's cohesive fictional worlds and posit diverse worldviews through foregrounding the literary building blocks of characters, images, narrator, and settings.

Instructors are invited to adapt the handouts and methodologies discussed depending on if they assign all of *Paradise Lost* for a reading-intensive unit or only one or two books plus the original Arguments, or synopses, for a close-reading unit—both approaches can work equally well.[5] This essay provides examples of just a few key passages, but instructors can and should select from any number of rich passages, from book 1, in which the epic narrator lays out a poetic thesis about mythical forces affecting humans—not simply Adam and Eve but also the epic narrator, biblical figures, and readers—to the last two hundred lines of the concluding book, which contains Adam and Eve's introduction to the fallen "world . . . all before them" (*PL* 12.646). Important factors in selecting the specific readings are the other texts on the syllabus, the instructor's areas of interest, campus resources including nearby special collections and campus events, and students' specializations, especially in institutions in which the course fulfills world culture, intercultural communication, or humanities requirements across disciplines.

The two following sections position *Paradise Lost* as a central node of textual, material, and digital resources focused on the topic of worldmaking. Each section offers discussion questions and miniassignments, in which pairs of students, or collaborating scholars, as I call them, are assigned to spend thirty to forty-five minutes of preparation before sharing their work in class or on a digital discussion board; a disciplinary and a general learning outcome are also specified for each question.[6] The first miniassignment for each question requires no additional resources beyond the text, the second requires an external resource, and the third involves a digital product. The questions and miniassignments are applicable to a variety of pedagogical circumstances, from low-tech (pencil and paper) to high-tech (rapid digital), in-person to asynchronous virtual classrooms, and are meant to be provocative since they cannot be comprehensive. This unit can lead to module projects that foster students' own making of expository, compare-and-contrast, or argumentative papers or multimedia projects; two examples are proposed at the end of each section. This organizational model demonstrates the agency that instructors and students can enact within the academic worlds or systems that many of us experience at the beginning of the twenty-first century.[7]

The Renaissance Literary World and Literary System

In the opening invocation of *Paradise Lost*, the epic narrator refers to evocative locales like "Eden" (*PL* 1.4), "Oreb," "Sinai" (1.7), "Chaos," "Sion hill" (1.10), "Siloa's brook" (1.11), and "th'Aonian mount" in close-up and panorama (1.15), in search of "my advent'rous song" that boldly "pursues / Things unattempted yet in prose or rhyme" (*PL* 1.13, 1.15–16). It is certainly a bold claim, but not a new one, since it is, in fact, an English translation of the same claim in the invocation of Ludovico Ariosto's Italian romance epic *Orlando Furioso* (*The Frenzy of Orlando*; 1.2), itself not entirely new—yet still entirely fresh—since it is, in turn, a continuation of a claim in Matteo Maria Boiardo's *Orlando Innamorato* (*Orlando in Love*) that its account of prodigious deeds is the most superlative "that verse or prose have ever told" (2.30.1).[8] Thus, worldly and otherworldly places are tethered in a literary system that enables them to accrue social and intensely passionate meaning in what Jo Ann Cavallo has called "the world beyond," and what is also a world "within."[9] The following sections are designed to most effectively enable these and related issues to unfold. Guided discussions and actitivites can energize intepretations about physical places and literary settings, "the general locale[s], historical time[s], and social circumstances in which the action of a narrative or dramatic work occurs" ("Setting" 294).

Question Set 1

How does this at once playful and serious one-upmanship constitute a convention within the larger conventions of proems and invocations in epics?[10] And how do one-upmanship and epic proems, invocations, and narrators fundamentally insert the human into the imaginative world-making at the onset of epics and interspersed throughout *Paradise Lost* (books 1, 3, 7, and 9)? How do two or more allusions affect each other? For this last question, and if the *Odyssey* or the *Iliad* is also on the syllabus (Homer, *Odyssey* and Iliad), students might consider the basis for Milton's being known as the Homer of Christianity.

Miniassignments

Practice an oral reading of one of the invocations of *Paradise Lost* or another epic (in English translation or the original, depending on students' skill sets), utilizing scansion, dictionaries, or the instructor to understand and pronounce unfamiliar words and to shape an engaging oral reading.[11]

194   *Paradise Lost*

Listen to an audio recording of one or all the invocations of *Paradise Lost*, from *Librivox* (Milton, *Paradise Lost* [Copeland]) or Hugh Richmond's *Milton Revealed* website, then describe two matters that emerge from experiencing the invocation or invocations aurally rather than textually; or select two footnotes from an invocation on the website *The John Milton Reading Room* or in the assigned material book, then read the relevant section of the source text and explain the deeper meaning to be derived from the aural experience or contextual information.

Create a six-degrees-of-separation chain, word cloud, or other digital audio file or visual, with explanatory commentary, based on the "Epic Beginnings" handout (Duran, "John Milton, *Paradise Lost*").[12]

Learning Outcomes

Question set 1 and the above miniassignments give due attention to prosody—since "prose or rhyme" (*PL* 1.16) foregrounds the matter of genre and language and, by extension, the human voice and cognition in representing worldmaking (the process) and worldviews (temporary or enduring ideologies)—and they foster recognition of how intermedial or multimodal practices cooperate with and respond to human understanding.

Question Set 2

What characteristics does Milton's epic narrator possess in book 1, and which of them are most relevant to the narrator's represented travels? What characteristics are drawn out and added to the narrator and the travels in the invocations in books 3, 7, and 9? What characteristics of a "fit audience" does the epic narrator imply or assume (*PL* 7.31)? What places are mentioned in each invocation, and how do they factor into the epic narrator's or the audiences' accruing characteristics?

Miniassignments

Make a chart, drawing, grid, or other representation to showcase your answers to any one of the questions in question set 2, then assess whether the characteristics are complementary or contradictory, affiliative or unattractive.

Read a brief biography of Milton from an open-access resource, such as *Wikipedia*, or limited-access one, such as *The Oxford National Biography*, or both, then assess which ascribed characteristics are shared by the author and epic narrator or what information overlaps in the two resources.

Create a digital map of the places in one or more of the invocations from books 1, 3, 7, and 9 in *Paradise Lost*, taking careful direction from the text and its footnotes and innovating on how to represent such unearthly settings as Hell, Chaos, and Heaven.[13]

Learning Outcomes

Question set 2 and the miniassignments focus on the strategies that the epic narrator uses to create a sense of coherence, authority, and affiliation or alterity with readers—and that have contributed to this epic's position in world literature—and on the tactics that readers, from the past to today, use to assess the epic narrator and author. These questions and miniassignments prompt students to understand the staying power of epic conventions and, by extension, other traditional discursive and representational structures, literary or otherwise.

Module Projects

The first module project treats the epic narrator or other characters in *Paradise Lost* as possessing identities and agency or constituting round characters—that is, characters with "particular moral, intellectual, and emotional qualities" expressed by "their speech and actions" in their settings ("Character" 33)—perhaps with an eye to the construction of gender. If the project's focus is on women characters, students could consider Sin and Eve in *Paradise Lost*, Angelica and Alcina in *Orlando Furioso*, and Florimel and Britomart in *The Fairie Queene*.

The second module project considers the network of temporal-regional cultures surrounding *Paradise Lost*, which might be limited to textual allusions, for example Italy, and thus to *Orlando Furioso* and *Orlando Innamorato* or to the "Tuscan artist," "Galileo" (*PL* 1.288, 5.262). Galileo is an important figure for considerations of human perspective, whether scientific or artistic, which can be explored in his "The Starry Messenger" (21–58) or "Letters on Sunspots" (59–144). This module project could also be limited to twentieth-century influences, thus to either Bertolt Brecht's play *Life of Galileo* or the folk rock song "Galileo," by the Indigo Girls, to draw out modern considerations about the figure of Galileo, or to the edition of *Paradise Lost* with extensive annotations by the science fiction author and chemistry professor Isaac Asimov (Milton, *Asimov's Annotated* Paradise Lost), to animate conversations about the connections between the arts and sciences or the modern genre of science fiction.[14]

196 *Paradise Lost*

Worldmaking through Storytelling

Epics are narratives mimetically conveyed through and about storytelling.[15] Like so many epics—for example, the *Odyssey*, in which Odysseus hears Demodocus sing the story of the Trojan War in which he fought (book 8)—*Paradise Lost* inscribes episodes of storytelling: the lead up to and harrowing account by the half-woman, half-serpent Sin to her father Satan of her birth from the left side of his head, their sexual union, then equally startling events before and after her arrival at the gates of Hell (2.629–814); Eve's loving iteration to Adam, overheard by Satan, of her creation and their marriage (4.440–504); the "full relation" of the war in Heaven by the "Divine instructor" and archangel Raphael to Adam and Eve (5.556, 5.546, 5.505–6.912), then "the work of Creation" to Adam (book 7 Argument, 7.70–640); Adam's account to Raphael of Adam's creation, naming of the animals, and marriage (8.203–560); and the archangel Michael's audiovisual account of future human history through the Noachian Flood then oral account through the Second Coming (11.370–901, 12.1–551). This essay takes its title from a passage in this last account, "Thus thou hast seen one world begin and end" (12.6), because it so succinctly grasps the relentless association of settings and agency in worldmaking. Over the centuries, readers have paid special attention to the multimedia of storytelling in *Paradise Lost* because of the fact that Milton became fully blind in 1654 and therefore spoke the verses of the epic, first published in 1667, to amanuenses, family members, and friends.[16]

My examples are broad when possible but focused on book 7, containing Raphael's story of the Creation, when specificity is warranted. This book is especially fruitful for considering the alliance of the natural world and the word of God, especially when Genesis 1–3 is on the syllabus and when students are encouraged to dip into the end of book 2 and beginning of book 3, when readers view "[t]his pendent world" for the first time as Satan makes his way there (*PL* 2.1052).[17]

Question Set 3

What kind of worldview does this embedded story express? Specifically, what elements of the social and physical world does it refer to and to what effect? What phrases indicate the characteristics of fictional worldmaking through storytelling?

Miniassignments

List the sequence of events, making sure to mention the settings, or retell a portion of the story as a graphic novel, lyric poem, or scene in a draft of a novel or young adult short story.[18]

Look up the categories of flora represented in the epic's third day of Creation (*PL* 7.307–38) in John Gerard's *The Herball*, animals created on the sixth day (*PL* 7.449–504) in Karen Edwards's *Milton's Reformed Animals*, or metals and metallurgy involved in the rebel angels' construction and use of Pandemonium in Hell (*PL* 1.670–798), then hypothesize how these elements operate in the story.[19]

Compile a digital visual that includes at least three illustrations of the same poetic scene from three different cited sources. Particularly rich sources are the twelve frontispieces in the first illustrated edition of *Paradise Lost* (Milton, Paradise Lost: *A Poem*); the fifty book illustrations by Gustave Doré (Milton, *Milton's* Paradise Lost); the anglophone translation Paradise Lost: *A Graphic Novel* (Auladell) of Pablo Auladell's hispanophone graphic novel El Paraíso perdido *basado en la obra de John Milton*; and the edited collection *Global Milton and Visual Art* (Duran and Murgia). Then assess how these images accurately translate or creatively innovate the written text.

Learning Outcomes

Question set 3 and the miniassignments track the building blocks of this narrative, as a case study for epic narrative more generally, and they build an understanding of intermedial systems or networks, particularly the role of collaboration in these systems, such as the collaborative voices represented in epic texts and epic tasks.

Question Set 4

Given that the source text for *Paradise Lost* is Genesis 1–3, what techniques does Milton utilize to expand the sparse narrative of the Old Testament, from direct quotation to wholesale invention? In particular, how do the characteristics and roles of God the Father and the Son in books 3, 7, or 9–10 of *Paradise Lost* resonate with God's role in Genesis 1–3? What is the relationship between the Creation by God the Father and the Son—in Genesis, *Paradise Lost*, or both—and the creative acts of storytelling by the various characters in *Paradise Lost*, especially given the emphasis on the divine as "Word" (*Bible*, John 1.1)? A related set of questions can be asked about the relation of imperialism and colonialism with religion, founded on scriptures and social codes, in this and other epics on the syllabus.[20]

198 *Paradise Lost*

Miniassignments

Sketch one passage or scene from *Paradise Lost*; aim to provide enough detail so that fellow students can guess the passage or scene.

Select either Genesis 1–3 or a storytelling scene from another epic and determine how various categories of imagery (visual, auditory, olfactory, tactile, gustatory, and kinesthetic) generate and maintain audience interest.

Given Milton's description of *Paradise Lost* as a "song" and his use of musical images, create a digital soundscape that includes the auditory imagery from a passage or scene, anything from the "Dorian mood / Of flutes and soft recorders" to the sound of the "night-warbling bird," the nightingale (1.13, 1.550–51, 5.40).[21]

Learning Outcomes

Question set 4 and the miniassignments reinforce the varied experiential, cognitive, and imaginative tools reflected in and honed through illustration, imagery, and intertextuality—components of the sibling arts of poetry and painting—and by Milton's readers, including students and artists. These questions and miniassignments foster students to define and consider the qualities of innovation, reformation, renewal, and revision.

Module Projects

The first module project for question sets 3 and 4 considers the interaction of characters and settings in *Paradise Lost*, with an eye to their qualitative and quantitative differences and similarities.

The second module project considers the representation of the ability to apprehend, comprehend, organize, and communicate fulsomely situations and events as heroic or not heroic—within the context of *Paradise Lost* or the epic's original literary, political, or religious context or in relation to today's global world or students' campus life.

The multiperspectival descriptions of the world of *Paradise Lost*—constituted by events, characters, settings, and poetic strategies—can resonate with students' experiences of ambivalence and instability and with the constant development of students' personal roles as scholars and global citizens. The prompts in this brief essay aim to enable instructors to relentlessly consider and readily meet capacious learning outcomes that matter to them, to ever-changing disciplines, and, frankly, to humankind; such an approach is only fitting for our deserving students and the equally deserving primary text of *Paradise Lost*.[22]

Notes

1. For early modern worldmaking, see Ramachandran, especially pp. 1–21, 182–220. For a historically panoramic discussion of aesthetic worlds, see Halyot. For the distinct aesthetic world of Milton's ten-book *Paradise Lost* of 1667 and the twelve-book *Paradise Lost* of 1674, see Lieb and Shawcross. For other rich topics, themes, and methodologies for teaching *Paradise Lost*, see Herman, *Approaches*.

2. Including the Arguments at the beginning of each book, there are six uses in book 1, twelve in book 2, seventeen in book 3, seven in book 4, nine in book 5, two in book 6, fifteen in book 7, six in book 8, four in book 9, twenty-four in book 10, thirteen in book 11, and thirteen in book 12. All citations to Milton's *Paradise Lost* (*PL*) are from the edition edited by John Leonard, which has excellent annotations and a pleasing format and is inexpensive and extensively available.

3. A stable, reliable digital *Paradise Lost* is on the website *The John Milton Reading Room*. Stanley Fish's *Surprised by Sin* remains useful on Milton's construction of imagined readers as fallen.

4. By *teaching unit*, I mean a series of readings, class discussions, and assignments on *Paradise Lost*. Two to five units constitute a module that fulfills a number of learning outcomes, and three to seven modules can be ably integrated into a fifteen-week semester.

5. The Arguments are in Milton, *Paradise Lost* [Leonard], and on the website *The John Milton Reading Room*. Instructors who have the library resources and interest in promoting digital archival practice can provide students with instructions to access digital copies from such resources as *Early English Books Online* or *The British Library Digital Collections*.

6. I thank the Purdue Center for Instructional Excellence and my collegial teacher-scholars for sharing their course materials and positively affecting my academic world.

7. For Milton's historically bound educational proposal, see Milton, "Of Education."

8. Ariosto 1.2; Boiardo 2.30.1.

9. "[W]ithin" refers to Michael's pointed term for the worldmaking of a "paradise within thee, happier far" that Adam and his descendants can achieve in the fallen world (*PL* 12.587).

10. See Duran, "John Milton, *Paradise Lost*," and go to the "Epic Beginnings" section.

11. *The Oxford English Dictionary* is useful especially for identifying historical changes in the meanings of words. *Merriam-Webster* provides current pronunciations of words, including for some proper names, such as "Zephyrus" (*PL* 5.16).

12. For familiarity chains in relation to Milton, see Greteman; Herman, "'Still Paying.'" Students may be aware of any relationship-mapping software and apps that are readily available and particularly useful to their cohort.

13. If library resources allow, the instructor can assign the commentary or footnotes from Milton, *Asimov's Annotated* Paradise Lost, or from any of the

200 *Paradise Lost*

editions listed in the "Major Editions" section of Evans, "Select Bibliography" (235–69). What I call an invocation in book 9 may be classified as a proem. For further reading for students or instructors on places and settings in the invocations, see Manguel and Guadalupi, which does not have entries on Chaos, Heaven, or Hell but provides a good approach and other examples.

14. Snow's *The Two Cultures* remains a useful touchstone for the divisions and overlap of the quadrivium and trivium, or today's STEM and humanities or liberal arts.

15. For a useful definition of *epic*, see Cavallo's introduction to this volume and "Epic."

16. For integrating into the classroom the genre of illustrations of blind Milton dictating, see Duran, "John Milton and Disabilities Studies."

17. The opening of the Gospel of John aligns God's speaking the world into being from Genesis and the new world inaugurated by Jesus in the First Coming, especially in the verses "[i]n the beginning was the Word, and the Word was with God, and the Word was God" and "the Word was made flesh, and dwelt among us" (*Bible*, John 1.1, 1.14).

18. For graphic novels based on *Paradise Lost*, see Auladell, Paraíso perdido and Paradise Lost; Milton, Paradise Lost: *A Graphic Novel*. For a vibrant analogue, see Mya Gosling's web comic *Good Tickle Brain*.

19. For the introduction to Edward's bestiary, see Edwards, "Milton's Reformed Animals." The remainder of the bestiary can be found in the following issues of *Milton Quarterly*: "A–C," vol. 39, no. 4, 2005, pp. 183–292; "D–F," vol. 40, no. 2, 2006, pp. 99–187; "G," vol. 40, no. 4, 2006, pp. 263–91; "H–K," vol. 41, no. 2, 2007, pp. 79–147; "L," vol. 41, no. 4, 2007, pp. 223–56; "M–O," vol. 42, no. 2, 2008, pp. 113–60; "P–R," vol. 42, no. 4, 2008, pp. 253–308; "S," vol. 43, no. 2, 2009, pp. 89–141; and "T–Z," vol. 43, no. 4, 2009, pp. 341–403. For further reading on the natural world, see Edwards, *Milton*; on mining in Hell and on Earth, see Cummins.

20. For further reading on this cluster of topics, see Quint; Evans, *Milton's Imperial Epic*. See also V. Turner and Ortiz in this volume.

21. The epic as song can be found readily through a keyword search for "song" on the website *The John Milton Reading Room* and for synonyms, as well as other auditory imagery, for example, "warning voice," "Heav'nly choirs," the "sound / Of leaves and fuming rills," and "Th' Archangel trumpet" (*PL* 4.1, 4.711, 5.5–6, 6.203).

22. For further reading, see Duran, "John Milton, *Paradise Lost*," and go to the "Bibliography" section.

Works Cited

Abrams, M. H., and Geoffrey Galt Harpham. *A Glossary of Literary Terms.* 8th ed., Thomson Wadsworth, 2005.

Ariosto, Ludovico. *Orlando Furioso (The Frenzy of Orlando)*. Translated by Barbara Reynolds, Penguin, 1975. 2 vols.

Auladell, Pablo. *John Milton's* Paradise Lost: *A Graphic Novel*. Translated by Ángel Gurría, Pegasus Books, 2017.

———. El paraíso perdido *basado en la obra de John Milton*. Sexto Piso, 2015.

The Bible. Edited by Robert Carroll and Stephen Prickett, Authorized King James Version, Oxford UP, 2008.

Boiardo, Matteo Maria. *Orlando Innamorato: Orlando in Love*. Translated by Charles Stanley Ross, U of California P, 1989.

Brecht, Bertolt. *Life of Galileo*. 1943. Grove Press, 1966.

Cavallo, Jo Ann. *The World beyond Europe in the Romance Epics of Boiardo and Ariosto*. U of Toronto P, 2013.

"Character and Characterization." Abrams and Harpham, pp. 33–35.

Cummins, Juliet Lucy. "The Ecology of *Paradise Lost*." Duran, *Concise Companion*, pp. 161–77.

Duran, Angelica, editor. *A Concise Companion to Milton*. Rev. ed., Wiley-Blackwell, 2011.

———. "John Milton, *Paradise Lost*." *World Epics*, edblogs.columbia.edu/worldepics/project/milton-paradise-lost/. Accessed 1 May 2021.

———. "John Milton and Disabilities Studies in Literature Courses." *Journal of Literary and Cultural Disability Studies*, vol. 6, no. 3, 2012, pp. 327–39.

Duran, Angelica, and Mario Murgia, editors. *Global Milton and Visual Art*. Lexington Books, 2021.

Edwards, Karen. *Milton and the Natural World: Science and Poetry in "Paradise Lost."* Cambridge UP, 1999.

———. "Milton's Reformed Animals: An Early Modern Bestiary: Introduction." *Milton Quarterly*, vol. 39, no. 3, 2005, pp. 121–31.

"Epic." Abrams and Harpham, pp. 81–84.

Evans, J. Martin. *Milton's Imperial Epic:* Paradise Lost *and the Discourse of Colonialism*. Cornell UP, 1996.

———. "Select Bibliography: Much Arguing, Much Writing, Many Opinions." Duran, *Concise Companion*, pp. 235–69.

Fish, Stanley. *Surprised by Sin: The Reader in* Paradise Lost. 2nd ed., U of California P, 1971.

Galileo. *Discoveries and Opinions of Galileo*. Edited and translated by Stillman Drake, Random House, 1957.

Gerard, John. *The Herball; or, Generall History of Plantes*. 1597. Dover Publications, 1975.

Greteman, Blaine. "Milton and the Early Modern Social Network: The Case of the *Epitaphium Damonis*." *Milton Quarterly*, vol. 49, no. 2, 2015, pp. 79–95.

Halyot, Eric. *On Literary Worlds*. Oxford UP, 2012.

202 *Paradise Lost*

Herman, Peter C., editor. *Approaches to Teaching Milton's* Paradise Lost. 2nd ed., Modern Language Association of America, 2012.

———. "'Still Paying, Still to Owe': Credit, Community, and Small Data in Shakespeare and Milton." *Digital Milton*, edited by David Currell and Islam Issa, Palgrave Macmillan, 2018, pp. 153–78.

Homer. *The* Iliad *of Homer*. Translated by Richmond Lattimore, U of Chicago P, 1992.

———. *The Odyssey*. Translated by Emily Wilson, W. W. Norton, 2018.

Indigo Girls. *Galileo*. 1992. Epic, 2000.

Lieb, Michael, and John T. Shawcross, editors. "Paradise Lost: *A Poem Written in Ten Books*": *Essays on the 1667 First Edition*. Duquesne UP, 2007.

Manguel, Alberto, and Gianni Guadalupi. *The Dictionary of Imaginary Places*. Harcourt Brace, 2000.

Marvell, Andrew. "On Mr. Milton's *Paradise Lost*." 1674. *Poetry @ Princeton*, 2021, poetry.princeton.edu/2008/12/09/on-mr-miltons-paradise-lost/.

Milton, John. *Asimov's Annotated* Paradise Lost. Edited by Isaac Asimov, Doubleday, 1974.

———. *Milton's* Paradise Lost. Illustrated by Gustave Doré, Cassell, Petter, Galpin, 1866?

———. "Of Education." *1643–1648*, edited by Ernest Sirluck, Yale UP, 1959, pp. 362–415. Vol. 2 of *The Complete Prose Works of John Milton*.

———. *Paradise Lost*. Narrated by Thomas A. Copeland. *Librivox*, 29 Nov. 2014, librivox.org/paradise-lost-by-john-milton-2/.

———. *Paradise Lost*. Edited by John Leonard, Penguin Books, 2000.

———. Paradise Lost: *A Graphic Novel*. Illustrated by Lucas Pastorfield-Li, Blurb, 2015.

———. Paradise Lost: *A Poem in Twelve Books*. Miles Flesher for Jacob Tonson, 1688.

Quint, David. *Epic and Empire: Politics and Generic Form from Virgil to Milton*. Princeton UP, 1993.

Ramachandran, Ayesha. *The Worldmakers: Global Imagining in Early Modern Europe*. U of Chicago P, 2015.

"Setting." Abrams and Harpham, pp. 294.

Snow, C. P. *The Two Cultures and a Second Look*. 2nd ed., Cambridge UP, 1964.

"Zephyrus, *N*." *Merriam-Webster*, 2022, www.merriam-webster.com/dictionary/Zephyrus.

Part IV

Oral-Derived Epics in the Sixteenth through Nineteenth Centuries

Nathan C. Henne

Stretching the Boundaries of Epic: *Popol Wuj*, Maya Literature, and Coloniality

The Maya K'iche' *Popol Wuj*[1]—often referred to as the oldest book in the Americas—presents both significant challenges and unique rewards to Western-educated students and to instructors of epics courses. The complications stem mostly from the fact that *Popol Wuj* evolved in complete isolation from European cultures and doesn't follow the logic or literary conventions that students in anglophone countries are used to. Of course, the work's differences are why it's worth reading and why it has so much to offer in terms of understanding alternative ways of seeing and living in the world today. Before getting into how best to bring these qualities of the work to the fore in a comparative epics course, instructors need to understand some unique aspects of both the historical and the literary context of *Popol Wuj* in Mesoamerica. These contexts are important not only because literature has such deep roots in pre-Contact Maya history but also because literature has played such a nefarious role in the colonization of the Indigenous Americas.

Historical and Cultural Context

Maya literature (and the people who wrote it) did not fare well upon first contact with the Western world early in the sixteenth century. The Spanish

206 *Popol Wuj*

armies and the clerics that followed them burned thousands of Maya books and whole Maya libraries in what is present-day Guatemala—where *Popol Wuj* was written—and Mexico (see Henne 38–39, 192–93 for specifics). Spanish officials outlawed writing in the hieroglyphic script the Maya had been using for almost two millennia, and most of the Maya intellectuals who read and wrote their ancient script either died of the rampant European plagues—as did about half of the general population before the Spanish even set foot in Guatemala—or were killed in the implementation of coloniality (directly, as punishment for heresy, or indirectly through forced labor). In all, about ninety percent of the Maya population—made up of several independent groups that spoke different languages—died in the first hundred years of contact (i.e., by about the end of the sixteenth century).

In the centuries that followed, the only known pre-Contact Maya books that survived the fires and other destruction were spirited off to Europe, where they now bear European names like Madrid Codex and Dresden Codex and sit in European museums. For the 450 years after contact, the Maya—one of only three cultures in the world that independently developed a comprehensive writing system—along with the rest of Mesoamerica were forced into illiteracy by race-based colonial policies (following the genocide described above). What's more, the Maya—a people with almost two thousand years of literary history—were portrayed to the outside world as barbaric in order to justify the civilizing and Christianizing mission of the European colonizers.

Several different Maya peoples survived the initial genocide and fought against all odds during the long colonial and so-called postcolonial period to keep specific concepts of their cosmovisions[2] alive in their material practice and in their Maya languages through the complex oral tradition that had flourished alongside the sophisticated Maya writing system (Acuerdo 71). Unlike classical philosophers and Renaissance (and, later, Enlightenment) Europeans—whom classical philosophy influenced so deeply—the Maya had never thought of writing and orality as binary opposites, much less thought of writing as a litmus test that could draw a stark line between prehistoric and civilized peoples. However, Europeans eventually justified their colonial power and the marginalization of Indigenous peoples in the Americas—at least in part—on the supposed fact that Indigenous Americans did not have writing (and, by extension, did not have history) and thus could not progress in the linear way modernity required to fuel the development imperative (Mignolo 306; Quijano 552–53; Arias 52).

By the end of the first century of the colonial project, most people in the new Spanish-controlled urban centers of power had bought the official story that pre-Contact Maya writing had been no more than a rudimentary pictographic system, incapable of the abstractions that alphabetic writing made possible. Since the Indigenous intellectuals—who knew better—had been silenced or were dead by this time, it was exceedingly difficult to pass down their knowledge of their writing system to the next generations. By the end of the second century of coloniality, a period of at least a couple of centuries began in which no one knew how to read much more than the numbers in the old hieroglyphic script.

In the last few decades, scholars have finally—and relatively rapidly—overcome those centuries of ignorance and figured out how to read the Maya hieroglyphics. It is now crystal clear that the Maya hieroglyphic system was phonetically based and that its surviving ideographic elements were stylistic choices among several options available to creative scribes. Unlike what scholars originally thought, the Maya writing system is as capable as any modern European alphabet of capturing any abstract notion that can be spoken (even made-up words). Because Maya hieroglyphics have a phonetic foundation, most of their graphic symbols represent the sounds of syllables (phonemes), like the combination of a consonant and a vowel in English alphabetic writing.[3] This phonetic basis is quite significant in exploding the myths underlying the logic of coloniality and writing because the range of the hieroglyphic writing system is only limited by utterable sound, just like the alphabetic system. It is also essential in terms of understanding the range of literature that the Maya produced over millennia. Dennis Tedlock's *Two Thousand Years of Mayan Literature* traces various forms of texts representative of the long literary tradition this writing system made possible, and it's worth including at least some of the visual images from this book in a slideshow on the first day of class. In addition, Justin Kerr's searchable *Maya Vase Database* (research.mayavase.com/kerrmaya.html) has hundreds of stunning pre-Contact images of Maya texts in less traditional media, such as painted vases. Many of these images include hieroglyphic and graphic elements that directly reference episodes in *Popol Wuj*. These two sources give instructors valuable options for showing students the sweeping scope of Maya literature across the millennia that—for centuries—virtually no one knew existed.

Popol Wuj provides a notable exception to the barren period that Maya literature endured during colonization. The highland Guatemala K'iche' is one of the many different language groups that together make up what

208 *Popol Wuj*

we now call Maya culture, though the Maya were never a unified empire like the Inca in the Andes or the Triple Alliance (known as the Aztec Empire) in northern Mexico. The K'iche' wouldn't have referred to themselves at the time of contact as Maya. The word *maya* comes from Yucatec—spoken more than five hundred miles away from the Guatemalan highlands—and was borrowed by scholars centuries later to name a broad group of cultures based on several key shared cultural characteristics, including related languages, writing and calendric systems, ballgame structures, cosmogonies, and so on (Restall and Asselbergs 4).

At the beginning of the eighteenth century, an Indigenous parishioner in Chichicastenango (Guatemala) loaned a K'iche' *Popol Wuj* to Francisco Ximénez, a Spanish Dominican parish priest and linguistics enthusiast. Ximénez transcribed the K'iche' text and then translated it into Spanish. The K'iche' authors of a *Popol Wuj* that has since disappeared (perhaps the one from which Ximénez was transcribing) were writing in the middle of the sixteenth century, just after the arrival of the Spanish in Guatemala, and they tell us explicitly (twice) in the text that their alphabetic *Popol Wuj* was based on an even earlier book, which would necessarily have been a hieroglyphic codex from pre-Contact times. These sixteenth-century K'iche' authors had written their version in the new Latinate alphabet that Spanish priests had recently adapted for writing catechisms in K'iche'. They explain in the preamble that they were doing this "because there is no longer a place to see it [i.e., "the original book"]," which contained the "root of everything K'iche'" (Sam Colop, *Maya Poetics* 70). Still, scholars remain surprisingly divided about whether a unified pre-Contact hieroglyphic *Popol Wuj* existed (Henne 37–39).

But the decolonial imperative—not only in reading *Popol Wuj* specifically but also in expanding the boundaries of the epic category as this collection of essays does—is much more important than resolving the technical terms that underlie this disagreement in Mayanist circles. Why wouldn't we take the word of these Indigenous authors who tell us twice, in no uncertain terms (Tedlock, Popol Vuh 63, 198),[4] that there was a book that can no longer be read, when we know the Maya had libraries with thousands of such books at the time of contact? Certainly, it would have been a different kind of book because the stark Western division between writing and orality didn't exist in Maya thinking. Maya books were written to include much more wiggle room in terms of adding or skipping over material in the book when performed publicly and in terms of leaving space for the performer to insert personal idiosyncrasies (27–28).

We might imagine the pre-Contact *Popol Wuj* more like a script that gave the reader or performer considerable agency in determining which details might appeal to particular audiences. We see residues of this kind of present-tense voice interrupting the story on pages 78 and 94, for example—the performer almost pointing at the page as he read aloud and embellished, crossing freely back and forth across the fuzzy oral/written divide. Given what we now know about the versatility of Maya writing— and given the clearly colonial rationale for drawing such writing/orality distinctions in the first place—this decades-long debate about the degree of orality determining the pre-Contact version should only matter in the context of this collection for two reasons: to facilitate comparisons with other epics that students will be reading and that contain varying levels of orality within the written version and to structure a class discussion about the role literature and writing have traditionally played in coloniality and in nation building. We'll probably never know for sure if most of *Popol Wuj* as it appears today ever coalesced into what we'd consider to be a book, but close parallels to many of the episodes we read in it are found separately in other kinds of Maya hieroglyphic texts from more than two thousand years ago, so the point is mostly moot anyway.

Charles Pigott efficiently sums up various elements that complicate any concrete classification of *Popol Wuj* in the confines of traditional literature: "Certainly, the evidence indicates that [*Popol Wuj*] is best understood as an evolving literary event formed through multiple acts of translation formed across diverse languages, materialities, regions, and dimensions (oral and literate, hieroglyphic and alphabetic, linguistic and non-linguistic)" (133). Combing with students through these various layers in Pigott's description provides a good way to conclude the first day of class.

Choosing a Translation, and Translating a Choice

Popol Wuj has been translated into English more than twenty times, so we're spoiled for choice compared to readers of many of the other epics in this collection. Unfortunately, none of those translations into English have been carried out by people who identify as K'iche' and grew up speaking K'iche'. The K'iche' intellectual and activist Luis Enrique Sam Colop wrote his dissertation in English, and in it he translates some selected passages from *Popol Wuj*, which I cite above (*Maya Poetics*). However, his only full translation of *Popol Wuj* is into Spanish; it is the best translation

210   *Popol Wuj*

in Spanish, and instructors teaching in a bilingual context should use Sam Colop's version as the base Spanish translation. This illuminating annotated *Popol Wuj* was reissued in hardback in 2021 and is available for the first time in the United States. The 2012 paperback edition doesn't include Sam Colop's extensive explanations, which are indispensable for a decolonial reading.

The English translation of *Popol Wuj* that best reflects the original K'iche' is Tedlock's *Popol Vuh*. Tedlock finds a way to carry across the poetic beauty of K'iche' discourse in many instances while at the same time mostly refusing to sacrifice alienating meaning-making structures that crucially provided K'iche' poets the scaffolding for their Indigenous cosmovisions. Tedlock went through the complete training cycle with the *aj qij* (ritual specialist) Andrés Xiloj in Momostenango and was officially authorized by the community of *aj qijaab* (ritual specialists) as an *aj qij* himself. Even if, as a result, he focuses too much on astronomical and astrological aspects of *Popol Wuj*, he worked over every word and passage of the K'iche' with Xiloj for years and clearly understands the Maya cosmovision underlying *Popol Wuj* more than the great majority of translators do. His extensive notes (160 pages of them) make the complications of translation transparent and open up the way *Popol Wuj* references a radically different way of living in the world. Students may not want to read copious notes, but instructors should go the extra mile when teaching a text from a culture that developed in complete isolation from the cultures of most students, to avoid their making a simple, structuralist interpretation of the text. Instructors can do this by assigning as part of the reading a few selected endnotes on the vagaries of translation choices that apply to the lecture or discussion material for the next class.

Unfortunately, most English translations of *Popol Wuj* still tend toward centering English poetics to facilitate consumption in the anglophone world. For example, Michael Bazzett tells us that he carried out his 2018 translation of *Popol Wuj* "with the end goal of creating a lucid poem that the modern reader can enter and disappear into with minimal framing" (x). The resulting so-called translation is indeed smooth and comfortable in terms of English poetics (and thus tempting to use). But *Popol Wuj* is an ancient text, written in an archaic form of K'iche' that grows out of a cultural trajectory radically different from that familiar to modern Western students. In choosing a translation for a class that purports to open up the nuances of other cultures' ways of seeing the world, we must challenge our students to confront awkward language differences that uniquely reflect and preserve fundamentally different cosmovisions. After all, the nuances of what can sometimes be alienating language and narrative structures partially reveal those cosmovisions, but they need framing—not bleaching out—in order to keep Western readers from finding facile and comfortable equivalences in their dominant cultures.

For this reason, I caution against using any one translation exclusively. An instructor should build in some translation comparison work because it helps students see that K'iche' cosmovisions lie mostly in the spaces between imprecise word choices in English. In the case of *Popol Wuj*, translation comparison is fairly easy to set up because Allen Christenson makes two of his translations available for free at mesoweb.com (Popol Vuh: *Literal Poetic Version* and Popol Vuh: *Sacred Book*). Although Christenson's translations are not the best to use as the primary reading text, they are an excellent resource for comparative translation exercises with the class's primary version. I have students prepare and perform in-class readings of the same passage from different translations, for example Christenson's literal, but rough, translation and either Tedlock's or Christenson's idiomatic version. Then I have the class discuss how the translations are different and why those differences might matter.

Even a brief comparison of the first few lines of the preamble works well to show students how translation choices affect our reading and subsequent understanding of K'iche' cosmovision. For example, readers can see that the second word in the preamble is "uxe," which in K'iche' literally means "its root" and which Christenson translates that way in his literal version (Popol Vuh: *Literal Poetic Version* 13). By contrast, his idiomatic version, and Tedlock's translation, render "uxe" as "beginning" (Christenson, Popol Vuh: *Sacred Book* 59; Tedlock, Popol Vuh 63), an abstract word that parallels Genesis but loses the way the rest of the preamble persistently builds the tight connection between K'iche' culture and the plant world (using words like "planting," "sowing," and so on [Popol Vuh: *Literal Poetic Version* 13]).

Glimpsing Key Elements of Maya Cosmovisions

Ultimately, instructors should help students learn to perform a reading that uses the narrative content of *Popol Wuj* to understand how literary works can preserve and pass along fundamental—though often opaque—elements of a culture's cosmovisions. This function of literary works becomes

212　*Popol Wuj*

even more important when the cosmovision that produced the work differs substantially from the students' own. This is especially true for the category of epic because the primary role of myth in Indigenous American societies is to renew the past. Renewal through myth matters more than ever now, as it empowers the cultures of the Americas to resist the relentless colonial logic of progress, a logic that tolerates the celebration of certain elements of Indigenous culture as exotic folklore but that regards the underlying Indigenous cosmovisions and philosophies as fundamental obstructions to universal development. The next section provides a way for instructors to get at this role of epic myth through a more properly narrative analysis.

Why *Popol Wuj* Splits the Hero Figure into Two

The most epic-like sections of *Popol Wuj* are consistently structured around pairs of heroes, primarily the Boys—brothers Junajpú and Xbalanqué. The narrative choice to pair them is puzzling because these hero brothers almost always act, think, and talk exactly in concert. Not until the end of an epic section do we find a scene where there is a clear narrative rationale for having two of them. At the end of their time in Xibalbá (the underworld), Xbalanqué sacrifices Junajpú and brings him back to life as part of their plan to defeat the lords of Xibalbá (136–37). This process takes two: Junajpú cannot sacrifice and resurrect himself. However, this narrative necessity could have been easily resolved otherwise, such as by introducing a temporary companion only in this scene. Instead, *Popol Wuj* insists that all the heroic action across the long narrative be carried out by both characters and uses the plural third person to describe almost everything they do jointly.[5]

Before students do the last reading assignment, I ask them to think about what rationale might explain the Boys as split heroes. Then, in the first few minutes of the next class, I ask them to offer possible explanations (using examples) in an informal writing exercise. In this exercise and the ensuing discussion, students come up with well-conceived narrative rationales for the split heroes, but none of the rationales are completely convincing when taken in the wider context of traditional K'iche' cosmovision. Since I don't have space to show the limitations of each rationale here, I only handle the most compelling argument and show how that can lead us to a fundamentally different cosmovision underlying the Boys' exploits.

After their exploits in Xibalbá, Junajpú and Xbalanqué go up into the sky and become the sun and the moon (141, 287n). Students point out that this ending requires two heroes. But we have to understand the unique relationship between the sun and moon in K'iche' thinking: to the K'iche' the sun and moon are parts of a whole, not a binary opposition. The full moon always rises directly facing the setting sun, and the moon's light is a result of the two bodies moving in synchronicity. (The K'iche' call the full moon *qij*, or sun.) As such, the individual ontologies of the sun and moon—as Western science separates them—don't make sense in K'iche' thinking, where the two bodies are inextricably connected, part of each other. The sun and moon form a complementary duality and cannot be thought of separately.

This same indivisibility expresses itself in K'iche' cosmovision in terms of people and their communities. That the hero cannot be one grows out of a cosmovision that refuses to lionize the individual as separate and unique. Instead, individuals are inextricable from their ongoing relationships with the other people in the community and, indeed, with all elements of the world. Traditional K'iche' thinking does not separate selfhood (as understood in the dominant Western worldview). Individuals achieve laudatory things only as a result of all they have learned from others and all they have been given by the community.

So Junajpú and Xbalanqué need to be two characters not because they become the sun and the moon but because they are like the sun and the moon and everything else: they are intricately interrelated such that no one person or thing is anything without its ongoing interactions with everyone and everything else. The idea of the chosen, unique hero doesn't make sense in traditional K'iche' cosmovision. The resulting split-hero characters in *Popol Wuj* open up the possibility of productive class work revolving around identifying similarities and differences with other epics that split the hero role, such as *The Legend of Ponnivala Nadu*. As Brenda E. F. Beck explains in her essay in this volume, the twins who share rulership in that epic work reflect and reinforce important elements of the South Indian worldview, in which "good rule requires mixed and complementary qualities and involves multiple dualities" and which ends up favoring "communal loyalty [over] individual initiative and success." What other epics offer variations on these two related positions, in *Popol Wuj* and in *The Legend of Ponnivala Nadu*? How are other epics similar to or different from *Popol Wuj* in other ways that might explain their splitting the role of the hero? Why might these similarities or differences matter?

Excerpting from and Reordering *Popol Wuj*

Part of the way of being in and seeing the world of other cultures that instructors can help students get a glimpse of through epics is these cultures' sense of order—chronological or deliberately not—which in many ways drives other key cultural perceptions. However, for a comparative course that can only devote three to six class sessions to each epic covered, I map out two itineraries below, which excerpt and necessarily reorder episodes from *Popol Wuj*.

But first I (somewhat reluctantly) order the readings chronologically and label them according to their distinct narrative levels in table 1, to make the abrupt narrative shifts in the story easier to follow. Our oldest extant version of *Popol Wuj* is structured on distinct narrative levels that are temporarily put on hold to move to lower narrative levels and are then picked back up later. The table identifies principal actors in each reading and explains briefly how the readings are most significant in the overall context. The table also allows instructors to choose their own itineraries through *Popol Wuj*, though I suggest two itineraries below.

Epic Reading Itineraries

Here are two options for reading schedules depending on the number of classes available for *Popol Wuj*. If I have only three class sessions, I group the material together as follows.

Day 1: Introduction, Preamble, Cosmogony

Preclass readings. The translator's introduction (21–60), the preamble (63–64), the last four lines of *Popol Wuj* (198), the shaping of the world (64–73), and the successful shaping of humans (145–49).

Key takeaways. The preamble makes a decolonial warning to read between the lines because it has been written within the colonial dictates of the Catholic Church. The last four lines of *Popol Wuj* match up with the preamble and emphasize literary continuity across the pre-Contact/post-Contact divide. In the K'iche' text, the episodes about the shaping of the world and the stuttering attempts by the Shapers to populate it with animals and humans are separated by dozens of pages from the scene that narrates successful emergence of humans. This suggested reading order links these episodes for clarity.

Table 1

Readings in *Popol Wuj* arranged chronologically

Pages in Tedlock, Popol Vuh	Narrative level	Actors	Description
63–64	Meta-discursive	The K'iche' authors of the 1550s copy of *Popol Wuj* and the Spanish colonizers	The preamble describes the historical and cultural context of the contact period and acknowledges the complications of the colonial era; this section matches up with the last six lines of *Popol Wuj*, described below.
64–73	Cosmogony	Various *k'abawil* or deities (also known as Formers or Shapers), earth, sky, and animals	The *k'abawil* talk together to figure out how to shape the world and its inhabitants out of the mass of material lying there, but their efforts lead to mixed results, including unsatisfactory humans.
73–88	Epic battles, tricks, and Xibalbá (the under-world)[a]	The Boys (the second generation of epic-like heroes in *Popol Wuj*) and the Wuqub Kaqix family (Mother, Father, and two sons)	The actors in this section work to adjust conflicting forces in the cosmos for ecological balance amid climate changes, earthquakes, and volcanic eruptions (see Henne 100–28 for complications of translation and supposedly epic hubris).
91–102	Epic battles, tricks, and Xibalbá[a]	The fathers (of the Boys), the lords of Xibalbá, and Blood Moon (the Boys' mother)	The fathers play ball on earth and in the underworld. In doing so, they lay the groundwork for humans to negotiate suffering and death by linking to cycles such as the agriculture cycle.
102–42	Epic battles, tricks, and Xibalbá[a]	The Boys, Blood Moon, the Boys' grandmother, the artisan half-brothers, the lords of Xibalbá	This section addresses the Boys' birth and life on earth and their defeat of the lords of Xibalbá. The Boys complete the cultivation of corn that will be used to make humans and feed them, and they overcome suffering.
145–49	Cosmogony	Animals, *k'abawil* and humans	The *k'abawil* finally find the right material to make humans successfully.
149–84	Cosmogony or mythistory	Maya ethnic groups, leaders, warriors, their *nawals*, and the fourth sun	Newly formed Maya cultural groups migrate to the highlands, fight for position, and wait for the fourth (current) sun. This section is on the same narrative level as the ones in which the *k'abawil* shape humans because these Maya leaders are similar to *k'abawil*.
184–98	Cosmogony or mythistory	The three branches of K'iche' culture, their leaders, Pedro de Alvarado, and his Spanish armies	This section narrates the rise and partial fall of the highland Maya cultures.
198	Meta-discursive	The K'iche' authors of the 1550s copy of *Popol Wuj* and the Spanish colonizers	The last four lines of *Popol Wuj* affirm that the work was copied from a book that is now lost.

a. These are the most epic-like sections in *Popol Wuj*. They involve larger-than-human but humanlike beings making the world ecologically feasible (including for humans) and modeling behavior for humans.

216   *Popol Wuj*

Day 2: Epic Battles, the Ball Game, and Xibalbá

Preclass readings. The battle between the Boys and the Wuqub Kaqix family (73–88); the flashback to the Boys' fathers, the ball game, and the trip to Xibalbá (91–102); the flash-forward to the Boys themselves, the ball game again, and their trip to Xibalbá, with better results (102–42).

Key takeaways. In two ways, the actions in this section are characteristic of those often found in epics, described in this volume's introduction as memorable deeds by larger-than-life characters whose actions carry great stakes for their communities. Through their actions the actors figure out how to balance the ecology and what to make humans out of (corn) so that they're an inextricable part of the ecology, but the actors also figure out how to see human death as regeneration (like the death of crops and death found in other natural cycles) in the bigger ecological picture.

Day 3: Underlying K'iche' Cosmovision and Comparison with Other Epics

Preclass readings. Students could examine comparative translation charts and related questions from *Reading* Popol Wuj on cosmogony and complications of inception-of-the-world parallels (Henne 69–75) and similar charts and related questions on epic battles and the complications of paralleling these with Western literary tropes of pride or hubris (105–10). Students could also compare specific crosses with paired characters from other epics in this volume such as the twins in *The Legend of Ponnivala Nadu*, mentioned above and discussed in the essay by Beck.

Key takeaways. The readings on this last day hammer home how *Popol Wuj* staunchly resists traditional comparisons with the biblical creation narrative and conventional Western literary tropes and requires persistent and active decolonial reading.

A window of six class sessions for *Popol Wuj* allows a class to read the text in its entirety without any reordering of the episodes because each class then allows time for the instructor to signpost the narrative breaks and to discuss notions of chronology and narrative order. The cosmogony discussion will be split over days 1 and 4—one day for the inception of the world (64–73) and the other for the forming of humans (145–49)—and divided, like the original text, by the epic sections, which are also split into two days: the battle on day 2 (73–88) and the flashback and flash-forward on day 3 (91–102, 102–42). The migration and rise of the K'iche' people (149–84, 184–98) and the discussion of comparative translation charts, cosmogony (Henne 69–75), and epic battles (105–10) will be handled on day 5. Day 6 wraps up with comparative work on other epics.

Notes

1. *Popol Wuj* is spelled here as K'iche' writers currently spell it in the nationally recognized K'iche' alphabet—which was standardized and officially adopted almost four decades ago. The great majority of English publications still use the colonial spelling of *wuj—vuh*—used by Spanish priests in the archaic Spanish alphabet, which serves as the first reminder in this essay of the pervasiveness of coloniality in the Indigenous Americas. *Wuj* means book; *vuh* doesn't mean anything. I also drop the customary article *the* since no article accompanies the title in the K'iche' and since using the definite article in English gives the mistaken impression that *Popol Wuj* is considered by the K'iche' to be absolutely authoritative, as the Bible, the Koran, and the Torah are considered in their associated belief systems. See Henne 21–24 for further discussion of the meaning of the title *Popol Wuj*.

2. I substitute *cosmovision* for the more familiar *worldview* because it reflects the added scope and depth (in time and space) that figures prominently in determining traditional K'iche' visions of possible human relations with the wide array of surrounding realms.

3. See Coe for an in-depth, but quite accessible, explanation of how the syllabary worked.

4. Citations to *Popol Wuj* refer to Tedlock's revised edition, Popol Vuh: *The Definitive Edition.*

5. The previous heroic generation, the Boys' fathers (or father-uncles), also follows this pattern with even less narrative rationale; Jun Junajpú becomes corn—which is essential to the rest of the *Popol Wuj* narrative and to K'iche' life and culture—but our extant *Popol Wuj* doesn't assign a key role moving forward for his brother, Wuqub Junajpú.

Works Cited

Acuerdo sobre identidad y derechos de los pueblos indígenas. MINUGUA, 31 Mar. 1995, www.almg.org.gt/wp-content/uploads/2020/05/j-Acuerdo -Sobre-Identidad.pdf.

Arias, Arturo. *Recovering Lost Footprints.* State U of New York P, 2017.

Bazzett, Michael, translator. *The Popol Vuh.* Milkweed Editions, 2018.

Christenson, Allen J., translator. Popol Vuh: *Literal Poetic Version.* U of Oklahoma P, 2008, www.mesoweb.com/publications/Christenson/PV-Literal.pdf.

———, translator. Popol Vuh: *The Sacred Book of the Maya: The Great Classic of Central American Spirituality.* U of Oklahoma P, 2007, www.mesoweb .com/publications/Christenson/PopolVuh.pdf.

Coe, Michael. *Reading the Maya Glyphs.* Thames and Hudson, 2016.

218   *Popol Wuj*

Henne, Nathan C. *Reading* Popol Wuj: *A Decolonial Guide*. U of Arizona P, 2020.

Mignolo, Walter D. "On the Colonization of Amerindian Languages and Memories." *Comparative Studies in Society and History*, vol. 34, no. 2, 1992, pp. 301–30.

Pigott, Charles M. *Writing the Land, Writing Humanity: The Maya Literary Renaissance*. Routledge, 2020.

Quijano, Anibal. "Coloniality of Power, Eurocentrism, and Latin America." Translated by Michael Ennis. *Nepantla: Views from South*, vol. 1, no. 3, 2000, pp. 533–80.

Restall, Matthew, and Florine Asselbergs. *Invading Guatemala: Spanish, Nahua, and Maya Accounts of the Conquest Wars*. Penn State UP, 2007.

Sam Colop, Luis Enrique. *Maya Poetics*. 1994. State U of New York, Buffalo, PhD dissertation.

———, translator. *Popol Wuj*. 2nd ed., F and G Editores, 2021.

———, translator. *Popol Wuj*. 2nd ed., F and G Editores / Biblioteca Guatemala, 2012.

Tedlock, Dennis, translator. Popol Vuh: *The Definitive Edition of the Mayan Book of the Dawn of Life and the Glories of Gods and Kings*. Rev. ed., Simon and Schuster, 1996.

———. *Two Thousand Years of Mayan Literature*. U of California P, 2011.

Thomas A. DuBois

Finland's *Kalevala*: Folk Songs, Romantic Nationalism, and an Enduring National Epic

Imagine growing up in the nineteenth century in a rural society bounded by a particular language, one taken for granted by everyone in your community but considered complex, inscrutable, and uncouth by virtually everyone from the outside. Imagine a society in which most administrative and intellectual duties were performed by members of an upper class speaking a different language than yours, officials with ties to one or another colonizing realm—first the Kingdom of Sweden (for some six centuries), then the Russian Empire (beginning in 1809). And imagine a context in which no one quite knew where your language or community came from: that is, no one could point definitively to any past empire or great historical battles that involved your so-called nation, and virtually no records of migration or voyages of discovery existed that could provide a sense of a beginning for your community, its language, and its culture. In a nineteenth-century romantic nationalist Europe fascinated by real or imagined histories of national origins and national destiny, your community would prove a puzzling conundrum or a trivial enigma, consigned to a footnote in the grand histories of nations to the east, south, and west. Such was the case for speakers of Finnish (Suomi) in the nineteenth century. And such was the context in which a district physician and romantic

220   *Kalevala*

nationalist, Elias Lönnrot, compiled and published in 1835 a text he named *Kalevala*, a work today known as the Finnish national epic. Drawn from narrative, lyric, and ritual songs performed in the Finnish language in rural village settings of Finland and Karelia (a culturally and linguistically related region east of the political boundary that separated the Grand Duchy of Finland from other parts of the Russian Empire), Lönnrot's epic would provide Finnish people with a heroic past, a present cultural identity, and a future claim to be counted among the nations of Europe. In 1917, less than a century after the first publication of the *Kalevala*, leaders of a galvanized Finnish nation declared national independence and sovereignty over their country, an act of defiance and self-confidence facilitated in its initial stages by the publication of the epic.

Students in modern college literature classrooms often harbor particular assumptions regarding cultures and countries around the world. They often project continuity into the past. And so while they will certainly be aware that the United States did not always exist, they can easily imagine that there has always been a Germany, a Sweden, an Italy, or a Finland. If one of the goals in a course on epics is to help make students critical interpreters of the world to which they belong, then an important lesson could be for them to understand the degree to which such European nation-state entities emerged in the nineteenth century, replacing earlier multiethnic empires and kingdoms, and the ways in which their novelty was camouflaged through references to national epics. While epics are works with their own narrative features and textual integrity, they have also been tools for political and cultural maneuvering, a process that scholars of history call nation building. The *Kalevala* as we have it today is a product of nineteenth-century nation building while at the same time a reflection of age-old Finnish cultural traditions and a work with its own aesthetic features and narrative appeal.

Including the *Kalevala* in a course on comparative epics offers much of interest. First, in comparison with many other oral-derived epics from the European cultural area, the performance mode of the often lengthy narrative, lyric, and ritual songs that became the basis of the *Kalevala* is well documented in easily accessible transcriptions, translations, and even sound files. Where scholars must often hypothesize concerning the musical rendition of medieval European epics, the *Kalevala* seems to offer a revealing glimpse into a past Europe in which sung poetry was a valued and common component of evening entertainment, an accompaniment to monotonous work, or a key tool in important rituals like weddings, funerals, and healings. Although published in the nineteenth century (with a first edition in 1835 and a revised and expanded edition in 1849), the *Kalevala* is not a literary text planned to be read as poetry, but rather an anthology of merged transcribed songs and charms that readers experience as a work of poetry in the absence of accompanying musical notation.

A second reason for including *Kalevala* in a course on epics is that it illustrates vividly the accretive, creative function that nineteenth-century literary and cultural leaders envisioned for national epics. Once a national epic became known through publication (and in the case of *Kalevala*, through translation into languages familiar to people outside Finland), subsequent Finnish writers, composers, and artists participating in the romantic nationalist project were enjoined to take up the materials contained in the epic and extol and extend them through new works. Understanding this enterprise in the context of Finnish nation building, particularly in the late nineteenth century and early twentieth century, allows for the exploration of great Finnish artists like the composer Jean Sibelius and the painter Akseli Gallen-Kallela and the explicitly political role art played in the cultural activism that eventually culminated in Finnish independence.

A third reason that including the *Kalevala* in a comparative epics course can prove valuable is the ways in which the epic recurs in postnationalist contexts of the later twentieth and twenty-first centuries. Once Finnish nationhood was secured by political recognition, as well as by participation in international networks like the League of Nations, the United Nations, and the European Union, and once the military threat of absorption into the Soviet Union subsided in the aftermath of World War II, it became possible for Finns to explore the *Kalevala* in a more playful or critical way, a process that continues unabated in Finland today in a manner that is both highly creative and sometimes surprising. Elements of the *Kalevala* were dramatized in 1970s television miniseries, performed by 1990s world music folk ensembles like Värttinä, and pastiched or parodied in popular literature of the early 2000s. They continue to be widely adapted in contemporary brand names, fantasy games, role-playing activities, and folk metal and heavy metal performances by bands like Amorphis, Ensiferum, and Korpiklaani. Using Michael Billig's notion of "banal nationalism" and Tim Edensor's examination of national identity, an instructor can help students explore the ubiquity of this epic in a country that continues to regard it as a cornerstone of national identity. Even when modern Finns listen to a heavy metal adaptation of lines from

222   *Kalevala*

the *Kalevala* that may sound different from the folk songs that were originally recorded by Lönnrot, it is possible for them to sense an enduring attention to the notion of Finnish nationhood, an attention celebrated and continued in *Kalevala*-related cultural products nearly two centuries after the epic's initial publication.

The *Kalevala* is easily accessed and widely available in accurate and readable English translations. Although early English translations by John Martin Crawford and W. F. Kirby can be found for free online (Lönnrot, Kalevala [Crawford] and Kalevala [Kirby]), a good and affordable modern translation for use in the classroom is Keith Bosley's 1989 translation (Lönnrot, Kalevala [Bosley]). Instructors will want to consult the useful introduction and appendices of Francis Peabody Magoun's 1963 prose translation, which provides a close and accurate glossing of the epic (Lönnrot, Kalevala [Magoun]). Art historians and lovers of modern verse will enjoy the 1988 translation by Eino Friberg (Lönnrot, Kalevala [Friberg]), which, although too expensive and inaccessible to assign in a class, contains illustrations by Björn Landström that can provide excellent counterparts to the more famous illustrations of Gallen-Kallela, as detailed below.

As this discussion suggests, understanding the genesis and nature of the *Kalevala* as a text is a crucial element to teaching it well to people who may know little about Finland or Finnish history. When Lönnrot began his collecting work in the late 1820s, folklore collecting as a scholarly activity was still in its infancy. Lönnrot had no recording devices other than a pen and paper, and his handwritten transcriptions of the songs he heard were full of gaps and abbreviations. The songs he was interested in were not common in nineteenth-century southern and western Finland (i.e., the areas of the country that had absorbed the greatest degree of influence from Swedish culture over many centuries) but rather were found mostly in small farmsteads or villages in eastern and northern Finland, as well as in the region of Karelia (Karjala) in Russia. Walking long distances from farm to farm, Lönnrot persuaded or cajoled peasant singers of varying ages and genders to take a break from their work duties and sit and dictate songs that they knew by memory. Over time, Lönnrot began to see the same songs recurring in repertoire after repertoire, but with varying details, characters, or turns of phrase. In his mind, he began to imagine a supposed right or original version of the songs he heard, out of which the singers' sometimes contradictory or confusing songs had developed. And he began to imagine a unified epic that he could construct, or reconstruct, from the various songs he had amassed.

Good discussions of the oral traditions that Lönnrot encountered and recorded are available in the excellent anthology by Matti Kuusi, Bosley, and Michael Branch, *Finnish Folk Poetry: Epic*, as well as in the anthology by Leea Virtanen and me, *Finnish Folklore* (Virtanen and DuBois). In both these works, readers can see the Finnish original songs alongside English translations and learn about the distinctive meter (trochaic tetrameter), alliterative poetics, formulaic phrasing, and line-pair parallelism that characterize the song tradition. The compact disc *The* Kalevala *Heritage* provides excellent audio examples of songs from the traditions Lönnrot encountered, albeit through performances recorded in the early twentieth century. The disc includes examples of solo-voice epic songs, lyric choral songs expressive of feelings and situations, and *loitsut* (charms) used in healing and the management of luck. Irma-Riita Järvinen's Kalevala *Guide* provides an excellent overview of these song traditions, Lönnrot's text, and adaptations of the epic over time. An earlier work of value, particularly in understanding Lönnrot's literary agenda, is Juha Pentikäinen's Kalevala *Mythology*.

Given that even today the *Kalevala* remains closely tied to its originating national project, in which it was asserted to be the product of the entire Finnish nation rather than the brainchild of a single literary author, scholars will often begin their discussions of the *Kalevala* with citations of numbers: the revised and expanded *Kalevala* of 1849 contains some 22,795 trochaic tetrameter lines, of which only 1,139 were composed by Lönnrot himself (Lönnrot, *Kalevala* [rev. ed.]). The vast bulk of the text is, in other words, built of quoted lines from songs that Lönnrot (or other collectors) recorded. Lönnrot's editorial process bears a resemblance to the sampling that happens in modern popular music, in which extant lines of music are recombined in creative ways to make new wholes. While respecting the nineteenth-century context in which Lönnrot conducted his editing, I have found it useful to challenge students to build a short mini-epic of their own out of five to ten existing songs from a genre of popular music of their choice. Students often enjoy such an activity, creating a rap epic, a country-and-western epic, or some other such amalgamation. The process underscores both the creativity and the challenges of Lönnrot's work better than a lengthy lecture could ever do.

A teachable selection of poems from the now standard 1849 edition of the epic includes the epic's opening mythic poems (Lönnrot, *Kalevala* [rev. ed.], poems 1–2); the poems of the hero Väinämöinen's dealings with Joukahainen and Aino (poems 3–5); poems having to do with the creation,

224 *Kalevala*

theft and destruction of the magic Sampo (poems 10, 39, 42, 43); and the epic's final poem, about the maiden Marjatta, the birth of the Christlike king of Karelia, and the final departure of Väinämöinen (poem 50).[1] This selection highlights the character of Väinämöinen, the epic's main hero, while limiting the attention paid to some of Lönnrot's ancillary male characters, Ilmarinen (a doughty but brooding smith), Lemminkäinen (a testy and impetuous philanderer), and Kullervo (an oppressed and ultimately self-destructive orphan). As noted below, female characters in the epic tend to occur in relation to the male protagonists: the above selection includes detailed depictions of Aino (a young woman consigned to marry the aging Väinämöinen against her will), Louhi (the farmwife-ruler of the land of the north called Pohjola), Louhi's unnamed daughter (the object of a courting contest between Väinämöinen and Ilmarinen, and the eventual victim of Kullervo's violent anger), and Marjatta (a virgin mother akin to the biblical Mary).

One of the recurrent characters that Lönnrot encountered most often in the songs he collected was an aged worker of magic and wisdom frequently (but not always) called Väinämöinen. This figure was often depicted in mythic events having to do with the creation of the world. Other songs depicted him employing word magic to build boats or heal ailments or traveling to places like Tuonela (the land of the dead) in the manner of a shaman. Lönnrot made Väinämöinen his epic's hero, recounting his birth at the outset of the world (poems 1–2), his triumph in a singing match against the rival Joukainen (poem 3), his unsuccessful courtship of two women (including the maiden Aino; poem 4), his expeditions to otherworlds in quest of magic words (poems 16–17), his creation of the *kantele* (the first harp; poems 41–42), and his final departure at the arrival of Christianity (poem 50).

In poems 4–5, Aino reacts to the proposal that she marry an aged Väinämöinen by preferring to become transformed into a fish. Lönnrot's adaptation of women's lyric songs (see DuBois, *Finnish Folk Poetry* 261–92) reflects a problematic sexual-textual agenda, which often led Lönnrot to revise his folk-song sources in favor of messages that reinforced a nineteenth-century patriarchal mindset, a topic that has been explored in Patricia Sawin's classic article "Lönnrot's Brainchildren." The sexism of the epic has been revisited and revised in postwar Finnish adaptations and parodies, reflecting the creative ways in which Finns have chosen not to banish the epic but rather to reappropriate it for continued modern use.

To build a narrative core for an epic built of many discreet songs, Lönnrot seized upon a relatively lengthy narrative song he collected from a number of different singers regarding the creation, theft, and eventual destruction of a magic object bearing the mysterious name Sampo. With its images of a struggle between the peoples of two lands—which Lönnrot came to call Kalevala (a land of heroes symbolizing Finland) and Pohjola (a bleak and magic land to the north)—the Sampo song seemed to evince the interethnic strife so common in classic European epics like *The Song of Roland* and *Poema de mío Cid*. Examples of the original songs Lönnrot adapted are available in the anthologies by Kuusi and colleagues and by Virtanen and DuBois. In *Kalevala*, the Sampo—a magic device that could produce whatever its owner desired—becomes the required betrothal gift that helps the hero Ilmarinen gain the hand of the maiden of Pohjola (poem 10). When hard times hit Kalevala later in the epic, Väinämöinen, Ilmarinen, and Lemminkäinen use magic to steal the Sampo back from Pohjola (poems 39, 42). They are pursued, however, by an enraged Louhi, who transforms into a bird and attempts to wrest the Sampo away from the fleeing heroes. The Sampo is thereby destroyed, ending an era of primordial plenty and accounting for the hard work and poverty in the world today (poem 43). In poem 50, Lönnrot adapted songs that were explicitly about the Nativity of Christ to create a more metaphorical ending to his epic (see DuBois, "From Maria"). Väinämöinen departs from Kalevala at the birth of a mysterious new king of Karelia, leaving behind the *kantele* and his songs for the Finnish people.

Thematically, Lönnrot's epic provides historicized and culturally specific takes on seemingly universal topics, like the relation of parent and child, the relation of individual to community, the workings of the supernatural, and the nature of the good life. Repeatedly in the epic, men turn to their mothers for guidance on whom to marry or what to do next, and farmwives act craftily and cannily to try to maneuver their daughters into good marriages or prevent them from entering into bad ones. The life of an orphan is the most miserable imaginable. Nearly every character makes use of magic spells—*loitsut*—to accomplish daily or special tasks, details that reflect Lönnrot's great fascination with the ubiquitous tradition of magic that he found among rural Finns and Karelians. Helping students recognize all the many *loitsut* included in the *Kalevala* for activities as diverse as baking, slaughtering, planting, harvesting, building, burning, traveling, or relaxing can prove a stimulating class exercise.[2] And in contrast with many loftier epics, the *Kalevala*'s characters aim by

226 *Kalevala*

and large to attain simple treasures: a good marriage, a warm place by the fire, a successful harvest, a functional boat, tasty beer, and so on. These elements of the epic make for excellent topics of discussion with students, as they distance the epic from some idealized realm of abstract or martial heroism and bring it into the ordinary and humble worldview of peasant folk songs.

Although first published in 1835, the *Kalevala* did not rise to real prominence as a tool of Finnish nationalism until near the end of the nineteenth century, when a mounting process of Russification in the Grand Duchy of Finland threatened to obliterate the cultural and social distinctiveness of Finns as autonomous subjects of the Russian Empire. In this political climate, artists like Sibelius and Gallen-Kallela began to draw on the *Kalevala* as a means of celebrating Finnish culture and protesting Russian incursions and pressures. Many of the evocative symphonic settings that Sibelius created in connection with details of the epic (e.g., his *Kullervo* and *Swan of Tuonela*), as well as the vivid and defiant paintings produced by Gallen-Kallela, became better known and more influential than the epic that they ostensibly referenced.[3] When looking at famous works by Gallen-Kallela like *The Forging of the Sampo*, *The Defence of the Sampo*, and *Kullervo Cursing*, we can easily sense the high seriousness and submerged political edge of these works produced in the final difficult years of Russification. It can then be useful to explore the more whimsical, frail, and human images that Björn Landström produced in 1988, which are available in the Friberg translation (Lönnrot, Kalevala [Friberg]). Landström's illustrations, characteristic of a postwar, postnationalist Finnish view of the epic, call attention to the songs' references to Väinämöinen's blubbering, duplicity, and lechery, details overlooked in nineteenth-century artistic portrayals. The comic writer and illustrator Mauri Kunnas has created a hilarious parody of both the epic and Gallen-Kallela's paintings in his *Koirien* Kalevala, translated as *The Canine* Kalevala, in which the heroes and villains of the *Kalevala* become dogs and cats and in which Gallen-Kallela's paintings are irreverently reworked.

Kimmo Laine and Hannu Salmi provide a fascinating overview of postwar film and television interpretations of the *Kalevala,* including the 1959 Finnish-Soviet *Sampo* and the avant-garde television miniseries *Rauta-aika* (*Age of Iron*), directed by Kalle Holmberg; the miniseries is based on a screenplay by the modernist poet Paavo Haavikko and has a symphonic soundtrack composed by Aulis Sallinen. Tina Ramnarine explores the uses of folk songs related to the epic by modern Finnish bands like Värttinä in her study *Ilmatar's Inspirations*. Karl Spraklen includes a chapter on Finnish folk-metal adaptations of the *Kalevala* in his study *Metal Music and the Re-imagining of Masculinity, Place, Race and Nation* (135–50). It can be valuable for instructors to challenge students to explore one or more such modern adaptations of the epic on their own or in groups and to offer a brief analysis of the ways the product transforms or interprets the epic. Doing so helps underscore the evolving nature of a national epic as community property—a vehicle aimed at expressing the identity of a nation as that nation endures and progresses through time.

Notes

1. Poem numbers mentioned in the essay refer to Lönnrot, *Kalevala* (rev. ed.).

2. The various spells in the *Kalevala* are noted textually in Lönnrot, Kalevala [Magoun], which can provide the instructor with a useful list.

3. For an overview of the place of *Kalevala* in Sibelius's work, see Wilson. For a discussion of Gallen-Kallela, see Wahlroos. For copyright-free images of many of Gallen-Kallela's most famous paintings, see "Search."

Works Cited

Billig, Michael. *Banal Nationalism*. SAGE, 1995.

DuBois, Thomas A. *Finnish Folk Poetry and the* Kalevala. Garland, 1995.

———. "From Maria to Marjatta: The Transformation of an Oral Poem in Elias Lönnrot's *Kalevala*." *Oral Tradition*, vol. 8, no. 2, 1993, pp. 247–88.

Edensor, Tim. *National Identity, Popular Culture and Everyday Life: Nations and Nationalisms*. Berg, 2002.

Gallen-Kallela, Akseli. *The Defence of the Sampo*. 1899. *Finnish National Gallery*, www.kansallisgalleria.fi/en/object/389962.

———. *The Forging of the Sampo*. 1893. *Finnish National Gallery*, www .kansallisgalleria.fi/en/object/389724.

———. *Kullervo Cursing*. 1899. *Finnish National Gallery*, www.kansallisgalleria .fi/en/object/384175.

Järvinen, Irma-Riitta. Kalevala *Guide*. Suomalaisen Kirjallisuuden Seura, 2010.

The Kalevala *Heritage: Archive Recordings of Ancient Finnish Songs*. Ondine, 1996.

Kunnas, Mauri. *The Canine* Kalevala. Otava Publishing, 1992.

Kuusi, Matti, et al., editors. *Finnish Folk Poetry: Epic*. Finnish Literature Society, 1977.

Laine, Kimmo, and Hannu Salmi. "From *Sampo* to *The Age of Iron*: Cinematic Interpretations of the *Kalevala*." *Journal of Finnish Studies*, vol. 13, no. 2, 1992, pp. 73–84.

228 *Kalevala*

Lönnrot, Elias. *Kalevala.* Rev. ed., Suomalaisen Kirjallisuuden Seura, 1849. *Suomalaisen Kirjallisuuden Seura,* nebu.finlit.fi/kalevala/index.php?m=1&l=1.

———. *The* Kalevala: *An Epic Poem after Oral Tradition.* Translated by Keith Bosley, Oxford UP, 1989.

———. *The* Kalevala: *Epic of the Finnish People.* Translated by Eino Friberg, Otava Publishing, 1988.

———. *The* Kalevala; *or, Poems of the Kaleva District.* Translated by Francis Peabody Magoun, Jr., Harvard UP, 1963.

———. Kalevala: *The Epic Poem of Finland.* Translated by John Martin Crawford, 1887. "The Project Gutenberg Ebook of *Kalevala,*" 1 Feb. 2004, www .gutenberg.org/cache/epub/5186/pg5186-images.html.

———. Kalevala: *The Land of the Heroes.* Translated by W. F. Kirby, J. M. Dent and Sons, 1907. 2 vols. *Project Gutenberg,* www.gutenberg.org.

Pentikäinen, Juha. Kalevala *Mythology.* Translated by Ritva Poom, Indiana UP, 1989.

Ramnarine, Tina K. *Ilmatar's Inspirations: Nationalism, Globalization and the Changing Soundscapes of Finnish Folk Music.* U of Chicago P, 2003.

Rauta-aika. Directed by Kalle Holmberg, YLE, 1982. Four-part miniseries.

Sampo. Directed by Aleksandr Ptushko, Suomi-Filmi/Mosfilm, 1959.

Sawin, Patricia. "Lönnrot's Brainchildren: The Representation of Women in Finland's *Kalevala.*" *Journal of Folklore Research,* vol. 25, no. 3, 1988, pp. 187–217.

"Search the Collections." *Finnish National Gallery,* www.kansallisgalleria.fi/ en/search. Accessed 28 Sept. 2022.

Spraklen, Karl. *Metal Music and the Re-imagining of Masculinity, Place, Race and Nation.* Emerald Publishing, 2020.

Virtanen, Leea, and Thomas A. DuBois. *Finnish Folklore.* Finnish Literature Society, 2000. Studia Fennica Folkloristica 9.

Wahlroos, Tuija. "Devoted to the *Kalevala*: Perspectives on Akseli Gallen-Kallela's *Kalevala* Art." *Journal of Finnish Studies,* vol. 13, no. 2, 1992, pp. 28–37.

Wilson, William A. "Sibelius, the *Kalevala* and Karelianism." *The Sibelius Companion,* edited by Glenda Dawn Goss, Greenwood Press, 1996, pp. 43–60.

Roberta Micallef

The Many Lessons
of the Central Asian Epic *Manas*

I first fell in love with Turkic epics listening to Ruhi Su, a wonderful Turkish musician, singing cycles of the epic *Köroğlu* (Micallef). His songs were moving and beautiful and took the listener to another time and place while teaching much about brigands, hierarchy, and human relationships to nature and animals, as well as power dynamics in the seventeenth-century Ottoman Empire. Little did I know that this interest would lead to a master's thesis on Anatolian Hızır tales and much later to teaching undergraduate courses on Turkic epics.[1]

Among the epics I have included in my syllabi, *Manas*, a Central Asian epic, stands out not only because of its content but also because of its history. This beautiful, rich, entertaining tale can teach us much about nomadic values and the sociopolitical milieu in which it would have been recounted. This essay opens with a brief description of the epic and available English translations before turning to a discussion of teaching it through the themes of gender and gender roles, friendship, and good leadership and community. The concluding section moves beyond the particular features within the epic to address the interplay between the arts and politics in its reception history. Especially in the last three centuries, intellectuals and the public at large have had to defend this epic as an important

229

230 *Manas*

treasure trove, while some politicians have used it to legitimize their agendas, and others have tried to ban it. Thus it seems important for students to examine both the internal characteristics of the epic and the varying political responses to it.

The Epic *Manas*

The main oral epic of the Kyrgyz, *Manas* is a vast collection of myths, tales, and legends constructed around the birth, life, and death of Manas, a great fighter credited with uniting the Kyrgyz tribes. The title *Manas* most frequently refers to a trilogy about the hero Manas; his son, Semetey; and his grandson, Seytek. Chokan Valikhanov, a Kazakh ethnographer who in 1856 compiled the earliest written text of a *Manas* cycle, described it as "[t]he encyclopedia which contains the tales, the mythology, the way of life of the Kirghiz and the history of their relations with their neighbors, and expresses them clustered around the name of a single hero, Manas" (qtd. in Başgöz, "Epic Tradition" 318).

Although the epic's millennium was celebrated in 1995, the oldest remaining fragment of *Manas* is found in an early-sixteenth-century Tajik historiographical work, the *Majmu'at-at-Tavarih* (*A Collection of Histories*; Chadwick and Zhirmunskiĭ 306).[2] The German-born Turcologist Wilhelm Radloff, who served as the director of the Asiatic Museum in St. Petersburg and did groundbreaking work with Kyrgyz oral epic poetry, printed five cycles from *Manas* and two from the epic *Semetey*. Karl Reichl describes how these cycles were discussed and reedited with an English translation by Arthur Hatto (Reichl, "'True Nature'").

English Translations

In addition to many recordings and academic translations of *Manas* available for specialists, there are two easily accessible English-language translations aimed at nonspecialist audiences: Elmira Köçümkulkïzï's *The Kyrgyz Epic* Manas and Akylay Baimatova's *Tales of* Manas (Baijiev).[3] Both translators are native speakers of Kyrgyz, but they have different backgrounds, and their translations are based on alternative sources. Köçümkulkïzï translated the first eight episodes of *Manas* as performed by Saiakbai Karalaev and published in a 1995 academic edition. Karalaev was one of the last "chong manashchïs" ("great bards of *Manas*")—the highest level attainable by such a singer—and has been called the "Homer of the twentieth century," as noted in Köçümkulkïzï's introduction. In fall 2022 a Penguin Classics edition of *The Memorial Feast for Kökötöy Khan*, by Sagymbaĭ Orozbak uulu, became available in English. Affordable and beautifully translated by Daniel Prior, this text is a welcome teaching tool.

Baimatova, a native Kyrgyz with a Russian education, chose to translate the Kyrgyz playwright Mar Baijiev's Russian-language version not only because it "conveyed the ideas and cultural nuances in full color" but also because it was in line with the recordings of great *manaschis* in Kyrgyz, according to Baimatova's foreword (Baijiev). Baimatova's translation takes the reader from the beginning of the epic, which is about what Köçümkulkïzï calls the ancestors of Manas, to the death of Manas. Baimatova's is a shorter, more concise rendition of the epic marketed to young readers (five to eighteen years of age) and emphasizes different aspects of the epic. It is a useful tool in introducing a generalist audience to the epic, but it lacks the details captured in the academic translations as well as in Köçümkulkïzï's translation. In this essay, I primarily work with the first five thousand lines provided by Köçümkulkïzï, but I address Baimatova's translation as well.

Approaches to Teaching *Manas*

The courses that I have taught on Turkic epics have been comparative in nature. In them students read different cycles from different epics organized around themes such as gender, sports, and rituals. My courses often include an analysis of societal gender norms, expectations, and performances. Given that the Kyrgyz state is investing much effort in linking its heritage to *Manas*, one might examine what possibilities this epic offers regarding notions of community, society, and gender roles, and more specifically what gender-specific role models are offered in this text. In addition, for those readers interested in exploring the interplay of literature and history, this text provides a valuable tool since its history of availability and suppression is closely linked to historical events.

Gender and Gender Performance

The first two sections of Köçümkulkïzï's translation of *Manas* can be used by instructors to plan a lesson around the social and cultural expectations for men and women in different stages of their lives in this ancient nomadic society. Early on, readers are introduced to how people are grouped in this society. Students can be prompted to look for categories, such as young men, warriors, old men, maidens, craft women, wives, and mothers.

232 *Manas*

Class discussion can also center on the different types of behavior deemed acceptable for people as they move from one category to the next.

An examination of the first two sections of Köçümkulkïzï's translation, "Ancestors of Manas (before He Was Born)" and "Birth of Manas and His Childhood" (the first 5,429 lines of the epic), provide us with ample evidence of the preference for boys in this society (lines 966–70). However, as in other Turkic epics, girls are also to be celebrated, even if to a lesser extent; it is childlessness that is ultimately represented as a terrible fate (2080).

In these first two sections, the reader is introduced to the idea that certain behaviors are considered appropriate for different phases of life. While the epic provides many examples of associations of masculinity with bravery, dominance, prowess in warfare, and the ability to commit violence, a closer glance demonstrates that these qualities are acceptable depending on where the protagonist is in his life cycle. A boy might be playful (Köçümkulkïzï, line 875), and a young man might be full of passion and fire, reckless, and at the same time brave, proud, and arrogant (1170), whereas an older man is charged with being wise and providing good counsel and balancing the young man's passion with sound judgment (1270, 1971–74). The variety of assigned roles provide guidance for men in their expectations of themselves and one another.

Expectations of behavior for women in the epic are dependent on age and social status. Young girls, for instance, might be shy and may shed tears, but mothers are expected to be wise and strong. The emphasis and value placed on motherhood is evidenced by how the pregnant woman Chiyirdi, Jakyp's wife, is treated in the cycle "Birth of Manas and His Childhood." Her husband and eventually the entire tribe work together to satisfy her cravings and keep her safe even when she asks for tiger meat. Once women have become mothers as well as wives, they are responsible for properly socializing their daughters and protecting their sons. They are extremely brave when it comes to protecting their sons from harm, even if the harm is coming from the child's father or his family. The Baimatova translation, which provides us with the complete *Manas* cycle, concludes with the death of the hero and his legendary wife, Kanikay, fleeing with her son, Semetey, to protect him from his uncles. As wives, women are expected to provide their husbands with sage advice. They are generous and hospitable. As befitting their position in the tribe, they can be mother figures for many and leaders among women.

Good Leadership and a Community in Harmony

A theme that is found in many Turkic epics is the importance of good leadership. A good leader, in addition to being a good warrior, is just and takes good care of each member of the community; such leaders are rewarded with wealth or a son. While certainly there are named characters and individuals who have roles to play and unique personalities, the reader becomes aware of the importance given to the well-being of the group from the opening lines of the epic. In the first two sections, when the Kyrgyz have lost everything, including their brave leader Karakhan, their land, and their accumulated wealth, we find several examples of the emphasis placed on the community. Jakyp, Manas's father, and Akbalty, an older wise man, raid the enemy, who are carrying riches to their leader, but don't keep what they steal; rather, they distribute it to their group (Köçümkulkïzï, lines 1040–50). When Jakyp and his wife both have prophetic dreams pointing to the potential arrival of the epic hero, Manas, they decide to host a feast for the entire community to ensure that the pregnancy takes place. When Jakyp's wife craves tiger meat during her pregnancy, the community members come together to obtain the meat and thereby secure the birth of the hero who will save them.

Friendship

While we find evidence of friendship in many epics, in *Manas* we find evidence of friendship with people who are not part of the core community. One important pattern found in *Manas* is the help offered by (or to) people who are not from one's group, an action that sometimes leads to either personal friendships or friendly relations with neighboring states. In Köçümkulkïzï's translation, a Chinese hunter provides the Kyrgyz with the tiger meat that Manas's mother is craving during her pregnancy (lines 3500–20). In the chapters "The Tale of Almanbet" and "The Tale of How Almanbet came to Manas" in the Baimatova translation, we learn how this outsider becomes a loyal and trustworthy friend to Manas.

The Interplay of History and the Arts

The story of *Manas*'s reception makes this epic a wonderful tool for teaching students about the history of the region and the links between foundational stories, cultural identity, and nation building. The display of pride in one's cultural heritage has been identified as an element in the social

234   *Manas*

construction of an imagined community or a nation (Anderson). Scholars of the Turkic epic tradition and of Central Asian studies have concluded that after independence in 1991, *Manas* was used to fill the ideological void left by the collapse of the Soviet Union by promoting national pride, community, and unity (Reichl, "Oral Epics" 327; Wachtel 8–10; Heide 288–91). Over the years, Kyrgyz intellectuals and the population at large have fought as valiantly to preserve the memory of *Manas* as the hero himself fights in the text against those who oppress the Kyrgyz people.

In the political turmoil in the final years of the Russian Empire, versions of the *Manas* epic were written down by Jadid folklore collectors who were dedicated to documenting the artistic expression of Turkic peoples (Heide 297).[4] After the Bolshevik revolution in 1917, the epic became controversial, and in 1925 attempts by Kyrgyz political figures to have it published were blocked. In the 1930s, the official attitude toward folktales and other forms of folklore changed from indifference to enthusiasm and control. As new borders and boundaries were drawn during the Soviet era, the existence of national epics was provided as evidence that an ethnic group was a nation (Heide 297). In the 1940s, requests for a celebration of an anniversary of the epic were turned down, or if they were granted, they never took place (Heide 297). While excerpts appeared in newspapers in Moscow in 1946, by the latter years of Stalin's rule, the Soviet regime labeled Central Asian epics as "obstacles to building socialism" (Bennigsen 464).

The Kyrgyz reaction to the attacks on *Manas*, in contrast to the response to attacks on epics from the other Soviet Muslim republics, was "bitter, passionate, outspoken" and came from all layers of Kyrgyz society (Bennigsen 468). In an essay based on biographies of the world-renowned Kyrgyz author Chingiz Aitmatov and interviews with his family members, Alva Robinson writes that Aitmatov remembered a tense conference of about three hundred scholars at the Kyrgyz Academy of Sciences in Frunze that was forced to convene by Communist Party officials. On this occasion, Aitmatov recalled, the Kazakh historian and scholar of *Manas* Mukhtar Auezov, after listening to speakers attacking *Manas* one after the other, stood up and declared, "To take this epic away from the life of its people is like cutting out the tongue of our whole folk" (qtd. in Robinson 10). Thirty years later, Aitmatov was the chief editor of the first Kyrgyz print edition, which was transcribed from a *Manas* recitation based on recordings made by Auezov (Robinson 10). By the 1970s, *Manas* supporters found more room to maneuver, and a new series of publications of the epic were less severely censored (Heide 297).

That a folk epic could become a foreign affairs question and an arena of conflict is also worth discussing with students. In the first decade of the twenty-first century, the Kyrgyz state found itself embroiled in a battle over the epic once again when China listed *Manas* on the UNESCO List of Intangible Cultural Heritage in Need of Urgent Safeguarding in October 2009. The reaction from the Kyrgyz government was swift, but condemnations by people of all strata, from intellectuals to the business sector, quickly followed. *Manas* was clearly not an empty signifier that was simply being used by the government. Announcements by Kyrgyzstan's UNESCO Commission that China had nominated the epic on behalf of its Kyrgyz minority and that the epic had been recognized by UNESCO as an endangered piece of intangible heritage because in China the epic was known only to the Kyrgyz minority, "which was in urgent need of protection and support by China's authorities," helped calm the situation (Jacquesson 325). Four years later, in December 2013, the *Manas* epic—presented for the occasion as a trilogy comprising the stories of Manas; his son, Semetey; and his grandson, Seytek—was added to the UNESCO Representative List of Intangible Cultural Heritage of Humanity, this time on behalf of Kyrgyzstan.

The multiple meanings available to different readings of various cycles in *Manas*, in historical contexts ranging from the czarist era to the Soviet era, are particularly useful in discussions of nation-building efforts. Since the nineteenth century, *Manas* has been used by politicians as an element of national pride, a unifier, and an artwork in need of protection. The epic continues to be recited on special occasions by Kyrgyz *manaschis* in Afghanistan, China, and Kyrgyzstan. Today there are roughly one hundred recordings by various *manaschis*—from a vast area including Kyrgyzstan, Afghanistan, and Xinjiang, China—of this epic, which has many elements in common with other Turkic epics that span from Central Asia to Anatolia.

Since the nineteenth century, scholars have been predicting that modernization would destroy the epic genre worldwide. A prominent Turkish folklorist, İlhan Başgöz, argued as recently as 2008 that urbanization, increased levels of literacy, and the blurring of the lines between high and low culture would result in the demise of the "hikâye" tradition (Başgöz, *"Hikâye"* 214). In defiance of such dire predictions, the postindependence *Manas* phenomenon, which recognizes and commemorates the epic and its hero, has become so prominent that some bloggers and scholars describe it as "Manasification," "Manas mania," and "Manaspulation" (Jacquesson 324). When UNESCO declared 1995 the year of the *Manas*

236 *Manas*

celebration, official delegations from many countries attended the celebration, and UNESCO's general director spoke at the closing ceremonies (Reichl, "Oral Epics" 327). In Kyrgyzstan the international airport was named after the epic hero, an enormous equestrian monument was erected in front of the Bishkek Philharmonic Hall, and the Manas village complex was created in the country's capital (Wachtel 9). The first president of Kyrgyzstan, Asqar Aqayev, gave a speech titled "Manas—the Non-Fading Star of the Kyrgyz Spirit" (Reichl, "Oral Epics" 327), at once claiming the epic and its hero as Kyrgyz and linking it to modern Kyrgyz identity. In Bishkek in 2011, in honor of the twentieth anniversary of Kyrgyz independence, a statue of Manas replaced Erkindik, the statue of a winged woman representing liberty and peace, which, in turn, had replaced Lenin's statue after independence. Last but not least, a 2012 decree by the Kyrgyz Ministry of Education made a course in *Manas* studies a graduation requirement for every university student in the country (Wachtel 10). However, the limits of *Manas* mania became clear in the debates on *Facebook* when the Kyrgyz government suggested that the capital be renamed Manas in 2019. Some participants expressed that they would prefer that the Kyrgyz government use its resources to solve tangible problems ("Kyrgyz"). While one might have pride in one's folklore and epic traditions, some participants suggested, an ancient hero does not necessarily make a viable role model for contemporary Kyrgyz citizens.

Notes

1. Hızır is a Muslim saint especially known for appearing to travelers in need.

2. There has been much discussion about this text. See Heide (163–66) for further information.

3. There are also scholarly translations of *Manas*, but they are not easily available or accessible for nonspecialist readers.

4. The Jadid were Muslim reformers within the Russian Empire in the late nineteenth and early twentieth centuries. See Khalid for further information.

Works Cited

Anderson, Benedict. *Imagined Communities: Reflections on the Origin and Spread of Nationalism*. Verso, 2016.

Baijiev, Mar. *Tales of* Manas: *Kyrgyz Epos* Manas. Translated by Akylay Baimatova, Kindle ed., 2018.

Roberta Micallef 237

Başgöz, İlhan. "The Epic Tradition among Turkic Peoples." *Heroic Epic and Saga: An Introduction to the World's Great Folk Epics*, edited by Felix J. Oinas, Indiana UP, 1978, pp. 310–35.

———. *"Hikâye": Turkish Folk Romance as Performance Art*. Indiana UP, 2008.

Bennigsen, Alexandre A. "The Crisis of the Turkic National Epics, 1951–1952: Local Nationalism or Internationalism." *Canadian Slavonic Papers / Revue canadienne des slavistes*, vol. 17, nos. 2–3, pp. 463–74.

Chadwick, Nora K., and V. M. Zhirmunskiĭ. *Oral Epics of Central Asia*. Cambridge UP, 2010.

Hatto, Arthur T., editor and translator. The Memorial Feast for Kökötöy-Khan *(Kökötöydün Aši): A Kirghiz Epic Poem*. Oxford UP, 1977. London Oriental Series, vol. 33.

Heide, Nienke van der. *Spirited Performance: The Manas Epic and Society in Kyrgyzstan*. 2008. U of Tilburg, PhD dissertation. Pure.uvt.nl/ws/portal files/portal/1000549/Spirited_Performance_proefschrift.pdf.

Jacquesson, Svetlana. "Claiming Heritage: The *Manas* Epic between China and Kyrgyzstan." *Central Asian Survey*, vol. 39, no. 3, July 2020, pp. 324–39. *Taylor and Francis Online*, https://doi.org/10.1080/02634937.2020.1765739.

Khalid, Adeeb. *Central Asia: A New History from the Imperial Conquests to the Present*. Princeton UP, 2021.

Köçümkulkïzï, Elmira. The Kyrgyz Epic Manas. *Silk Road Foundation*, 4 Mar. 2005, www.silkroadfoundation.org/folklore/manas/manasintro.html.

"Kyrgyz Debate Renaming Capital." *BBC News*, 26 Mar. 2019, www.bbc.com/news/blogs-news-from-elsewhere-47700161.

Micallef, Roberta. "The Epic of Köroğlu." *World Epics*, edblogs.columbia.edu/worldepics/project/koroglu/. Accessed 7 July 2021.

Orozbak uulu, Sagymbaĭ. The Memorial Feast for Kokötöy Khan: *A Kirghiz Epic Poem in the* Manas *Tradition*. Translated by Daniel Prior, Penguin Classics, 2002.

Reichl, Karl. "Oral Epics into the Twenty-First Century: The Case of the Kyrgyz Epic *Manas*." *Journal of American Folklore*, vol. 129, no. 513, summer 2016, pp. 327–44.

———. "'The True Nature of the "Aoidos"': The Kirghiz Singer of Tales and the Epic of *Manas*." *John Miles Foley's World of Oralities: Text, Tradition, and Contemporary Oral Theory*, edited by Mark Amodio, 2020, pp. 185–206. *Project Muse*, muse.jhu.edu/book/79368.

Robinson, Alva. "After Manas, My Kyrgyz, Your Chingiz." *Aramco World*, Jan.-Feb. 2019, pp. 6–13.

Wachtel, Andrew. "A Tale of Two Heroes: Kyrgyzstan in Search of National Role Models." *Region*, vol. 5, no. 1, 2016, pp. 1–16. *Project Muse*, https://www.doi.org/10.1353/reg.2016.0004.

Barlow Der Mugrdechian

The Armenian National Folk Epic
David of Sassoun

David of Sassoun is the Armenian national folk epic, which represents the ethos of the Armenian people in an age-old struggle for freedom from invasion and oppression. Several important themes are recurrent in all four cycles of the epic. The epic portrays the Armenian heroes as the defenders against all foreign efforts to subjugate their people. In each cycle a hero is faced with a challenge, usually against a foe of great strength who seeks to bring the people of Sassoun under their domination. The epic's center is Sassoun, a sacred place that represents not only the home of the heroes but also Armenia itself. *David of Sassoun* came to represent an Armenian worldview that anchored the Armenians to a place and encapsulated their identity as a people constantly defending its beliefs. The heroes represent the highest values of the Armenian people, as they are always willing to sacrifice themselves to protect their way of life. The heroes are thus not only defending their own families and homes, they are also defending an entire people and culture.

Historical Background

Armenian history extends back some three thousand years, and there is a continuous historiographic tradition that dates from the fifth century AD, when the Armenian alphabet was invented. Armenia has time and again been in the path of great empires and military aggressors, including the Achaemenid Persians, Alexander the Great, the Romans, the Sasanid Persians, the Byzantine Empire, the Arab Empire, the Seljuk Turks, the Mongols, and many more.

Armenians have been a Christian people since the fourth century AD. Although many foreign powers have tried to convert the Armenians to other religions, they have been unsuccessful. In the fifth century AD, Armenians successfully defended themselves from the Persians, who sought to forcibly convert them to Zoroastrianism. The main Armenian protagonist, General Vartan, lost his life in the battle, but the outcome was that the Armenians were able to continue to freely practice Christianity. General Vartan's decision to sacrifice himself in the defense of his people became a shining example to future generations. The Armenian historian Yeghishe immortalized General Vartan's sacrifice, and even today the anniversary of the battle is marked as an Armenian national holiday.

Movses Khorenatsi, commonly referred to as the father of Armenian history, was the first to record the history of the Armenians from their origins to the fifth century AD. In his *History of the Armenians*, Khorenatsi relates oral tales but does not identify their sources. Among these tales is the foundational epic tale of Hayk and Bel. Hayk is the eponymous father of the Armenian people. Bel wanted to dominate Hayk and his people, offering not to attack if Hayk were to accept Bel's dominion over him. Refusing to be intimidated, Hayk fought and slew Bel in single combat. Thereafter Hayk and his people moved to the region of Mount Ararat, and the Armenians were free to lead their own lives. This recurring theme of resisting domination, rather than submitting, became an inextricable component of the Armenian ethos.

The epic *David of Sassoun* is part of the tradition first established by the tale of Hayk and Bel. The epic was not composed by a single author and was, unlike most other national epics, exclusively transmitted orally for more than a thousand years before it was published in 1874 by the priest and ethnographer Garegin Srvandztiants, under the title *Grots u brots yev* Sasuntsi Davit *kam* Mheri tur (*Notes and Observations and* David of Sassoun; or, Mher's Door). Multiple versions of the epic were transmitted in various areas throughout historic Armenia by *gousans*, or troubadours. Srvandztiants became the first to transcribe the oral epic when, after a three-year search, he found a villager named Krpo from the town of Moush who recited it to him. Part of the enigma of the epic is that it was recited orally for over a millennium before it was first put to paper. There is mention of the epic in a twelfth-century Arabic text and by sixteenth-century Portuguese travelers, but there is no mention of the epic in classical Armenian literature. Why this is so remains a mystery.

The tradition of reciting *David of Sassoun* continued well into the early twentieth century, when it was cut short by the 1915 Armenian genocide. The genocide ruptured the oral tradition of the epic, as those who could recite it by heart were either killed or forced to leave their homeland permanently. Fortunately, some survivors were able to escape to the Republic of Armenia, later Soviet Armenia. There, those who could still remember the epic were asked to recite it so that it could be transcribed. Some sixty-five variants were thus saved and eventually became the basis for the first critical edition of the epic published in the Armenian capital of Yerevan in 1939.

This official version is referred to as the jubilee edition because the origin of the epic was arbitrarily attributed to the year AD 939—even though scholars realized that there could be no specific date of inception for an oral epic. The edition was compiled by a small team of scholars led by Manuk Abeghyan, who compared the transcribed oral versions and produced a unified rendering. In 1964, Artin Shalian translated this jubilee edition into English, and this publication was followed by translations into other languages (Shalian, *David*; Kouymjian, "Ethos"). However, additional versions of the epic were discovered after 1939 that were not incorporated into the critical edition and have yet to be fully studied (Kudian; Surmelian; Tolegian). They are a rich source for further study because comparison of the variants sheds light on the significance of each of the epic's cycles.

The manner in which the epic was finally recorded is also significant because the ethnographers who transcribed it were able to gather details about the lives and backgrounds of the reciters, including when and where they were born, and information about the dialects they utilized. The question of language is important because the wide variety of Armenian dialects used in the recitation of the epic indicates the extent to which the epic had spread through the centuries. The diversity of the variants, some of which remain unstudied, adds valuable insight into the development of the epic.

Suggested Reading for a Survey Course

Shalian's 1964 English metrical translation is entitled David of Sassoun: *The Armenian Folk Epic in Four Cycles*. Although its 377 pages would prove daunting for a one-to-two-week segment on the epic, instructors can easily assign specific episodes. Shalian's introduction gives an overview with valuable background information (xv–xxxvi). The first cycle explains how Sassoun was established (4–25). This section also includes some of the miraculous elements of the epic and introduces the attitude of the Armenians with respect to their enemies. The core of this cycle is represented by the heroic efforts of Sanasar and Baghdasar against the caliph of Baghdad (77–105). In the second cycle, the story of Lion Mher illustrates the importance of making and keeping oaths in the epic (111–49). The third cycle focuses on David and his conflict with his main enemy, Msra Melik (see, in particular, 154–65). This cycle also shows the hero David defending the people of Sassoun from their various enemies (204–13). The climactic moment of this cycle is the duel between David and Msra Melik and David's eventual victory (252–85).

Since Shalian's translation is expensive, another option for instructors would be to use an English version available online. Especially recommended is a version of the third cycle by Hovhannes Toumanian, often referred to as the national poet of Armenia. This version can be covered in one to two weeks and includes many of the epic's most important episodes, namely, the life of David and the challenges he faces. The English translation is also in verse, allowing students to enjoy the rhythms of poetry even if not in the original language.

To give students an idea of what this epic sounds like when sung in Armenian, instructors can play in class a segment of a performance available online through the *UNESCO Intangible Cultural Heritage* website ("Performance").

Features of the Epic

An alternative name of the epic is *Daredevils of Sassoun*, and here the word *daredevil* includes those who are eccentric, are sometimes reckless, and take unexpected risks. This fits in with one Armenian self-image as an individualistic and nonconformist people. The daredevils are willing to face enormous odds as underdogs and to embark on quests that many would see as foolish or crazy. But it is precisely these qualities that have endeared

242   *David of Sassoun*

the heroes of Sassoun to all Armenians and can explain why the epic flourished orally for over a millennium.

The epic, as noted above, comprises four cycles. Each cycle represents one generation of an extended family: Sanasar and Baghdasar, Lion Mher, David, and Little Mher (Kouymjian and Der Mugrdechian, "Sassounts'i Davit"). The heroes of each generation perform heroic exploits and face similar challenges, which must be overcome before they can take their rightful place in society (Anderson; Hazarabedian). Thus, students may compare episodes from these cycles to each other as well as to any number of epic narratives worldwide in which heroes undertake valiant deeds in high-stakes situations.

Sanasar and Baghdasar are divinely born and establish the town of Sassoun. Sanasar is endowed with unusual strength, which he utilizes to battle all who would threaten his domain. His son, Lion Mher, so named because he killed a lion with his bare hands, must prove himself a worthy successor to his father. Lion Mher's son, David, is the epic's most famous hero, born at the moment his parents die and therefore raised as an orphan. The cycle of David is the longest and the most elaborate of the cycles and is the one most frequently included in oral recitations, thus it gives its name to the entire epic. David's most important foe is his half-brother, Msra Melik, the king of Egypt, who seeks to subjugate Sassoun. David's encounters with Msra Melik form the core of the epic. David's son, Little Mher, must also fight against injustice in the world. He does not die in the epic but rather awaits the moment when the world is cleansed of its iniquity and he can take his place as the rightful heir of Sassoun. Thus, there is no real conclusion for the epic, as Little Mher is imprisoned within a rock that opens only twice a year. He can come out of the rock only when there is no evil left in the world. There is a sense of timelessness to the epic that renews its vitality and relevance with each generation.

For students studying the epic, there are many interesting aspects that can be discussed. Women play a significant role in the epic, as their interaction with the main heroes is important to the plot. Women are usually portrayed as the virtuous upholders of family life, whereas often the men break their vows and are punished accordingly. Women in the epic are strong, can stand up to the heroes of Sassoun, and have agency. The role of female characters in the epic can be compared to the role of women in contemporary society, thus raising issues of equity in the family and beyond.

Another interesting facet of the epic is the question of identity and its corollary of how to distinguish between those who are within your group and those who are not. For the heroes of Sassoun, it is imperative to defend their home against all outsiders, who neither share their beliefs nor their outlook on life. Difference can be noted in language, religion, and customs. The epic portrays the Armenians as tolerant of difference, whereas those who seek to dominate them are not tolerant.

This tension begins early in the first cycle when the Armenians encounter the caliph of Baghdad, who wishes to wed the Armenian king Gagik's daughter. This event is an echo of the period of the Arab invasion and eventual conquest of Armenia in the eighth and ninth centuries. It would not have been possible in these circumstances for the king's daughter to marry a non-Armenian, and the king states, "I am an Armenian, you are an Arab. I am a cross-worshipper, you are a pagan. How can I give my daughter to you? I will never give my daughter to you" (Shalian 6–7). The epic clearly draws the boundaries of family for its protagonists and reminds readers how a foreign ruler's marriage proposal may be a thinly veiled attempt at political dominance.

One interpretation of this encounter deals with the religious aspect, as the heroes of Sassoun are Christian, while the invaders are Muslim or from other religions. In the epic, the Armenians have maintained the memory of their earlier defense of their country against the Assyrians and subsequently the Persians. The Armenians express their own identity and do not want to intermarry into foreign cultures. The epic provides a means to inspire future generations of Armenians to maintain their identity against any challenges. Following the example of the brave exploits of the heroes of Sassoun, each new generation can learn from the epic how to fortify themselves against new aggressors.

Magical beings also inhabit the world of *David of Sassoun*. Children find these magical elements enchanting, and they add color to the epic. These magical beings include *devs* (monsters), dragons, and *pehlevans* (brave warriors). Often these magical creatures have exploited the people of Sassoun, for example, by stealing treasure or by terrifying the population, but the heroes are able to overcome the challenges and defeat the magical creatures. Such beings may also guide the heroes. Of particular interest for his positive qualities is Kourkig Jelali, a supernatural marine horse associated with many of the heroes. He is endowed with the ability to speak and can thereby impart his wisdom. Kourkig Jelali rarely speaks during the epic, but each time he conveys important advice to the heroes.

244   *David of Sassoun*

When David is preparing to duel his foe Msra Melik, Kourkig Jelali senses that David is wavering and thus encourages him by saying, "Why are you frightened? My breath will slay as many as your sword can slay . . ." (Shalian 271).

Another major theme that resonates throughout the epic is the inner strength of the heroes, who are often seemingly ordinary and who must muster the courage to defeat their enemies. This is often accomplished with the help of divine intervention, as the epic reflects the strong Christian values of the Armenians. The heroes utilize oaths to God to achieve their goals—even if they often break their oaths in moments of weakness.

The heroes are not portrayed in the epic as perfect. One recurrent flaw, repeated in each generation of the house of Sassoun, is their temporary abandonment of their wives for other beautiful women, who are often outsiders. This behavior means that the heroes are open to foreign influence and that they are able to adapt that influence to make it Armenian. In the end, they return to their wives after having broken their vows. Students may compare these episodes to Odysseus's dalliances with Circe and Calypso in the *Odyssey* or Aeneas's love affair with Dido in the *Aeneid*. Lion Mher, for example, is married to Armaghan but sleeps with Ismil Hatoun, who bears him a son, Msra Melik, who becomes the archenemy of the Armenians (Shalian 140–44).

Given the epic's Christian elements, students may seek connections to biblical figures and stories. The hero and namesake of the epic, David, most clearly evokes the hero who defeated the giant Goliath, but he is often also compared to Moses, and some of the other main figures likewise have biblical figures as their prototypes. Sanasar and his brother Baghdasar are born from a mother (Dzovinar) who gives birth after drinking from a divine spring. Sanasar, the firstborn son, is stronger than his brother because his mother drinks a cupped handful of water from the spring before he is born and only half a handful before his brother's birth. This miraculous episode evokes the story of the birth of Jesus since the twins are conceived through water (representing the Holy Spirit) and the heroine Dzovinar takes the role of Mary, the mother of God (see Alishan).

Students will notice, in fact, that many parts of the epic are informed by Armenian religious beliefs and that the epic evokes a sense of identity based on a common language and literature. Throughout the epic students can note specific references to Christianity—from the construction and establishment of major worship sites such as churches and monasteries to the heroes' frequent consultation with clergy before making important decisions. At the same time, however, students may also detect vestiges of the pre-Christian religions of the Armenians. The heroes, in fact, embody some features of early Armenian gods such as Vahakn, the god of thunder, and thus reflect the long history of the Armenian people.

In sum, the epic *David of Sassoun* stands out as an example of world literature because it encompasses more than a thousand years of Armenian history (from the ninth to the nineteenth century) and thus reflects on extraordinary events over various eras in its verses (Khatchadourian; Kouymjian and Der Mugrdechian, David). It continues to provide new generations of Armenians with the means to connect with their ancestors and to maintain their language, culture, and religion. In a course on world epics, this timeless work can provide students with valuable insights not only into the ethos of the Armenian people but also into the workings of the epic genre in western Asia more broadly.

Works Cited

Alishan, Leonardo P. "The Sacred World of Sasna Tsrer: Steps toward an Understanding." *Journal of the Society for Armenian Studies*, vol. 2, 1985–86, pp. 107–39.

Anderson, Earl. "The Armenian Sasun Cycle: Folk Epic, Structure and Theme." *Revue des études arméniennes*, vol. 13, 1978–79, pp. 175–86.

Hazarabedian, Margit Anahid. *Functional Transformation in Traditional Oral Narrative: An Interdisciplinary Study and Personal Interpretation of the Codification of the Armenian Epic* David of Sassoun. 1998. U of California, Berkeley, PhD dissertation.

Khatchadourian, Arpine. David of Sassoun: *An Introduction to the Study of the Armenian Epic*. Wipf and Stock, 2016.

Kouymjian, Dickran. "The Ethos of a People." *Ararat*, vol. 6, no. 3, summer 1965, pp. 55–58.

Kouymjian, Dickran, and Barlow Der Mugrdechian, editors. David of Sassoun: *Critical Studies on the Armenian Epic*. The Press at California State U, Fresno, 2013.

———. "Sassounts'i Davit: The Synopsis of the Official Version of the Epic." Kouymjian and Der Mugrdechian, David, pp. 21–33.

Kudian, Mischa. The Saga of Sassoun: *The Armenian Folk Epic Retold*. Kaye and Ward, 1970.

"Performance of the Armenian Epic of 'Daredevils of Sassoun' or 'David of Sassoun.'" *UNESCO Intangible Cultural Heritage*, ich.unesco.org/en/RL/performance-of-the-armenian-epic-of-daredevils-of-sassoun-or-david-of-sassoun-00743. Accessed 29 Sept. 2022.

246 *David of Sassoun*

Shalian, Artin K., translator. David of Sassoun: *The Armenian Folk Epic in Four Cycles.* Ohio UP, 1964.

Srvandztiants, Garegin. *Grots u brots yev* Sasuntsi Davit *kam* Mheri tur. Ye. M. Dndesian, 1874.

Surmelian, Leon, translator. Daredevils of Sassoun: *The Armenian National Epic.* A. Swallow, 1964.

Tolegian, Aram, translator. David of Sassoun: *Armenian Folk Epic.* Bookman Associates, 1961.

Toumanian, Hovhannes. *David of Sassoon.* Translated by Thomas Samuelian, 1997.

Part V

The Enduring Oral Tradition

Frederick Turner

To Drink from the Source:
Teaching the *Mwindo* Epic

Why teach the *Mwindo* epic? This question is bound up in a deeper question—why teach epics at all? And to answer it already points to how to teach such works. It is beginning to become clear that narratives are not mere fictions or fantasies, distracting us from reality, but the means by which we organize any coherent understanding of the world. Science cannot operate without testable hypotheses, and hypotheses are essentially stories. Stories underpin families, and they do the same for cities, nations, and religions. Of course, stories may be useful or not: the less useful ones tend to constrain the choices and narrow the affordances of those that hold to them, and the more useful ones tend to open up worlds of possible action and understanding. Epics are usually stories whose survival and wide acceptance warrant their value as providers of coherent alternatives and scenarios whose exploration clarifies our picture of the world.

In the past, when the nation or the religious community was the largest viable human unit of cooperation, a single epic cycle provided most of the root stories needed by the citizen. Think of the matter of Troy; the matter of Britain, with its Arthurian core legends; the matter of the crusades that furnished so many European nations the images of Roland and

250 *Mwindo*

Orlando; the matter of the ring and the dragon in the Nordic world, and the matter of the great Bharata.

But today that largest viable human community must be the human race as a whole if we are to survive as a species and not go down to a catastrophic ecological disaster or final military apocalypse. We must look beyond the celebration of a single creed or nation that we find in individual epics and seek the deeper human story that underlies all the truly great epic narratives. The study of several epics together is the best way to disentangle the universal human truths and values and beauties from the local loyalties and partisanships that sometimes obscure them. Teaching epics may be the most important of all literary teaching—it is no coincidence that all the great literatures of the world have at their root some founding epic story.

To teach the *Mwindo* epic in particular, especially today and especially to young multicultural students, is both a challenge and an opportunity. It is a challenge because the best written form in which it exists—Daniel Biebuyck and Kahombo Mateene's transcription and translation—though an excellent piece of anthropological scholarship and a painstaking work of linguistic expertise, is a rather formidable proposition for students accustomed to user-friendly editions of the traditional epic canon. *Mwindo* has not yet gone through the process that *Gilgamesh* has since Nancy K. Sandars's first good but bare-bones translation, which has resulted in a dozen excellent translations with illustrations, glossaries, and real literary polish.

But *Mwindo*, even or perhaps especially in its forbidding anthropological guise, is also an extraordinary opportunity for the teacher of the epic genre. Here we not only see but take part in the crucial crossover from oral to literary modes, in which a good anthropologist serves as both the scribe and a witness of the ritual and performative context of the original oral bardic presentation. Accordingly, the student, with guidance from the instructor in visualizing the event, can be a virtual witness to the performance itself; or, analogously, it is as if the student had a time machine and could hear some proto-Homer sing Odysseus's struggle in an Aegean chieftain's hall.

Mwindo also happens to contain a larger-than-usual collection of the basic epic tropes and themes and a strong combination of narrative, metanarrative, and performative ornamentation such as musical, lyric, and celebratory passages. In other words, like *Popol Wuj* and the *Mahabharata*, it introduces students to a much wider selection of the fundamental elements of the epic genre than do many other epics in the world canon. In some ways Western epic scholarship has been limited by its foundation in the written *Iliad*, whose perfection is achieved at the cost of excluding many themes and motifs that are found elsewhere in the genre. The wager scene in *Mwindo* (Biebuyck and Mateene 108–09) is a good example: compare the similar scene in the *Mahabharata* where Yudhishthira wagers all against Duryodhana (Buck 55–61), or the fatal horse-fight wager in *Njal's Saga* (98–101), the ball-game wagers in *Popol Wuj* (*Popol Vuh* 91–98, 119–32), or even the wager between God and the devil in Job and *Faust* (Job 1.6–12; Goethe 48–50). Another example is the baby abandoned to and rescued from the river (Biebuyck and Mateene 59–72), which has parallels in Exodus, *Journey to the West*, and the Korean epic of *Jumong*, briefly discussed below.

Mwindo vigorously opens the student up to a fresh set of perspectives on how an epic story can be told. I myself remember the shock of first encountering Eschenbach's playful, teasing tone in *Parzival* and the grotesque slapstick of the Monkey King's adventures in *Journey to the West*. *Mwindo*'s rap or rock concert format and style is similarly startling and defamiliarizing—this is not your grandparents' epic! And it is precisely this aspect of the poem that might, with the right teacherly guidance, introduce a culturally suspicious student to a whole world of artistic and philosophical experience. The long passage on pages 84–87 (Biebuyck and Mateene; see 165–68 for the equivalent passage in the Nyanga original) is a classic rap, with its insistent rhymes (in the original), its self-referential implication that Rureke and his performance band need to be fed and paid, and its final celebration of the drum to which the whole piece is sung.

Mwindo's existence dispels several canards, such as that epic is predominantly a Western genre and that to teach it reinforces ideas of racial or civilizational superiority. *Mwindo* gives voice to Bantu sensibility while expressing a fully recognizable common humanity. It also demonstrates that the critique of absolute political power that is implicit in many great world epics exists robustly in the sub-Saharan African context and can provide a model for emerging states there. In *Mwindo* there is a bloodless transfer of political power, the beginnings of limited government, popular participation in governance, and a strong sense of the rightful power and status of women. Shemwindo's patriarchal oppression of his wives is replaced by his son's much more egalitarian relationship with Iangura, Kahindo, and the other female personages in his life. Those who would

252   *Mwindo*

cast doubt on Africa's future, citing its troubled postcolonial history, might reflect on the final law-giving passages of *Mwindo*. Biebuyck's humility and respect before the *Mwindo* bard and teacher Shekarisi Rureke properly models the mindset of the Euro-American researcher when approaching the wisdom and art of another culture.

Further, the later parts of the story suggest an emerging spiritualized environmentalism that is relevant today. The slaying of Kirimu (or Dragon, as Biebuyck and Mateene translate it; 129–36), like the slaying of Humbaba in the *Epic of Gilgamesh* (80–84), is plainly a recognition of the dangers of taking more from nature than is just. Much of the poem suggests a cultural awareness of sustainability and renewability analogous to that of the Balinese water-temple culture made famous by J. Stephen Lansing and others. The passage where Mwindo must plant a banana grove (at the behest of Muisa and as a marriage test) is a textbook example of sustainable rainforest horticulture (Biebuyck and Mateene 97–99). Mwindo does not burn the forest: he plants the banana stipes first then fells the trees and lets them both decompose and continue to shade the saplings as they grow, thus preserving the soil's fertility and mimicking nature's own ways.[1]

But *Mwindo* is more than a highly instructive cultural object lesson. It is also a celebration, inviting students to join in its spirit, and the work's strong parallels to rap poetry offer lively possibilities for classroom performance. In particular, the ethnodrama method of teaching anthropology pioneered by Richard Schechner and Victor Turner might suggest ways of bringing the epic to life in the classroom (or even perhaps in a theater or musical performance space). Rap expresses the indefatigable ebullience of downtrodden youth and celebrates the emerging ego and the pathos of youth's heroic defiance. *Mwindo* does the same, and if I were teaching it now with a serious budget I would try to get a good rap artist to coach my students in a performance of scenes from the poem, beginning with the banana-grove passage (Biebuyck and Mateene 97–99).

What makes great works of literature great is that which makes them belong, not just to the canon of their own nation but to the emergent human canon. *Mwindo* is a case in point. Certainly, it is deeply rooted in the practices and ideas of the Nyanga people of the Democratic Republic of the Congo (formerly Zaire), whose culture is extremely different (on the surface) from that of most readers of this volume. But it is also relevant to the titanic struggle of Africa as a whole for a humane and beautiful social order in the context of Africa's own characteristic cultural strengths and flaws. And beyond Africa, *Mwindo* is one of the great panhuman documents, like all the major epics of the world, an account from the inside of how we humans became human. It has a rightful place in our global canon.

Epics do many things: they define the nature of the human storyteller; directly or indirectly, they recall the creation of the world and of the human race; they describe the paradoxical role of the hero as both an ordinary person and a radical exception; they establish the complex quest underlying all human action and tell the story of the journey that it entails; they get to the bottom of the kin strife that both blocks and inspires the quest; they distinguish the three worlds of nature beneath us, society around us, and heaven above us; they recount the tragicomic fall of our race from nature to culture, wild creature to knowing human; they take us shamanically into the underworld and back; they recount the basic principles of the founding of a polity's laws and rituals and give a representative history of its people; they provide by example a set of fundamental virtues, values, and vices; they embrace and understand the new medium of communication of their time; and they teach us how to deal with the boundaries of the psychological, social, and cosmological world, especially the mystery of time. All these elements are in *Mwindo*, many with a clearer and stronger articulation than is found in other epics.

Biebuyck and Mateene's translation—or rather, their trot of the great storyteller Rureke's oral memorized version of the poem—is clearly the fullest and best version of the story to which a Western reader has access (roughly one hundred pages of translated text). That version is profoundly reflexive, in the sense that the storyteller, in playing out the part of the hero, is also himself performing a shamanic journey into the underworld. He is explicitly taking Biebuyck and Mateene, the scribes, and his helpers and hearers—and us, the readers he knows will read him—along for the ride. The exhaustion, thirst, and hunger he feels in this enormous recitation—and its astonishing intellectual and artistic effort—are openly introduced into the songs that Mwindo sings as he makes his great journey (a brilliant device that no other epic poet I know of uses so directly and effectively). Rureke takes on the paradoxical authority of the storyteller—he is only a servant, passing along a tradition he inherited from the Babuya lineage of Ihimbi, whence the story cycle came; but he is also a shaman, channeling the ancestral and divine beings of whom he tells. The hero's power comes from his songs; the singer's ordeal is itself a heroic journey.

The birth of the epic hero is almost always bizarre and marvelous. In telling the story of Mwindo's miraculous birth and his refusal to be

254 *Mwindo*

destroyed by his father Shemwindo, Rureke is recapitulating in similar terms the Greek myth of the primal gods, who again and again attempt to eat or smother or abort their offspring and who are thwarted by the heroic intransigence of their young. In his journey Mwindo encounters the great forces of the universe—the animal spirits, the sun, the moon, and the rivers and storms—often embodied in the major characters he encounters. This is a cosmogenesis, a myth of the hope of growth, evolution, and new things breaking in on the old—the amazing ability of time to create a new moment every moment, the ability of life to give birth to new beings. We find it in the birth of the Chinese hero Tripitaka, the Maya hero twins, the Egyptian Osiris, the Korean hero Jumong, and Moses, who similarly escape an evil father figure by floating down a river (a theme in many world epics, as noted above). Jesus escapes Herod's massacre of the innocents by leaving with his mother for the land of the Nile. The Malian hero Sun-Jata escapes his own tyrants and goes into exile with his mother, Sugulun, as Mwindo escapes his father by finding refuge with his beloved aunt Iyangura. Time, and the human story, is an escape from the fixity or recycling of eternity. As Rhea saves Zeus from Chronus, his father, Iyangura offers sanctuary to her nephew, allowing the time of his future regime to flow forth, to the rhythm of Mwindo's drum (and Rureke's recitation).

Mwindo is not only an epic but also a bildungsroman, a story of personal and moral formation and development. Mwindo's search for revenge on his father changes the epic's goal and meaning radically as it brings to Mwindo an encounter with death and the experience of lived life. The hero finds that those who have most betrayed him and most deserve his wrath are also those most closely tied to all those he has loved, that the greater the offense to him, the more its revenge will damage him and his dear ones. He finds that his heroic ebullience and self-assertion—essential to being a person, a somebody—must be humbled and chastened to really come into their own. Odysseus, too, must hubristically challenge Polyphemus in order to make his name—literally to get into trouble, since *Odysseus* (Ὀδυσσεύς) means "trouble" in Greek—but he must also learn patience and self-control so as to be able to regain his wife, son, and home. Students might be asked to compare Mwindo's vaunting defeat of the dragon Kirimu, who is dear to the lightning god Nkuba, to Odysseus's vaunting defeat of the giant Polyphemus, who is dear to his father, the sea god Poseidon. Both heroes—like Parzival, Cuchulain, and the Monkey King, in their respective epics—must repent of their hubris.

Likewise, Gilgamesh's triumph over Humbaba leads to the death of the hero's friend Enkidu, and Gilgamesh's humiliation in the quest for eternal life is the very thing that makes him a good king and city builder. In these archetypal moral equations *Mwindo* is not just an epic but part of the eternal human epic, told again and again with a different dialect, but always in what Steven Pinker calls "humanese."

Epics often recount the tragic conflict of close kin as we humans continually struggle with the paradoxes of the human kinship system: selfish care of our own genes versus unselfish sacrifice for the genes of our kin, blood kinship versus affinal love, father against son, women against men. The explicitness of *Mwindo*'s oedipal theme is an important gloss on the many world epics in which the hero must contend for his existence and identity with a tyrannical male figure. Yes, in epics men must struggle with their fathers (as women with their mothers) to find their own heroic stature—Cuchulain with Conchobar, Sohráb with Rostám, Achilles with Agamemnon and Priam, Hamlet with Claudius, the Pandavas with the blind king Dhritarashtra, and Moses with Pharaoh. But usually the conflict is, in Sigmund Freud's terms, more or less repressed and symbolically redirected; *Mwindo*, however, blurts it out.

But what is truly remarkable about the poem is that Mwindo forgives his father. The truth-and-reconciliation ritual in which Shemwindo confesses his crimes and Mwindo refuses to accept his father's abdication and reinstates him as a king but under law is a deeply moving solution to the Freudian problem. Mwindo embraces him as the father without whom he could not be a true son. The search for a lost and criminal father is eerily relevant today in the context of the war on drugs and the consequent warehousing of Black men in the American legal system. I believe *Mwindo*, properly taught, might well become a mythic narrative for the recovery of Black fathers.

Mwindo is also an extraordinary political example to Africa, where former presidents who are free in their own countries are extremely rare and where the transfer of political power is often appallingly bloody. Mwindo always repents of the slayings that he as hero must perpetrate; and the greatest power of his *conga*, a symbolic object like a caduceus or thyrsus, is not to kill but to bring back to life.

The central drama of all epics is the fall of human beings from the naked, innocent, deathless, simple, and unashamed state of nature into the clothed, prurient, death-obsessed, wandering, conflicted, and self-conscious state of culture. We see Mwindo grow from a naked baby, full of ebullient

256   *Mwindo*

strength, unconscious boastful self-assertion, and oedipal passion for his aunt, into the wise, self-aware, well-traveled, and fully clothed king and husband at the end, who, in Wordsworth's words, "hath kept watch o'er man's mortality." Like the Monkey King in *Journey to the West*, Mwindo grows from a trickster figure into a sort of bodhisattva—even though the trickster is essential to the process. Mwindo achieves this transformation— as in different ways do Odysseus, Aeneas, and Dante in the Greek, Latin, and Italian epic traditions and the Pandavas and the hero twins in the Hindu and Maya epics, respectively—by means of the journey into the underworld. In contention with the lords of the underworld, Mwindo must submit to death but rise again through the power of his invincible *conga*; he must transcend death by internalizing it.

Mwindo's ordeals are, in a common epic trope, intended to prepare the hero for marriage with divine Kahindo. Significantly, one of the marriage tests imposed on him by her kin is to cultivate and harvest a crop of the staple food of the tribe (bananas) in one day. That is, he must demonstrate the technology of postlapsarian civilized culture (as Hunahpu and Ixbalanque must do in *Popol Wuj*, with an instant crop of corn, to be recognized as the true sons of the first pair of hero twins [*Popol Vuh* 109–10, 116]). In transferring his love from the mother figure Iangura to Kahindo, Mwindo has achieved full human, fallen adulthood. But he is not to enter a divine wedding. In an important twist, he will marry not the goddess but rather a mortal woman. He is instituting not a theocracy but something like a participatory democracy.

On his second great journey, with Nkuba, the lightning god, into the chilly realms of heaven, Mwindo shows himself to be not only the shaman of the subterranean journey but the shaman of the sky journey. He returns, like Moses from Sinai, with the legal and moral laws of Nyanga polity and the liturgies and founding rituals of his society. His is to be a kingship bound by laws and limits and prohibitions, in which he is not the master but the servant of his people: his kingship is no more than the stamping feet of his people's assent. Why should not Africa, which has in this epic perhaps its clearest definition of the spirit of democracy, find here its own founding political myth? The story is, after all, that of an insurrection: but it is one that, unlike recent insurrections, replaces despotism with popular participation, hatred with forgiveness, and a personality cult with a culture of compromise.

Rureke himself is well aware that in transmitting his poem into what are for him the alien media of the recorded, written, and translated text, he is joining myth to history. He simultaneously makes fun of the incomprehension and naivety of his European scribe, Biebuyck, and acknowledges the profound new meanings that emerge from the transcription of his story into another culture and a future time. The teacher can become another link in the chain of storytellers that memorialize the work of becoming human.

Note

1. Hayao Miyazaki, the great Japanese animated film director, deals with the same theme in his epic environmentalist movie *Princess Mononoke*, which many students will know; there, moreover, the killing of the sacred stag has the same valence as the killing of Kirimu in *Mwindo* (*Princess Mononoke* 1:40:20–2:05:15).

Works Cited

Biebuyck, Daniel, and Kahombo C. Mateene. *The* Mwindo *Epic from the Banyanga (Zaire)*. U of California P, 2021.

Buck, William. *Mahabharata*. New American Library, 1973.

The Epic of Gilgamesh. Translated by N. K. Sandars, Penguin Books, 1973.

Freud, Sigmund. *The Psychopathology of Everyday Life*. General Press, 2018.

Goethe, Johann Wolfgang von. *Faust: Part One*. Translated by Zsuzsanna Ozsvath and Frederick Turner, Deep Vellum, 2020.

Lansing, J. Stephen. *The Balinese*. Wadsworth Publishing, 1994.

Njal's Saga. Translated and edited by Robert Cook, Penguin Books, 2001.

Pinker, Steven. Personal communication with the author.

Popol Vuh. Translated by Dennis Tedlock, Touchstone, 1985.

Princess Mononoke. Directed by Hayao Miyazaki, Studio Ghibli, 1997.

Schechner, Richard. *The Future of Ritual: Writings on Culture and Performance*. Routledge, 1995.

Turner, Victor. *From Ritual to Theater: The Human Seriousness of Play*. PAJ Publications, 1982.

Wordsworth, William. "Ode: Intimations of Immortality from Recollections of Early Childhood." *Poetry Foundation*, 2022, www.poetryfoundation.org/poems/45536/ode-intimations-of-immortality-from-recollections-of-early-childhood.

John William Johnson

The Epic of *Sun-Jata* in the Light of Abrahamic and Mande Traditions

The West African epic of *Sun-Jata* was first introduced to French-speaking audiences in 1960 by Djbril Tamsir Niane in a small book, *Soundjata ou l'èpopèe mandingue.*[1] It took another five years for this volume to find English-speaking audiences through G. D. Pickett's translation, *Sundiata: An Epic of Old Mali.* Until these publications, this epic was largely unknown outside West Africa, but since then the story of this culture hero has entered the canon of the great epics of world history. Sun-Jata's exciting, heroic adventures celebrate his rise to power as the founder of the Mande Empire in the late twelfth or early thirteenth century.[2]

But the story of Sun-Jata is much more than a West African adventure story, useful in comparative literature classes. It has also inspired scholars to investigate actual performances of the epic by the Mande peoples in Mali, Guinea, Gambia, and sections of Burkina Faso and northern Ivory Coast. It might be noted in passing that interest in oral literature in general led to the European school of oral literature in Britain and Western Europe, which began during the colonial period. New methodologies and terminology have developed, such as replacing the term *oral literature* with *orature.*

The study of orature involves investigating more than the text. This school is also interested in the social context of orature: the society, the raconteurs, and the functions of performance. In Mali, for example, the bards who keep extensive cultural knowledge, including several epics, for Mande peoples are professionals, whose right to sing about their culture in public is inherited and protected by their caste position in society. To protect their right to this knowledge, bards only marry within bardic families. People outside are prohibited from marrying a caste member. Bards are called *jeli* (or *jali*) in the Mande-kan languages spoken by regional ethnic speakers called Mandinka, Maninka, Manding, Mandingo, Bamana, Bambara, and Jula. These bards are known widely in print as *griot* (fem. *griote*) in French.

The recitation of the epic of *Sun-Jata* in sung, poetic form is a living oral tradition about the principal culture hero of the Manden and those he encounters in his quest for power. A performance of all the core episodes about Sun-Jata occurs every seven years in the town of Kela in southern Mali, now recognized as a UNESCO Intangible Cultural Heritage event ("Septennial Re-roofing Ceremony"). Kela is a cultural center of bards, as most of its inhabitants are from bardic families. The festival lasts several evenings, when the epic of *Sun-Jata* is formally addressed to representatives of Sun-Jata's own family, the Keïta. Other families may also be present. Most of the time, however, one only hears individual episodes from the epic in contextual performances relevant to social and cultural events, such as festivals, weddings, and funerals. The bard or bards will relate episodes involving the families included in those events and their relationship to Sun-Jata. It is also possible to encounter a relatively complete set of episodes relating the whole story of Sun-Jata when local officials engage a bard to sing at a gathering of their choosing or when a researcher records a live performance for transcription and publication.

The performance of this oral text is never repeated word for word, as the choice of words may differ from one performance to another. The basic narrative events in each episode, however, are part of each bard's memory, and the episodes are performed using linguistic formulas and themes that given bards have heard and learned informally for years from other bards in their town and in other towns. The epic version described in this essay was sung by the bard Fa-Digi Sosòkò, who sang his epic as though addressing friends named Bèmba and Garan.[3] The audience listened in as though eavesdropping. The performance was recorded in what is known as an induced natural context, and the research methodology involved continuous recording without interruption. This method records the bard's actual words, unedited by the researcher, to a gathering of local people

260 *Sun-Jata*

who are all acquainted with the basic plot, keeping the bard from changing anything to please the researcher. Short of collecting a performance meant only for a local audience, this technique is the most reliable collection method possible for obtaining an authentic, unaltered text that exhibits the bard's language skill and narrative prowess, almost as if the researcher were not present to influence the text.

The lines of Sosòkò's epic are divided into three modes. The *narrative mode*, sung by a male bard, carries the plot. Major events in the narrative are celebrated in the *song mode* and may be sung by the male bard or by female bards. The *praise-proverb mode* is sung only by the male bard. The episodes of the story usually entail a change of location, and the praise-proverb mode acts as an interlude between episodes. It may comprise praise names, proverbs, incantations, prayers, curses, genealogies, and other genres in the Mande repertoire. Thus, epic is a multigeneric form. Audiences discern these modes by their performance style. The narrative mode is slow with regular rhythm. In song mode each melody is unique. The praise-proverb mode is sung rapidly at a higher pitch, giving the bard time to recall the next segment of the plot by reciting lines that do not require intense concentration. Remarkably, these modes are similar to those in grand opera, where recitatives advance the plot; arias celebrate important ideas, emotions, or moments; overtures introduce works; and interludes divide scenes. American musicals are similar, though in them the recitative is spoken rather than sung.

Together with contextual performance to enhance social events, other cultural functions of epic are evident, such as enumerating the roles of people in society, in which function the epic serves as a sort of handbook for appropriate social behavior. Moreover, the epic helps audiences connect to the place of their families in the history of the Manden and their relationship to the Manden's greatest culture hero, Sun-Jata.

Indigenous audiences share the same worldview and culture with the bard, and most of them will be acquainted with this epic, because they have listened to variants of it many times. Foreign readers of a printed version of the epic, however, will need an introduction and extensive footnotes explaining obscure passages to understand more than the barest parts of the plot.[4] This essay isolates key issues and important backstories in the epic that teachers may use in inspiring students for discussion beyond the surface adventures of the culture hero.

Before describing key issues, one more point concerning orature must be clarified. If teachers are to present the epic of *Sun-Jata* as a living epic participating in the contextual orature of several West African societies, an authentic text should be assigned, such as Sisòkò's version. This translation is inexpensive and easy to read in one or two class periods and represents a version of the epic that was sung in an oral performance to a live audience. Although it may be somewhat more difficult to read than some other translations, it represents an authentic performance in a specific place, recorded as the bard performed it in real time. A plethora of other translations have been published since Niane's 1960 book.[5] Some of them are reconstructed (rewritten) in the words of the editor rather than an authentic word-by-word, line-by-line translation of a recorded version of the poetic text. Other translations are composite texts, combining several versions inclusive of all or most of the episodes of Sun-Jata's life story recited by several bards. The least authentic are reconstructed translations written in prose.

Historians have determined that Islam arrived in sub-Saharan Africa as early as the eighth century. It took another century for Islam to make its way south and into the Manden, nearly three hundred years before the reign of Sun-Jata.[6] As is common in many places where Islam has spread, a syncretized version of Islam developed that was mixed with indigenous Mande religion and that has continued in Mali to this day, playing a part in the memory and celebration of Sun-Jata. The sources of power in the epic—one Islamic, one indigenous—reflect this syncretism, and all the episodes lead to Sun-Jata's acquisition of power.

The Islamic source involves a backstory that is not dealt with in the epic but that needs to be described if students are to understand the origin of Sun-Jata's power inherited from the Abrahamic tradition shared by Jews, Muslims, and Christians. That power is called *baraqah* in Arabic and means "grace."[7] The story goes back to the biblical and Qur'ānic versions of the rivalry between Abraham's two wives, Sarah and Hagar, together with the quarrel over the legitimacy of their sons (see the genealogy chart in the appendix). Students can compare the two versions of the story. Co-wife rivalry, common in societies that practice polygyny, is a major issue in the epic of *Sun-Jata*, as described below.

The Islamic concept of grace is seen as a divine power or covenant originating with Abraham, the patriarch of both Hebrew and Muslim peoples. *Baraqah* is believed to be attained in two ways, the first of which is by genealogical inheritance from Abraham's sons. It is important to note that Judaism and Islam differ over the legitimacy of Abraham's firstborn son, Ishmael.[8] In the Bible, Abraham's wife, Sarah, is barren and suggests

262   *Sun-Jata*

to Abraham that he take her Egyptian handmaiden, Hagar, for a wife so that he may have an heir by her. This he does, and they have a son named Ishmael. Much later, after Abraham is visited by three strangers (Gen. 18.1–15), Sarah bears Abraham a son named Isaac. In the Genesis account the status of Ishmael, as the son of a concubine, is lowered when Abraham blesses Isaac. Isaac becomes the forefather of the Hebrew nation and passes God's covenant of grace through his progeny to Jacob, Judah, and David—and, according to Christian tradition, Jesus.[9] Thus Hebrew doctrine elevates Sarah's progeny as God's chosen people. But Qur'ānic scripture grants Ishmael equal status with Isaac, if not actually elevated status, as Abraham's firstborn. Likewise, in the Qur'ān Hagar is considered equal to Sarah as a wife, not a concubine. Ishmael is twelve years old when Isaac is born, and the Qur'ān names Ishmael, not Isaac, the son whom God commands Abraham to sacrifice. Ishmael's legitimacy is crucial to Sun-Jata's inheritance of *baraqah* because Ishmael's genealogy leads to Muḥammad, Islam's most important prophet, who inherited *baraqah* in the sixth century.[10]

The second way to attain *baraqah* in Islam is to inherit it from an *aṣ-ṣaḥābah* (companion) of the Prophet.[11] In Sisòkò's version of the epic of *Sun-Jata*, Bilāl bin Rabaḥ was Muḥammad's first convert and most important companion, and Bilāl is recognized as the ancestor of Sun-Jata's father's family, the Kònatè, and of Mande peoples. It was he who passed *baraqah* on to Sun-Jata.

The power Sun-Jata inherits from his mother's family, the Kòndès, is the traditional Mande source of strong occult power called *nyama*. It is here where Islam is mixed with indigenous Mande religion. Like *baraqah*, *nyama* can be passed on to progeny and may also be acquired by other means. Several secret societies in Mali initiate their members to teachings that empower them with *nyama*. One of the most important of these societies is the hunters' society, made up of men who denounce ties to family and normative society and live together in the *wula* (bush), defined as any area beyond the borders of a *bò-kè-yòrò* (town). The bush is a dangerous place because it is filled with wild animals and, according to local beliefs, uncontrolled spirits and dangerous forces. Hunters are observably feared by most townspeople, who believe hunters can control *nyama*.

Another important trait of *nyama* illustrated in the epic is the acquisition of power by the deliberate violation of normative behavior. At one point, Sun-Jata sacrifices the unborn child of a *mansa* (ruler), Tulunbèn of Kòlè, to his fetish (Sisòkò, lines 1725–67). Strong and dangerous *nyama* is believed to be released on a person who violates social rules, but if the perpetrator survives the release of *nyama*, as Sun-Jata does, control over it is believed to be acquired. Building a supply of *nyama* strengthens one's power over time. Thus, Sun-Jata must stockpile *nyama* to add to his inheritance of *baraqah*.

Throughout Sun-Jata's struggle for power, women play a major role, particularly with regard to *nyama*. Sun-Jata inherits *nyama* from his mother, Sugulun, who inherited it from her aunt, the buffalo woman Du Kamisa. The episodes about Du Kamisa explain the origin of the family's strong *nyama*. Witness the Tarawere hunters' failed attempt to have sex with Sugulun, which she foils by using *nyama* (lines 963–96). After the death of Sun-Jata's mother, her daughter, Sun-Jata's sister Sugulun Kulunkan, takes her mother's place and plays a major role by seducing Sun-Jata's archenemy, the blacksmith wizard Susu Mlountain Sumamuru Kanyè, and learning the secrets of his powerful *nyama* (2668–745).

Not all women in the epic, however, are helpful to Sun-Jata. Their roles range from subservient to outright antagonistic toward him. The women who reverse the sequence of birth of Sun-Jata and his half brother (1048–84) are responsible for the onset of the cowife rivalry in Mansa Fata Magan Kònatè's family. Sugulun's cowife, Saman Berete, cripples Sun-Jata through a hex and later demands that her own son drive him away from the Manden. She continues to pressure the rulers of the Manden's neighboring countries to refuse sanctuary to Sun-Jata during his exile until Sumamuru conquers the Manden and drives Saman Berete and her son away (1880–902).

Daughters are treated like gifts to reward success in parts of the epic. Mansa Magan Jata Kòndè offers the Tarawere hunters any maiden of their choice in compensation for having killed the Buffalo Woman. The hunters shock everyone by choosing the *mansa*'s daughter Sugulun, who is considered ugly; the hunters make this choice because the defeated Du Kamisa revealed to them that Sugulun has inherited *nyama* from her aunt (905–25). Mansa Fata Magan Kònatè trades his sister Nakana Tiliba to the Tarawere hunters for Sugulun (1027–44), and in another episode Dankaran Tuman gives his daughter as a gift to Sumamuru in exchange for help in killing Sun-Jata.

Female characters can also wield great power, however, especially if they are outside the normative society. In one extended scene, the exiled Sun-Jata meets his match with the nine Queens of Darkness (1768–77). By this time, Sumamuru has overthrown Mansa Dankaran Tuman, and

264 *Sun-Jata*

Sumamuru sends the gift of a buffalo to the queens, asking them to kill Sun-Jata (1910–61), but Sun-Jata counters with a larger gift of nine buffalo to the queens (1965–87), and he escapes to his final sanctuary, Mèma (2037), where he again performs more sacrifices to increase his *nyama*.

Perhaps the most dramatic episode concerning women in the epic is the cowife rivalry between Saman Berete and Sugulun, again involving a reversal. The reversal of the birth announcements of Fata Magan's sons, causing the rivalry between Fata Magan's wives, can be likened to the reversal of the legitimacy of Abraham's sons, as discussed above. The structure of the Mande nuclear family can help explain this rivalry.

In Islam, a man may have up to four wives, a practice that often ensures rivalry between cowives, which is common in societies that practice polygyny. In these families, sequence in marriage and birth reflects social hierarchy. The first wife takes precedence over any future cowife. Likewise, the eldest male child becomes the father's heir and is owed deference by all his half and full siblings. In Mali, the eldest son reserves the right to marry first, hoping his son will be born first in the next generation and inherit primary rights as he did (see 951–61).

Mande *den-baya* (nuclear families) include all cowives and both full and half siblings. A *ba-den* (mother's children) are all full siblings and live with their mother in her dwelling, separated from the other cowives' domiciles. These children receive her comfort and love, and they share support and affection, called *ba-denya* (mother-child-hood). All *fa-den* (the father's children), both full and half siblings, encounter each other when they enter the walled courtyard of their father's compound, where they may compete for their father's attention. Based on these relationships, rivalry in the Mande nuclear family is given the name *fa-denya* (father-child-hood), implying competition and disharmony. Cowife rivalry is also marked by *fa-denya* and is actually expected. The Mande worldview expands nuclear family terminology so that *fa-denya* also means discord and chaos in the world in general and *ba-denya* means the opposite: cohesion and harmony.[12]

Cowife rivalry in Fata Magan's family begins when both wives give birth on the same day, Saman Berete first, Sugulun second (1048–122). But the announcements of their children's births are reversed, placing Sun-Jata as the apparent eldest. Immediately, an omen of Sun-Jata's eventual primacy is revealed when his grandmother discovers his body covered with hair. She gives the boy, whose name is Narè Magan Kònatè, his first praise name, Sun-Jata, meaning "Lion Thief" (lion for his strength, and thief for his eventual higher rank over his elder brother). What follows is a series of events and omens supporting Sun-Jata's eventual primacy.

Although the accurate sequence of births is eventually revealed, placing the child Dankaran Tuman first, Saman Berete is alarmed by Sun-Jata's praise name. She first summons her omen master, who places a curse on Sun-Jata to hamstring him (1151–59), causing him to have to crawl on the ground for several years. Despite this curse, Sun-Jata's personal jinn miraculously transports him to Mecca to perform the Muslim obligation of pilgrimage, beginning his long journey to accumulate *baraqah* (1160–77).[13]

The portents of Sun-Jata's supremacy continue to add up, as the hero performs his own sacrifices and gains enough *nyama* to enable him to stand up. He furthers his quest for *nyama* by becoming a hunter (1403–535), seriously upsetting the Saman Berete wife. Even though Dankaran Tuman eventually ascends to the throne, his mother pressures her son into expelling Sugulun's *ba-den* from the Manden. And so begins Sun-Jata's exile (1647).

The exile of heroic figures in scripture, mythology, literature, and human history is recognized as an archetype of human behavior. Both Lord Raglan and Stith Thompson acknowledge exile, whether forced or voluntary, as a motif of heroic behavior, and Sun-Jata is no exception.[14] His exile is forced on him by his father's jealous cowife, although it serves an important purpose, which is to increase his accumulation of *nyama* and strengthen him for his final goal.

After many vicissitudes that increase his *nyama*, Sun-Jata is invited back to the Mande, and he attacks Sumamuru but is unsuccessful because his rival's *nyama* is too powerful for him to overcome. Meanwhile, Sun-Jata's mother dies, passing her occult power on to her daughter, who succeeds in seducing Sumamuru to learn the secret of his power (2668–741). Counter fetishes are placed around the boundaries of the Manden by Sun-Jata's new ally Fa-Koli, who has abandoned his master, Sumamuru (2770–94). The last battle at Kirina finds Sun-Jata finally achieving the throne of his father, fulfilling all the portents of his youth, and beginning his reign over the growing Manden Empire.

Since Niane first drew attention to the epic of *Sun-Jata*, a floodgate of information about this culture hero has opened. Bards sing his epic in many contexts and have even exported versions of the whole epic and praise songs to France, other places in Europe, and America. West African and foreign scholars have published core episodes of the epic in books and articles.

266 *Sun-Jata*

A feature-length film highlights Sun-Jata's story and the bard who told it. Versions of the epic have appeared in children's books, comic books, and graphic novels. Even outside the Mande areas of West Africa, Sun-Jata appears in legends under different names. Articles about Sun-Jata and the art of bards are available, as are images depicting the hero. Performances featuring parts of the epic can be found on CD and on *YouTube*. The actor Daniel Sunjata Condon, who performs in film, television, and theater, has incorporated *Sun-Jata* as a part of his stage name. In the relatively short period of time since it first became known beyond West Africa, the story of Sun-Jata Keïta has taken its place among the great epics in world history.

Notes

1. Sun-Jata (Lion Thief) is the praise name of Narè Magan Kònatè, also known as Mari Jata I, who became so powerful that he earned his own surname, Keïta. Praise names are like Western military medals earned for bravery. Several variant spellings of *Sun-Jata* appear in publication, such as *Sunjata*, *Soundiata*, *Soundjata*, *Sundiata*, and *Son-Jara*.

2. Manden is the ancient name for the present-day country of Mali and its multiethnic peoples. *Manden* refers to the country, *Mande* is the adjective, and *Mande-kan* refers to the language family. The Empire of Gāna (Wagadugu) preceded the Mande Empire, and the Empire of Songhay followed.

3. They may have been the musicians who accompanied him on a dobro, a metal-faced guitar, during his performance. Sisòkò, *Epic*, is an inexpensive student text. Johnson, Son-Jara, is a more detailed edition that includes the original Mande-kan, my introduction, and my analytical notes and footnotes and that may be more suitable for teachers.

4. In addition to the introduction and extensive footnotes in Sisòkò, *Epic*, students can consult my detailed episode-by-episode exegesis of the difficult parts of the plot; see Johnson, "Epic": scroll down to the "Summary" section under "Resources."

5. For a complete list of translations of the epic of *Sun-Jata*, see Johnson, "Epic": scroll down to the "Bibliography" section under "Resources."

6. For information on this topic, see "Islam."

7. The concept of grace is shared by all three Abrahamic faiths, but each lends a different understanding of its meaning. Students can prepare for class discussion on this topic by consulting Benner; "Grace"; "Barakah."

8. Students can review "Ishmael"; "Isaac" to learn about the different versions of Abraham and his sons.

9. The synoptic Gospels of Matthew (1.1–17) and Luke (3.23–38) list Jesus's genealogy. As messiah, Jesus is not necessarily considered divine in these gospels. The Gospel of John names Jesus the son of God.

10. Most Muslims trace their genealogy, actual or imagined, to Hussein, one of the Prophet's twin grandsons, in order to secure *baraqah* for themselves. The father of the forty-fourth president of the United States was a Muslim from Kenya and may well have had these notions in mind when he named his son Barack Hussein Obama.

11. The Prophet's companions hold a position similar to the apostles of Jesus.

12. Mande nuclear family terminology might be used to stimulate class discussion related to students' families. For example, *fa-denya* could be applied to mixed marriages when one or both spouses bring children from a previous marriage into their new household. Going further, the dysfunctional atmosphere of American politics could also be referred to as *fa-denya*.

13. In Islam, there is a belief in jinns, spirits of lower rank than angels, who are capable of becoming invisible.

14. Lord Raglan's item 7 concerns exile of the hero (174). The Thompson motifs are "Expulsion and return of culture hero" (A516; 1: 119) and "Exile returns and succeeds" (L111.1; 5: 9).

Appendix: Sun-Jata's Inherited Sources of Power

The genealogy chart below shows how *baraqah*, the Abrahamic power of grace, was passed down from Abraham through Hagar to Muḥammad to his companion Bilāl bin Rabaḥ to the Kònatè family to Sun-Jata. It also shows how *nyama*, the Mande power, was passed down through the Kòndè family to Du Kamisa to Sugulun to Sun-Jata. In the diagram, | represents one generation, and : represents several generations.

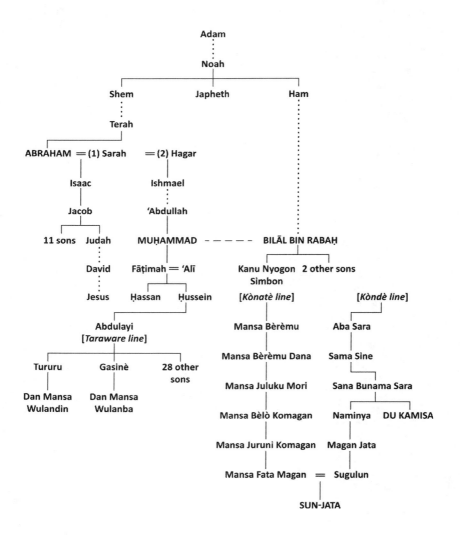

Works Cited

"Barakah." *Wikipedia*, 28 Aug. 2022, en.wikipedia.org/wiki/Barakah.

Benner, Jeff A. "The Meaning of Grace from a Hebrew Perspective." *Ancient Hebrew Research Center*, 2022, www.ancient-hebrew.org/studies-words/meaning-of-grace-from-a-hebrew-perspective.htm.

"Grace in Christianity." *Wikipedia*, 13 Nov. 2022, en.wikipedia.org/wiki/Grace_in_Christianity.

"Isaac in Islam." *Wikipedia*, 12 Dec. 2022, en.wikipedia.org/wiki/Isaac_in_Islam.

"Ishmael in Islam." *Wikipedia*, 4 Dec. 2022, en.wikipedia.org/wiki/Ishmael_in_Islam.

"Islam in Mali." *Wikipedia*, 26 June 2022, en.wikipedia.org/wiki/Islam_in_Mali.

Johnson, John William. "Epic of Sun-Jata." *World Epics*, edblogs.columbia.edu/worldepics/project/epic-of-sundiata/.

———, translator. *Son-Jara: The Mande Epic*. New ed., Indiana UP, 2003.

Niane, Djbril Tamsir. *Soundjata ou l'èpopèe mandingue*. Éditions Présence Africaine, 1960.

———. *Sundiata: An Epic of Old Mali*. Translated by G. D. Pickett, Longmans, 1965.

Raglan, Lord. *The Hero: A Study in Tradition, Myth, and Drama*. 1936. Dover Publications, 2003.

"Septennial Re-roofing Ceremony of the Kamablon, Sacred House of Kangaba." *United Nations Educational, Scientific and Cultural Organization*, 2009, ich.unesco.org/en/RL/septennial-re-roofing-ceremony-of-the-kamablon-sacred-house-of-kangaba-00190.

Sisòkò, Fa-Digi. *The Epic of Son-Jara: A West African Tradition*. Translated by John William Johnson, Indiana UP, 1992.

Thompson, Stith. *Motif-Index of Folk-Literature: A Classification of Narrative Elements in Folktales, Ballads, Myths, Fables, Mediaeval Romances, Exempla, Fabliaux, Jest-Books, and Local Legends*. Indiana UP, 1966. 6 vols.

Thomas A. Hale

Orality and History in
The Epic of Askia Mohammed

The Epic of Askia Mohammed is about Askia Mohammed, the man who conquered an area six times the size of Texas to create the Songhay Empire, the largest empire in West Africa, and then ruled over it from 1493 to 1528. This vast region included parts of today's Niger, Mali, Senegal, Burkina Faso, Benin, Nigeria, and Mauritania, and its capital was Gao, a city in eastern Mali on the left bank of the Niger River. For the Songhay, the story of Askia Mohammed is a *deeda* (long narrative) that includes *ceyan* (calling out the names of heroes). For those familiar with the Western literary tradition, it is an epic.

I recorded Nouhou Malio's version of the epic in Saga, Niger, in two forty-five-minute sessions, one on 30 December 1980 and the other on 26 January 1981. The long break between the sessions was caused by Nouhou Malio's illness. Saga was a village about five miles south of Niamey, the capital of the country. It has since been absorbed into the expanding city. Nouhou Malio was a farmer and also a *jeseré* (plural *jeserey*), or keeper of the oral tradition. He was known locally as a *jeseredunka*, or master *jeseré*, because he taught boys and other bards who came to him to learn about the past. *Jeseré* is the Songhay term for *griot*, used by Africans to designate keepers of the oral tradition in the Sahel, a 3,600-mile-wide

270

band that runs from Senegal to the Red Sea, between the southern edge of the Sahara and the northern edge of the forest zone.

Nouhou Malio, in his performance, told of love, infanticide, fratricide, patricide, sibling rivalry, religion, murder, magic, sorcery, family conflict, deception, and warfare. But there are also written versions of the story he told. African chroniclers in the seventeenth and eighteenth centuries recorded in Arabic the biographies of Askia Mohammed and many other rulers who reigned before and after him. Two of the manuscripts were translated and published in France: the *Tarîkh el-fattâch* (*Chronicle of a Seeker of Knowledge*), by Mahmoud Kâti, in 1913, and the *Tarîkh es-Sudan* (*History of the Sudan*), by Abderrahman es-S'adi, between 1898 and 1900. For an English translation of Kâti's work, see *Timbuktu Chronicles,* by Christopher Wise and Hala Abu Tala. Scholars refer to them as the Timbuktu chronicles because they are associated in many ways with that ancient city, the intellectual capital of the Songhay Empire.

While having students read episodes from the chronicles is not the best assignment for a unit on *The Epic of Askia Mohammed*, it is worth noting key differences with respect to the epic version.[1] The volumes by Kâti and by es-S'adi add up to 850 pages (including the original Arabic and the French translation) of dry prose providing extensive coverage of all events and historical figures of the Songhay Empire. By contrast, the 1,604 verses of the epic focus only on major events and people in a loosely organized narrative that is episodic, hermetic, and poetic. In addition, the chroniclers see events through an Islamic lens that tends to obscure pre-Islamic Songhay values. The *jeseré*, on the other hand, gives the listener deep insights into Songhay culture. This different perspective is apparent, for example, in the reasons given for the decline of the empire after a Moroccan invasion in 1591. The chroniclers attribute the defeat to corruption, adultery, incest, and the failure of nobles to adhere to Islamic values. But for Nouhou Malio there were two causes for the debacle: the violation of traditional practices regarding relations between different strata of Songhay society and collaboration with the enemy.

Nouhou Malio's version of the epic—the only one available in English—was published as *The Epic of Askia Mohammed*.[2] Instructors and students can find a detailed outline of the plot in the introduction, but a brief synopsis may nonetheless be useful here for instructors considering the epic for a course. Askia Mohammed was known as Mamar, which is the diminutive of *Mohammed*, and his last name was Kassaye, the name of his mother. He was conceived in mysterious circumstances and grew up to

272   *The Epic of Askia Mohammed*

kill his uncle, the Songhay ruler Si, or Sonni Ali Ber in the chronicles. He then took the Songhay throne and successfully expanded the empire. He was deposed by his son Moussa in 1528 and died in 1538 (Hale, *Scribe* 94). His children and grandchildren ruled the empire for forty-three years. In 1591, the Moroccan sultan Moulay Ahmed sent an army to conquer the Songhay Empire. For the next century, the Songhay mounted a series of campaigns to dislodge the invaders. Moroccan leaders eventually tired of supporting the army, and some of the Moroccan soldiers returned home, while others blended into the local population.

The Epic of Askia Mohammed is short and can be read in a few hours, thus making it highly suitable for a survey course. There are, however, three challenges to teaching it. First, the lack of knowledge about Africa has led to negative stereotypes about its peoples. Some topics and terms should therefore be mentioned briefly before students start to read the epic—or any other African work of fiction.

> *Geography.* There is a tendency to associate North Africa with the Middle East and to separate the sub-Saharan part of the continent. Today, Africanists and the fifty-four member states of the African Union see the continent as a whole. It is essential that instructors review a map of Africa with students.
>
> *Verbal art.* The fact that there is a strong oral literary tradition in African cultures may reinforce the misconception that Africans are illiterate. Tarzan, the best known fictional character in Western narratives set on the continent (Burroughs), contributes to that stereotype. But *The Epic of Askia Mohammad* is part of both oral and written traditions. That vast corpus ranges from ancient love poetry recorded by Egyptian scribes to dramatic works by the Nigerian playwright Wole Soyinka, winner of the Nobel Prize for literature in 1986.
>
> *Social organization.* When used in discussions of African societies, the term *tribe* may wrongly imply that the people in a given society are unified and illiterate. The Songhay are a diverse collection of peoples, not a tribe, and some of them write in Arabic.
>
> *Language.* The common use of *dialect* in reference to the speech of Africans may be misconstrued as suggesting that Africans do not speak separate languages. Approximately 1,800 languages are spoken in Africa—and also thousands of local variants (Pereltsvaig

105–23). The Songhay speak a common language that has seven dialects or variants.

Superstition. Superstition is a pejorative term for an unfounded belief. Africans have religions, beliefs, and myths, as well as superstitions. The participant-observer anthropologist Paul Stoller in the book *In Sorcery's Shadow* offers evidence that some Songhay beliefs are well founded and not mere superstitions (Stoller and Olkes).

Second, how can the instructor elicit responses from students about a subject that is so far from their own experience? One solution is to ask them to write one-page reaction papers to be handed in on the first day of discussion of the text. The papers could focus on two subjects: the content and the form of the epic. The instructor can then draw from these brief essays shared interests or concerns about the epic and use them for discussion in class. The papers need not be graded, but if handed in on time they may count as an activity that contributes to the final grade.

Third, how can the instructor explain the cultural traditions of the Songhay in the Sahelian context? These traditions are rooted in many factors, including hierarchical social structure, complex family relations, Islamic and pre-Islamic values, delineated gender roles, magical practices, and regional history, as well as the ambiguous status of the *jeserey* and other artisans. But a presentation on all this information would delay a discussion of the narrative threads in *The Epic of Askia Mohammed*.

One solution is to approach the epic in both a linear fashion, beginning with the supernatural conception of the hero, and in a thematic mode, considering references to examples of extraordinary events throughout the narrative. This recursive approach requires a return to some episodes from a different thematic or stylistic angle, thus inviting students to examine the epic as a whole. Students can be asked, for instance, "What examples of magic and the supernatural did you find, and what is their role in the narrative?"

A discussion of the supernatural in the epic could begin with two countervailing prophecies. First, seers who serve the ruler Si predict that a nephew born of Si's sister Kassaye will kill him (*Epic*, lines 10–12). Second, a well-dressed man emerges from a spirit world under the Niger River to predict that if Kassaye has sex with him, she will give birth to a son who will overthrow Si (30–38). The spirit man impregnates Kassaye, a son is born, and she protects him from being killed by Si by switching

274 *The Epic of Askia Mohammed*

him with her servant's infant. Kassaye's son, Mamar, works as a servant for Si. But when Mamar steps on the feet of Si and pulls his beard, Si declares that the child is suspect and should be killed. Thanks to the intervention of Kassaye, Mamar is spared. He grows up, receives weapons from his spirit father, who returns from under the river, then kills Si during an Islamic religious ceremony (115–85).

These events raise two sets of questions. First, what other examples of magic or the unusual occur in the epic? Students should pay particular attention to the following: a stone, seeds, and an egg (437), a flying sorcerer (393–462), a levitating city (1269–302), and talking horses (1540–43). What is their function in the narrative? The second set of questions focuses on archetypal situations, such as a mother protecting her baby by switching it with another child and a boy killing his father or uncle. Are there other examples with which students are familiar? At least some may recall that in *Star Wars: The Return of the Jedi* Luke Skywalker almost kills his father, Darth Vader, and that in *Star Wars: The Force Awakens* the evil Kylo Ren kills his father in the course of efforts to stop resisters trying to bring down the First Order.

Another fruitful theme for class discussion is the social structure typical of societies in the Sahel as presented in the epic. There are nobles, free people, and those of captive heritage. This last group does not consist of chattel slaves, as in the antebellum southern United States. Instead, these individuals—some of whom come from villages taken in battle—have a lower status compared to the nobles they serve. Students can be asked to trace the role that captives play in the narrative and to ascertain the epic's perspective on the issues that arise when individuals are differentiated according to the status of certain groups. Fruitful examples include the Bargantché servant of Kassaye (*Epic*, lines 48–81) and the woman who reveals to Yefarma the reason he has been sent on a mission away from the battlefield (1499–523).

Students may be asked to delve more deeply into a complicated but fascinating story in the second half of the epic that involves the violation of customs governing relations between nobles and captives (807–1047). The problem begins when Soumayla Kassa marries a woman from a family of captive origin attached to the ruler of Gao but does not free her. They subsequently have a son named Amar Zoumbani, who (unbeknownst to him) technically remains a captive even though he is raised as a prince. Soumayla Kassa then marries a second wife, Sagouma, the daughter of the ruler of Gao, and they have twin sons. When Sagouma's father dies,

Soumayla Kassa assumes the throne. During a competition between young men for the hand of the most beautiful woman in Gao, Amar is very generous to the *jeserey* who sing the praises of the suitors. Sagouma then tells her brother that Amar is of captive origin and encourages him to offer Amar as a gift to the *jeserey*. When Amar learns that he is not a prince, he is devastated. Soumayla Kassa tries to assuage Amar's feelings by having Sagouma's brother killed, but the matter is not resolved since Soumayla is later reminded of his son's low status during a battle with the Moroccan forces. For Nouhou Malio, Soumayla Kassa violates the social structure both by failing to free his first wife and by raising his captive son as a prince.

The class discussion of social relations within the family could include attention to the kind of distinction that occurs in a family where a father has several wives. There is a close relationship between children of the same father and the same mother. In Songhay it is called *nya-ize-taray*, or mother-childness. Milk symbolizes that relationship. Cooperation and emphasis on the family mark the behavior of these children. *Baba-ize-taray*, or father-childness, refers to the relationship of a son with his half brothers and his father. Blood symbolizes that relationship. Individual achievement is what counts. Rivalry with his half brothers and with his father characterizes the actions of that son, who wants to challenge his half brothers for leadership and wants to outdo his father's achievements. If he succeeds, he will earn a place of greater distinction in the family chronology. In times past, this place could be earned by heroism in battle. Today it could be earned by the award of a doctorate from the Sorbonne. The epic relates a notable example of rivalry that invites close attention. Daouda, a son of Askia Mohammed, demands the Songhay throne. His brothers reply that he can have it if he can kill two lions. It would normally take a team of hunters to track, encircle, and kill a lion. The plan of the brothers is to commit fratricide by beast, but Daouda succeeds in killing the lions single-handedly. He thereby takes the throne, reigning from 1549 until 1582 or 1583 (515–88). The instructor can ask students what character traits distinguish Daouda from Askia Mohammed's other sons.

Students may also focus on female characters in the epic from the perspective of gender roles. Although women receive scarce mention in the chronicles, they play a far more important part in the epic. In fact, the success of Mamar depends on women, beginning right after his birth, when his survival is due to his mother's ruse. His mother's essential role continues when Kassaye quells the anger of the crowd after Mamar kills his uncle

276 *The Epic of Askia Mohammed*

(187–95) and when she subsequently provides the means for him to escape the Bargantché (378–420). The episode of Soumayla Kassa, referenced above, can likewise be examined in terms of its female characters. The princess Sagouma demonstrates that a woman does not have to accept mistreatment, in this case the murder of her brother. First, she takes revenge against her husband by killing their twin sons (1077–83). She then promises her hand to any man who can lead an army to attack Gao and kill both Soumayla Kassa and his son Amar Zoumbani (1084–171).

Other women in key roles will no doubt elicit students' interest. In addition to the abovementioned captive woman who reveals to Yefarma the purpose of his mission (1499–523), instructors can direct attention to the woman who reveals the secret of the levitation of Gao (1272–96) and the women who send boatloads of supplies upstream for the army planning to kill Soumayla and Amar (1203–12). These examples of women's roles in Songhay society are not exceptions from the past. Today Songhay women express in songs their sentiments about child raising, education, sports, politics, belief, love, courtship, marriage, sex, men, mothers-in-law, and divorce. Some of these songs frighten and embarrass the men who hear them. Instructors who would like to bring examples of this lyric genre into a discussion of gender in the *The Epic of Askia Mohammed* can find eighty Sahelian songs in *Women's Voices from West Africa* (Sidikou and Hale).

No discussion of an African epic would be complete without some attention to the *jeseré*, an important figure not just as the storyteller but sometimes also as a character within the narrative. Students should look for the *jeseré* to emerge as a character at various moments in *The Epic of Askia Mohammed*, beginning with the scene in which Mamar kills his uncle (lines 209–18). When the children of the former ruler react by accepting the new leader, one of them sings the praises of Mamar, thereby becoming the first *jeseré*. This is one of several origin tales about griots in the Sahel (Hale, *Griots* 59–64). Later, that *jeseré* accompanies Mamar to Mecca as a companion and advisor (*Epic*, lines 309–51). *Jeserey* also appear as praise singers of the suitors in the competition for the most beautiful woman of Gao (890–916).

The importance of *jeserey* in *The Epic of Askia Mohammed* reflects the many functions that griots have in Sahelian societies, effectively serving as historians, genealogists, spokespeople, diplomats, interpreters, musicians, composers, tutors, and exhorters. Today, they draw on their musical and verbal skills to perform around the world. Audiences range from

Students should look for rhetorical devices used by the *jeseré* to capture the interest of listeners and to draw them into the story. Repetition is a common device not only in the genealogies but also in the action of the narrative itself. To emphasize the passage of time, for example, Nouhou Malio in his performance often repeated a single word, "until" (*Epic*, line 23), or an entire phrase, "Si continued to have the child work" (101–03). Another rhetorical device is metaphor, often used to describe a character—particularly one with a bad reputation—without going into detail. For example, after Askia Moussa deposes his father, he kills many of his rival relatives. Rather than describe him, Nouhou Malio simply listed a series of metaphors that gave the audience some sense of what the man was like, including "iron," "the horn of the great ram," and "the hat of the wild boar" (654, 648, 658). Students can also discuss the meaning conveyed through metonymy. At several points Nouhou Malio relied on this rhetorical device to underline the close relationship of two beings, such as a horse and its rider (1311). A horse designates the cavalry, while the rider and mount designate a military unit more powerful than a foot soldier. In addition, comparisons in the epic help to explain events in terms that listeners can understand today. The flying *sohanci* (sorcerer) is compared both to a hawk and to an airplane (406–08).

Nouhou Malio employed his most striking device to shorten the distance between the narrative and the listeners, bringing them into the story and bringing the story to them. When he described Mamar approaching the prayer ground where Si and his entourage are sitting, he added that the crowd wonders if the well-dressed horseman is a prince and if he should be invited to join the group. Nouhou Malio then shifted to the present tense, as if he were in the story, and commented that the prince looks a bit like Mamar, the little captive of Si. He then turned to his listeners and asked, "Did you see him! When I saw him he looked like the little captive

278   *The Epic of Askia Mohammed*

of Si" (178). The listeners thus became witnesses to the most dramatic moment in the epic: Mamar's killing of his uncle. This event marks in breathtaking fashion the beginning of Mamar's reign and the reason for his militant piety.

It should be pointed out that despite *The Epic of Askia Mohammed*'s engaging narrative and Nouhou Malio's expert storytelling, the style sometimes presents challenges for local listeners as well as for those outside the Songhay world. Many verses are in Silance, an archaic form of Soninke that sorcerers also employ. One theory for the use of Silance is that Askia Mohammed was of the Touré clan that hundreds of years earlier migrated from Ghana, a thousand miles west of Gao. When Askia Mohammed Touré came to power in 1493, Soninke griots gravitated to Gao to sing his praises (Hale, *Scribe* 175–76). But in the course of five centuries, the language evolved. Today, even the *jeserey* cannot always explain the meaning of certain Silance terms. For this reason, there are numerous lines listed in the translation as "undecipherable" (*Epic*, line 4). In the genealogies, Nouhou Malio gave listeners some clues by often alternating in poetic fashion between Silance and Songhay words. For example, he used the Silance term for village, *ndaba*, followed by the Songhay term *kwara* (Hale, *Scribe*, lines 749–58) and the Silance verb *sarra* (to father) with the Songhay equivalent, *hay* (733–36).[3]

Instructors can bring Nouhou Malio's original 1980 and 1981 performances of *The Epic of Askia Mohammed* to their students by playing an audio recording available online (see Hale, "*Epic*").[4] The clip moves from the prophecy prior to Mamar's birth to the youth's killing of his uncle and thus includes Nouhou Malio's abrupt shift noted above, in which the narrator directly addresses the audience (*Epic*, lines 176–78). What do the features of the performance, such as the sound of Nouhou Malio's voice, the rhythms of the recitation, and the musical accompaniment of a three-stringed *molo* (lute), add to students' experience of this epic?

The Epic of Askia Mohammed is one of many epics from West Africa that are rooted in centuries of history. *Oral Epics from Africa* includes excerpts from nineteen of them (Johnson et al.). It is probable that less than one hundred people have read the original Songhay transcription in my book *Scribe, Griot, and Novelist: Narrative Interpreters of the Songhay Empire* (Hale, *Scribe*). It is likely that no more than a thousand have read the English translation in the same volume or in the student edition produced by Indiana University Press in 1996 (*Epic*). But when griots narrate epics on the radio or on television in the Sahel region of West Africa, they are heard by millions of people. For this reason, we can say that West African epics are among the most widely disseminated forms of African literature today.

Notes

1. Assigning episodes from the chronicles is impractical for several reasons, including the fact that the English translations of one of the chronicles are incomplete and not readily accessible.

2. Nouhou Malio's version was one of ten that I recorded in western Niger in 1980–81. In the local context, griots are rewarded for their performances. I paid all the *jeserey* whose versions of the epic I recorded an amount equivalent to what they might receive at a village wedding. I chose Nouhou Malio's version for publication after scholars at the University of Niamey confirmed that it was indeed an excellent example. With assistance from Mounkaila Maiga, Fatima Mounkaila, Abdoulaye Dan Louma, Moussa Djibo, and Ousmane Tandina, I spent nine years on the difficult task of transcribing, translating, and annotating the epic. When it appeared in Hale, *Scribe*, and in *Epic*, I shared the meager royalties with Nouhou Malio and his family.

3. Words in Silence are italicized in the English translation; see *Epic*.

4. The first 194 lines of the audio recording and the accompanying transcription and translation of the twelve-minute clip can be found in the "Resources" section under the "Performance" tab.

Works Cited

Burroughs, Edgar Rice. *Tarzan of the Apes*. McClurg, 1914.

The Epic of Askia Mohammed. Edited by Thomas A. Hale, Indiana UP, 1996.

Es-S'adi, Abderrahman. *Tarikh es-Sudan*. Translated by Octave Houdas, 2nd ed., Adrien-Maisonneuve, 1964.

Hale, Thomas A. "*The Epic of Askia Mohammed*." *World Epics*, edblogs .columbia.edu/worldepics/project/the-epic-of-askia-mohammed/. Accessed 4 Oct. 2022.

———. *Griots and Griottes: Masters of Words and Music*. Indiana UP, 1998.

———. *Scribe, Griot, and Novelist: Narrative Interpreters of the Songhay Empire*. U of Florida P, 1990.

Johnson, John William, et al. *Oral Epics from Africa: Vibrant Voices from a Vast Continent*. Indiana UP, 1997.

Kâti, Mahmoud. *Tarikh el-fattâch*. Translated by Octave Houdas and Maurice Delafosse, 2nd ed., Adrien-Maisonneuve, 1981.

Pereltsvaig, Asya. *Languages of the World: An Introduction*. Cambridge UP, 2012.

Sidikou, Aissata G., and Thomas A. Hale. *Women's Voices from West Africa*. Indiana UP, 2012.

280 *The Epic of Askia Mohammed*

Star Wars: The Force Awakens. Directed by J. J. Abrams, written by Lawrence Kasdan et al., Bad Robot Productions / Lucasfilm, 2015.

Star Wars: The Return of the Jedi. Directed by Richard Marquand, Lucasfilm / 20th Century Fox, 1983.

Stoller, Paul, and Cheryl Olkes. *In Sorcery's Shadow: Memoir of an Apprenticeship among the Songhay of Niger.* U of Chicago P, 1987.

Wise, Christopher, and Hala Abu Tala, translators. *The Timbuktu Chronicles, 1493–1599: Al Hajj Mahmud Kati's* Tarikh al-Fattash. Africa World Press, 2002.

Brenda E. F. Beck

The Legend of Poṉṉivaḷa Nadu: A South Indian Oral Folk Epic

Epics are not just long stories. They are especially memorable because they provide a grand vision of the world and attempt to explain the place of human life within the wider cosmos. Folk epics, in particular, vividly depict how core human relationships, heroic adventures, and concepts of power relate to the nature of existence. *The Legend of Poṉṉivaḷa Nadu*, a folk epic popular in the Kongu Nadu region of Tamil Nadu (in South India), recounts the evolution of one heroic farming family over the course of three generations. This essay first describes some of the rich threads that make up the warp and woof of this narrative, including details about the story's geographic and historical background, its important gender dynamics, its key characters and their kinship bonds, embedded concepts of good governance, and the belief in a range of divine powers that influence human life, both from above and below. The focus then turns to a variety of teaching strategies that can be used in multiple settings, ranging from the third grade up to and including undergraduate lectures and postgraduate and faculty seminars.

Origin, Transmission, and Available Versions

We do not know much about this story's beginnings, but a good guess is that the epic acquired its current shape and structure between the fourteenth and sixteenth centuries, a period during which many local Tamil legends were first recorded on palm leaves. Nonetheless, some of this story's central components are demonstrably much older, displaying a close affinity with several well-known Hindu myths, the ancient *Epic of Gilgamesh*, and ancient Babylonian ideas about the constellations.[1] Because of its oral transmission, *The Legend of Ponnivala Nadu* varies somewhat from teller to teller as well as across the several schools of bards who sing it. Although various palm leaf manuscript versions exist, all are limited in length and in scope, and none have yet been fully authenticated or made available for broad academic study.

The extended version of the epic discussed here was first committed to writing in 1965, while the author was doing research in a remote village in Tamil Nadu. A local bard, who had sung this story in front of a live audience just a few weeks earlier, then dictated it over many days to a local scribe, who patiently set down his exact words on paper.[2] My English translation of his version of this grand legend first appeared in 1992 and was republished in 2023 with the title *Land of the Golden River* (Beck, *Land*). This new edition, available in both paperback and e-book, has a lengthy introduction, extensive index, maps, diagrams, and a twenty-six-part story summary. In addition, the epic has been adapted as an animated video and as a set of twenty-six graphic novelettes, published in two parts (Beck, "Legend"; Beck and Cornall, *Legend of Ponnivala: Part 1* and *Legend of Ponnivala: Part 2*).[3] There are also three websites devoted to this story: www.ponnivala.com, www.sophiahilton.ca, and, for children, www.annanmarkathai.com.

A Three-Generation Family of Heroes

The Legend of Ponnivala Nadu revolves around a unique three-generation family. A pioneer farmer named Kōlattā is the hero of the first generation. A prominent king from a neighboring area ordered this experienced plowman to open up Ponnivala Nadu, a remote upland plain in northwestern Tamil Nadu, so that it would produce abundant crops. Unfortunately, this clan founder accidentally causes the death of seven cows just as he is about to harvest his first fine field of sugarcane. Shiva curses Kōlattā's descent line for this grave mistake, leaving Kōlattā's wife barren, but eventually softens because of Vishnu's pleas and creates a magical baby named Kuṇṇuṭaiyā. Signalling the start of the second generation, this magical son is hidden by Shiva under a rock pile and eventually discovered by Kōlattā. Orphaned at age six, Kuṇṇuṭaiyā gradually matures and in time manages to claim back his family's lost lands and become a respected and beloved local leader. Unfortunately, however, he inherits his family's curse of infertility. His wife, Tāmarai, remains barren until Shiva intervenes and immaculately sires twin sons and one daughter on her. This begins the third generation: two boys named Poṇṇar and Caṅkar, plus one sister named Taṅkāi. The twin boys are determined to become skilled warriors, whereas their father, now a minor king, remains a landlord who has never lifted a sword. Meanwhile, the daughter remains a virgin who serves as her twin brothers' visionary protector and guide.

In the first two generations, Kōlattā and Kuṇṇuṭaiyā confront a range of antagonists who claim that the family has wronged them: rival cousins who believe that the new Poṇṇivaḷa territory was split unequally, the finest portion being allocated to Kōlattā and the other, lesser piece given to Kōlattā's eight younger siblings; assorted craftsmen who are angry at having been demoted to the status of service workers when the nine immigrant brothers begin to forcibly plow local lands in an area these residents continue to consider theirs; and a group of Veṭṭuvā hunters, nearby hill dwellers, who believe that their pristine forest homeland has been violated by these newly arrived immigrants.

Vishnu supports the heroes' family in the face of all these challengers until near the end of the epic. Then this important god secretly switches sides and starts to lead the attackers against the twin heroes Poṇṇar and Caṅkar. Initially, things appear to go well when a huge wild boar that has wreaked havoc by flooding the heroes' fields is hunted down, killed, and offered up as a sacrifice. Vishnu then suddenly steals that boar's now-severed head, angering the forest hunters who had always treated the boar almost as a family member. Vishnu sets the scene by leading their attack but then, sheltering the forest hunters from the heroes' swords by using a major illusion, makes the heroes believe they have won. When the twin heroes then go to bathe, Vishnu shoots a flowered arrow at one of them. This is the signal, from this god, that their time on earth is over. As a result, the two warriors commit suicide, falling forward on their own sword points, making a gift of their own lives to the gods (Beck, *Land* 338–47).[4]

284 *The Legend of Poṇṇivaḷa Nadu*

Vishnu, meanwhile, drags off the boar's head while disguised as a humble washerman and offers that magical vessel of life to the earth goddess Bhudevi. Symbolically, this severed head becomes the seed that Bhudevi will use to renew the entire world. Several background myths that intertwine with this epic account serve to heighten the emotion stirred up by the sacrifice of both the great boar and the twin heroes. The final song sung by bards when they perform this epic suggests that a new cosmic era is about to begin and that all life on earth will soon be refreshed (367). Some bards recommend at this point that listeners perform a common local ritual used to celebrate new beginnings, known as the Poṅkal ceremony. In fact, annual rituals that commemorate this epic story occur each year in this epic's core area, and the death and rebirth of devotees possessed by the twins' spirits is a major event that locals celebrate.

Social Roles

The twin Poṇṇivaḷa heroes have a prominent assistant in their employ named Cāmpukā. He is a Dalit, meaning that his family occupies a very low (technically, untouchable) position in the caste hierarchy. Although Cāmpukā is described by means of stereotypes—he is black-skinned, drinks a lot, lives in a corner of the horse stable, and is miraculously strong and fit—his character is given considerable dimensionality. Like his father before him, Cāmpukā is respected and admired by the heroes' family members, who rely on his vital services. The epic also includes scattered references to a few high-status Brahmin males, who represent the other end of the social spectrum. Unlike Cāmpukā, however, who has a mother and, early on, a father, prestigious, high-ranking Brahmins, when mentioned, are given no family context at all. These nameless men are simply invited to perform specific ceremonial tasks as required. By contrast, inside the heroes' family, the story is filled with rich detail: women desire children, and fathers worry about their sons, while loving brothers struggle to confront perceived rivals and to contest each other's prowess. Brother-sister bonds, plus kinship rules and parent-child ethical obligations, are given particular importance.

Nowhere in this epic account do we learn the caste identity of the all-powerful Chola kings who once backed these farmers, nor do we gain any information about the Chola queen of the time. However, certain basic social shifts that occur over this three-generation story are obvious. While the first Chola monarch is a supporter, two generations later his unnamed successor becomes pompous and demands the heroes' unconditional submission. Poṉṉar and Caṅkar resist this demand, believing such behavior will demean them. Matters degenerate from there, and eventually the twin heroes kill that overbearing Chola king (239–55). Their violent act wins the brothers independence and the freedom to enter a nearby forest area, where the Veṭṭuvā hunters had previously lived out their lives more or less undisturbed. It seems likely that the Chola family, whose initial orders directed the plow farmers to Poṉṉivaḷa, treated this prime woodland as its private hunting ground. The Veṭṭuvās, in turn, appear to have served as these Chola kings' hunting guides, fighters, and animal keepers. The kings' finest horses and elephants were likely grazed in these hunters' thickly wooded hills.

The artisans play a somewhat different role. The local craftsmen, who are the hunters' allies, are rivals whom the family of immigrant farmers, now warriors, must confront. The artisans belong to one of the area's early local communities. They resist the newly arrived plowmen at first, meeting with them in a magical confrontation Vishnu himself sets up. Although the disgruntled craftsmen have little means of recourse when they suffer defeat, they continue to believe that they have been wronged. Vishnu soon redefines this contentious relationship in the farmers' favor, outlining a contract the farmers can enforce. It promises fixed fees, paid in grain, for each service these craftsmen provide. The unhappy artisans struggle against this oppression and the fixed wage structure the farmers install, but they never manage to regain their former pride and independence (41–42). Similarly, the Veṭṭuvā hunters living in the nearby hills suffer repeated wrongs (theft, kidnapping, tree cutting, etc.), now carried out by Kōḷatta's grandsons, that they are helpless to consistently prevent.

From a sociological perspective, this story describes the gradual development of a new power hierarchy in the Poṉṉivaḷa area over a period of three generations, a hierarchy that features the domination of a newly established agricultural economy that devalues and exploits earlier forms of subsistence still prevalent in the area. Although Vishnu stands with the heroes until near the end of the story, he ultimately switches sides and prevents them from killing their key rivals, the Veṭṭuvā hunters. Vishnu knows that the wild landscapes and less assertive first peoples of this area need protection from the aggressive farmers who live on the plains. In the end, this great god tries to foster harmony and mutual tolerance between those two opposing groups. These several themes clearly correspond to patterns familiar to aboriginal groups around the world. Those who exit

286 *The Legend of Ponnivala Nadu*

the forest usually manage to assimilate but often end up as low-status members of a greatly transformed social order. *The Legend of Ponnivala Nadu* provides a unique opportunity to discuss these important issues that remain relevant today.

Geography and History

The Ponnivala area is basically an upland alluvial bowl cut in half by the Kāveri River. A ring of mountains and high hills nearly surround this area, known today as Kongu Nadu. The great Chola Empire once lay just beyond its boundaries. Ponnivala was an attractive but primitive and remote area during the hegemony of that famous line of kings. Those rulers commanded a huge territory that they were always hoping to expand. They wanted to incorporate Ponnivala Nadu and control its resources. That is why the first Chola king described in this story sends a knowledgeable group of plow farmers there to start cutting trees and initiate widescale plowing (40–41).[5] The pristine Kongu area was thought to be a potential food bank for the Cholas, while its forested fringe was labeled a valuable hunting preserve and a place to graze and house the Chola army's large animals, especially elephants and horses.

Historically, the Cholas had some initial success in their dynasty's expansion efforts. Later, however, other powerful competing kingdoms, the Cheras and the Pandiyas, contested Chola rule. As a result, the Kongu area was frequently invaded but never successfully controlled by any of these three great South Indian monarchies for any significant length of time. The people of this area have always resisted outside domination. *The Legend of Ponnivala Nadu* is one important way the intrepid residents of this upland plain have found to react to their sidelined status. The epic glorifies the Kongu region's unique history and its brave ancestors, thus playing to local pride. Essentially, the epic declares that "[w]e, the fierce and warlike farming community in the Kongu area, have a history of bravery that demonstrates why we deserve respect in the wider world."

The Role of Twin Rulers

Central to *The Legend of Ponnivala Nadu* is the importance of twinship. Twinship has ancient roots in the Indo-Iranian figures of Mitra and Varuna. The idea is that good rule requires mixed and complementary qualities and involves multiple dualities: bright versus dark, sensitive versus assertive, benign versus dangerous, and communal loyalty versus individual initiative and success. These oppositions can all be clearly seen in this epic, where Poṉṉar, the firstborn twin, represents the first pole of each of these dualities, and Caṅkar, the second-born twin, represents the second pole. These underlying concepts are threaded through the entire legend and provide a key to understanding its broader symbolism. In a classroom these oppositions can be used to debate the nature of good, successful leadership. Which twin would make the better ruler? Or is compromise, something in-between, more desirable?

The Gods

There are two central gods in this story, Shiva and Vishnu, who are considered brothers-in-law. A friendly rivalry exists between them. But there is also a key difference between them, a contrast that somewhat resembles the contrast between the earth-based heroes Poṉṉar and Caṅkar, who rule together. Shiva and Vishnu have different responsibilities and distinct personalities. Vishnu is empathetic and always trying to help the heroes, whereas Shiva is not approachable but determines each protagonist's ultimate fate. Instructors can ask students to compare these two gods and to consider their differing responsibilities in the light of a belief system that insists each individual is shadowed by a fate that has been predetermined by divine forces. Students can also be asked to find references in the text to personal fate being written on a person's forehead such that only others are able to see what is written there. Of course, a character can use a mirror to view the fate. But mirrors reverse the letters of whatever words are written there. Instructors should also consider asking students if the fates described for male characters differ, in a consistent way, from those assigned to female characters and, if so, what those differences are.

Women

Women in the story, though less visible at first glance, are in some ways more important than the men. In the second generation, Kunnutaiya's wife, Tāmarai, is a representative of the Pleiades constellation. She was sent to earth to help direct her brothers' actions but is endowed with a magical

288   *The Legend of Poṉṉivaḻa Nadu*

dimension in her own right. Tāmarai gives birth to triplets. Her daughter Taṅkāi also has special powers, including an ability to see into the future. Of all the characters described in this epic, Taṅkāi is the one whose fears and emotions have the most impact on the heroes' decision-making. Equally interesting is the fact that only divine females, and not their male counterparts, have clear human forms. Pārvati, the story's key female divinity, exists on earth in the form of Cellāttā, guardian of Poṉṉivaḻa's fine lands. In a fiercer manifestation, known as Kāḷi, this key goddess is worshipped by all the key characters, including the heroes' in-laws and the Veṭṭuvās, the heroes' adversaries. Instructors can ask students to examine how the earthly form of this goddess changes as she tries to mediate disputes between various rival groups. Instructors can further ask students to explore female behavior in various contrastive settings. For example, does the heroine Tāmarai's behavior on earth as a sister, wife, and (eventually) mother reflect her similar kinship roles in heaven? There she is simultaneously Vishnu's sister and Shiva's wife, making her the logical go-between when those two brothers-in-law argue. Does Pārvati's strategy, when the goddess attempts to mediate between two gods, differ from the techniques she employs on earth, when she tries to help human relatives negotiate?

Pārvati must also be recognized as the creatrix who starts the story off by placing nine plowmen in an unspecified forest and ordering them to begin to work (38). At the end she is briefly referenced as Korravai (346), an early and fierce forest goddess described by some of Tamil's early Sangam poets. All in all, there is much to explore regarding the important roles of women in this story, in both their divine and human forms. Asking students to consider which gender is more significant in this legend will lead them to look more deeply into the worldview that lies behind this epic account and encourage them to appreciate its significance in a variety of creative ways.

Symbolism of Drought, Rain, and Cows

The Legend of Poṉṉivaḻa Nadu presents a rich tapestry for students interested in metaphors and symbolism. The epic's many poetic songs present beautiful, heart-wrenching images meant to elicit the precise emotions a particular storyteller wants listeners to feel. Many passages, for instance, make reference to abundant rain and its key result: happy, healthy cattle (79). Cows are some of a farmer's most valued possessions, and they fatten and thrive after a good rain. Indeed, cows are also metaphors for good women in the epic, while bulls are used to describe strong, aggressive men. Drought is also mentioned several times and is something that the residents of Poṇṇivaḷa fear. Kongu is basically a dry region, one heavily dependent on natural precipitation during the monsoon season. This rainy period of the year brings relief from the baking heat and promises a greening of the landscape. It also softens the land so that it can be easily plowed. Dark clouds bring joy as a harbinger of rain. Some men in Tamil Nadu are actually given the name Dark Cloud by their parents. Parents consider this term to be a positive moniker that suggests their child will grow up to be filled with blessings and goodwill toward others. This folk epic, then, is first and foremost a story about the origins of agriculture in the dry, often rain-deprived Poṇṇivaḷa region. Love for the region is expressed through poems about abundant rain, fine crops, and handsome, contented cows. The prime focus of the heroes throughout is to protect and promote this beloved area with pride, while at the same time showcasing their own remarkable courage.

Further Topics for Discussion and Comparative Analyses

This epic is well suited to Socratic teaching techniques. It does not provide answers but rather paints scenes that beg further thought and raise such questions as, Which protagonist was right? Could a better solution have been found? What underlying values were at play in this contest of wills? In addition, this epic invites discussion of relevant contemporary and universal topics, including immigrant pioneers versus first peoples, emigration and starting over, fence building, being a good person, believing in hidden truths, living with a disability, suddenly becoming orphaned, the plight of the underdog, family violence, denial of social rights, breaking a gender stereotype, climate change, environmental protection, animal rights, charity, structural inequality, respect for others, family bonds, terrorism in school, bullying, outcasts, refugees, scapegoats, strategies for talking with a suicidal person, infertility anxiety, and facing one's personal fate. In addition, the comparison of episode 13 (179–92) with the story that the Tamil author Perumal Murugan presents in his modern novel *One Part Woman* would make an excellent student assignment, especially for anyone expressing special interest in female empowerment.

In a course on world epics or world literature more generally, *The Legend of Poṇṇivaḷa Nadu* can be compared to any number of canonical

290 *The Legend of Ponnivala Nadu*

works. My new volume, *Hidden Paradigms*, suggests similarities between this account and *The Epic of Gilgamesh*, the *Mahabharata*, the Bible, an Icelandic saga, and a North American story cycle celebrating the Ojibwa hero Nanabush (Beck, *Hidden Paradigms*). Students who have read *The Epic of Gilgamesh* will find many parallels to discuss, not the least of which are the role of the forest, the importance of killing a great wild boar, and the significance of Gilgamesh's close friend Enkidu, who strongly resembles the character Cāmpukā in *The Legend of Ponnivala Nadu*.

Selection of Episodes

It is recommended that students sample at least one or two episodes from *The Legend of Ponnivala Nadu* involving each of the three generations featured in the story. Students should be able to complete such readings in one to two weeks. In the new edition of my translation, *Land of the Golden River*, the relevant episodes are as follows: for generation 1, episode 1 and part of episode 2 (Beck, *Land* 38–49); for generation 2, the remainder of episode 2 through the first part of episode 14 (59–195); for generation 3, the remainder of episode 14 through episode 26 (192–366). The twenty-six episode summaries found at the start of *Land of the Golden River* can fill in the details concerning the story's progression. A more abstract and conceptually oriented summary is in the first chapter of Beck, *Hidden Paradigms* (11–38).

In sum, this South Indian folk epic has many features that position it exceptionally well for inclusion in a range of world epic and world literature courses:

It is an oral legend that contrasts in informative ways with literary epics.

It comes from an area of the world, South Asia, that is relatively understudied in English-language scholarship on epics.

Its content covers a wide range of teaching topics, allowing instructors to choose from a vast range of relevant historical, economic, sociological, religious, and philosophical themes, any of which can be used for essay assignments and discussion planning.

The story's Babylonian overtones allow for probing comparisons to be made with a wide range of similar epic and religious accounts of heroism, suffering, leadership, saintly behavior, and more.

Using a little ingenuity, instructors can teach the story at any level and ensure that it is appreciated by students who embrace a widely contrastive range of political, ethical, and religious views. Each reader will find something to identify with, enjoy, and embrace.

The story is told in a Socratic way (i.e., without interpretation of its events) that invites debate about its many characters' ethics, norms, and philosophical assumptions.

The story emphasizes immigration and the confrontation of aboriginal and colonial perspectives, and it tackles how families change over several generations. Moreover, it describes a variety of leadership styles. These characteristics make this epic account easy for instructors to relate to modern-day issues that many students will be interested in and already knowledgeable about.

Internal comparisons can be made between characters from different generations. The family history presented in the epic features both divine and human characters and provides multiple attractive, easy-to-use contrasts in status, personality, and more, all of which a teacher can organize student assignments around.

In addition to having these features, *The Legend of Ponnivaḷa Nadu* is available in the various formats discussed earlier, allowing students to explore and enjoy the epic's rich imagery in a multitude of ways.

Notes

1. See Beck, *Hidden Paradigms* 245–404. The book's second half presents a variety of symbolic overviews and interpretive frameworks relevant to understanding this epic legend in additional ways.

2. The version that the bard performed before a live village audience took thirty-eight hours over eighteen nights to complete. That version was taped, later transcribed, and then typed in its original language, Tamil. See "Annanmar Katai" for a digital file of a few excerpts (with translations) that can be listened to online. While the performed version contains more emotional color, many additional mythical references, and more humor, the dictated version is shorter, is better structured, and presents a clearer sequence of key events. See Beck, *Three Twins*, for an in-depth comparison of the two versions.

3. See Beck, "Legend," for free online access not only to all twenty-six animated segments of this story but also to all twenty-six graphic novel segments, in both English and Tamil.

292　*The Legend of Ponnivala Nadu*

4. Citations to *The Legend of Ponnivala Nadu* refer to Beck, *Land*.

5. See Beck, *Peasant Society*, especially 29–41, for more background information.

Works Cited

"Annanmar Katai—the Birth of the Queen's Triplets (Six Excerpts)." Performed by Erucanampalayam Ramasami and Olappalayam Palanisami. *Smithsonian Folkways Recordings*, 2022, folkways.si.edu/erucanampalayam-ramasami-and-olappalayam-palanisami/annanmar-katai-the-birth-of-the-queens-triplets-six-excerpts/india-world/music/album/smithsonian.

Beck, Brenda E. F. *Hidden Paradigms: Comparing Epic Themes, Characters and Plot Structures*. U of Toronto P, 2023.

———, editor and translator. *Land of the Golden River*. Friesen Press, 2023.

———. "Legend of Ponnivala." *University of Toronto Scarborough Library*, 2013, collections.digital.utsc.utoronto.ca/islandora/object/tamil:ponnivala.

———. *Peasant Society in Konku: A Study of Right and Left Subcastes in South India*. U of British Columbia P, 1972.

———. *The Three Twins: The Telling of a South Indian Folk Epic*. Indiana UP, 1982.

Beck, Brenda E. F., and Cassandra Cornall. *The Legend of Ponnivala: Part 1: A Kindgom Constructed*. Ponnivala Publishing, 2012.

———. *The Legend of Ponnivala: Part 2: A Kingdom Contested*. Ponnivala Publishing, 2012.

Murugan, Perumal. *One Part Woman*. Translated by Aniruddhan Vasudevan, Penguin Random House, 2013.

Part VI

World Epics
in Various Contexts

Zachary Hamby

Epic Engagement:
Giving Ancient Stories New Life in
the Secondary School Classroom

Nine years of war has come down to this climactic moment: Amid swirling clouds of dust, Achilles and Hector face one another on the arid Trojan plain. Achilles tightens his grip on his spear and springs forward in a deadly advance while Hector steels his spirit for the onslaught of the godlike warrior. But as soon as the two are about to make contact, a nasal voice fills the air, and Achilles skids to a stop. The overhead intercom is paging Achilles to the office to pay his library fine. The illusion broken, Achilles turns to me (his teacher) with a look that says, "Do I have to?" I doom Achilles to his fate, sending him grudgingly on his way, and issue a battlefield promotion, elevating another student to the role of Achilles. We ease back into the world of Homer's *Iliad*, and the battle continues.

Most high school students do not correlate *ancient* with *engaging*. In fact, one humorist goes so far as to say that *epic* is a code word for "boring" used by English teachers (Barry). For most young people, simply mentioning ancient epics stirs up only one image: dusty books wherein characters with unpronounceable names perform one tedious deed after another. Add in the expectation of ponderous descriptions and the absence of any relevancy to real life, and ancient stories seem to have nothing to offer; however, nothing could be further from the truth. Ancient epics are

296 Secondary School Classroom

filled with exciting action, compelling characterization, and timeless life lessons. It just takes a bit of work for teachers to make this apparent.

Admittedly, there are many challenges to teaching ancient stories in the secondary school classroom. First, students struggle to connect with civilizations hundreds (and often thousands) of years removed from their own, which seem to have little relevance to their lives. Second, since ancient epics are well above the average reading level of secondary school students, reading comprehension is an issue. Character names alone pose a problem; Astyanax, Agamemnon, and Neoptolemus do not exactly roll off the tongue for students unaccustomed to ancient Greek names. Third, there are roadblocks for teachers as well. Teaching epics with any degree of fidelity takes a great deal of class time, and most course syllabi are already tightly packed as it is. As daunting as these challenges may seem, they can be overcome through epic engagement, a methodology designed to engage and enlighten students through four strategies: giving students a voice in the story, putting them in the action, connecting them to the deeper themes of the story, and empowering them to play with the story.

Giving Students a Voice in the Story

Halfway through my student teaching experience, I learned that I would be taking over as the full-time classroom teacher, and coupled with this shock was the jarring news that I would be teaching a course called Mythology—a subject about which I knew next to nothing. The textbook for this course was Edith Hamilton's *Mythology*, which provides accurate (but largely unengaging) summaries of the Greek and Roman myths. My first semester of teaching Mythology using this text was not a success. I quickly learned that summaries, no matter how accurately they reflect the original works, are not the stories themselves. They lack the subtle characterization and storytelling power of the originals. My students were unengaged, and their comprehension suffered. Although I vowed to make the course experience better, I kept coming up against the same obstacle: the text itself. I knew that trapped behind these stilted summaries were vibrant, exciting, *epic* stories, but how could I bring them to life?

In a last-ditch effort to engage my students, I decided to try my hand at adapting the Hamilton summaries into reader's theater script-stories. I was familiar with this approach as a teaching strategy for younger learners, but I was unsure of its effectiveness with secondary school students. I just needed something—anything—to engage them. The result was transformational. By adapting the story into spoken lines of dialogue, I allowed my students to participate in the events as never before. Rather than simply reading a story, they were experiencing it. Even more, they were enjoying it—so much, in fact, that they were asking when they could read the next one. Realizing that there was no next one, I went home that day and immediately began to adapt the next story in the curriculum. I repeated the process time and again, spurred on by my students' continued engagement.

Although I felt that I had solved the engagement problem, I wondered how my students' comprehension was affected by this approach. To my relief, when the time for assessment arrived, the students were exponentially better at recalling events, analyzing plots, examining characterizations, and determining themes than they had been before. Script-stories were a hit—for both engagement and comprehension.

As I continued to analyze the script-story effect, I had an important insight: When students inhabit character roles, they are much more likely to think deeply about those characters, their motivations, their world, and the story as a whole. Even students who were not reading a character role were more actively engaged in the story simply because it was their classmates who were bringing the characters to life. Achilles and Aphrodite were no longer archaic, abstract characters; they were now students from a few desks over. I observed this happening in real time during our lessons: students who had never before spoken in class were interrupting the action of the story to ask me questions like, "Why does Achilles want his comrades at arms to fail without him?" "Why is Zeus trying to stay neutral in the conflict?" and "Why are the gods so petty?"

Before proceeding further, a moment should be spent explaining how script-stories work in the classroom. I use the term *script-story* to avoid the more common term *reader's theater play* since many students associate a play with sets, costumes, and physical acting, which are not part of the script-story approach. The absence of physical acting frees up the students to focus on the language—reading their dialogue with the proper inflection through provided dialogue tags (e.g., *softly* or *angrily*). I never force any student to take a reading part; students readily volunteer for these parts since the alternative means that they must read silently. Even students without a reading part participate in the storytelling through group sound effects such as cheering, collective gasps, and the fan favorite, snicker-snack. I also keep on hand an arsenal of noisemakers (a pair of hollowed-out

298   Secondary School Classroom

coconut halves for hoofbeats, a recorder, a plastic trumpet, a thunder can, etc.) and sometimes designate a student to be the sound-effects technician for a particular script-story. The full-class participation results in a living, breathing experience—a collective creation from the combination of our unique voices. Even I have a role—often as the part of the ubiquitous narrator, but on occasions I have been known to take a character part and show off my acting talents (or lack thereof). Moving through the story together at the same pace creates a safe space, where students feel comfortable asking a question about a particular event that they might not ask if they were reading silently.

The success of script-stories taught me that engaging students with ancient epics is only possible when students are given a voice in the story. Script-stories transform my students, previously passive spectators, into active participants. The characters' lines may be printed on the page, but the students are the ones who bring them to life as modern voices embodying ancient figures. As one student explained in an anonymous end-of-the-year course survey, "We understand the characters better because we *are* the characters. It's like they are actually alive." Students have likewise commented on the "family" group-learning atmosphere that script-stories create as well as their heightened ability to remember character names and plot details from the stories they have read.

As engaging as they are, script-stories are not meant to replace the original works that they adapt; instead, I intersperse excerpts from the original epics among the script-story adaptations. For example, while studying Homer's *Odyssey*, we will read excerpts from the original epic poem between each of the five script-story adaptations.[1] With other epic selections such as *Beowulf*, I use three script-stories to relate the full plot of the epic poem before students approach the original text, freeing them up to appreciate the poem's language and analyze its deeper themes. Often historical background is necessary for appreciating an epic, and script-stories make students much more motivated to dive into the world of the story. And dive they do.

Putting Students in the Action

Giving students a voice in the story is only the first step of the epic engagement methodology. For students to be fully engaged, they must also experience the action of the story. Fortunately, ancient epics are filled with thrilling action—climactic duels, bloodthirsty monster attacks, descents into the underworld—and this is where strategies such as gamification, role-playing, and hands-on learning transport students into these action-packed worlds.

Some of my favorite action-oriented activities are those that I use in conjunction with the study of the *Iliad*.[2] At the beginning of the Trojan War unit, I divide my Mythology class into Greeks and Trojans by changing the physical layout of my classroom. Splitting the room right down the middle, I ask students to turn their desks toward each other to accentuate the confrontational nature of the conflict, and the resulting seating arrangement is one they will keep for the entire three-week unit. I then assign each student a character role in the Trojan War. Some roles are thrilling, such as the coveted role of Achilles, Greece's greatest warrior, while others are as underwhelming as Astyanax, the young son of Hector. Immediately, this role-playing aspect increases the interest students have in their assigned characters as they begin to wonder about the backstory of their characters, the role their characters will play in the conflict, and whether their characters will live or die. All of a sudden they have a vested interest in the events that are about to unfold.

Many students are unfamiliar with ancient warfare, so in addition to a healthy dose of historical background, I give them a visual aid for the fighting style of the Trojan War. Holding up a pair of shields and long spears that I constructed from cardboard and yardsticks, I ask for a pair of volunteers to demonstrate exactly how ancient warriors would attack one another. A pair of Halloween-shop Greek helmets completes the makeshift armor. Since I based the dimensions of the weapons on historical sources, the sight of the volunteers pretending to jab at one another over or under the shields gives students an accurate visual for the duels they will encounter in the *Iliad*.

To further invest my students in the stakes of the Trojan War, I gamify the unit so that by its end there will be a clear winner between the classroom Greeks and Trojans, an outcome determined by what I call the Trojan War Game. Setting aside two or three days throughout the three-week unit as battle days, I use the game to accentuate the action of the *Iliad*. The game is played using dice and game sheets, on which students individually plan their strategies by buying a series of warriors using a predetermined number of troop points. Listed on the game sheets are four types of troops, each with a different cost. Chariot warriors cost more than the javelin throwers, which cost more than foot soldiers, and so on. Of course, the costlier the troop type is, the harder it is to kill. Some troop types can only be killed by rolling a five or six on the dice, while others can be killed by lower numbers. Each player also chooses a patron deity from a list of gods and goddesses, separated out by Greek or Trojan loyalty. Patron deities protect the players from a specific number in a dice roll when they are attacked.

When the students have spent their troop points, they are prepared to do battle. Taking turns, the students call out an opponent from the opposing side for single combat. They choose a troop type from the opposing player's game sheet to attack, noting which numbers are required to kill that type of troop. Each player takes a turn attacking then retreats to their side. This action is performed time and again, and players die in the game when all their troops are eliminated. It does not take long for the battle (and my classroom) to reach fever pitch. Rolling a dice becomes a matter of life and death.

This may seem like a frivolous activity in the midst of the study of one of the world's greatest epics, but apart from achieving off-the-charts engagement from students, it is a subtle teaching tool. Students learn the names of the Trojan War's sea of characters, their affiliations (Greek or Trojan), and the loyalties of the gods; furthermore, the game drives their curiosity to find out the outcome of the story. Many a time the Trojan victors of the Trojan War Game are crestfallen to find that their literary counterparts did not achieve the same success.

This gamification technique is not limited to the study of the Trojan War, and there are many classroom games of this nature that I use in conjunction with other ancient stories: Battlefield, based on Virgil's *Aeneid*, recreates the war between Aeneas and Turnus in a strategic one-on-one Battleship-meets-Risk style of game play; Lord of the Labyrinth pits one player acting as Theseus against another as the Minotaur; and an *Odyssey* escape-room-type challenge asks students to solve puzzles related to Odysseus's various obstacles. These games are a simple way to draw students into the action of the epics, pique their interest, and reinforce crucial information. They bring students one step closer to the next goal of the epic engagement teaching methodology: forging personal connections to the story.

Connecting Students to the Story

Although script-stories allow students to inhabit character roles, and classroom games build their excitement, students can only engage with an epic when they make meaningful connections between the fictional lives of the epic characters and their own life experiences. This is no easy feat considering how far removed these characters are from the students' own time and culture; nevertheless, through thoughtful questions and creative assignment design, these all-important connections can still occur. Ancient epics, it turns out, are much more relevant to high school students than those students might initially think. The heroes of myth are often young adults brimming with potential and eager to prove themselves yet at the same time burdened with mighty expectations. The obstacles they face, while outwardly different from those faced by students, embody universal struggles of loss, self-doubt, failure, and fear. Recognizing these similarities is revelatory for my students, and thoughtful questions make these connections apparent.

Ancient stories can be even more meaningful to students when they use them to process their real-life choices. One of my go-to characters for this purpose is Achilles, who faces a dilemma of competing destinies: Achilles knows that if he goes to the Trojan War, he will forever be remembered as the world's greatest warrior but will die young. Conversely, if he chooses to stay home, forgoing war for peace, he will live a long and happy life but die in obscurity. So I ask my students, "What would you do if you were Achilles? Which destiny would you choose?" At its heart Achilles's choice is between a short, glorious life and a long-lasting, humble one. The students' responses are always interesting, and their justifications reflect their ambitions and values. Asking students to step into the mind of Achilles for a moment forges a link between them and the character. They equate his dilemma with the choices that they face. Of course, their choices look different—perhaps between college and the leap of faith necessary to follow an acting career against the advice of their parents—yet these shared moments of decision develop students' empathy for the characters.

Achilles's dilemma is just one of many points at which students' connections to characters in the story can be forged through creative questioning. Questions can also help build these connections to moments in other epics: Is it right for Odysseus to lie to his own men? Should Penelope have remained faithful to her husband? Did Aeneas make the right choice when leaving Queen Dido behind, choosing duty over love? Was Gilgamesh foolish to seek immortality? Time and again, I attempt to make meaningful connections by inviting students to analyze real-world choices through the fictional lives of epic characters.

Although student-character connections are meaningful, perhaps the most important connection I attempt to make is between my students and the elements of the epic itself. Stories are mirrors of realities—lenses

302 Secondary School Classroom

through which readers see themselves more clearly—therefore, viewing life as a story yields many important connections. An activity titled Make Your Life Epic takes common elements of the epic such as the hero, mighty purpose, vast setting, supernatural aid, mentors and allies, and elevation of style and asks students to apply the elements directly to their own lives. A series of prompts guide students through the epic-life connection. Students are the heroes of their own lives, so what are some of their strengths that could make them successful or flaws that could trip them up? All epic heroes have a quest—a mighty purpose that sends them on a journey. What is an epic goal that students have for their lives? Epic heroes go on incredible journeys to distant (and dangerous) lands. Where do students think their life journey will take them? Epic heroes receive motivation and assistance on their quests. When students are confused and discouraged, where do they find strength and wisdom? To answer these questions, students delve into their past, analyze their present, and anticipate their future. Their responses never fail to give me new insights into their hopes, fears, and dreams. Their responses also serve as a reminder that my goal as an educator, more than simply teaching stories for their own sake, is to use stories as a tool to help my students live better lives. These connections allow students to forge deeper bonds with ancient stories, but students will never adopt these stories as their own until they are empowered to play with them.

Empowering Students to Play

Play, a surprisingly analytical activity, is such an important part of learning, but playing with a story may seem problematic. On the surface stories appear so rigid—solidified plot, established characters, and inflexible themes—especially the ancient texts, enshrined and revered by generation after generation. Yet students can only engage with an epic if they are empowered to play with the story through adaptation, interpretation, and transformation. Through the use of creative project design, stories that were once solid and immutable can become fluid and moldable.

The power to play begins with creative projects that allow students to reinterpret the epic narrative in imaginative ways: If there were a video game based on *Beowulf*, what would it be like? What new level should be added to Dante's concept of hell, and who would be punished there? What would a doll or action figure based on a character from the *Odyssey* look like? If an epic were to be reimagined as a musical, what would some of the song titles be? These types of projects could easily descend into the realm of fluff, but as students playfully adapt an epic story, I require that they include evidence from the original epic that justifies their choices.

Another creative way to play with stories is by changing their plots through branching-pathways storytelling (similar to the Choose Your Own Adventure series). I give my students the challenge of creating a branching-pathways version of an ancient story we have read. To model this activity, I created a digital version of the Greek myth of Theseus that allows the students to make choices for the hero, which often result in a variety of gruesome deaths but ultimately lead Theseus to his mythic destiny. Their versions of an ancient story can lead in any direction they choose—stimulating their creativity but also developing an appreciation for the original plot structure. They accomplish this work by writing out a short section of the story on a note card and then giving the reader choices that lead to other note cards with additional story segments and further choices.

Another playful project I utilize when teaching the Trojan War involves asking students to write a deleted scene from the *Iliad* in the form of dialogue between two characters. This gives students a chance to demonstrate their understanding of the story as well as their abundant wit. One deleted scene showcased a pair of Trojans planning to end the war by assassinating Paris, the weak-willed Trojan prince. Another dramatized how Hebe and Hestia, two goddesses who did not figure heavily in the action of the Trojan War, at last decide to enter the fray, with hilarious results.

Ultimately, play brings ownership. Once the students have made their own mark on these ancient stories, they are much more likely to adopt them as their own. Since one goal of teaching epics is that students will pass them on to the next generation, feeling ownership is a key step in this process. Thus, the epic engagement methodology brings ancient stories full circle. Those who first received them are inspired to treasure them and empowered to impart them to the next generation. By giving students a voice in the story through reader's theater script-stories, letting them experience the action through classroom games and activities, forging meaningful connections through thoughtful questioning, and empowering them to play with the story, teachers can give ancient stories new life.

Notes

1. Excerpts from the *Odyssey* appear in Hamby, *Greek Mythology*.

2. Students read script-stories based on the *Iliad* in Hamby, *Reaching Olympus*.

304   Secondary School Classroom

Works Cited

Barry, Dave. "The Funny Side of 'Beowulf.'" 16 Nov. 1997. *Chicago Tribune*, www.chicagotribune.com/news/ct-xpm-1997-11-16-9711160429-story .html.

Beowulf. Translated by Burton Raffel. *Elements of Literature: Sixth Course: Literature of Britain*, edited by Richard Sime, Holt, Rinehart, and Winston, 1997, pp. 18–46.

Hamby, Zachary. *Greek Mythology for Teens.* Prufrock Press, 2011.

———. *Reaching Olympus: The Greek Myths: The Saga of the Trojan War.* Hamby Publishing, 2012.

Hamilton, Edith. *Mythology.* Little, Brown, 1942.

Ana Grinberg

Epic Youth Narratives in an Active Learning World Literature Course

The Epic of Gilgamesh, Homer's *Odyssey*, and the *Chanson de Roland* (*Song of Roland*) are often taught in world literature survey courses that stretch from antiquity to the early modern period. These and other epics that are sometimes included, such as Valmiki's *Ramayana* and *Popol Wuj* (Popol Vuh), expose students to a broader view of heroism around the world. Nevertheless, the fact that these canonical epic narratives tend to focus on adulthood creates the false impression that children and adolescents were not included in premodern heroic literature. Yet early narratives centering on young heroes do exist across cultures, even though most have not been translated into English and are not even mentioned in Frederick Turner's "loose list of epics" (17). This essay engages with epic youth narratives taught in a culturally diverse sophomore world literature course using engaged, active approaches.[1] Several types of activities have been developed based on active pedagogical techniques, such as student-led ludic discussions and asynchronous debates, but the emphasis in this core literature course is on a collaborative multimodal assignment dealing with young heroes' texts. The evaluation of active learning upon completion of the course has demonstrated that this pedagogical approach goes beyond

305

306   Youth Narratives

the institutional learning objectives, as students develop strong collaborative skills and expand their understanding of the world.

Heroic narratives offer a window into historical expectations about specific social attitudes. Often students are surprised to find that some protagonists in epics written before 1600 CE do not follow the behavioral patterns anticipated today in a hero. What makes the comparative approach even more appealing to students is the realization that diverse cultures share a focus on companionship as the basis for individual prowess while emphasizing specific deeds based on a cultural worldview, a focus found in *The Epic of Gilgamesh*, the *Ramayana*, and *Popol Wuj*. A chronological ordering of assigned epic works, from antiquity to the early modern period, encourages the class to investigate shifting perspectives on gender, familial duty, honor, and glory according to specific societies. In other words, we approach epics synchronically as well as diachronically to explore this specific set of themes.

I used to start the course by introducing cosmogonies that tie into the epic genre, drawing out the clear connection between *Enuma Elish* and *The Epic of Gilgamesh*, for example, and reading *Popol Wuj* as both a creation myth and a heroic narrative. More recently, however, I decided to share with my students some narratives about the childhood of heroes to help explain the fan fiction aspect of literary creation before 1600 CE.[2] In spring 2020, students compared foundational epics, particularly the complete *Epic of Gilgamesh* and selections about Rama's adult exploits in Valmiki's *Ramayana*,[3] to infancy heroic narratives such as the boyhood deeds of Cú Chulainn from the medieval Irish *Táin Bó Cúailnge* (*The Cattle Raid of Cooley* [Táin 35–50]) and the youth of Roland included in the medieval Franco-Italian *Geste Francor* (Morgan), whose title might be translated as *The Story of the Franks*. *Táin Bó Cúailnge* is the central epic in the Ulaid (Ulster) cycle, relaying the battle between Queen Medb of Connaught and the seventeen-year-old hero. The section we read deals with the feats of Cú Chulainn as a young child. *Geste Francor* is an anthology of medieval chansons de geste (Carolingian epic poems) belonging to the *cycle du roi* (cycle of the king), as it centers on the deeds of Charlemagne and his paladins. Roland's youth, the section from *Geste Francor* that we considered in class, is one of many prequels to other chansons de geste, which are known as *enfances* (childhood or youth stories) because they tell of the first martial and sentimental exploits of established heroes.[4] Recalling Phillis Gaffney's observation that *enfances* have a structure similar to the lives of Christian saints (159), I also had students compare the boyhood deeds of

Cú Chulainn and Roland to the childhood of Jesus (in the Infancy Gospel of Thomas) and Buddha (in Ashvaghosha's *Life of Buddha*).

We used two active learning assignments to study these six texts. First, individually and before class, students read and annotated the texts through *Perusall*—a social-learning platform accessible through our institutional learning management system.[5] This collaborative engagement with the material allowed students to consider diverse perspectives on the issues we were going to discuss in class. Then they prepared reading-journal entries—which students in the class write about once a week. An early journal entry asked them to consider how *The Epic of Gilgamesh* diverges from the monomyth, as explained by Joseph Campbell in his *The Hero with a Thousand Faces*, and rejects the "claims of universality" of the monomyth mentioned by Turner (10).[6] For the following journal entries, students explored the use of the *Ramayana* as didactic literature and later on examined the similarities between heroes and religious figures. With this background, as part of our customary classroom activities, a team of students facilitated a ludic discussion in which their classmates attempted to apply the monomyth model to the young heroes' journeys. Evidently, as groups of students created comparative visual representations of the heroes' paths, they discovered the monomyth to be insufficient for describing heroic childhood narratives.

The comparison of foundational epics to youth narratives was still the goal during the fall 2020 iteration of the course, but in this course *Egil's Saga* replaced the childhood lives of religious figures. This Icelandic family saga, which is closer to a chronicle than to an epic, narrates the life of Skallagrim and his descendants. We focused on the sections about Egil's birth, first deeds in the ball court, and voyages to Norway and the Baltic.[7] With all of his juvenile quirks, Egil became a great comparison for young Cú Chulainn and Roland. Besides the fact that *Egil's Saga* has not received attention from the creators of learning guides and those who write and sell essays for students, a particular advantage to teaching the work is its availability in several translations and the existence of some great websites that enrich the students' experience of medieval Iceland.[8] We explored together Emily Lethbridge's *Icelandic Saga Map* website, which is an interactive map showing the locations mentioned in all the sagas of the Icelanders.[9] As a team activity, students had to find certain locations on this map. In looking for Skallagrim's farm, the site of the ball game, the places where Egil and his brother Thorolf land in Norway and travel around the Baltic, students realized that Icelandic people journeyed to distant regions. In spring 2021, students engaged with the same activity with similar results: in a brief discussion after exploring the map, they agreed that seafaring is a distinguishing element of Egil's culture, whereas other heroes did not travel by ship in their childhood.

During the seventy-five-minute sessions devoted to each of the boyhood narratives in *Egil's Saga*, *Táin Bó Cúailnge*, and *Geste Francor*, we went over the historical and cultural background, then discussed some crucial themes in the works. The class noticed commonalities, such as the emphasis on lineage, the (expectation of) early submission to rules of fealty, and the prominence of physical strength and cunning as qualities needed by the heroes to gain glory. Students then had the opportunity to do some teamwork and be creative. The Timeline Project assignment required them to work collaboratively with two classmates. Each team member chose a different heroic narrative and worked with one of the heroes: young Cú Chulainn in the *Táin Bó Cúailnge*, young Roland in *Geste Francor*, and young Egil in *Egil's Saga*. The students separately created a timeline of their hero's actions using representative events and quotations and contextualized them culturally or historically. The individual timelines somewhat work as the first step in a reversed approach to the revised Bloom's taxonomy. The revised model, developed by Lorin Anderson, begins with the Remember step (which is aligned with the transmission pedagogical model).[10] My students instead started with the Create step (which helps to build on previously acquired knowledge). Teams subsequently compared their three timelines, finding commonalities such as the heroes' invincibility, disregard of parental advice, and quick tempers. Students emphasized the importance given to competition, pointing to the heroes' innate leadership skills. Moreover, they recognized that, despite the similarities between the texts, the cultural expectations of heroism and childhood were different, even though all three narratives were composed during the Middle Ages. Following the reversed Bloom's taxonomy model, the Evaluate and Analyze steps became the second and third steps in this process and gave students the opportunity to pause and consider their findings. Finally, each student wrote a reflection—known in pedagogical scholarship as a metacognitive component—about the assignment.[11] A common remark in the reflections was that students' views on heroism, which they found were influenced by contemporary ideals, had to be dismantled. The reversed Bloom's taxonomy worked well, as the class would understand and remember the information they gathered in order to create and analyze their timelines. The Timeline Project not only provided peer-to-peer learning opportunities but also ensured that students individually performed close readings and, most importantly, enabled the formation of rich learning communities through collaboration, support, inquisitiveness, and creativity.

As shown with the Timeline Project, the main goals of active learning techniques can be summarized as to encourage active engagement, strengthen and assess understanding, reflect on learning, establish connections for future application of knowledge, and provide or get peer feedback (as practice).[12] In a core literature course, where often students have to fulfill an academic requirement, this exploration of young hero narratives generates a productive and dynamic engagement with literature while helping to satisfy the learning outcomes dictated by universities: reading effectively and thinking critically, as well as analyzing and valuing artistic creations. Collaborative work, though not included in my institution's required learning outcomes, happens to be "a life-long skill that we will need," according to the students. Moreover, these assignments promote respectful attitudes toward a broadly defined diversity.

New translations have become available that enable the inclusion of other childhood epic narratives in the course. One such example is the recent translation of parts of the *Sirat al-amira Dhat al-Himma* (*The Tale of Princess Fatima, Warrior Woman*), including the childhood of the *amira* (commander or warrior woman) as she develops into a full-blown hero.[13] Fatima is a self-made warrior and clan leader, and her example demonstrates that even during the Middle Ages the role of women was not set in stone. This text particularly appealed to my female students, who mentioned while discussing Fatima in class that they appreciated reading about a strong female warrior. A student comments in the reading journal for that week that "Fatima is a great warrior and she also has the strong build that all heroes had." The same is true of Bodhmall, in *Macgnímartha Finn* (*The Boyhood Deeds of Finn*), as she is not only a druidess but also Finn McCumall's tutor during the boy's childhood. Neither of these women warriors can be seen following the monomyth, further demonstrating that youth narratives contain specific steps and might not even be aligned with Gaffney's idea that heroes' stories resemble saints' lives. *Macgnímartha Finn*—which belongs to the Fianna cycle of early Irish literature but is only extant in one example dated to the fifteenth century—takes *Táin Bó Cúailnge*'s place among the youth epics in some iterations of my course, as it is actually the only *macgnímartha* (tales of boyhood deeds) that is not grouped with other stories of Irish heroes.

310   Youth Narratives

Moreover, instead of Finn being the clan leader's nephew (as are Roland and Cú Chulainn in their respective narratives), he is a liminal character like Fatima. Both youths are brought up by foster mothers, ignorant of their true identity. For my spring 2022 course, *The Tale of Princess Fatima, Warrior Woman* and *Macgnímartha Finn* join the syllabus with *Egil's Saga* and Roland's story in *Geste Francor*, offering further depth to students' understanding of heroism in diverse cultures. The search for childhood epics does not end here. The youth of the hero Yamato dake no Mikoto, as narrated in the *Nihon Shoki* (also known as *Nihongi* [*Japanese Chronicles*]), will soon be part of the course's exploration of heroes' youth.[14]

While Turner claims, in the introduction of his *Epic: Form, Content, and History*, that his book is intended to demonstrate that epics are not "just a 'Western' genre . . . [or] an outdated historical relic" and that "epic is the basic story that the human species tells to itself about itself," he devotes almost no attention to the childhood of heroes (13). Epics such as *Chanson de Roland* or the *Nibelungenlied* served for a long time to promote nineteenth- and twentieth-century nationalisms, but this is not necessarily true of the other texts discussed here. Stories of youth deeds—as *enfances*, *macgnímartha*, and similar texts—have hardly been used with these intentions. Roland, in *Geste Francor*, is brought up in the woods, where his parents are hiding from Charlemagne; the boy is oblivious to his social status. Since his birth, Finn, in *Macgnímartha Finn*, lives with two druidesses and is unaware of the perils he might face approaching others. Moreover, Finn's father is a *fénnid* (outlaw), and his mother the daughter of a druid. In *The Tale of Princess Fatima, Warrior Woman*, Fatima is the rejected daughter of a Banū Kilāb leader and is raised by a Turkish slave in the Ṭayyibi tribe's camp, where she is ignorant of her social station. In depicting the young future heroes as liminal in diverse ways, premodern composers of epics were interested in the development of heroism, despite gender, place of origin, and even social station. That lesson is central to teaching a culturally diverse, active survey course embracing strong collaboration among students to further expand their worldview.

Notes

1. As Brame explains, active pedagogies "often embrace the use of cooperative learning groups, a constructivist-based practice that places particular emphasis on the contribution that social interaction can make."

2. While the *Oxford English Dictionary* defines fan fiction as "fiction, usually fantasy or science fiction, written by a fan rather than a professional author," the term is especially appropriate to convey that *enfances*, stories about the childhood of established heroes, are "based on already-existing characters from a television series, book, film, etc." ("Fan Fiction").

3. The *Ramayana* is one of the main Sanskrit epics, consisting of 24,000 verses divided into seven *kandas* (books). Each *kanda* contains a number of *sargas* (chapters) of different length, similar to *laisses* in Old French epics. Though "Bala Kanda" ("Book of Bala"), the first of these books, narrates the miraculous birth of Rama, it does not depict Rama as a child. Students read "Ayodhya Kanda" ("Book of Ayodhya"), chs. 15–31; "Aranya Kanda" ("Book of Aranya"), chs. 14–18, 32–37, 42–68; "Kiskindha Kanda" ("Book of Kiskindha"), chs. 56–67; "Sundara Kanda" ("Book of Sundara"), chs. 1–38; and "Yuddha Kanda" ("Book of Yuddha"), chs. 109–23, 130–31.

4. Unfortunately, because many *enfances* deal not with the childhood but with the youth of heroes, texts like Adenet le Roi's thirteenth-century *Enfances Ogier* (*Ogier's Youth*) cannot be paired with the deeds of Cú Chulainn in *Táin Bó Cúailnge*. Other narratives such as *Mainet* (the *enfances* of Charlemagne), *Enfances Garin de Monglane* (*Garin de Monglane's Youth*), *Enfances Vivien* (*Vivien's Youth*), and *Enfances Guillaume* (*Guillaume's Youth*) are not available in English translation.

5. *Perusall* is a social annotation platform through which "students interact together on assignments . . . honing their critical thinking skills and developing a deeper understanding of the material" (as stated on the site's home page at the time of this writing).

6. Instead of reading Joseph Campbell's *The Hero with a Thousand Faces*, early on in the course students watch a video by Matthew Winkler that summarizes Campbell's argument.

7. *Egil's Saga* is divided into *kaflar* (chapters). Those focusing on Egil's youth are 29–31 and 40–48.

8. The *Vikingeskibs Museet* website provides background on Viking ships. Most important, the "Education" portal on the site has information about the Vikings, including written sources and runic writing, clothing, weapons, and navigation. Jesse Byock's *Mosfell Archaeological Project* contains several videos and multimedia links, in addition to reports on the findings in Hrísbrú, Iceland (the location of Egil's burial), among other sites.

9. The texts of all these sagas appear on the website in Old Norse, which gives the students a visual sense of the language.

10. The transmission model—what Freire calls the "banking concept of education" (72)—assumes a passive attitude in the student and the memorization of information.

11. For findings on the benefits of metacognitive activities, see Weimer; Chick.

12. For more information about active learning, see Karmas; Kember and Leung; and Tomcho and Foels.

312   Youth Narratives

13. This text, also known as *Sirat al-Mujāhidīn* (loosely translated as *The Epic of Those Fighting in the Way of God*), is a northern Syrian text created between 1100 and 1143. Further information is available in Melanie Magidow's introduction to her translation (*Tale* ix–xxii).

14. I have considered using *Digenis Akritis* (*Two-Blood Border Lord*; the title is an epithet), though Elizabeth Jeffreys's outstanding scholarly parallel translation of the two earliest existent manuscripts of this work is not suitable for undergraduate readers because of the extensive footnotes on the versions' details.

Works Cited

Adenet le Roi. *Ogier's Youth (Les enfances Ogier): A Thirteenth-Century Epic.* Translated by Anna Moore Morton, Arizona Center for Medieval and Renaissance Studies, 2020.

Anderson, Lorin W., et al. *A Taxonomy for Learning, Teaching, and Assessing: A Revision of Bloom's Taxonomy of Educational Objectives.* Longman, 2001.

Ashvaghosha. *The Life of Buddha.* Translated by E. B. Cowell. *Bedford Anthology of World Literature: The Ancient, Medieval, and Early Modern World*, vol. 1, edited by Paul Davis et al., Bedford/St. Martin's, 2003, pp. 1549–58.

Brame, Cynthia J. "Active Learning." *Vanderbilt University Center for Teaching*, 2016, cft.vanderbilt.edu/active-learning.

Campbell, Joseph. *The Hero with a Thousand Faces.* 1949. Joseph Campbell Foundation, 2020.

Chick, Nancy. "Metacognition." *Center for Teaching*, Vanderbilt U, 2013, cft.vanderbilt.edu/guides-sub-pages/metacognition.

Digenis Akritis: *The Grottaferrata and Escorial Versions.* Translated by Elizabeth Jeffreys, Cambridge UP, 1998.

Egil's Saga. Translated by Hermann Pálsson and Paul Edwards, Penguin Books, 1976.

Enuma Elish. Translated by Benjamin R. Foster. *Norton Anthology of World Literature*, Martin Puchner, general editor, 4th ed., vol. A, W. W. Norton, 2018, pp. 29–34.

The Epic of Gilgamesh. Translated by Benjamin R. Foster, 2nd ed., W. W. Norton, 2019.

"Fan Fiction, *N.* (2)." *Oxford English Dictionary Online*, Oxford UP, draft addition Sept. 2004, www.oed.com/view/Entry/68000.

Freire, Paulo. *Pedagogy of the Oppressed.* 1968. Translated by Myra Bergman Ramos, Continuum Books, 2000.

Gaffney, Phillis. *Constructions of Childhood and Youth in Old French Narrative.* Ashgate, 2011.

The Infancy Gospel of Thomas. Translated by Bart D. Ehrman. *Lost Scriptures: Books That Did Not Make It into the New Testament*, by Ehrman, Oxford UP, 2003, pp. 57–62.

Karmas, Cristina. "School to Work: Using Active Learning to Teach Business Writing." *US-China Education Review*, vol. 8, no. 3, 2011, pp. 302–16.

Kember, David, and Doris Y. P. Leung. "The Influence of Active Learning Experiences on the Development of Graduate Capabilities." *Studies in Higher Education*, vol. 30, no. 2, Apr. 2005, pp. 155–70.

Macgnímartha Finn. Translated by Joseph Falaky Nagy. *The Wisdom of the Outlaw: The Boyhood Deeds of Finn in Gaelic Narrative Tradition*, by Nagy, U of California P, 1985, pp. 209–21.

Morgan, Leslie Zarker. "Italian Literature: *Geste Francor.*" *The ORB: On-line Reference Book for Medieval Studies*, 7 July 2006, the-orb.arlima.net/encyclop/culture/lit/italian/morganintro.html.

Nihongi: Chronicles of Japan from the Earliest Times to A.D. 697. Translated by W. G. Aston, George Allen and Unwin, 1956.

Popol Vuh: The Mayan Book of the Dawn of Life. Translated by Dennis Tedlock, rev. ed., Simon and Schuster, 1996.

The Táin*: A New Translation of the* Táin Bó Cúailnge. Translated by Ciaran Carson, Viking Penguin, 2008.

The Tale of Princess Fatima, Warrior Woman: The Arabic Epic of Dhat al-Himma. Translated by Melanie Magidow, Penguin Classics, 2021.

Tomcho, Thomas J., and Rob Foels. "Meta-Analysis of Group Learning Activities: Empirically Based Teaching Recommendations." *Teaching of Psychology*, vol. 39, no. 3, July 2012, pp. 159–69.

Turner, Frederick. *Epic: Form, Content, and History*. Transaction Publishers, 2012.

Valmiki. *The Concise* Ramayana *of Valmiki*. Translated by Swami Venkate-sananda, State U of New York P, 1988.

Weimer, Maryellen. "Assessing and Developing Metacognitive Skills." *Faculty Focus*, 21 Jan. 2011, www.facultyfocus.com/articles/teaching-and-learning/assessing-and-developing-metacognitive-skills.

Winkler, Matthew. "What Makes a Hero?" *TEDEd*, ed.ted.com/lessons/what-makes-a-hero-matthew-winkler. Accessed 11 Oct. 2022.

Dwight F. Reynolds

Middle Eastern Epics across the Millennia: *The Epic of Gilgamesh, Sirat Bani Hilal,* and the *Shahnameh*

This essay explores ways of presenting three Middle Eastern epics—*The Epic of Gilgamesh*, the Arabic *Sirat Bani Hilal*, and the Persian *Shahnameh*—in the context of an introductory course in comparative literature titled Major Works of Middle Eastern Literatures, which forms part of a series of courses at the University of California, Santa Barbara, that cover the literatures of Asia, Africa, North and South America, and Europe. The course is designed to present freshman and sophomore college students with various methods of comparative literary analysis as well as a generalized understanding of the peoples, languages, and literatures of the Middle East from ancient to modern times. This course can be taken to fulfill the literature requirement (two courses for the bachelor of arts degree, one for the bachelor of science degree) as well as the one course in world cultures that is required for both degrees. Major Works of Middle Eastern Literatures also counts as one of the six required writing courses for all undergraduates; in the course students write three essays during the ten-week quarter, in addition to completing quizzes and both a midterm and a final exam. The fact that the course fulfills three general education requirements increases its popularity (it now regularly enrolls over 150 students) but also means that many of the students select the course for that

314

reason, and not from any special interest in the Middle East or in literature. I often advise my teaching assistants that the majority of these students have most likely stumbled into this class because it fits their general education needs or their schedules and that our task is to make it interesting enough that by the end of the term they will be glad to have taken it. In particular, since a large percentage of the students are from the sciences, I make a special effort to appeal to their interests at several points in the course.

Although the course does not focus exclusively on epic as a genre of literature, the three texts cited above constitute a substantial portion of the course. There are five primary objectives in teaching these texts: to think about epic as a genre, particularly in contrast to folktales (see below), various hero and heroine patterns, the interface between oral and written literature, the concept of performance, and literary portrayals of intimate psychological bonds between same-sex friends and within families, particularly father-son and mother-daughter relations. I have found that centering some of the discussions on types of relationships allows even first-year students to share their opinions, which they might not be able to do with the same confidence if they were asked questions of a more literary nature. If there is a principle at work here, it is to ask students to reflect on and discuss things they can readily understand and then to teach different approaches to literary analysis in the interstices of those discussions.

The first week of the quarter is devoted to lectures that give a basic introduction to the Middle East, starting with a survey of different peoples and languages and an explanation of how those languages relate to one another. This survey includes identifying well-known groups such as Arabs, Armenians, Iranians, and Turks but also lesser-known groups such as Imazighen (Berbers), Nubians, Copts, and so on. We also discuss the overlapping relationships between these categories and religious communities. It comes as a surprise to many students, for example, to find out that there are Jewish, Christian, and Muslim Arabs and that in the Middle Ages the majority of Jews in the world spoke Arabic as their mother tongue, as do many Jews even today.[1]

In the second week of the term, students take a map quiz of the modern Middle East to assure me that they understand references to geographic locations, and they then take a detailed quiz about Middle Eastern languages that includes placing all of the major languages in their language families (Indo-European, Semitic, Turkic, etc.) and identifying examples

316   Middle Eastern Epics

of different scripts (cuneiform, Hebrew, Aramaic, Arabic, Coptic, modern Turkish, etc.). One could imagine jumping immediately into reading the texts and discussing them purely for their content; however, I choose to use this course to provide students with a basic understanding of Middle Eastern cultures. This is not information that American students have normally encountered in secondary school, and, in most cases, they will not study this in other classes during their college careers.

The Epic of Gilgamesh

The first reading of the course is *The Epic of Gilgamesh*; having explored and taught various different translations, I have used Stephen Mitchell's Gilgamesh: *A New English Version* a number of times.[2] Any translation or edition has strengths and weaknesses, but this version offers an extremely readable text with a useful introduction. Its weakness is that it does not give a sense of the fragmentary nature of any one of the original texts, since it fills in missing passages from other versions. We discuss the missing passages in lecture, but I am more interested in encouraging students to read the narrative carefully and to analyze it than I am in pushing them to read a more so-called authentic but difficult edition.[3] In future iterations of the course, however, I plan to use Sophus Helle's Gilgamesh: *A New Translation of the Ancient Epic*, which I find to be admirably eloquent and readable.

The introductory lecture gives a sense of the ancient world of the Sumerian, Akkadian, and Babylonian empires, with a particular focus on the Sumerian city of Ur. In a happy coincidence, the archaeological remains of Ur are almost exactly the same size as the main campus of my institution (roughly 450 hectares, which equals 1,100 acres), and the supposed height of the city walls (forty to fifty feet) is comparable to the heights of several of the university buildings, so it is easy for me to ask students to imagine the ancient city and picture it filled with the bustling populace and commercial activity described in the text. Although I offer a somewhat detailed time line for the Sumerian, Akkadian, and Babylonian cultures as background, I ask students to focus on and remember one key point: The tale of Gilgamesh was told and retold, written, rewritten, edited, redacted, and copied for 2,500 years then lapsed into oblivion for two thousand years, until it was rediscovered in the nineteenth century.

Dwight F. Reynolds 317

In a nod to the many science students in the course, at some point I often pose the question, What aspect of Sumerian culture do we still use every second, minute, and hour of every day of our lives? The answer of course is the Sumerian sexagesimal (base-sixty) mathematical system, which is the reason our modern seconds, minutes, and hours are divided into sixty units. I then ask students to think of other uses of this same system: geometry (e.g., there are 360 degrees in a circle, and an equilateral triangle has three sixty-degree angles) and also geography and mapmaking (latitude and longitude are divided into degrees, minutes, and seconds). I then ask the mathematics students to explain the special qualities of the number 60 (e.g., it is divisible by the numbers 1, 2, 3, 4, 5, and 6) and teach students to count on their fingers Sumerian style (using the outer three knuckles of each finger to count from 1 to 12 on one hand, then using one finger on the other hand as a place marker, repeating for all five fingers to reach 60). Some may think this is an odd topic to raise while teaching literature, but I think it is the type of quirky knowledge that helps students engage with the course materials. I also think many students are intrigued by the fact that we still use a mathematical system that emerged at a time when *The Epic of Gilgamesh* was first being written down, despite all the advances in mathematics and science since then.

As students read through the first half of the epic, they are asked to make comparisons to other narratives. We compare the portrayal of Shamhat, the woman who leads Enkidu into self-knowledge and civilization, to that of the biblical Eve, who leads Adam into self-knowledge and exile from paradise. For the section of the text that describes the rivalry and then close friendship of Gilgamesh and Enkidu and their subsequent travels (*Gilgamesh: A New English Version* 69–150), students are asked to bring examples of bromance and road-trip tales from books, movies, television programs, comic books, and other sources to their discussion sections, which are led by teaching assistants. They are also asked to think of examples of similar stories based on close female friendships, such as the movie *Thelma and Louise*. While they are reading the second half of *The Epic of Gilgamesh*, various themes, such as the confrontation with death, the search for eternal life, and the Great Flood, are discussed in lectures and sections. We end with an examination of Gilgamesh as a hero figure, contrasting his almost supernatural characteristics with his very human flaws. This discussion often leads to a discussion of modern heroes and superheroes and the classic combination of superhuman powers with one

318   Middle Eastern Epics

or more critical weaknesses (e.g., Superman and kryptonite, Indiana Jones and his fear of snakes).

The flood story provides our first comparative leap to the dual, intertwined accounts of the Flood in Genesis in the Hebrew Bible. Most students have never been confronted with the contradictory passages in the biblical account, but we consider, for example, how Noah is first instructed to choose "two of every kind" of animal for his ark (*Holy Scriptures*, Gen. 6:19–20), while one chapter later he is instructed to choose "seven pairs of every kind" (7:2). This discussion provides room for an initial comparison between Judaic, Christian, and Muslim concepts of scripture, as well as how scripture is accessed by these three communities (e.g., in the original language or in translation, in daily or weekly readings or piecemeal through sermons, primarily through silent reading or through oral recitation, and so forth).

The next pair of texts that students read in depth are the biblical and Qur'anic accounts of Joseph. I always assign versions of these texts that show the translation alongside the original language—Hebrew and Arabic, respectively.[4] We read and analyze different passages in detail, puzzling, for example, over why the story of Tamar and Judah (Gen. 38) is embedded in the biblical story of Joseph, noting that it presents a counternarrative in which the female protagonist is virtuous and the male figure is the wrongdoer, and recognizing that this counternarrative appears before the story of pious Joseph and Potiphar's lustful and scheming wife. The first writing assignment in the course is to compare the versions of the Joseph story in the Qur'an and the Bible by selecting three differences that can be marshaled into a coherent argument. Students are instructed not to make generalizations about Jews and Muslims, or about Judaism and Islam, but only to compare the two texts as versions of the same story.

Before we take up the comparative reading of passages from the Arabic epic of the Bani Hilal Bedouin tribe and the Persian *Shahnameh*, we read a handful of Middle Eastern folktales that feature female protagonists. This provides an opportunity to talk about the role of oral and folk traditions, explore written literature as a gendered phenomenon, and think about the sometimes shockingly harsh world of folktales and the admonitory lessons passed down through generations of female storytellers. We do one miniature case study by reading two versions of a ghoul story, one narrated by a young Muslim Palestinian woman in the West Bank, and the other by an elderly, Arabic-speaking Jewish woman from the Atlas Mountains of Morocco (Reynolds, *Arab Folklore* 93–98). Through these two stories we learn that many folk traditions of the Middle East are shared across geographic, linguistic, and sectarian boundaries, including the tradition of the ghoul—a being that is able to assume different shapes and forms—later imported and completely reconceived in the West, starting with Antoine Galland's translation of the *One Thousand and One Nights* (see Al-Rawi). In each of these folktales, the father is taken in by the ghoul's wiles and, due to his desire for food or wealth, places himself, his wife, and his daughters in grave danger of being eaten by the ghoul. The womenfolk become aware of the truth and figure out how to escape, but the father pays no heed. Eventually, the women escape, and the father is eaten after reciting verses that instruct the ghoul to start by eating his ears "because I did not listen to my wife's advice!" (Reynolds, *Arab Folklore*, 97). We discuss the contrast between typical heroic tales, such as epics that laud physical prowess and bravery, and folktales that often feature female or child protagonists and that offer examples of intelligence and cunning.

Sirat Bani Hilal

The Epic of Gilgamesh is of course a staple text in many different university classes, and there are multiple translations and a large bibliography of works analyzing it from many different angles. The Arabic epic tradition is far less known, so it is worth offering a short survey of the texts and some of the most useful secondary sources. Beginning in the eleventh to thirteenth centuries, a cluster of lengthy heroic narratives began to emerge in Arabic literature and came to be referred to as *siyar* (singular, *sira*), a term that has variously been translated into English as *epic, folk epic, romance, geste*, and other terms. Some of the written versions of these tales are thousands of pages in length, and many of them are rooted in historical events and even feature known historical figures. Most of them appear to have roots in oral traditions, particularly in various forms of public recitation or performance. Edward Lane, for example, writes that in the coffee shops of Cairo in the 1830s there were some fifty professional epic singers who sang *Sirat Bani Hilal*, or the *sira* of the Bani Hilal Bedouin tribe, while accompanying themselves on the *rabab* (spike-fiddle) without written texts; thirty storytellers who recounted the *sira* of the Mamluk Sultan Baibars, also from memory with no written text but without musical accompaniment; and a half dozen reciters who read the *sira* of the Black warrior-poet 'Antar aloud from books (386–419).[5] An overview of the Arabic epic tradition is available in M. C. Lyons's *The Arabian Epic*.

320   Middle Eastern Epics

My dissertation research on the performance tradition of the Bani Hilal epic resulted in a book (Reynolds, *Heroic Poets*), a number of articles (e.g., Reynolds, "Sirat Bani Hilal," "Epic," and "Abū Zayd al-Hilālī"), and also the creation of the Sirat Bani Hilal *Digital Archive* website. The archive includes a general introduction to *Sirat Bani Hilal*, audio recordings of epic performances recorded in 1986–88, English translations of the opening episodes of the epic, photographs of the epic singers and their village in Egypt, and a video where students can hear an epic singer while the Arabic text and English translation appear line by line ("Virtual Performances"), giving a sense of how the story unfolds in real time and the interaction between the singer and his listeners.

Students read a version of the opening episode of the Arabic epic featured in the Sirat Bani Hilal *Digital Archive* ("Virtual Performances"), which narrates the birth of the Black hero Abu Zayd (Reynolds, "Start").[6] Since I recorded this text during my doctoral research, I offer the students a summary of how that research was conducted and of the findings published in my book *Heroic Poets, Poetic Heroes*, with a focus on the work of Milman Parry and Albert Lord and the concepts of "oral-formulaic composition" and "composition in performance" (Reynolds, "Composition"). The version of *Sirat Bani Hilal* that the students read includes all of the audience's reactions and interactions, so they are able to get a sense of the role of audience responses in shaping the performance. They can also listen to the performance with subtitled translation ("Virtual Performances"). In the opening episode, the hero's mother is accused of adultery and expelled from the Bani Hilal Bedouin tribe with her newborn child in her arms. She is found by a Sufi dervish who guides her to safety in a rival tribe where she is granted asylum. Her son grows up not knowing the true identity of his father. After many youthful adventures, the young hero finds himself on the battlefield face to face with his father, though neither of them knows this. After seven days of battle, during which neither fighter is able to defeat the other, the young hero's sister realizes the truth of the situation, and their identities are revealed. Father and son are reconciled when the father welcomes his wife back into the tribe with full honors. The two tribes unite to form the tribal confederation that will play the central role in the remainder of the epic. A study of the various facets of the main hero, Abu Zayd, can be found in my work "Abū Zayd al-Hilālī: Trickster, Womanizer, Warrior, Shaykh" (Reynolds, "Abū Zayd al-Hilālī"), which also highlights some remarkable parallels between this Arabic oral epic hero and the young Jesus as portrayed in the Infancy Gospel of Thomas.[7]

Dwight F. Reynolds 321

A wonderful new translation of a different Arabic epic that features a female heroine is found in *The Tale of Princess Fatima, Warrior Woman: The Arabic Epic of Dhat al-Himma*, translated by Melanie Magidow. I plan to incorporate readings from this work into this course and to have students engage in a discussion of male versus female models of heroism in Arabic epic works.

The *Shahnameh*

Our reading from the great Persian *Shahnameh* (*Book of Kings*), composed by Ferdowsi (or Firdawsi) around the year 1000 CE, is the tale of Sohrab and Rostam, perhaps the most famous—and heart-rending—episode in the overall story. Jerome Clinton's translation of this section of the epic is available as a paperback that includes facing-page Persian text and English translation (*Tragedy*). An excellent introduction to the text and its history is found in Hamid Dabashi's *The* Shahnameh: *The Persian Epic in World Literature*, although some may take issue with Dabashi's interpretation of this section of the epic (126–38). In this episode in the *Shahnameh*, the great hero Rostam fathers a son while in a foreign land but departs before his child's birth, leaving behind a talisman for the mother to put on the child when it is born. As the son, Sohrab, grows up, he is told that Rostam is his father, but he has never seen him. After a number of youthful exploits, the young hero unknowingly faces his father in battle. Ironically, Sohrab's goal is to join forces with his father to oust the corrupt shah and put his father on the throne. The battle lasts for days, and at one point the young Sohrab is tricked into giving his opponent (his father) a second chance, instead of killing him. In the end, it is Rostam who delivers the fatal blow. As Sohrab lies dying, Rostam leaps off his horse to pay his respects to this valiant young warrior. As he cradles Sohrab in his arms, the youth's shirt falls open, revealing the talisman that Rostam left for his child to wear. Horrified, he realizes that he has killed his only son, and the episode closes with a description of the grief of the father and everyone in the kingdom of Iran. Since the full story is lengthy, I sometimes shorten it by having students read the first section, about Sohrab's birth (*Tragedy* 4–25), and the final battle scene with Sohrab and Rostam (138–75), along with a synopsis that summarizes the intervening tales of Sohrab's youthful adventures and early battles.

Using the two contrasting conclusions to father-son struggles (reconciliation or the killing of the son) offered by *Sirat Bani Hilal* and by the

322 Middle Eastern Epics

tale of Sohrab and Rostam, respectively, we begin to explore possible meta-phoric or psychological interpretations. At some point I ask if students know stories of father-son struggles where the father dies, and we soon add the story of Oedipus and *Star Wars* (featuring Darth Vader and Luke Skywalker) to the mix. The *Star Wars* example adds an additional dimension because Darth Vader (aka Anakin Skywalker) dies protecting his son, an act that brings him back from the "dark side" and provides a form of redemption.

While the students are reading the Sohrab-and-Rostam episode from the *Shahnameh*, they are introduced in lectures to the various hero patterns presented in the work of Lord Raglan, Otto Rank, and Joseph Campbell. We then discuss these contrasting models in reference to our epic readings and also to the folktales students have read that feature female protagonists.

Ultimately, from the study of *The Epic of Gilgamesh*, *Sirat Bani Hilal*, and the *Shahnameh*, I try to impart a sense of the richness of Middle Eastern literary traditions. I repeat key ideas and themes during my lectures and our discussions and ask students to write short explanations for the following concepts in their exams: epic, oral-formulaic composition, composition in performance, the various hero models, the interaction between oral and written literature, and the gendered nature of certain literary genres in certain societies. I also ask them to write short essay answers to questions about epics versus folktales, male versus female protagonists, and same-sex intimate friendships, as well as father-son and mother-daughter relationships as portrayed in the texts we have read.

Notes

1. Toward the end of the course, when we are dealing with modern texts, I emphasize that the facile Jews-versus-Arabs binary is rooted in twentieth-century politics and is not valid culturally for earlier historical periods.

2. I find Gilgamesh: *A Reader* to be a helpful survey of various approaches to the text.

3. Other commonly taught translations include *Epic of Gilgamesh* [Foster]; Gilgamesh: *Translated*; Epic of Gilgamesh [George]; and Gilgamesh: *A New Rendering*.

4. I prefer editions where the original language is centered and the English translation is presented in the margins, such as in *Holy Scriptures*. Multiple versions of Arabic-English Qur'ans are available, including *Qur'an; Meaning*. Since only

"Surat Yusuf" ("Chapter of Joseph") is taught in this course, the differences between editions do not matter a great deal. Choosing an English translation for a course in Islamic studies, however, would entail a much more complex decision.

5. One fascinating characteristic of Arabic epics is that several of the main heroes are Black. For a discussion of race, see Schine.

6. An excellent study of *Sirat Bani Hilal* is found in Slyomovics.

7. The Infancy Gospel of Thomas is thought to date to the second century CE and was perhaps composed to provide an account of that portion of Jesus's life that is only partially recounted in the canonical gospels. It is an entirely different work from the Gospel of Thomas. See Hock.

Works Cited

Al-Rawi, Ahmad K. "The Arabic Ghoul and Its Western Transformation." *Folklore*, vol. 120, no. 3, 2009, pp. 291–306.

Dabashi, Hamid. *The* Shahnameh: *The Persian Epic in World Literature*. Columbia UP, 2019.

The Epic of Gilgamesh. Translated and edited by Benjamin R. Foster, W. W. Norton, 2001.

The Epic of Gilgamesh: *The Babylonian Epic Poem and Other Texts in Akkadian and Sumerian*. Translated by Andrew George, Penguin Books, 1999.

Gilgamesh: *A New English Version*. Translated by Stephen Mitchell, Free Press, 2004.

Gilgamesh: *A New Rendering in English Verse*. Translated by David Ferry, Farrar, Strauss and Giroux, 1992.

Gilgamesh: *A New Translation of the Ancient Epic*. Translated by Sophus Helle, Yale UP, 2021.

Gilgamesh: *A Reader*. Edited by John Maier, Bolchazy-Carducci Publishers, 1997.

Gilgamesh: *Translated from the Sin-Leqi-Unninni Version*. Translated by John Gardner and John Maier, Vintage Books, 1985.

Hock, Ronald F. *The Infancy Gospels of James and Thomas*. Polebridge, 1995.

The Holy Scriptures of the Old Testament, Hebrew and English. British and Foreign Bible Society, 1950.

Lane, Edward. *Manners and Customs of the Modern Egyptians*. Cosimo Classics, 2005.

Lyons, M. C. *The Arabian Epic: Heroic and Oral Story-telling*. Cambridge UP, 1995. 3 vols.

The Meaning of the Holy Qur'an. Translated by Abdallah Yusuf Ali, 11th ed., Amana, 2006.

The Qur'an. Translated by M. A. S. Haleem, Oxford UP, 2004.

Reynolds, Dwight. "Abū Zayd al-Hilālī: Trickster, Womanizer, Warrior, Shaykh." *In Memory and Honor of Pierre Cachia*, special issue of *Journal*

324 Middle Eastern Epics

of Arabic Literature, edited by Elizabeth Holt, vol. 49, no. 1, 2018, pp. 78–103.

———. *Arab Folklore: A Handbook*. Greenwood Press, 2007.

———. "Composition in Performance Arab Style." *Classics@ Journal*, vol. 14, classics-at.chs.harvard.edu/classics14-reynolds/.

———. "Epic and History in the Arabic Tradition." *Epic and History*, edited by David Konstan and Kurt A. Raaflaub, Wiley-Blackwell, 2010, pp. 392–410.

———. *Heroic Poets, Poetic Heroes: The Ethnography of Performance in an Arabic Oral Epic Tradition*. Cornell UP, 2001.

———. "Sirat Bani Hilal." *Cambridge History of Arabic Literature: Postclassical Period*, Cambridge UP, 2006, pp. 307–19.

———. "Start." Sirat Bani Hilal *Digital Archive*, 2017, siratbanihilal.ucsb.edu/start.

Schine, Rachel. "Conceiving the Black-Arab Hero: On the Gendered Production of Racial Difference in *Sīrat al-amīrah dhāt al-himmah*." *Journal of Arabic Literature*, vol. 48, 2017, pp. 1–29.

Slyomovics, Susan E. *The Merchant of Art: An Egyptian Hilali Oral Epic Poet in Performance*. U of California P, 1988. U of California Publications in Modern Philology 120.

The Tale of Princess Fatima, Warrior Woman: The Arabic Epic of Dhat al-Himma. Translated by Melanie Magidow, Penguin Classics, 2021.

The Tragedy of Sohráb and Rostám. Translated by Jerome Clinton, 1987. U of Washington P, 1996.

"Virtual Performances." Sirat Bani Hilal *Digital Archive*, 2017, siratbanihilal.ucsb.edu/virtual-performances.

Atefeh Akbari

World Epics in Comparison: The *Odyssey*, *Kebra Nagast*, and the *Shahnameh*

I believe it apropos to begin this final essay in a volume discussing an expansive and extraordinary range of world epics by explaining some of the preliminary, contextual work my students and I conduct in a course titled World Literature Revisited I. In this class, in which we read and discuss the *Odyssey*, *Kebra Nagast* (*The Glory of Kings*), and the *Shahnameh* (*Book of Kings*), among other texts, we question and challenge implicit and explicit power structures in the category of world literature and try to come up with solutions that will allow us to work ethically within a category that is imperfect, but invaluable nonetheless.

When students first see the title of the course, many of them inform me that they expect to walk away at the end of the semester (or earlier) with a clear definition of world literature, but most find after the course that their preconceived ideas and conceptions are, at worst, upended and, at best, complicated. What's more, they don't expect to learn or care so much about translation. Before taking this course, most of them would not have noted the issue of translation or the translator of a work, they tell me; rarely, if ever, have they read a text's introduction, let alone a translator's introduction. I start the class by posing numerous questions, with

325

the understanding that we will work together to seek answers throughout the semester: What or who constitutes the world in world literature? Where is this world located? Why have some types of inscription been traditionally privileged over others when determining the category of literature? How can we read and trace literary influence across different literatures without reducing them to a mere repetition of the same themes and ideas? In other words, how do we read the similarities and differences in texts from different literatures in their particular contexts?

I also invite students to think about the difference between world literature as a category and as a discipline. The establishment of the disciplinary formation is what we investigate and critique while acknowledging that any type of narrative, inscribed or oral, from any corner of the globe, can be included in world literature as a category. Some students are surprised to learn that they'll read Jane Austen's *Pride and Prejudice* during the second semester of this course and may ask the following questions: Is Great Britain considered a part of the world in the discipline of world literature? Doesn't the discipline involve a study of non-Western texts and a preoccupation with diversity? Mustn't the literature we read in this course always be in translation to English? Though aspects of David Damrosch's "threefold definition" of world literature in his conclusion to *What Is World Literature?* can be interrogated (281), it offers an excellent framework for our conversation and for calling students' assumptions about the topic into question.

After discussing Johann Wolfgang von Goethe's theory of weltliteratur as the precursor to our topic of study in a Western literary tradition,[1] I end the first session by writing Damrosch's definition on the board:

1. World literature is an elliptical refraction of national literatures.
2. World literature is writing that gains in translation.
3. World literature is not a set canon of texts but a mode of reading: a form of detached engagement with worlds beyond our own place and time. (281)

I ask students to think about this definition in anticipation of our second class, when we'll begin to read Emily Wilson's remarkable translation of Homer's *Odyssey*. Most students require clarifications of all three points of the definition (especially the first two), which is to be expected. The point of this exercise is for them to grapple with this definition out of context and to emerge with a rudimentary idea of what the topic entails.

After I place the definition in the context of Damrosch's book and larger conversations about world literature as an institutional discipline, we think about the potential limits of work completed under this rubric in an English department. We discuss what Emily Apter, in *Against World Literature*, refers to as "the 'Eurochronology problem' . . . arising from the fact that critical traditions and disciplines founded in the Western academy contain inbuilt topologies—'epic,' 'classicism,' . . . —adduced from Western literary examples" (8).[2] We discuss this "problem" in reference to *Kebra Nagast*, a prose narrative that is known in some scholarly circles as an Ethiopian national epic, in the sense that it is "a myth about the founding of the Ethiopian state" (Tiruneh 55), but that is referred to by Wendy Laura Belcher, who is working on a new translation of the text with Michael Kleiner and a monograph about it, as a "fourteenth-century Egyptian and Ethiopian novel." I invite students to think about these categorizations, asking them to reflect on why we must categorize the text as an epic or novel and what we would gain by discussing the text on its own terms, rather than by forcing it to fit within a Western genre. Yet I also explain the merits of Damrosch's disciplinary rubric, in particular the notion of world literature as "writing that gains in translation" (281). Wilson's *Odyssey* is a great example with which to begin, as discussed below.

For a lecture class that meets twice a week for seventy-five minutes each session, we read the *Odyssey* over three sessions and selections from *Kebra Nagast* and the *Shahnameh* over two sessions each.[3] We read chronologically throughout the semester, thus Homer's epic is first on our list of readings. Chronological placement is not as straightforward, however, when it comes to *Kebra Nagast*. Though many scholars date this Ethiopian epic to the mid–fourteenth century, there is textual and material evidence that supports its having been composed in the sixth century AD. I therefore choose to teach it earlier in the semester and immediately after Genesis (*Bible*), creating an epistemological continuum in our conversations. We read the medieval Persian epic *Shahnameh* about two-thirds into the semester, immediately after we have read a few suras from the Quran (including "The Cow" [*Quran* 4–33], "The Ants" [239–44], "Sheba" [272–76], "Ranged in Rows" [285–89], and "The Clinging Form" [428]) and before we read excerpts from *The Arabian Nights* (including the foreword, prologue, and first fourteen tales [1–112]).

328 World Epics in Comparison

Reading in Translation

Before reading a translated text, we spend a few minutes discussing words or concepts for which there are no apt equivalents in English and how we might work through this potential loss in meaning. For example, in Dick Davis's translation of the *Shahnameh* (the edition I use in class), *farr* remains untranslated in the text. Davis explains in his introduction that it is "a God-given glory, and inviolability, bestowed on a king, and sometimes on a great hero. Its physical manifestation was a light that shone from the king or hero's face" (Ferdowsi xxxvi). The incommensurability of *farr* with glory is something that non-Persian-speaking students will miss, but it is in the space of this untranslatable word, this loss, where student creativity can flourish. While students are encouraged not to domesticate the text—not to, say, simply equate *farr* with glory—they're simultaneously encouraged to practice their agency and make connections between the texts and subject matters that have piqued their interest; in cases where there are unresolved contentions, these contentions can be productive. An interested student could therefore study the differences (and intersections, if any) between *farr* in a medieval Persian epic and *kleos* in a classical Greek epic. Wilson, who never leaves *kleos* untranslated, defines it in the introduction to her translation as "the honor that comes from being the named subject of heroic legend" (67).[4] It's worth noting that I've emphasized students' interest; I do not dictate which connections between texts they should investigate. By giving students the freedom to compare texts based on their individual readings, I've found that they become ethical readers of translated texts, highly cognizant of contextual differences and attuned to gaps in their comprehension due to these differences.

The *Odyssey*

Chances are many students have already read a different translation of the *Odyssey*. I therefore set up the first framework for a comparative reading of texts by asking students to read Wilson's comprehensive introduction and translator's note (Homer, *Odyssey* [Wilson] 1–79, 81–91). After discussing how an in-depth, thoroughly researched introduction to a translation can frame it in important ways, we turn to the equally important question of who writes the introduction, foreword, or preface to a translated text. These discussions help set up our later, similar investigations for *Kebra Nagast* and the *Shahnameh*. We discuss why it matters that Wilson is the first woman to translate this epic into English. In her essay in *Homer's Daughters*, Wilson provides a critical rationale:

> if no feminists translate classical texts, then students and general readers will have to rely on translations that inscribe uncritical modern assumptions about sex and gender. I felt a responsibility to provide Greekless readers with a reliable, authoritative substitute for the Greek texts that would take its complex representations of social inequality, including gender inequality, more seriously than I felt had been done before. ("Epilogue" 282)

In this essay, Wilson also suggests reading certain scenes from previous translations in comparison with hers. An example she gives is from book 22, lines 461–71. I provide copies of these lines from Richmond Lattimore's 1965 translation (Homer, Odyssey [Lattimore]), and we spend some time comparing the two translations. Students immediately recognize the bias and violent sexism in Lattimore's version of the epic. As one student, Aynika Nelson, remarks in a weekly response paper:

> Why was it so commonly accepted for past translators of the *Odyssey* to refer to non-Western/non-Greek people in their translations as "savages" and the enslaved women who were killed en masse for sleeping with Penelope's suitors [as] "sluts" and "whores" as if that justified their murder, when all of these terms weren't even equivalent to the descriptive language used in the original Greek version of the *Odyssey*?

Such responses show how crucial it is for students to read a translation such as Wilson's as well as the importance of instructors supporting and promoting new, ethical translations of classical texts when teaching world literature. As Wilson explains, "A very clear, direct, sometimes markedly 'modern' style seemed to me the best strategy for inviting readers to take the text seriously, not only as a historical document; many of the social inequalities and double-standards evoked by the *Odyssey* are present, perhaps in different ways, in our own societies" ("Epilogue" 285). Indeed, her translation demonstrates how instructors can continue to teach these canonical texts in engaging and relevant ways to students, many of whom question the cultural relevance of the texts.

Kebra Nagast

When searching for an edition of *Kebra Nagast* that I could use in the classroom, I found that the only available English translation of the full

330 World Epics in Comparison

text is A. E. Wallis Budge's 1922 secondhand translation from German, which Budge titled *The Queen of Sheba and Her Only Son Menyelek*. I assign this edition, published as an e-book by Routledge (*Queen*), yet I opt to bring to class a hard copy of the text from my institution's library—the only on-site hard copy of the text available for borrowing. I start the class by drawing attention to the copy in my hand: it's a xeroxed copy with a glued binding, published by African Islamic Mission Publications in 1988. Students note how, as an artifact, it pales in comparison with the exquisitely annotated scholarly editions of the previous books we've read, and this comparison allows us to reflect on the diminished value that non-canonical and non-Western texts have in a world literary marketplace and, by extension, in what we study as world literature in an English department. The African Islamic Mission's foreword to the text similarly strikes the students with its message of knowledge as liberation for Black people:

> These books are being produced to be able to combine the old with the present and the present with the future. It is because of the situation of our race that it is necessary to put so much emphasis on knowledge. Knowledge is the one thing that will lead us out of this oppression. We must first start with what happened to us as a people and how we developed along with the Earth. . . . We must then bring out the facts from these books and teach them to the world. This is the only way we will achieve the knowledge that we need. We can no longer wait for others to teach us. (Kebra Nagast)

In their weekly response papers, in which students are invited to reflect on the week's reading, many of them focus on this foreword as a part of the text they would like to discuss. Students notice how the foreword frames the text in a manner similar to Wilson's translator's note. They discuss how institutional obstacles to the dissemination of knowledge are recognized in the foreword; one student, Minori Ito, writes, "How textbooks depict Black people should not be how they are defined, but we can only reach that point by first addressing it."

By this point in the semester, students are working on their first graded assignment, a textual annotation. For this assignment, students heavily annotate two pages of text, paying close attention to details of language and literary devices; they include a written reflection on this annotation practice. Students have been preparing for this assignment through our targeted close readings conducted in class. They are therefore quick to notice shared motifs across disparate texts. For our sessions on *Kebra*

Atefeh Akbari 331

Nagast, we read chapters 1 through 67 (1–110); scenes that I ask students to focus on include the journey of the Queen of Sheba to Jerusalem to meet King Solomon, their conversations and intimate interactions, and the birth of her son and his subsequent meeting with his father, King Solomon. Many students immediately get drawn to the discussion of wisdom by King Solomon and the Queen of Sheba and compare it to manifestations of wisdom in the *Odyssey*. One student, Isabelle Snow, thoughtfully remarked on the distinct responses of Odysseus and the Queen of Sheba vis-à-vis wisdom: "While Odysseus has a tangible representation of wisdom in Athena, he refuses at times to acknowledge her contributions. In contrast, the Queen of Sheba is in such awe of wisdom that she personifies wisdom herself, transforming the intellectual into the tangible and associating it with her livelihood." Another student, Mirabella Mannray, reflected on the differences in the meaning of wisdom across the *Odyssey*, Genesis, and *Kebra Nagast*:

> Throughout *Kebra Nagast* the word "wisdom" is decorated with lavish language to emphasize its heavenly meaning. The Queen is "smitten with the love of wisdom, and constrained by the cords of understanding," so she decides to visit Solomon because he has this said "wisdom" (21). The Ethiopian national epic does not articulate what specific wisdom Solomon has. The Queen considers wisdom to be "sweeter than honey" and "the best of all treasures," but what exactly does wisdom look like (21, 22)?

Such comparative readings push the students to pose larger, critical questions about the purportedly universal values in world literary texts by focusing specifically on the language associated with this seemingly universal concept.

The *Shahnameh*

On our first day of reading Abolqasem Ferdowsi's *Shahnameh*, students work on the first draft of their second graded assignment, a close comparative analysis of two texts. In addition to the translator's introduction (xiii–xxxvii), I assign the following sections from Davis's translation: "Rostam, the Son of Zal-Dastan" (104–09), "The Beginning of the War between Iran and Turan" (110–30), "Rostam and His Horse Rakhsh" (131–33), "The Seven Trials of Rostam" (152–73), "The Tale of Sohrab" (187–214), "Bizhan and Manizheh" (306–45), "The Death of Rostam"

332 World Epics in Comparison

(423–40), "Sekandar's Conquest of Persia" (456–71), and "The Reign of Sekandar" (472–528). In the prompt for this assignment, I write the following:

> We've thought about the texts we've read as being on a continuum of literary, historical, and sociopolitical traditions, but we've also discussed their differing contexts, their parallel histories, and the tensions that mark the relations between them. After considering the broader conversations we've had in class, choose two of the texts that you feel address each other on a more granular level—whether in terms of their form or structure, their genre, their thematic content, or a combination of these elements. Come up with a logic of and framework for comparison, explain your framework using textual evidence, and offer reasons for the significance of your comparison. Your framework could include a variation on the following: a shared motif (e.g., wine, descriptions of flowers, crying, or the color purple); theme (e.g., death, marriage, desire, heroism, or faith); simile (e.g., a lion signifying something in both texts); historical context (e.g., a war, famine, revolution, or other event surrounding the texts); or poetic technique.

At this stage in their work, I am pushing students to offer structured arguments for comparative readings based on details in literary texts, bringing their observations down from broader, more abstract conversations to the level of concrete textual evidence. Student work has ranged from a comparison of Rudabeh's and the Queen of Sheba's experiences of childbirth, including the associated pain (both physical and emotional), to godlike men in the *Odyssey* versus lion-like men and women in the *Shahnameh*, and from the treatment of royal subjects in *Kebra Nagast* and the *Shahnameh*, to the ending of Homer's and Ferdowsi's epics and their conceptions of sovereignty.

Not surprisingly, this level of textual scrutiny makes the students hyperaware of the issue of translation. Their work, subsequently, demonstrates a healthy dose of skepticism and critical inquiry vis-à-vis the text's language. This change does not, however, result in a debilitating abstention from engaging with translated texts writ large, for students have learned strategies for discerning a translator's conscientious efforts to preserve "the rhetoricity of the original," to use Gayatri Chakravorty Spivak's rendering in "The Politics of Translation" (313). In his introduction to the *Shahnameh*, Davis offers justifications for translating an epic poem into prose and continues, "Given the poem's immense length, some passages have inevitably been omitted, and others are presented in summary form (the italicized prose passages are summarized translations of sections of Ferdowsi's text)" (Ferdowsi xxxiv). In response to this practice, one student, Melani Estevez, wrote, "It was interesting to find out that the parts of the stories I found most intriguing had been simply a shortened summary. It really goes to show that in translation the parts that you may choose to shorten can be the most interesting to others."

We also read Azar Nafisi's short foreword to the epic (Ferdowsi ix–xi), which I preface with an introduction to Nafisi's memoir, *Reading* Lolita *in Tehran*, coupled with a summary of Mitra Rastegar's and Sunaina Maira's critical responses to it. These readings underline Nafisi's Orientalist representation of Iranian women and the palpable dangers that such representation and the writer's related institutional and public work pose to the lives of Iranians and Muslims. In stark contrast to the prior forewords and introductions that students have read, Nafisi's contribution thus provides an example of the adverse power that such textual supplements can have, further underlining the importance of upholding ethical standards for both translators and their readership.

On the first day of class, I inform students that my syllabus is in no way an exhaustive survey of canonical texts in the discipline and that it is, rather, a sample, an imperfect introduction based on one person's expertise. By the end of the semester, most students will have grasped the value and truth of Damrosch's definition of world literature as "a mode of reading" rather than a "set canon of texts" (281). As a final project, I ask students to create their own world literature syllabi. They are equal parts excited and nervous about this assignment: How is it possible to do justice to the topic? How do they choose what to include and exclude? While quickly realizing the near impossibility of this task, they nonetheless proceed to create original syllabi that include a good balance between the breadth and depth of material covered.

By taking ownership of their learning process and thinking actively and critically about what they learn and how they learn, students arrive at an understanding of the institutional structures of world literature as a discipline. In discussing whether world literature anthologies are good choices for a class like this one, for example, I draw their attention to the fact that the excerpt chosen from the *Shahnameh*, an epic of approximately fifty thousand verses, for the fourth edition of *The Norton Anthology of World Literature* pertains solely to Alexander the Great's story, thus highlighting the part of the epic that would ostensibly be of interest to

334 World Epics in Comparison

a Western readership. Reading the final projects for my class, I am heartened by my students' efforts at imagining a discipline that is infinitely more democratic and less Eurocentric in its proclivities and methodologies.

Notes

1. The following selections from Goethe are assigned for the first day of class: "The Production of a National Classic" (83–88), "Goethe's Theory of a World Literature" (89–99), and the "*Weltliteratur*" entry (267) from "Extracts from the Conversations with Eckermann."

2. Apter attributes the phrase "Eurochronology problem" to Christopher Prendergast, who, she adds, has adopted the term from Arjun Appadurai (8).

3. This is a small, student-centered class, capped at twenty-five students, in which class time is divided equally between lecture and discussion.

4. Beck translates *kleos* as "report," "reputation," or "fame," and Martin adds "glory bestowed by poetry" to his translation of *kleos* as "report" or "fame."

Works Cited

Apter, Emily. *Against World Literature: On the Politics of Untranslatability.* Verso Books, 2013.

The Arabian Nights. Translated by Husain Haddawy, W. W. Norton, 2010.

Beck, William. "Kleos (κλέος)." *The Homer Encyclopedia*, edited by Margalit Finkelberg, Wiley, 1st ed., 2011. *Credo Reference*, ezproxy.cul.columbia.edu/login?qurl=https%3A%2F%2Fsearch.credoreference.com%2Fcontent%2Fentry%2Fwileyhom%2Fkleos_kleos%2F0%3FinstitutionId%3D1878.

Belcher, Wendy Laura. "The Black Queen of Sheba: A Global History of an African Idea." *Wendy Laura Belcher*, wendybelcher.com/african-literature/black-queen-of-sheba/. Accessed 15 June 2021.

The Bible. New Oxford Annotated Version, 4th ed., Oxford UP, 2010.

Damrosch, David. *What Is World Literature?* Princeton UP, 2003.

Ferdowsi, Abolqasem. Shahnameh: *The Persian Book of Kings.* Translated by Dick Davis, Penguin Classics, 2006.

Goethe, Johann Wolfgang von. *Goethe's Literary Essays: A Selection in English.* Arranged by J. E. Spingarn, Harcourt, Brace, 1921. *HathiTrust*, catalog .hathitrust.org/Record/006056319.

Homer. *The Odyssey.* Translated by Emily Wilson, W. W. Norton, 2018.

———. *The* Odyssey *of Homer.* Translated by Richmond Lattimore, Harper Perennial, 1965.

Kebra Nagast: *The Queen of Sheba and Her Only Son Menyelek.* Translated by E. A. Wallis Budge, African Islamic Mission Publications, 1988.

Maira, Sunaina. "'Good' and 'Bad' Muslim Citizens: Feminists, Terrorists, and U.S. Orientalisms." *Feminist Studies*, vol. 35, no. 3, 2009, pp. 631–56. *Gale Academic OneFile*, link.gale.com/apps/doc/A215244338/AONE.

Martin, Richard. "Glory." *The Homer Encyclopedia*, edited by Margalit Finkelberg, Wiley, 2011. *Credo Reference*, ezproxy.cul.columbia.edu/login?qurl=https%3A%2F%2Fsearch.credoreference.com%2Fcontent%2Fentry%2Fwileyhom%2Fglory%2F0%3FinstitutionId%3D1878.

Nafisi, Azar. *Reading* Lolita *in Tehran: A Memoir in Books*. Random House, 2003.

The Norton Anthology of World Literature. Edited by Martin Puncher, 4th ed., W. W. Norton, 2018.

The Queen of Sheba and Her Only Son Menyelek: The Kebra Nagast. Translated by E. A. Wallis Budge, Routledge, 2010. *Taylor and Francis*, www.taylorfrancis.com/books/mono/10.4324/9780203039533/queen-sheba-budge.

The Quran. Translated by M. A. S. Abdel Haleem, Oxford UP, 2016.

Rastegar, Mitra. "Reading Nafisi in the West: Authenticity, Orientalism, and 'Liberating' Iranian Women." *Women's Studies Quarterly*, vol. 34, nos. 1–2, spring-summer 2006, pp. 108–28. JSTOR, www.jstor.org/stable/40004743.

Spivak, Gayatri Chakravorty. "The Politics of Translation." *The Translation Studies Reader*, edited by Lawrence Venuti, 3rd ed., Routledge, 2012, pp. 312–30.

Tiruneh, Gizachew. "The *Kebra Nagast*: Can Its Secrets Be Revealed?" *International Journal of Ethiopian Studies*, vol. 8, no. 1, 2014, pp. 51–72. JSTOR, www.jstor.org/stable/10.2307/26554817.

Wilson, Emily. "Epilogue: Translating Homer as a Woman." *Homer's Daughters: Women's Responses to Homer in the Twentieth Century and Beyond*, edited by Fiona Cox and Elena Theodorakopoulos, Oxford UP, 2019, pp. 279–97.

Part VII

Resources

Jo Ann Cavallo

Critical Studies

Following his unabridged English translation of Matteo Maria Boiardo's 35,440-verse *Orlando innamorato*, Charles S. Ross begins his section "Notes to the Poem" by stating that "[n]otes to a long poem should be short" (Boiardo 851, 851–56). Such advice seems equally pertinent to the present volume. This concluding section offers a brief overview of mostly recent studies available in English to complement the readings recommended in the essays. Although the scholarly works suggested may cross various categories, they are grouped under distinct headings for reference.

Comparative Perspectives

Attempting to engage with the epic genre on a global scale is an undertaking not for the faint of heart. In *Epic: Form, Content, and History*, Frederick Turner explores such topics as the epic storyteller, the creation myth, the hero, the quest, kinship and kinship troubles, the descent into the underworld, the founding of the city, and definitions of core values to argue that epic is not so much the history of particular societies as "the history in symbol and story of the human species itself" (13). In considering epic "the most fundamental and important of all literary forms," Turner underscores "the remarkable underlying commonalities in epic across the globe" (8) in a probing way that avoids the overgeneralizations that some scholars have criticized in earlier studies seeking comprehensiveness, such as Joseph Campbell's *The Hero with a Thousand Faces*.

Dean A. Miller's *The Epic Hero* is not as global in scope as Turner's *Epic* but well beyond the Homer-to-Milton trajectory emphasized by some scholarship. Miller delineates his field of inquiry as the epic literature of the Indo-European linguistic group, which includes Greek, Slavic, Celtic, Nordic, Persian, and Indian languages, among others. Drawing on anthropology, psychology, and literary studies, Miller covers such topics as the birth, parentage, familial ties, sexuality, character, deeds, death, and afterlife of the hero. Attention is also devoted to figures who modify or accompany the hero along the way (partners, helpers, foes, foils, and antitypes). Although Miller posits a trajectory or evolution of the heroic narrative from ancient to modern times and across languages, readers need not subscribe to this teleological perspective to appreciate his critical insights and attention to historical context.

Another thought-provoking and ambitious work is Masaki Mori's *Epic Grandeur*. Although it likewise does not cover the range of epics discussed

339

340   Resources

by Turner, it does attempt to redefine the genre by expanding the scope of the term *epic*. After first outlining theoretical considerations from Plato and Aristotle to György Lukács and Mikhail Bakhtin, Mori aims to capture the essence of epic by concentrating on three core themes in epic works: the hero's mortality, the stakes for the larger community, and the breadth of time and space. In addition, in positing an ongoing historical transformation of epic narratives from martial concerns to peace, he devotes particular attention to what he considers representative transitional epics from England and Japan.

From the perspective of folklore and religious studies, Lauri Honko has used the Finnish *Kalevala* as a point of reference to comparatively examine a wide range of epics from around the world. His edited volumes *Religion, Myth, and Folklore in the World's Epics* and *The* Kalevala *and the World's Traditional Epics* bring to bear many epic traditions, including Ainu, Arabic, Chinese, eastern Uralic, Mongolian, Russian, South Slavic, and West African traditions. In a similarly comparativist vein, Brenda Beck's *Hidden Paradigms* places the South Indian *Legend of Ponnivala Nadu* in conversation with the *Mahabharata, The Epic of Gilgamesh*, the Bible, the Icelandic *Vatnsdaela Saga*, and the North America Ojibwa cycle of hero tales about Nanabush.

Some literary scholars have juxtaposed canonical epics from two different traditions without necessarily claiming that they have influenced one another. Wendy Doniger's various comparative studies analyze corresponding myths in ancient Indian and Greek epics (see especially *The Implied Spider* and *Other Peoples' Myths*). More recently, Shubha Pathak, who wrote her dissertation under Doniger, has continued the cross-cultural investigation of Greek and Indian epics in her *Divine yet Human Epics*. In this study Pathak contrasts the *Iliad* and the *Ramayana*, "affirmative" epics that exhibit "the divine ease with which a core ideal is achieved," with the *Odyssey* and the *Mahabharata*, "interrogative" epics that demonstrate "the human difficulty with which the same ideal is attained" (1).

Collections of Essays

More frequent in scholarship on the epic genre are edited volumes that draw on the expertise of several scholars working in their respective epic traditions. Many of these concentrate on a specific theme, time period, or subcategory. John Miles Foley's edited volume *A Companion to Ancient Epic* offers forty-two essays dealing primarily with ancient Greek, Near

Eastern, and Roman epics. As Foley notes in his introduction, "Epic is the master-genre of the ancient world. Wherever and whenever one looks, epics had major roles to play in ancient societies, functions that ranged from historical and political to cultural and didactic and beyond" (1). Despite the volume's focus on antiquity, there are also forays into later centuries (Davidson), including modern oral epics (Foley, "Analogues"). The volume's opening section, "Issues and Perspectives," contains essays by Richard P. Martin and Gregory Nagy on epic as a genre and the epic hero, respectively, as well as considerations of topics such as the ancient reception of epic works, archaeological contexts, the gods, history, myth, performance, physical media, translation, and women.

Epic and History, edited by David Konstan and Kurt Raaflaub, narrows the scope of its inquiry to the relation between epic and history while at the same time expanding the breadth of coverage to include Akkadian, Arabic, Hittite, Indian, Mediterranean, northern European, Persian, Southern African, and Sumerian epic traditions, as well as the Bible. The volume's privileging of ancient epics reflects its origin in a project investigating oral and written epics in ancient societies (developed under the auspices of Brown University's Program in Ancient Studies).

Heroic Epic and Saga, edited by Felix J. Oinas, is a collection of fifteen scholarly essays on folk epic, which is rigidly distinguished from literary epic. The volume's restriction to folk epic has the advantage of paying serious attention to epic traditions that were less known by English-language scholars at the time of the volume's publication in 1978 (and perhaps even today), including African, Balto-Finnic, Russian, Serbo-Croation, and Turkic epic traditions.

The Epic Cosmos, edited by Larry Allums, "undertakes to examine epics of Western and other cultures upon the assumption of the genre's importance to a people's desire to understand both their origins and their destiny," according to Allums's preface (x). The prominent placement of Western epics in Allums's description is maintained in the selection of essays themselves, since the first nine (of the eleven) feature Homer's *Iliad* and *Odyssey*, Exodus, Virgil's *Aeneid*, Dante Alighieri's *Divine Comedy*, John Milton's *Paradise Lost*, Herman Melville's *Moby Dick*, William Faulkner's *Go Down, Moses*, and Caroline Gordon's *Green Centuries*. In her introduction to *The Epic Cosmos*, Louise Cowen associates epic with an urgent striving toward the fulfillment of a collective destiny (23) and includes within the genre any work that "demonstrates the cosmic scope of epic," including many late-twentieth-century novels (9).

342   Resources

Epic Traditions in the Contemporary World, coedited by Margaret Beissinger, Jane Tylus, and Susanne Wofford, focuses on both oral and literary epics from antiquity to today, with particular attention to the political and poetic aspects of contemporary epic performance from an ethnographic perspective. According to the editors, "To look at the position of epic in the contemporary world is to pose, not to evade, the question of epic ideology and its relation to nationalism, national identity, and the politics of gender" (Beissinger et al., Introduction 3).

The Western Canon

By far the most prolific studies in English concern European epics, sometimes acknowledged as a regional grouping but all too often implicitly treated as representative of the epic genre *tout court*—at least until recently. David Quint's *Epic and Empire* focuses on the political and ideological dimensions of "epics of the Latin West." The study identifies two opposing political perspectives: on the one hand, "epics of the imperial victors," and on the other, "epics of the defeated, a defeated whose resistance contains the germ of a broader republican or antimonarchical politics" (8). Adeline Johns-Putra's monograph *History of the Epic* and Catherine Bates's edited volume *The Cambridge Companion to the Epic* both begin with *The Epic of Gilgamesh* and subsequently focus mostly on European epics through the centuries. The four-volume *Structures of Epic Poetry,* edited by Christine Reitz and Simone Finkmann, addresses a multitude of themes and situations in ancient (mostly Greek and Roman) epics.

As noted in the introduction to this volume, Carolina López-Ruiz and Mary Bachvarova brought a fresh perspective to the study of the Western canon by viewing the ancient Mediterranean as an interconnected world with cultural continuities across wide areas. López-Ruiz's *When the Gods Were Born* examines how ancient Greek myths emerged in relation to their Near Eastern counterparts, while the selections of primary texts in López-Ruiz's subsequent *Gods, Heroes, and Monsters* offer students the opportunity to study firsthand Greek and Roman mythology as part of a broader Mediterranean world that includes the Near East. In her massive volume *From Hittite to Homer,* Bachvarova investigates the prehistory of Homer's epics from a new direction, meticulously revealing how bilingual Syro-Anatolian poets conveyed a set of narrative traditions to the Greeks in the late Bronze and early Iron Ages.

The medieval epics of Western Europe have traditionally been the subject of intense scholarly activity. Among recent studies, Luke Sunderland's *Rebel Barons* explores the Carolingian epic tradition in its historical context, with particular attention to political conflict—from civil war, feud, and rebellion, to holy war. In *Epic and Romance: A Guide to Medieval European Literature*, edited by Leonard Neidorf and Yang Liu, twenty-three contributors newly engage with works and topics that were central to W. P. Ker's influential study *Epic and Romance: Essays in Medieval Literature*, first published in 1897.[1]

Considering the modern period, Robert Crossley's *Epic Ambitions in Modern Times* invites us to reconceptualize the Western epic canon by including within the genre a variety of forms and media, including fantasy and science fiction novels, history writing, drama, opera, film, music, and painting. The volume explores a selection of pioneering large-scale works from the past three centuries that have engaged with ancient and medieval epics in deeply original ways, including Richard Wagner's Ring cycle; J. R. R. Tolkien's *Lord of the Rings*; the eighteenth-century bestsellers *Clarissa*, by Samuel Richardson, and *The Decline and Fall of the Roman Empire*, by Edward Gibbon; Jacob Lawrence's *Migration Series* paintings from the 1940s; Tony Kushner's drama *Angels in America*; and Madeline Miller's novels *The Song of Achilles* and *Circe*.

African Epics

Perhaps the most dramatic expansion of the epic literature canon has taken place in African studies. Until the 1970s Anglo-American scholars did not seem to be aware of the existence of the epic genre on African soil. Following the groundbreaking publications of John Johnson ("Yes") and others, however, a number of critical studies, anthologies, and translations have made African epics much better known worldwide. Decades of field research have brought to an international public a rich ongoing epic tradition relating imperialist struggles among the African empires predating European colonialism. Especially valuable in this regard is *Oral Epics from Africa*, an anthology of excerpts from twenty-five African epics edited by Johnson, Thomas A. Hale, and Stephen Belcher. In their introduction to the volume, the editors state that "the oral epic in Africa represents one of the most vibrant voices from this vast continent today" (Johnson et al., "Introduction" xxii). Two years later, Belcher published *Epic Traditions of Africa*, combining textual analysis with attention to the ethnographic,

344   Resources

historical, and performance contexts of epic traditions across various regions of Africa. Since his dissertation, *The Hero in the African Epic*, Joseph Mbele has published several essays on African epics, in particular, on the East African *Liyongo* epic (e.g., Mbele, "Identity"). By far the African epic that has received the most scholarly attention has been the West African epic of *Sun-Jata*, with several translated retellings as well as critical studies devoted to it, including the volume edited by Ralph A. Austen, *In Search of* Sunjata.

In addition to the extensive work of the abovementioned scholars, further studies and translations have been undertaken to bring epics from the African continent to the attention of academics and the general reading public. Dwight F. Reynolds has made it possible to learn about the epic *Sirat Bani Hilal*, as performed in Egypt, through both an extensive online resource (Sirat Bani Hilal *Digital Archive*) and his printed volume *Heroic Poets, Poetic Heroes*. Dan Ben-Amos has studied storytelling events, including tales about heroic characters, in Benin culture.

Asian Epics

There is a wealth of scholarship on both oral and written heroic narratives across the expanse of Asia that has a sustained focus on storytelling in performance. Karl Reichl's *The Oral Epic: From Performance to Interpretation* draws from the author's fieldwork on the oral traditions of the Turkic peoples of Central Asia and Siberia to address theoretical issues regarding the sociocultural context of performance and the performance elements that contribute to the meaning of oral and oral-derived epics. Critical studies and English translations of oral epics in India include, respectively, *Oral Epics in India*, edited by Stuart Blackburn and colleagues, and *Strings and Cymbals*, edited by C. N. Ramachandran. Bernard Arps has recently examined key characteristics of epics from Afghanistan to the Philippines and Indonesia, addressing several intersecting themes and topics, such as the centrality of "love, leadership, and land," kinship, emotion, multiple threads, exile, contrasting values, genealogies, and sequels (351).

Orality and Textualization

In the wake of Albert Lord's 1960 work *The Singer of Tales*, countless studies have emerged that explore and expand on the questions of orality and textualization with respect to the epic tradition. Issues range from how to decipher the process of textualization in the most ancient past to how to best collect and record living oral epic traditions in the present. Honko's edited volume *Textualization of Oral Epics* offers essays on various interrelated issues concerning African, European, Indian, Siberian, and Turkic epics. Published the same year, Reichl's edited volume *The Oral Epic: Performance and Music* devotes attention to a variety of musical traditions of African, Albanian, Greek, Mongolian, Old Norse, Philippine, Romanian, South Slavic, and Turkic epics. Reichl's subsequent edited volume, *Medieval Oral Literature*, gathers together twenty-seven essays on Western European, Russian, Arabic, Persian, and Turkish oral epics, including his own extensive introductory essay, "Plotting the Map of Medieval Oral Literature." In addition, Jonathan L. Ready's *Orality, Textuality, and the Homeric Epics* uses perspectives drawn from linguistic anthropology and folkloristics, as well as from religious, medieval, and performance studies, to consider the trajectory of the Homeric poems prior to the emergence of standardized written texts.

Women and Gender

Sara S. Poor and Jana K. Schulman's coedited volume *Women and Medieval Epic* offers eleven essays exploring "the place, function, and meaning of women as characters, authors, constructs, and cultural symbols in a variety of epic literatures from the Middle Ages" (Poor and Schulman, Introduction 1). The focus is mostly on epics from Western Europe, namely, English, French, German, Icelandic, Latin, Norse, Occitan, and Spanish epics, but there is also an essay on the Persian *Shahnameh*.

Doniger's *Splitting the Difference* focuses on gender issues in epics from ancient India and Greece, not only maleness and femaleness, but also androgyny and bisexuality. The volume's cross-cultural comparisons of related plots, beginning with alternative accounts of Sita, in the *Ramayana*, and Helen, in the *Iliad*, include stories of bisexual transformations, self-impregnating androgynes, and transposed body parts.

Maeve Hughes's published thesis also uses Indian epics as a point of comparison, in this case to the female protagonists of Irish epics. *Epic Women: East and West* focuses primarily on Medb and Deirdre from the medieval Irish *Táin Bó Cúailnge* and Draupadi and Madhavi from the ancient Sanskrit *Mahabharata*. Drawing from the theoretical work of Georges Dumézil, Hughes analyzes these four women as avengers of injustice, shapers of destiny, and mother figures.

346   Resources

Pedagogy

Volumes dedicated to teaching world literature more generally may offer a useful methodological framework for the epic genre as well. David Damrosch's *Teaching World Literature* contains over thirty essays centered on issues and definitions as well as program and teaching strategies. Among the almost forty contributions in Foley's *Teaching Oral Traditions* are many essays dedicated to teaching both ongoing epic traditions across the globe and epics with roots in oral traditions. The previously mentioned *Epic Traditions in the Contemporary World*, edited by Beissinger and colleagues, contains a final section, "Epic and Pedagogy," whose essays address the teaching of epic narratives today (Farrell; Wofford). In addition, Marie Lazzari and Elizabeth Bellalouna have edited separate slim volumes entitled *Epics for Students*.

When the focus of study is a single national or linguistic epic tradition, English epics have unsurprisingly received the most attention in anglophone publications. There are entire volumes dedicated to the teaching of *Beowulf* (Chickering et al.; Bessinger and Yeager; Swain and Hostetter), the Arthurian tradition (Fries and Watson), Edmund Spenser's *Faerie Queene* (Miller and Dunlop), Milton's *Paradise Lost* (Crump; Herman), and Tolkien's *The Lord of the Rings* (Donovan).

Concerning the Western canon more broadly, one can find volumes on teaching individual epics, including the Homeric poems (Myrsiades), Virgil's *Aeneid* (Anderson and Quartarone), and *The Song of Roland* (Kibler and Morgan), as well as particular epic traditions, such as the Italian Renaissance romance epic (Cavallo).

With respect to the epics of Africa and Asia, Hale addresses various issues related to teaching African oral epics ("*A Siin de Mé*"), and Charles B. Dodson shares his strategy of using the more familiar Homeric epics as a bridge to introduce students to the *Ramayana*.

Publishers' Series

Some university presses have series that feature epic texts and traditions. Boydell and Brewer's imprint, Bristol Studies in Medieval Cultures, is publishing a series of volumes about Charlemagne, under the direction of Marianne Ailes. The volumes on Charlemagne in English, German and Dutch, Spanish, and Latin traditions are already in print, and the Italian, Norse, Celtic, and French volumes are either forthcoming or in progress.

Since 1992 Indiana University Press has published its African Epics series under the direction of Johnson and Hale. In addition, Anthem Press has a new book series under my direction, World Epic and Romance, that specializes in epics and chivalric romances from across the globe, both written and oral, in poetry and prose, as well as adaptations in theater and cinema. The series seeks to foster new comparative understandings of heroic narratives, focusing on literary and geopolitical contexts, from antiquity to contemporary society.

Academic Journals

While journals devoted to scholarship on oral traditions, folk studies, and comparative literature are open to studies of epic narratives, there are also journals that focus exclusively on the epic genre either within a regional tradition or more broadly. The journal *AOQU: Achilles Orlando Quixote Ulysses* publishes essays in English, Italian, French, or Spanish that explore "the role of the Epic model (either as a genre proper or as a register) in different cultures up to our days, including non-literary approaches." This biannual journal, which also welcomes proposals for special issues on specific topics, "aims to be a forum for scholars from multiple disciplines to discuss Epics beyond linguistic, cultural and chronological boundaries" ("About"). *The Yearbook of Ancient Greek Epic*, edited by Jonathan L. Ready and Christos C. Tsagalis, is an annual publication devoted to the study of Greek epics and their interactions with other genres, from the Archaic period to late antiquity (fifth century CE). *Letteratura cavalleresca italiana (Italian Chivalric Literature)* is an annual journal that publishes essays examining Italian chivalric literature in poetry and prose, including Franco-Italian literature, from the Middle Ages to the nineteenth century.

Reference Works

The most complete and useful reference works on the epic genre that I have encountered are the two volumes edited by Guida M. Jackson, *Encyclopedia of Traditional Epics* and *Encyclopedia of Literary Epics*.

Websites

In the comparativist and polycentric spirit of this volume, I have been developing a collaborative website entitled *World Epics*. The site includes oral and literary epics from across the globe, from the ancient world to today, and it features adaptations of epic narratives in film, music, puppetry,

348   Resources

theater, and visual art. It aims to showcase websites and teaching resources developed by colleagues and is continuously updated as I receive contributions, syllabi, news, announcements of opportunities, and links to online epic-related materials. *National Epics* is another collaborative website devoted to epic narrative on a global scale; the site is currently being developed by David Wallace, whose parallel project, a multivolume book edited by him, will be published by Oxford University Press.

Various websites feature individual or regional epic traditions. The "Epic Poems" section of the *African Poems* website offers introductions, written excerpts, and oral performances of several epic poems. The main focus of the website *eBOIARDO* is the representation of Boiardo's *Orlando innamorato*, Ludovico Ariosto's *Orlando furioso*, and other Italian chivalric epics in musical, artistic, and theatrical traditions, especially Sicilian puppet theater and the *maggio epico* (epic folk opera) tradition of the Tuscan-Emilian Apennines. The *Japanese Performing Arts Research Consortium* website, currently under construction, will contain materials on adaptations of Japanese epic narratives in Nogaku, Kabuki, and Bunraku theater. Emily Lethbridge's *Icelandic Saga Map* website provides the texts of Icelandic sagas and identifies locations mentioned in them to help students envision the breadth of cultural contact of the Icelanders. The website *Charlemagne: A European Icon*, part of a "network project examining the ways in which the different linguistic cultures of medieval Europe appropriated Charlemagne material from chronicle and epic" (Home page), features virtual exhibitions, activities, research groups, and further reading.

Note

1. As of this writing, Neidorf and Yang is not yet commercially available outside China. I am grateful to Leonard Neidorf for providing an advance copy.

Resources Cited

"About the Journal." *AOQU: Achilles Orlando Quixote Ulysses*, riviste.unimi.it/index.php/aoqu/about. Accessed 3 Jan. 2023.

Allums, Larry, editor. *The Epic Cosmos.* Dallas Institute, 1992.

———. Preface. Allums, pp. ix–xi.

Anderson, William S., and Lorina N. Quartarone, editors. *Approaches to Teaching Vergil's Aeneid.* Modern Language Association of America, 2002.

Arps, Bernard. "Epics in Worlds of Performance: A South/Southeast Asian Narrativity." *Monsoon Asia: A Reader*, edited by David Henley and Nira Wickramasinghe, Leiden UP, 2023, pp. 351–75.

Austen, Ralph A. *In Search of Sunjata: The Mande Oral Epic as History, Literature, and Performance*. Indiana UP, 1999.

Bachvarova, Mary R. *From Hittite to Homer: The Anatolian Background of Ancient Greek Epic*. Cambridge UP, 2020.

Bates, Catherine, editor. *The Cambridge Companion to the Epic*. Cambridge UP, 2010.

Beck, Brenda E. F. *Hidden Paradigms: Comparing Epic Themes, Characters and Plot Structures*. U of Toronto P, 2023.

Beissinger, Margaret, et al., editors. *Epic Traditions in the Contemporary World: The Poetics of Community*. U of California P, 1999.

———. Introduction. Beissinger et al., pp. 1–17.

Belcher, Stephen. *Epic Traditions of Africa*. Indiana UP, 1999.

Bellalouna, Elizabeth, editor. *Epics for Students: Presenting Analysis, Context, and Criticism on Commonly Studied Epics*. Vol. 2, Gale Research, 2001.

Ben-Amos, Dan. *Sweet Words: Storytelling Events in Benin*. Institute for the Study of Human Issues, 1975.

Bessinger, Jess B., Jr., and Robert F. Yeager, editors. *Approaches to Teaching Beowulf*. Modern Language Association of America, 1984.

Blackburn, Stuart H., et al., editors. *Oral Epics in India*. U of California P, 1989.

Boiardo, Matteo Maria. *Orlando Innamorato*. Translated by Charles Stanley Ross, Parlor Press, 2004.

Campbell, Joseph. *The Hero with a Thousand Faces*. 1949. 2nd ed., Princeton UP, 1968.

Cavallo, Jo Ann, editor. *Teaching the Italian Renaissance Romance Epic*. Modern Language Association of America, 2019.

Chickering, Howell, et al. *Teaching* Beowulf *in the Twenty-First Century*. Medieval and Renaissance Texts and Studies, 2014.

Cowen, Louise. "Introduction: Epic as Cosmopoesis." Allums, *Epic Cosmos*, pp. 1–26.

Crossley, Robert. *Epic Ambitions in Modern Times: From* Paradise Lost *to the New Millennium*. Anthem Press, 2022.

Crump, Galbraith M., editor. *Approaches to Teaching Milton's* Paradise Lost. Modern Language Association of America, 1986.

Damrosch, David, editor. *Teaching World Literature*. Modern Language Association of America, 2009.

Davidson, Olga M. "Persian/Iranian Epic." Foley, *Companion*, pp. 264–76.

Dodson, Charles B. "Using Homer to Teach *The Ramayana*." *Teaching English in the Two Year College*, vol. 28, no. 1, Sept. 2000, pp. 68–73.

350 Resources

Doniger, Wendy. *The Implied Spider: Politics and Theology in Myth.* Columbia UP, 1998.

———. *Other Peoples' Myths: The Cave of Echoes.* U of Chicago P, 1988.

———. *Splitting the Difference: Gender and Myth in Ancient Greece and India.* U of Chicago P, 1999.

Donovan, Leslie A., editor. *Approaches to Teaching Tolkien's* The Lord of the Rings *and Other Works.* Modern Language Association of America, 2015.

"Epic Poems." *African Poems,* africanpoems.net/category/epic/. Accessed 17 Oct. 2022.

Farrell, Joseph. "Walcott's *Omeros*: The Classical Epic in a Postmodern World." Beissinger et al., *Epic Traditions,* pp. 270–300.

Foley, John M. "Analogues: Modern Oral Epics." Foley, *Companion,* pp. 196–212.

———, editor. *A Companion to Ancient Epic.* Wiley-Blackwell, 2009.

———. Introduction. Foley, *Companion,* pp. 1–6.

———, editor. *Teaching Oral Traditions.* Modern Language Association of America, 1998.

Fries, Maureen, and Jeanie Watson, editors. *Approaches to Teaching the Arthurian Tradition.* Modern Language Association of America, 1992.

Hale, Thomas A. "*A Siin de Mé*: Learning to Teach the African Oral Epic in African Literature Courses." *Women's Studies Quarterly,* vol. 25, no. 3, fall 1997, pp. 188–200.

Herman, Peter C., editor. *Approaches to Teaching Milton's* Paradise Lost. 2nd ed., Modern Language Association of America, 2012.

Home page. *Charlemagne: A European Icon,* U of Bristol / Leverhulme Trust, www.charlemagne-icon.ac.uk.

Honko, Lauri, editor. *The* Kalevala *and the World's Traditional Epics.* Finnish Literature Society, 2002.

———, editor. *Religion, Myth, and Folklore in the World's Epics: The* Kalevala *and Its Predecessors.* Reprint ed., De Gruyter, 1990. Religion and Society 30.

———, editor. *Textualization of Oral Epics.* De Gruyter Mouton, 2000. Trends in Linguistics: Studies and Monographs 128.

Hughes, Maeve. *Epic Women: East and West: A Study with Special Reference to the* Mahabharata *and Gaelic Heroic Literature.* 1994. Asiatic Society, 2015.

Jackson, Guida M. *Encyclopedia of Literary Epics.* ABC-CLIO, 1996.

———. *Encyclopedia of Traditional Epics.* ABC-CLIO, 1994.

Johnson, John William. "Yes, Virginia, There Is an Epic in Africa." *Genre and Classification in African Folklore,* special issue of *Research in African Literatures,* edited by Lee Haring, vol. 11, no. 3, autumn 1980, pp. 308–26. *JSTOR,* www.jstor.org/stable/3818278.

Johnson, John William, et al. "Introduction: The Oral Epic in Africa." Johnson et al., pp. xiii–xxii.

Resources   351

————, editors. *Oral Epics from Africa: Vibrant Voices from a Vast Continent.* Indiana UP, 1997.

Johns-Putra, Adeline. *The History of the Epic.* Palgrave Macmillan, 2006.

Ker, W. P. *Epic and Romance: Essays in Medieval Literature.* 1897. Macmillan, 1905.

Kibler, William W., and Leslie Zarker Morgan, editors. *Approaches to Teaching the* Song of Roland. Modern Language Association of America, 2006.

Konstan, David, and Kurt Raaflaub, editors. *Epic and History.* Wiley Blackwell, 2014.

Lazzari, Marie, editor. *Epics for Students: Presenting Analysis, Context, and Criticism on Commonly Studied Epics.* Vol. 1, Gale Research, 1997.

López-Ruiz, Carolina, editor. *Gods, Heroes, and Monsters: A Sourcebook of Greek, Roman, and Near Eastern Myths in Translation.* 2nd ed., Oxford UP, 2018.

————. *When the Gods Were Born: Greek Cosmogonies and the Near East.* Harvard UP, 2010.

Lord, Albert. *The Singer of Tales.* 1960. Edited by David F. Elmer, 3rd ed., Center for Hellenic Studies, 2019.

Martin, Richard P. "Epic as Genre." Foley, *Companion*, pp. 9–19.

Mbele, Joseph. *The Hero in the African Epic.* 1986. U of Wisconsin, Madison, PhD dissertation.

————. "The Identity of the Hero in the Liongo Epic." *Swahili Verbal Arts,* special issue of *Research in African Literatures,* edited by Carol M. Eastman, vol. 17, no. 4, winter 1986, pp. 464–73.

Miller, David Lee, and Alexander Dunlop, editors. *Approaches to Teaching Spenser's* Faerie Queene. Modern Language Association of America, 1994.

Miller, Dean A. *The Epic Hero.* Johns Hopkins UP, 2000.

Miller, Madeline. *Circe.* Little, Brown, 2018.

————. *The Song of Achilles.* Ecco, 2011.

Mori, Masaki. *Epic Grandeur: Toward a Comparative Poetics of the Epic.* State U of New York P, 1997.

Myrsiades, Kostas, editor. *Approaches to Teaching Homer's* Iliad *and* Odyssey. Modern Language Association of America, 1987.

Nagy, Gregory. "The Epic Hero." Foley, *Companion*, pp. 71–89.

Neidorf, Leonard, and Yang Liu. *Epic and Romance: A Guide to Medieval European Literature.* Nanjing UP, 2021.

Oinas, Felix J., editor. *Heroic Epic and Saga: An Introduction to the World's Great Folk Epics.* Indiana UP, 1978.

Pathak, Shubha. *Divine yet Human Epics: Reflections of Poetic Rulers from Ancient Greece and India.* Center for Hellenic Studies, 2014.

Poor, Sara S., and Jana K. Schulman. Introduction. Poor and Schulman, pp. 1–14.

————, editors. *Women and Medieval Epic: Gender, Genre, and the Limits of Epic Masculinity.* Palgrave Macmillan, 2007.

Quint, David. *Epic and Empire: Politics and Generic Form from Virgil to Milton.* Princeton UP, 1993.

Ramachandran, C. N., editor. *Strings and Cymbals: Selections from Kannada Oral Epics.* Translated by Ramachandran and Padma Sharma, Center for Translations, Kannada U, 2007.

Ready, Jonathan L. *Orality, Textuality, and the Homeric Epics: An Interdisciplinary Study of Oral Texts, Dictated Texts, and Wild Texts.* Oxford UP, 2019.

Reichl, Karl, editor. *Medieval Oral Literature.* De Gruyter, 2012.

———. *The Oral Epic: From Performance to Interpretation.* Routledge, 2021.

———, editor. *The Oral Epic: Performance and Music.* Verlag fur Wissenschaft und Bildung, 2000. Intercultural Music Studies 12.

———. "Plotting the Map of Medieval Oral Literature." Reichl, *Medieval Oral Literature*, pp. 3–67.

Reitz, Christine, and Simone Finkmann, editors. *Stuctures of Epic Poetry: Foundations, Configuration, Continuity.* De Gruyter, 2019. 4 vols.

Reynolds, Dwight F. *Heroic Poets, Poetic Heroes: The Ethnography of Performance in an Arabic Oral Epic Tradition.* Cornell UP, 1995.

Sunderland, Luke. *Rebel Barons: Resisting Royal Power in Medieval Culture.* Oxford UP, 2017.

Swain, Larry, and Aaron Hostetter. *Teaching* Beowulf: *Practical Approaches.* Western Michigan U, 2022. Studies in Medieval and Early Modern Culture.

Turner, Frederick. *Epic: Form, Content, and History.* Transaction Publishers, 2012.

Wofford, Susanne L. "Epics and the Politics of the Origin Tale: Virgil, Ovid, Spenser, and Native American Aetiology." Beissinger et al., *Epic Traditions*, pp. 239–69.

Notes on Contributors

Atefeh Akbari is term assistant professor at Barnard College. Her current book project, tentatively titled "From the Caspian to the Caribbean: Toward a Planetary Comparison of Literatures," is a cross-cultural literary study of twentieth-century Iranian and Caribbean fiction and poetry. She has published in the *Cambridge Journal of Postcolonial Literary Inquiry* and *Philosophy and Global Affairs* and has work forthcoming in *Spirit and Defiance: Ali Shariati in Translation*.

Brenda E. F. Beck is a social anthropologist who has spent a lifetime studying South Asia, in particular the Kongu Nadu area of Tamil Nadu. She has published eight books and written over sixty journal articles. In recent years she has lectured around the world, including in Tokyo, Taiwan, Malaysia, Poland, Latvia, and the United Kingdom. She has thrice been a guest lecturer sponsored by the Government of India.

David T. Bialock is associate professor of Japanese literature in the Department of East Asian Languages and Cultures at the University of Southern California. He is the author of *Eccentric Spaces, Hidden Histories: Narrative, Ritual, and Royal Authority from* The Chronicles of Japan *to* The Tale of the Heike (2007) and articles on classical and medieval Japanese literature.

Jo Ann Cavallo is professor of Italian and current chair of the Department of Italian, Columbia University. Author of *The World beyond Europe in the Romance Epics of Boiardo and Ariosto; The Romance Epics of Boiardo, Ariosto, and Tasso: From Public Duty to Private Pleasure*; and *Boiardo's* Orlando Innamorato: *An Ethics of Desire* and editor of *Teaching the Italian Renaissance Romance Epic,* she has published widely on Italian literature and culture, including popular traditions dramatizing epic narratives.

Albrecht Classen is university distinguished professor of German studies at the University of Arizona. He has published 122 scholarly books and circa 840 articles, covering vast stretches of medieval literature and culture and extending into the sixteenth and even seventeenth centuries. He has received numerous awards for teaching, research, and service. He is the editor of two journals: *Mediaevistik* and *Humanities Open Access*.

Barlow Der Mugrdechian is the Berberian Coordinator of the Armenian Studies Program and director of the Center for Armenian Studies at California State University, Fresno. Since 1985 he has taught courses in Armenian language, history, literature, and art in the program. He is editor of

353

354   Notes on Contributors

the Armenian Series for the Press at California State University, Fresno, and is coeditor of David of Sassoun: *Critical Essays on the Armenian Epic*.

Thomas A. DuBois is the Halls-Bascom Professor of Scandinavian Studies, Folklore, and Religious Studies at the University of Wisconsin, Madison. His research and publications focus on folk culture and identity, particularly in the Nordic region.

Angelica A. Duran is professor at Purdue University, where she has been on the English, comparative literature, and religious studies faculties since 2000. She is the author of more than fifty shorter publications and two monographs, including *Milton among Spaniards* (2020). She is the editor or coeditor of five volumes, including *Milton in Translation* (2017) and *Global Milton and the Visual Arts* (2021).

Ana Grinberg is the Ruth T. Faulk Distinguished Lecturer at Auburn University. Her research intersects with her global premodern and early modern literature classes. Besides publications on medieval depictions of contact between Islam and Western Christendom in epics and chivalric romances, her recent chapter "A Portrait of an Enemy as a Young Man? Intimate Contacts of Charlemagne in Spain," included in *The Legend of Charlemagne: Envisioning Empire in the Middle Ages*, edited by Jace Stuckey, deals with *enfance* narratives.

Thomas A. Hale is the Edwin Erle Sparks Professor Emeritus of African, French, and Comparative Literature at Pennsylvania State University. He recorded *The Epic of Askia Mohammed* in Niger in 1980. It was published in a bilingual Songhay-English format as *Scribe, Griot, and Novelist: Narrative Interpreters of the Songhay Empire* (1990) and in English as *The Epic of Askia Mohammed* (1996).

Zachary Hamby was a 2020 Missouri Teacher of the Year finalist. He is the author of the Reaching Olympus series, *World Mythology for Beginners*, *The Hero's Guidebook*, and *Introduction to Mythology for Kids*. He maintains the website *Creative English Teacher* and teaches high school English in rural Missouri, where he resides with his wife and two children.

Nathan C. Henne was born and raised in Guatemala. He is the Rev. Guy Lemieux, SJ, SAK Distinguished Professor of Latin American Studies at Loyola University, New Orleans. His publications and teaching focus a decolonial lens on cultural and philosophical traditions of the historical and contemporary Maya and other Indigenous American peoples. His recent book is *Reading* Popol Wuj: *A Decolonial Guide* (2020), and his current book project centers on Indigenous ecologies.

John William Johnson is a member of the Cherokee Nation and has both Indian and Scottish heritage. He spent three-and-a-half years in the Peace

Corps; taught two years at Michigan State University and thirty-two years at Indiana University; conducted fieldwork in Somalia, Mali, Bolivia, and the United States; and has published four books and fifty-two articles. In 1998 he was elected to the Finnish Academy of Sciences and Letters.

Carolina López-Ruiz is professor of the history of religions, comparative mythology, and the ancient Mediterranean world at the University of Chicago Divinity School and the Department of Classics. Her books include *When the Gods Were Born: Greek Cosmogonies and the Near East* (2010); *Gods, Heroes, and Monsters: A Sourcebook of Greek, Roman, and Near Eastern Myths in Translation* (2nd ed., 2018); and *Phoenicians and the Making of the Mediterranean* (2021).

Jason Lotz is assistant professor of English and humanities at Farmingdale State University of New York, where he engages the means and motives of global citizenship through courses in world literature, poetry, and composition. His research interests focus on the intersections of tragedy, narrative, and emotion within early modern and postcolonial literature.

Roberta Micallef is Professor of the Practice in World Languages and Literatures and professor of women's, gender, and sexuality studies at Boston University. As an active scholar of Turkish language and literature she has contributed articles on Turkish literature and cultural products and on pedagogy to journals and edited volumes. Since 2007 she has participated in a research group on travel literature, and she has edited, coedited, and contributed to volumes on travel literature.

Joseph M. Ortiz is associate professor of English at the University of Texas, El Paso, where he teaches Renaissance and comparative literature. He is the author of *Broken Harmony: Shakespeare and the Politics of Music* as well as several essays on classical reception and the relation between literature and music in early modern culture. He is currently working on a book-length study of the figure of translation in Renaissance epics.

Katherine Oswald is assistant teaching professor of Spanish at the University of Notre Dame, where she teaches language, culture, and literature. She is also a contributing faculty member to the Moreau College Initiative, a degree-granting program out of Holy Cross College, through which qualified incarcerated individuals at the Westville Correctional Facility pursue an associate or bachelor's degree in the liberal arts. Her research centers on the development and transmission of the Spanish epic tradition, with an emphasis on the legend of Bernardo del Carpio.

Elizabeth Oyler is associate professor of Japanese in the Department of East Asian Languages and Literatures at the University of Pittsburgh. She is the author of *Swords, Oaths, and Prophetic Visions: Authoring Warrior Rule in*

356 Notes on Contributors

Medieval Japan (2006) and coeditor of *Cultural Imprints: War and Memory in the Samurai Age* (2022).

Emrah Pelvanoğlu is chair of the Department of Turkish Language and Literature Teaching at the Yeditepe University in Istanbul. He is the author of *Tanzimat and Metahistory: Poetics of Namık Kemal's Historical Narratives* (2018). He was a visiting researcher at the Center for Middle Eastern Studies at Harvard University in 2018–19. His principal research interests are the beginnings of modern prose in Turkish literature and anthropologic approaches to literature.

Christine G. Perkell is emerita professor of classics at Emory University. She is editor of *Reading Vergil's* Aeneid: *An Interpretive Guide* and author of *The Poet's Truth: A Study of the Poet in Vergil's* Georgics; Aeneid *3: A Commentary*; Aeneid *12: A Commentary* (forthcoming); and articles on Virgil's *Eclogues* and *Georgics*, women's laments in the *Aeneid* and Homer's *Iliad*, and the underworlds of Virgil and Dante.

Dwight F. Reynolds is distinguished professor of Arabic language and literature at the University of California, Santa Barbara. His books include *Heroic Poets, Poetic Heroes: The Ethnography of Performance in an Arabic Oral Epic Tradition* (1995), *Interpreting the Self: Autobiography in the Arabic Literary Tradition* (2001), *Arab Folklore: A Handbook* (2007), *The Cambridge Companion to Modern Arab Culture* (2015), *The Musical Heritage of al-Andalus* (2021), *Medieval Arab Music and Musicians* (2022), and *Bestsellers and Masterpieces: The Changing Medieval Canon* (2022).

Paula Richman, William Danforth Professor of South Asian Religions, emerita, at Oberlin College, has published widely on the *Ramayana* tradition: *Many Rāmāyaṇas: The Diversity of a Narrative Tradition in South Asia* (1991); *Questioning Ramayanas: A South Asian Tradition* (2000); Ramayana *Stories in Modern South India* (2008); and *Performing the* Ramayana *Tradition: Enactments, Interpretations, and Arguments* (2021), coedited with Rustom Bharucha. She is completing a book on Tamil tellings of the *Ramayana*.

Moss Roberts, professor of Chinese in the East Asian Studies Department of New York University, has translated several Chinese literary and philosophical works and authored numerous articles about Chinese literature, philosophy, and contemporary Asian events (wp.nyu.edu/mossroberts). Recent publications include The Analects: *Conclusions and Conversations of Confucius* (2020) and *A Journey to the East: From Brooklyn 1945 to China ca. 500 BCE* (2021).

Charles S. Ross, a former Fulbright-Hays Scholar in Italy, is professor emeritus of English and comparative literature at Purdue University. His books include the first English translation of Matteo Maria Boiardo's Italian romance *Orlando Innamorato* (1989); *The Custom of the Castle: From Malory to* Macbeth (1997); *Elizabethan Literature and the Law of Fraudulent Conveyance: Sidney, Spenser, Shakespeare* (2003); and a verse translation of L. Paninius Statius's Latin *Thebaid* (2004).

Luisanna Sardu is visiting assistant professor of Italian and Spanish at Manhattan College. Her academic interests include the role of emotions in society: specifically, the use of anger in the texts of early modern women writers. She has published in *Emotions: History, Culture, Society*; *Teaching Italian Language and Culture Annual*; and *International Journal of Childhood and Women's Studies*.

Arshia Sattar teaches classical Indian literatures at various institutions in India and abroad. Her abridged translation from Sanskrit of the Valmiki *Ramayana* (1996) has remained continuously in print. Her other publications include collections of scholarly essays and adaptations of Hindu myths and epics for younger readers.

Stefan Seeber is a lecturer and adjunct professor at Freiburg University in Germany. His main areas of teaching and research are medieval and early modern German literature with an emphasis on poetics, reception studies, and rhetoric. He also works on medievalism of the early twentieth century.

Roberta Strippoli is associate professor of Japanese literature in the Department of Asian, African, and Mediterranean Studies at the University of Napoli "L'Orientale." She is the author of *Dancer, Nun, Ghost, Goddess: Giō and Hotoke in Traditional Japanese Literature, Theater, and Cultural Heritage* (2017) and has published studies and translations of medieval Japanese literature.

Frederick Turner, Founders Professor Emeritus of Arts and Humanities at the University of Texas, Dallas, was educated at Oxford University. He is a poet, critic, interdisciplinary scholar, philosopher, translator, and former editor of *The Kenyon Review*. He has published over forty books, including recently *Paradise: Selected Poems, 1990–2003*; *Epic: Form, Content, and History*; *Apocalypse: An Epic Poem*; *More Light: Selected Poems, 2004–2016*; and *The Golden Goblet: Selected Poems of Goethe*, translated with Zsuzsanna Ozsváth.

Victoria Turner is senior lecturer in French at the University of St Andrews. She is the author of *Theorizing Medieval Race: Saracen Representations in Old French Literature* (2019) and coeditor of *Inscribing Knowledge in the Medieval Book: The Power of Paratexts* (2020) and *Words in the Middle Ages / Les mots au moyen âge* (2020). She is currently working on the use of story, including folktales and fairy tales, to retell crusading ideologies in chansons de geste of the thirteenth to fifteenth centuries.